S0-AYE-116

Mixed Messages

Mixed Messages

Multiracial Identities in the "Color-Blind" Era

edited by David L. Brunsma

LYNNE
RIENNER
PUBLISHERS

BOULDER
LONDON

Published in the United States of America in 2006 by
Lynne Rienner Publishers, Inc.
1800 30th Street, Boulder, Colorado 80301
www.rienner.com

and in the United Kingdom by
Lynne Rienner Publishers, Inc.
3 Henrietta Street, Covent Garden, London WC2E 8LU

Library of Congress Cataloging-in-Publication Data
Mixed messages : multiracial identities in the "color-blind" era / edited by
    David L. Brunsma.
        p.   cm.
    Includes bibliographical references and index.
    ISBN 1-58826-372-X (hardcover : alk. paper)
    ISBN 1-58826-398-3 (pbk. : alk. paper)
    1. Racism. 2. Equality. 3. Social justice. 4. Racially mixed people—
United States. 5. Minorities—United States—Social conditions.
I. Brunsma, David L.
HT1521.M58   2006
305.8—dc22   2005018523

British Cataloguing in Publication Data
A Cataloguing in Publication record for this book
is available from the British Library.

Printed and bound in the United States of America

        The paper used in this publication meets the requirements
   ∞   of the American National Standard for Permanence of
        Paper for Printed Library Materials Z39.48-1992.

    5 4 3 2 1

For Nina, my punkin
and
Rachel, my constant amazement

Contents

Acknowledgments

This book is a meta-dream of sorts, wherein conversations about issues close to my scholar-activist heart are continued, and paths of inquiry about race, identity, inequality, and justice are illuminated and traversed. I am truly honored to have been able to engage with the stellar group of scholars in the book and eternally grateful that they were willing to share in this effort with me. It is with the deepest sincerity that I acknowledge their work—for without their ideas, their insights, their challenges, their openness, their timeliness, their critical lenses, and their willingness, this project would never have been possible.

Other scholars who were with us during the formation and implementation of the vision behind this book deserve thanks as well: Inna Altschul, Constance Backhouse, Adrian Blackledge, Marilynn Brewer, Philip Brown, James Cote, Kay Deaux, Nadine Dolby, Ian Christopher Fletcher, David Gilbert, Joshua Goldstein, Ellington Graves, Ronald Hall, Monica Hardesty, Janet Helms, Roger Herring, Dennis Howitt, Verna Keith, James O'Donnell, Daphna Oyserman, Alvin Poussaint, Wendy Roth, Jon Michael Spencer, William Swann, Ronald Taylor, Jewell Taylor-Gibbs, Cathy Thompson, Henry Trueba, Sarah White, and Howard Winant. These individuals' comments on early versions of the book led to significant reconceptualizations and rearticulations of the thematic material contained within these pages. Though some on this list may not know why they are included or in what way they contributed, they did—and their work made this a better book.

The staff at Lynne Rienner Publishers is fabulous, and their pursuit of cutting-edge scholarship is an important endeavor. I must first and foremost give a huge and serious thanks to Bridget Julian. I came to Bridget with a vision; she listened, read, and gave much thought to that vision and then came to the table with the most amazing ideas and challenges, delivered in the most amiable way; and through her well-honed editorial abilities and passion for the project, we pushed it further and clarified its core contentions. Bridget, thank you so much—and enjoy parenthood! Next, Lynne Rienner herself is a formidable and astounding publisher and editor. Going beyond the call of duty, Lynne spent time with me on the phone, in person, and through letters to continue to push this project forward—again, with passion and an understanding of the issues (and the audiences). Should I ever have the opportunity to work with Lynne again, I would welcome it. I would also like to thank Leanne Anderson, Lisa Tulchin, and Karen Williams at Lynne Rienner Publishers, as well as Beth Partin; their gracious and invaluable work is appreciated. The thorough and critical reviews from anonymous reviewers were top-notch and exceedingly helpful in moving through the final stages of this process—they made this book better. Thank you.

The process of developing the emerging contours of the book took place in several contexts, but most notably at annual meetings of the Association of Black Sociologists, the American Sociological Association, and the Southern Sociological Society. In addition, colleagues, staff, and students at both the University of Alabama in Huntsville and the University of Missouri at Columbia provided unstinting support for my work. Thank you to Dipa Basu, Cliff Beacham, Mitch Berbrier, Rebecca Brambach, Wayne Brekhus, Rodney Coates, Kevin Cokley, Glenna Colclough, Anamaria Csizmadia, Manndi DeBoef, Melissa Dixon, Marlese Durr, Nancy Finley, Walda Katz Fishman, Tyrone Foreman, Debbie Friedrich, Stephanie Grimes, Jay Gubrium, Annie Harris, Paige Hendrix, Melissa Herman, Joan Hermsen, Cedric Herring, Jan Howard, Sue Kirkpatrick, Amy Lane, Jackie Litt, Alan McClare, Veronica Medina, Suzanne Nevels, Bob Newby, Yvonne Newsome, Mary Oakes, Arthur Paris, Tola Pearce, Desiree Robertson, Steve Rosenthall, Lori Rounsvall, Bhavani Sitaraman, Rachel Sullivan, Amy Wilkins, Jeff Williams, and Tukufu Zuberi.

My family has been with me through this endeavor and, bless their hearts, they have had to deal with quite a lot. To my children, Karina, Thomas, and Henry, thank you so much for being understanding, in whatever ways you could (even listening to Mommy and Daddy talking about "Daddy's book" stuff when you really wanted to talk about *Lord of the Rings*), of the time Daddy had to devote to this book—heck, Thomas, you even made a book of your own alongside mine. To the extended family who, over dinner, visits, holidays, and so on, were kind enough to both ask about and then listen to me talk about this exciting project—Mom and Dad, Grandpa and Grandma, Brian and Mark, Anthony and Lynn, Olly, Juju, Jenny, Colin, Simon, Becky, David, and Lisa (even Katherine Taylor in utero), and Katherine Enfinger—thanks! Finally, words cannot express my gratitude to my partner in crime, my best friend, my companion along this road, Rachel. Thank you so much! You have been so kind, understanding, and supportive, as well as conceptually, organizationally, and logistically helpful concerning this project. Actually, Rachel, you were this project's "cheerleader," and as always you provided me with the space to complete this book. You never cease to amaze me; I am in awe of and in love with you. Thank you for being you!

1

Mixed Messages: Doing Race in the Color-Blind Era

David L. Brunsma

Theories of race—of its meaning, its transformations, the significance of racial events—have never been a top priority in social science.
—Michael Omi and Howard Winant (1986: 9)

Maria P. Root's groundbreaking collection, *Racially Mixed People in America,* published in 1992, was the first serious volume devoted to assessing the state of our understanding of mixed-race people in the United States. Before this publication, scholarship was far from objective in its attempt to unravel the issues surrounding racial identity and multiracial individuals. Although Root's anthology was indescribably important in the overall scholarship on multiraciality, in this book we present quite a different story about racial identity, racial ideology, racial social structure, and the multiracial individual through a much-needed critical lens.

A perennial starting point for research into multiracial identity and experience is the often cited *Who Am I?* question. In response to this central question, some scholarship has responded with a resounding "Black!" or "Asian!" and others with an equally resonant "Biracial!" or "Multiracial!" Root's anthology did attempt to place these scholarly and culturally rooted responses within the larger context of the meaning of race in the United States while still attending to the central multiracial question of *Who Am I?*

After decades (actually centuries) of negotiating the color lines of the most central axis of difference in the United States—black and white (or white and nonwhite)—multiracial Americans certainly have received (and produced, and provided data for scholars and journalists to produce) mixed messages. Root's anthology, predicated on a presupposed "biracial baby boom" following the Supreme Court decision in *Loving v. Commonwealth of Virginia v. Loving,* covers a lot of personal, multiracial ground. Root's

1

intentions were clear and actually ahead of their time, as seen in these opening lines:

> The emergence of a racially mixed population is transforming the "face" of the United States. The increasing presence of multiracial people necessitates that we as a nation ask ourselves questions about our identity: Who are we? How do we see ourselves? Who are we in relation to one another? These questions arise in the context of a country that has held particular views of race—a country that has subscribed to race as an immutable construct, perceived itself as White, and been dedicated to preserving racial lines. Thus such questions of race and identity can only precipitate a full-scale "identity crisis" . . . that this country is ill-equipped to resolve. Resolving the identity crisis may force us to reexamine our constructions of race and the hierarchical social order it supports. (1992a: 3)

The question of *Who Am I?* was central to the Root collection, as its contributors sought to understand how multiracial Americans from a multitude of combinations negotiate their hybridity—how they understand themselves racially, how they develop their identities. However, the underlying focus was more about *individual* multiracial strategies of "doing race" and less about the macro, political, cultural, and historical processes of structured (and contested, restructured) racial meanings within which these very individual negotiations are embedded. The larger questions of race, racism, and racial justice, though implicit in Root's anthology and her subject matter (and still embryonic and implicit in much of the literature on multiracial identity), remained largely untapped, leading to a mixed *message.* Instead of understanding the culturally, politically, and structurally located mixed messages that multiracial Americans have received (and professed) and how they have affected their own lives, Root and her colleagues entered a new message into the discourse—a *mixed* message—that mixed-race people, as a group, had something to say to all of us. Thus Root and her colleagues began to raise the question: *Who Are We?* This question cuts closer to the core for those of us interested in larger questions of race, racism, and racial justice; yet, even this question remains largely unexplored until now (but see Spencer 1999; Daniel 2000b; and, most recently, Dalmage 2004b).

    Racially Mixed People in America was both a watershed in research on race and racial identity and a symbol of a nascent social movement. This new "multiracial movement" was beginning to redefine and discursively criticize racial classification systems in the United States (Daniel 2002; Rockquemore and Brunsma 2002a; Spencer 1999). Such discussions corresponded to similar endeavors within academia. However, at the same time that the multiracial movement and multiracial advocates were criticizing classification schemes, they also desired to have their members *classified* as *unambiguously multiracial.* Here was a burgeoning movement arguing *against* the essentialism and inheritability of race—again, in line with much academic literature of the 1980s—while at the same time *reinscribing* essentialism and immutability onto multiraciality itself. With so many decontextualized, culturally contraband, and highly political messages and meanings associated with race and racial identity being pushed to the fore by this multiracial movement, what will be the result for the study of race and racial identity or the pursuit of social and racial justice for oppressed people of color in the United States? It is the answer to that question that the contributors to this book seek.

■ Outside the Frame

It is interesting to note that the Root anthology was nestled betwixt and between two other important publications: Michael Omi and Howard Winant's *Racial Formation in the United States: From the 1960s to the 1980s,* published in 1986 (some six years before Root), and Stephen Steinberg's poignant *Turning Back: The Retreat from Racial Justice in American Thought and Policy,* published in 1995.

Omi and Winant's work is important to highlight here as the backdrop to Root's anthology on multiracial people in the United States. Omi and Winant provide a detailed and strident critique of the three major paradigms of "racial theory"—ethnicity models, class-based models, and nation-based theories—in order to more effectively flesh out their theory of racial formations. The theoretical scaffolding rests upon a central concept of "racial formations"—consider the following brief discussion of the racial formation process:

> The meaning of race is defined and contested throughout society, in both collective action and personal practice. In the process, racial categories themselves are formed, transformed, destroyed, and re-formed . . . *racial formation* . . . is the process by which social, economic and political forces determine the content and importance of racial categories, and by which they are in turn shaped by racial meanings. Crucial to this formulation is the treatment of race as a central axis of social relations which cannot be subsumed under or reduced to some broader category or conception. (Omi and Winant 1986: 61–62)

The importance of this theoretical formulation for the study of multiracial identity and multiracial politics is undeniable, but it has been underutilized. Racial formations theory recognizes that, at the micro-interactional level, race is a matter of individuality and the formation of identities, whereas, at the macrolevel, race is a matter of the collective body focused on the formation of structured "sites" of contestation (economic, political, ideological, etc.). What this theory provides is a unique view of how the racial order is organized and enforced by the continuity and reciprocity *between* these two levels of social relations within a society and is politically, culturally, and ideologically rearticulated through the governing body of that society (the "racial state"). Ultimately, here was a theory, proposed in the mid-1980s, that underlined the purposeful, ideological, and political social construction and contestation of race as an "unstable and decentered complex of social meanings constantly being transformed" (Omi and Winant 1986: 68). Indeed, at the microlevel multiracial identities are about rearticulating meanings about betwixt and betweenness, but so too do racial movements (multiracial, color-blindness, etc.) rearticulate racial meanings, preserving the racist social structure (Bonilla-Silva 2001) and the racial state (Mills 1997).

Providing a thought-provoking bookend to the Root anthology, Stephen Steinberg published *Turning Back* during Office of Management and Budget debates over the addition of a multiracial category to the US Census. Though Steinberg discusses neither Root nor the ongoing debate over racial classification in the United States, he does describe a general trend in US thought at the time. Steinberg painstakingly details a climate in which scholars and policymakers consistently turned away from interpretations of racial dynamics that highlighted racism and the structure of white privilege in the United States. Instead, these same people embarked on discussions of "anything but racism" (Horton and Sykes 2003), offering conclusions that blamed the victim, a largely euphemistic discourse, and a plethora of racial verbiage that did *not* advance notions and strategies of racial justice but "retreated" from them and hailed their "end."

Although Root and her contributors could not have been aware of the specific concerns and arguments raised by Steinberg in his book—though the academic and political conditions discussed in *Turning Back* were extant at the time—the authors in Root's collection most certainly would have been aware of the new, critical theoretical formulation contained within Omi and Winant's pages. Both *Racial Formation* and *Turning Back* underscore the theoretical and empirical possibility that social construction of race (and "ethnorace") can and does change via political, cultural, ideological, and academic routes. In addition, their arguments should give serious reflective pause to scholars interested in *all things multiracial* because it remains highly probable that such micro- and macrolevel alterations/rearticulations of racial formations help preserve white privilege and the structure of that privilege. Given this, it might be argued that the multiracial movement—the interactionally situated "doing" of race—is in very important ways epiphenomenal to the underlying racist social structure of the United States.

So, Root's book was indeed an important starting point in the study of multiraciality. However, though the issue of multiracial identity is theoretically interesting, the move from a multiracial *Who Am I?* to a multiracial *Who Are We?* to an American (structural) *Who Are We?* has *not* been a central focus.

Investigations of multiraciality as a racial formation have *not* been of central importance. Questioning the impact of multiracial identity and the politics of the multiracial movement on racial justice pursuits in the United States have also *not* been foci. In fact, concerning "racial justice," Root and her colleagues (and indeed the more general movement that her early work helped to spawn) seem to imply that the primary "injustice" for multiracial people is a classification system that forces them to choose. Although that view may be to some extent correct, it really misses the larger and more important links between racial identity, racial inequality, and racial justice—this book addresses these links.

■ A New Call

In the decade or so since *Racially Mixed People in America* first appeared, it has become increasingly clear that "race" is not something one *is,* but rather an elaborate, lived experience and cultural ritual of what one *does.* It is also clear that race and racism are embedded within the very social and cultural structures that make up society and that they are very real in the ways they structure our lives and futures—in Eduardo Bonilla-Silva's highly relevant terminology, the processes of negotiating racial identities occurs in "racialized social systems" (2001). The time has come to explore the structures behind the patterns we have uncovered since the mid-1990s and come to grips with critical models of negotiations, strategies, and tactics that occur on the color line (or even a "color-blind color line").

The existence, experience, and voices of multiracial individuals are challenging (rearticulating) the current categorizations of race, altering the meaning of racial identity, and in the process changing the cultural and structural fabric of race in the United States. The question is *how?* Earlier assumptions in the literature, beginning largely with *Racially Mixed People in America,* assumed that these "changes" could only be for the "better"— whatever that meant. The trajectory of multiracial research desperately needs to be self-critical, to be willing to adopt new lenses with which to view the phenomena at hand; in sum, the field of multiracial identity is at a place where those investigating such processes must begin to answer the classic "so what?" question. It is my hope that the contributions in the present volume will take this field into the realm where we can begin to address that question and push toward new and innovative investigations aimed at understanding the shifting racial terrain and how that will affect the prospects for racial equity and racial justice. Indeed, a key component of all the contributions in the volume is their critical reflection on how racial identity and the correlate racial identity politics will either help to alleviate or further reinforce the unrelenting structure and culture of racism and racial inequality.

▪ Mixed Messages:
Multiracial Identities in the "Color-Blind" Era

The chapters that follow focus on one of four broad dimensions: (1) detailed arguments and investigations into the historical, present, and future structural and cultural racial hierarchy in the United States and how racial identities (re)articulate these "shifting color lines"; (2) theoretically and empirically rich explorations into the ways that groups, movements, institutions, and the state have used multiraciality to expand, redraw, rearticulate, and commodify racial boundaries and the meanings of those boundaries; (3) in-depth analyses of how the socialization processes in families (largely interracial) translate shifting racial formations and changing meanings of race into ideologies of identity for mixed-race children; and (4) critical microlevel, interactional models of how race, interrace, and multiraciality are negotiated in context. All of the chapters also attend to the important implications of these processes for the pursuit of racial justice.

Part 1: Shifting Color Lines

The first section of the book is devoted broadly to investigations into how racial lines are drawn and challenges to and reformations of the racial lines that illuminate the complex context from/within which the multiracial movement (and multiracial identity negotiations) can be more fruitfully examined.

Leading off this important contextualization is an insightful and theoretically valuable chapter by the author of the seminal and now classic *Who Is Black? One Nation's Definition* (1991): F. James Davis. In Chapter 2, Davis lays out his historically and comparatively grounded typology of statuses that mixed-race people can hold in modern societies. Here, he gives particular emphasis to the role of the US multiracial movement since the 1980s in reorganizing racial structures and challenging the one-drop rule; he also predicts which of the six alternatives in his model might be the path that multiracial Americans will pursue.

Resting upon this history, in Chapter 3 Eduardo Bonilla-Silva and David G. Embrick provide a rarity in sociological inquiry: they predict the future racial structure of the United States. These authors provide initial empirical glimpses into the earlier claim of Bonilla-Silva (2001) that the United States is moving from a bifurcated "biracial" system to a racial stratification system that is "triracial."

Chapter 4, "Racial Justice in a Black/Nonblack Society," outlines George Yancey's deeply discerning and theoretically important argument predicting a society in which all nonblack peoples will align with the dominant groups in the United States, leaving blacks "alone in their struggle for racial justice." This chapter, through specific critiques of previous models and strong arguments centered on the continuing and strengthening alienation of black Americans, provides an interesting counterpoint to Bonilla-Silva and Embrick's chapter.

Jeffrey Moniz and Paul Spickard detail the specific case of racial formations in Hawaiian society, how they have changed, and the resulting racial discourse in Chapter 5. Important lessons can be learned from the history presented in this wonderfully original chapter—how multiraciality operates in current racial hierarchies and how colonized groups use essentialist ideologies. Specifically, the authors' conceptual and theoretical development of the "midaltern" offers us new ways to actually look at fluid identity negotiations embedded within macrolevel racial formations and ideologies. In this chapter, the new theory of the midaltern promises to influence the next generation of identity scholars.

Rainier Spencer's *Spurious Issues: Race and Multiracial Identity Politics in the United States* (1999) remains one of the most scholarly, intellectually stimulating, and epistemologically challenging treatises on multiraciality in recent years. In this spirit, Spencer, in Chapter 6, continues to seriously challenge assumptions that have run rampant in the scholarly and popular literature on multiraciality in the United States, arguing that in the end multiracial discourse serves to further reinforce the idea of race and the idea of the immutability of things racial. This chapter demands that we dig deeper and engage in much more critical analyses of the phenomena at hand.

Chapter 7 brings us Charles A. Gallagher, an expert in the symbolic boundaries of whiteness. Gallagher here pays close attention to the current racial formation of "color blindness" so closely linked to the multiracial movement. Ultimately, he considers how in the future multiracial identities will follow a "which drop rule," in which certain offspring of certain interracial unions will be "privileged while others are relegated to the bottom of the racial pecking order." Thus the distribution of resources may be tied in complex ways to a more complex racial order, but a *racial* order nonetheless—even within a so-called "color-blind" formation—with disturbing implications for the pursuit of racial justice.

Rounding out Part 1 of this volume, Hayward Derrick Horton reiterates the role of racism and offers a reappraisal of the emergence of the "neo-mulatto" population in the United States. By putting forth an idea of "whitespace," Horton underscores the importance of racism and the structural nature of the term "neo-mulatto."

Part 2: Manipulating Multiracial Identities

The authors in Part 2 investigate how relevant institutional, political, and cultural actors have collectively transformed the ideas of race, multirace, and racialized beings into particular racial formations and how these actors deploy formations of "color-blindness," multiracial identities and ideologies, and symbols and images of multiraciality to pursue certain political, ideological, and economic ends. Thus, the authors in Part 2 investigate how multiraciality has been manipulated, looking deeper into the connections between the parameters set by racial formations; the social, political, and cultural racial projects that interacted with these parameters; and how these projects did or did not pursue racial justice.

Readers unfamiliar with G. Reginald Daniel's work in *More Than Black: Multiracial Identity and the New Racial Order* (2000) are in for a treat as Daniel and Josef Manuel Castañeda-Liles consider the Racial Privacy Initiative, or Proposition 54, which in 2003 asked California voters to decide whether racial data would be collected by California governmental agencies. In Chapter 9, these two authors assess the multiracial movement, the census debates, and the rise of the Racial Privacy Initiative in the larger context of a struggle for racial justice, concluding that it "remains to be seen whether a greater coalition can be built between multiracial and traditional civil rights organizations," given the evidence of the links between the multiracial movement and notions of essentialism, hierarchy, and inequality.

Interracial sexuality has been fundamental to the construction and maintenance of the symbolic boundaries of whiteness. In Chapter 10, Abby L. Ferber, author of *White Man Falling: Race, Gender, and White Supremacy* (1998), investigates the ways in which white supremacist discourse has theorized multiraciality. Arguing that the construction of race cannot be fully grasped without a discussion of boundary work and race mixing, she sheds a bright light on the racial project of white separatism and how notions of multiraciality and whiteness help to define such a project.

Johanna E. Foster's chapter, "Defining Racism to Achieve Goals: The Multiracial and Black Reparations Movements," presents a cutting-edge, thought-provoking, and inspiring analysis of how two social movements (which both articulate their ideologies as distinct from that of traditional civil rights movements) define and incorporate notions of race and racial identity differently in the pursuit of their objectives. Foster focuses on the complex and intriguing discursive correspondence between the politics of racial classification and white structural privilege. Her luminous analysis concludes by describing how movements could attack global white supremacy.

In Chapter 12, Kimberly McClain DaCosta shifts our focus to the marketplace and the ways in which images of multiraciality and ideologies of color blindness are being used to bolster profit margins. Hers is a truly innovative analysis of an extensive set of practices of marketing to, by, and of multiracials. From descriptions of reinscribed essentialism in hair products to broader ideological rearticulations of color blindness, DaCosta's chapter is a unique study in the commodification of the body, target marketing, and the processes of racialization.

Part 3: Socialization in Multiracial Families

Since families in many important ways link the broader macrolevel racial formations and microlevel processes of negotiating racial identities, they are crucial to understanding how existing racial paradigms and racialized parameters of the self are reproduced and can be challenged. Interracial families, through parenting practices, racial socialization, and in some cases antiracial socialization practices, may mediate these broader structures and create a space for understanding how race is taught, done, and maintained in the familial context and, perhaps, in other institutionalized contexts as well.

In their book *Raising Biracial Children* (2005), Kerry Ann Rockquemore and Tracey Laszloffy synthesizes the vast literature on racial identity among mixed-race people and translates those ideas into concrete applicable strategies for nurturing multiracial children. In Chapter 13, Rockquemore, Tracey Laszloffy, and Julia Noveske look at how racial socialization processes in interracial families are comparable to and/or different from those of monoracial families. One highly pertinent finding from this important contribution is that a parent's racial ideology may be an infinitely more essential component of determining racial socialization processes than the parent's race.

No volume such as this one would be complete without the work of France Winddance Twine. She has written a truly original contribution to address the focal questions of this section to be sure, but the illuminating research she presents in Chapter 14 also speaks volumes to the larger questions motivating this book. Using data from black/white multiracial families in England, she asks how these family members translate the logics of race and racism while also attempting to transfer particular racialized identities to their children. She discusses this subject through an original theoretical lens of "racial literacies."

In "Black and White: Family Opposition to Becoming Multiracial," Erica Chito Childs, author of *Navigating Interracial Borders: Black-White Couples and Their Social Worlds,* approaches the dilemmas faced by interracial couples in the current color-blind era. The empirical mismatch between attitudinal support for interracial relationships/marriage and actual, on-the-ground opposition to such unions leads Childs to interrogate the classic question of "concern" raised by opposing family members: "What about the children?" Through extensive in-depth interviews and keen insight, this chapter underlines the fact that broader collective fears and notions about race and racial difference are central components to our constructions of families and identities.

Part 4: Dilemmas of Multiracial Identity

Departing from the macro- and mesolevel contextualizations of multiraciality in society explored in the previous sections, Part 4 focuses on the microlevel, sociopsychological processes of "doing race" in social interactions. The chapters herein look at various "dilemmas" surrounding racially, interracially, and multiracially tinged circumstances. This broad approach leads us down several interrelated paths: how racial identity can be seen as a resource, how it is manipulated and altered across various contexts, when and how it remains consistent in different "identity markets," how culture affects strategies of racial identity through empirical and theoretical considerations of the role of appearance, clothing, and language.

R. L'Hereux Lewis and Kanika Bell begin this section with a chapter that develops a much-needed theoretical model, taking into account the various levels of analysis presented throughout the flow of this book and providing researchers interested in racial and multiracial identities with a way to understand how identities are deployed and negotiated in social interactions. Combining individual characteristics, social context, reference group orientation, and situation of encounter, their intersectional model of identity is a fresh addition to scholarship on identity negotiation. Their conclusion provides important insights into the role of threat and coping in identity work and pursuits of racial justice in a society.

In Chapter 17, readers are in for a treat as Kathleen Korgen, author of *Crossing the Racial Divide: Close Friendships Between Black and White Americans* (2002), and Eileen O'Brien, author of *Whites Confront Racism: Antiracists and Their Paths to Action* (2001), look closely at how color-blind racial ideology plays itself out in long-term, close, black/white friendship dyads. Their intriguing research design and immensely rich data allow them to pursue investigations into the ways in which these interracial friendships produce or do not produce significant antiracist activism within these individuals. They find that "simply becoming friends, even *close* friends, with black Americans will not motivate most white Americans to combat or even recognize racism in U.S. society."

Benjamin Bailey's "Black and Latino: Dominican Americans Negotiate Racial Worlds" uncovers a great deal of the complexities underlying racial identity strategies. In Chapter 18, Bailey looks at a sample of Dominican Americans, whose appearances range from individuals matching the African phenotype to those aligning more closely with the European phenotype. Despite their physical appearance, these individuals negotiate their identity somewhere outside the traditional U.S. black/white dichotomy. By looking at the subjective and performed aspects of race, Bailey uncovers many tertiary symbolic systems (i.e., linguistic, etc.) undergirding how these Dominican young adults navigate their identities. His work here is an important contribution to our knowledge of microprocesses of racial projects that both inform/alter and are informed by/altered by racial formations in the United States.

In Chapter 19, Heather Dalmage, whose clear and critical voice has influenced many of the authors in this volume through works such as *Tripping on the Color Line: Black-White Multiracial Families in a Racially Divided World* (2000) and *The Politics of Multiracialism: Challenging Racial Thinking* (2004), brings us an autoethnographic, personal, and analytical account of the color line in the United States and the implications for those who cross such a potent symbolic boundary—even in the color-blind era. Through a specific look into the housing market, she investigates the dilemmas faced by multiracial families in the search for a home—both literally and figuratively. She ends up with a poignant discussion about the struggle to weave a new "garment" that we can don in the struggle for racial justice in the United States.

An eminent scholar known for his work in both the psychology of racism and the racism of psychology, Kwame Owusu-Bempah engages in a discussion in Chapter 20 concerning the dilemmas faced by multiracials and critically assesses the possible racial projects occurring in the counseling office. His contribution adds a slew of strong questions for both scholars and those in professional therapeutic practice to consider when we write about, think about, and involve ourselves in the lives of multiracial people—calling people to "unflinching, resolute commitment to racial justice."

Rounding out the volume is a grounded contribution by Debbie Storrs, who pursues the shifting of racial boundaries by mixed-race women in their identity work. Interestingly, her respondents reject the option of identifying with the category "multiracial"; the women favored a nonwhite identity and challenged community and institutionalized notions of racial belonging through linguistic and other cultural markers. In the end, the ideological root of their cultural identity work is essentialism that, unfortunately, does more to reproduce our racial terrain than fracture it.

Part 1

Shifting Color Lines

2

Defining Race: Comparative Perspectives

F. James Davis

A black person in the United States has long been defined as a person with any known African black ancestry, no matter how little or how distant. The aphorism for this so-called one-drop rule is that "one drop of black blood makes you black." So deeply rooted in the American psyche is this rule that a person can have predominantly white ancestry and even look white, yet unquestionably be defined as black. Such people as Halle Berry, Lena Horne, Julian Bond, or Muhammad Ali come to mind. Is it any wonder that foreign visitors and television viewers have trouble understanding why we define such people as black? No other nation defines blacks in this way, and our one-drop rule does not apply to any minority other than African Americans.

Walter White, president of the National Association for the Advancement of Colored People (NAACP) from 1931 to 1955, had blue eyes, blond hair, and fair skin, and his ancestry was no more than one sixty-fourth African black (Ottley 1943). He had been raised in Georgia in the black community and had been subjected to white discrimination and violence (White 1948). He passed as white in order to investigate lynchings in the Jim Crow South. White's second marriage, to a brunette white woman, provoked outrage from the black press for his betrayal. He had married outside the black community, across the ethnic barrier. When the White family made an international goodwill tour and were publicized as an interracial couple, White was often asked how he happened to marry a black woman (Cannon 1956).

A former law professor, now a university president, grew up in a white, middle-class neighborhood in Virginia and had always thought he was white until he was ten years old. He certainly looks white. His father, after a financial collapse and a broken marriage, took him and his younger brother to live in his home community in Muncie, Indiana, in the 1950s. While en route there by bus, their father told the boys that he had passed as white and they would be living in a black neighborhood. There the boys were discriminated against and harassed by both whites and blacks. Against all odds, this older brother's abilities, both in the classroom and in athletics, enabled him to achieve outstanding success. When asked why he does not pass as white, he answers that he has been taught through bitter experience that in the United States he is black (G. H. Williams 1995).

Although there are average differences in visible physical traits in human populations, there are no pure races. When I use the term "unmixed African black," I mean someone whose entire ancestry derives from populations in sub-Saharan Africa. Originally the term "mulatto" meant half African black and half white, but it came to mean any degree of mixture. Often people now say that a child of an African American and a white is "half and half," which correctly describes the child's racial background. However, one such child may have a parent whose ancestry is three-fourths African, whereas another's is one-fourth. The ancestry of the first child would be three-eighths black, the second one-eighth. Regardless of the ancestral fractions and physical appearances, both children are black under the American one-drop rule. Due to strong social conditioning, most light-hued African Americans identify themselves as black, but as we shall see, some do not.

Because of the one-drop rule, mixed offspring with any African ancestry are assigned to the black community. The result of over 350 years of miscegenation in the United States is a "new people," derived predominantly from African black populations but with a large infusion of genes from European whites and a substantial amount from Native Americans (Reed 1969; Williamson 1980). Estimates of the number of African Americans who have some white ancestry range from three-fourths to above 90 percent, and as many as one-fourth have Native American ancestry. The color spectrum in the black community ranges from ebony to lighter than most whites, and other visible physical traits show a similar range of variation.

The one-drop rule is unique in the world because it has resulted from our particular experiences with slavery and racial segregation in the United States. The social statuses and identities of racially mixed people are determined by group power dynamics, just as those of their parent groups are. The varying social structures and histories of societies around the globe have produced sharply contrasting status positions and terms of identity for mixed-race people. Seven different status positions are identified here to help readers gain perspective on current issues of racial identity in the United States. First, we need to examine further the development and effects of the one-drop rule.

■ The Hypodescent Status

Anthropologists call our one-drop rule a hypodescent rule because mixed black/white children are assigned the status position of the lower status parent group—that of blacks. Evidently this first occurred in the mid-1600s in the Chesapeake area of Maryland and Virginia, where miscegenation between white indentured servants and slaves from Africa became widespread. The mixed persons generally were assigned the status of slaves and the same racial identity as African blacks (Williamson 1980). By the early 1700s, the one-drop rule had become the social definition of a black person in the upper South, and from there it spread southward.

Also in the 1600s, a competitor to the one-drop rule emerged. In Louisiana and South Carolina, free mulattoes came to have an in-between, buffer status. These free mulattoes were allied with whites and not considered to be blacks (Williamson 1980). Until the 1840s in South Carolina, mulattoes could become white by behavior and reputation and could marry into white families (Catterall 1926–1937). Louisiana also rejected the one-drop rule, accepting miscegenation and the intermediate status of mulattoes until 1808, when the Louisiana Civil Code prohibited "free people of color" from marrying either whites or blacks (Domínguez 1986).

In a number of states before the Civil War, there were court cases in which persons who had as much African ancestry as one-fourth were declared to be white. The United States had not yet lined up solidly behind the one-drop rule. Finally in the 1850s, in order to preserve slavery, the South came together in firm support of the one-drop rule (Williamson 1980). Although the competing rule was put down, for several decades there were statutes and court decisions that limited the definition of a black person to at least one-fourth, one-eighth, or some other fraction of ancestry.

The Civil War and Reconstruction accelerated the alienation of mulattoes from whites, who made it clear that mulattoes of all shades would be defined as blacks. The one-drop rule gained support in the North as well as the South and was further strengthened at the turn of the twentieth century by the passage of Jim Crow laws in the southern states. These segregation laws were reinforced by extralegal threats and terrorism. Light blacks were as likely as darker ones to pay the ultimate price for alleged violations of the master-servant etiquette for "getting out of their place" (Vander Zanden 1972). The lynching of blacks peaked from 1885 to 1909, and the peak of passing also occurred during this period, although most of those who could pass permanently did not do so (Burma 1946; Eckard 1947). By World War I, the one-drop rule was backed uniformly by US whites.

The one-drop rule was crucial to maintaining Jim Crow segregation, in which widespread miscegenation, not racial "purity," prevailed. The racial double standard of sexual relations gave white men access to black women but protected white women from black men. The entire system of white domination would be threatened by a mixed child living in a white home. Mixed children fathered by white males, defined as black by the one-drop rule, stayed with the mother in the black community (Blaustein and Ferguson 1957; Myrdal, Sterner, and Rose 1944; Rose 1956). US senator Theodore Bilbo of Mississippi trumpeted in a 1947 book that protecting white women from black men was preventing "mongrelization," keeping the white race pure (Bilbo 1947).

By 1925, the African American community had fully accepted the one-drop rule and was giving it strong support. The black community had developed a vested interest in a rule used for centuries to preserve slavery and legalized segregation. The rule had forced all shades of mixed persons into the black community, where, over time, white oppression and other common experiences created a common culture and a sense of ethnic unity and pride. Lighter mulattoes, discriminated against and terrorized by whites, allied themselves more firmly than ever with blacks. Many leaders of the Harlem Renaissance of the 1920s, including Langston Hughes and A. Philip Randolph, were light mulattoes.

The civil rights movement of the 1950s and 1960s put an end to the Jim Crow laws and saw major civil rights legislation passed in Washington, D.C. At the same time, white backlash to the movement strengthened African American support for the one-drop rule. In the 1960s, lighter blacks often felt heavy pressure to affirm their blackness (Williamson 1980). In 1972, the National Association of Black Social Workers (NABSW) strongly endorsed the one-drop rule by passing a resolution against the adoption of black children by white parents (Day 1979). Rejecting the terms "biracial" and "racially mixed," the Association insisted that mixed children be taught to acknowledge their blackness and raised to survive as blacks (Ladner 1977). By the mid-1970s, "cross-racial" adoption had almost stopped, and by 1987, thirty-five or more states had a policy against it. Although the issue has been revived, the NABSW has not changed its position.

In general the one-drop rule has had the support of law. The rule was challenged often in court in the nineteenth century and earlier but not much in the twentieth. State laws defining who is black in terms of fractions of ancestry, or an explicit one-drop rule, have generally been rescinded in recent decades. However, the courts have not invalidated the one-drop rule. In 1983, the rule was upheld by a district court in Louisiana in a lawsuit brought by Susie Phipps (*Jane Doe v. Louisiana*), whose application for a passport was denied because she checked "white" as her race. She looks white, had always lived as white, and thought she was white (Trillin 1986). Lawyers for the state produced evidence that Mrs. Phipps was three thirty-seconds black, and by a 1970 statute, one thirty-second was enough. Before 1970, a "traceable amount" was enough in Louisiana. In 1986 the US Supreme Court refused to review this decision on the ground that no substantial federal question was involved (107 Sup.Ct.Reporter, interim ed. 638). Louisiana has abolished the one thirty-second criterion, but its courts have not ruled against the one-drop rule.

Despite the general support for the one-drop rule by both whites and blacks, there are long-standing examples of rejection of it in both communities (Daniel 1992). Some of the African American children adopted by whites and some children of mixed marriages are socialized to reject the black-only identity. Many Creoles of color in New Orleans and vicinity still reject both the black and the white identity (Domínguez 1986: 163–164). Many Hispanic Americans with some black ancestry resist the rule if they can and embrace a Latino identity (see Chapter 18, this volume). Although a majority of Puerto Rican immigrants have some African ancestry, few of them were identified as black when they were still on the island (Jorge 1979).

Native Americans with some African ancestry generally try to avoid the one-drop rule, usually by staying on a reservation (Bennett 1962). Those who leave the reservation are often treated as blacks. In Virginia, persons who are one-fourth or more Native American and less than one-sixteenth African black have been defined as Indians while on the reservation but as blacks when they leave (Berry 1965). States and tribes differ in their definitions of who is Indian. In the East and South, there are 200 or so small triracial communities that have long evaded the rule by remaining isolated (Berry 1963).

The most common response to deviations from the rule in both the black and the white communities is to condemn the deviations and affirm the rule. Deviant acts and rhetoric call attention to a violated rule and can strengthen the consensus that supports it (Durkheim 1960). For most African Americans of all hues, apparently, the rule gets such constant reinforcement that it provides a clear sense of black ethnic identity. After the US Census Bureau offered respondents the opportunity to designate their own race in 1960, the percentage who checked "black" did not decline significantly.

Problems engendered by the rule, some of them painfully distressing, are borne primarily by the black community. Public concern about these problems does not rise very high because the one-drop rule is so taken for granted by both blacks and whites. All the problems stem from defining as black a mixed population with a rainbow of physical characteristics. The ambiguity of the racial identity of very light blacks often leads to everyday strains and embarrassments, even to traumatic experiences and deep dilemmas of identity.

The rule has other costs, including conflicts in black families and communities over differences in color, hair, and other traits. Darker and "nappier" blacks often receive stinging criticism of their appearance, and the lightest ones are also often harassed and humiliated (Gwaltney 1980). As filmmaker Spike Lee has shown in *School Daze* and later in *Jungle Fever,* intense conflicts among blacks over color and hair accompany dating, sexual relations, and marriage. Color discrimination among blacks also occurs in the workplace, in the media, and elsewhere (Russell, Wilson, and Hall 1992). Is discrimination based on racial traits not a violation of civil rights laws?

Among still other problems are collective anxieties of whites about "invisible blackness" (Williamson 1980) and of blacks about persons who "deny their color." Many white parents of mixed children worry about the suppression of their white ancestry. There is profound anxiety about the rare resort to passing to gain opportunities. There are complex administrative and legal problems in implementing the one-drop rule. The rule causes gross misperceptions of the racial classification of very large populations in Asia, the Middle East, Latin America, and elsewhere. It poses problems of sampling and interpretation in medical and scientific research on racial differences (Davis 1991).

Elsewhere in the world, persons whose ancestry is part African black are perceived as mixed, not as just black. However, the status positions of mixed-race persons vary greatly from one society to another, reflecting different group power dynamics. We now examine six other status and identity positions.

■ The In-Between Status

Remember that the one-drop rule assigns to mixed-race persons the identical status position occupied by the lower status parent group. A second rule assigns persons of mixed heritage a status between that of the parent groups, as occupied by the mulattoes of South Carolina and Louisiana before 1850. Such groups are seen as marginal to both parent groups, but often there is a firmer tie with one than the other. Some middle groups develop a strong separate identity.

Many, if not most, in-between minorities, whether racial hybrid groups or not, meet special occupational needs the dominant community is unable or unwilling to meet. "Middleman minorities," as the economists call them, may or may not have had previous experience with such work. Often the work is onerous, highly stigmatized, or very risky, or it involves long hours. This in-between group serves as a buffer between the groups above and below it. Political and economic changes, especially when they eliminate the group's special occupations, can have drastic consequences for the middle minority. When crises come, the dominant group rarely protects the middle group from the animosity of lower-status groups (Blalock 1967). The vulnerability of the middle minority is especially great when it is occupied by a mixed-race group because of special problems with identity and group acceptance.

Under the apartheid system in the Republic of South Africa, there were two buffer groups between the dominant whites and the native blacks: the Asians and the Coloureds. This system of fourfold segregation was legalized in 1948 (Van den Berghe 1971) and lasted for half a century. During the prolonged crisis that preceded the downfall of the system and of white domination in 1994, the two buffer groups experienced much harassment and violence. Major adjustments in group statuses in recent years are complex and have been proceeding with much less conflict than was expected.

The definitions of the four "race groups" in South Africa remain essentially as they were under the apartheid system. Blacks are unmixed Africans. South African whites often explain who the Coloureds are by saying they are not black and not Asian. Coloureds are any "mixed-blood" persons, including children and descendants of black/Asian and white/Asian unions, not just those of black/white and black/Coloured unions. The bulk of the Coloureds are mulattoes, ranging from very dark to very light, and thus are very similar to most African Americans. Under apartheid, both legal and informal controls were designed to prevent or punish all white/nonwhite sexual contacts, not just those involving white women. There was no double standard. White men were punished as severely for white/nonwhite sexual contacts as black, Asian, and Coloured men were.

Under apartheid, passing as white was facilitated by the infinite gradations of racial traits among the Coloureds, with many mixed persons appearing white. However, far from being secret as in the United States, passing was open, legalized, and administered by a complex bureaucracy. Passing required official reclassification to a different "racial" category, usually from Coloured to white. Some individuals and couples were reclassified more than once, and different members of a family were sometimes classified differently (Watson 1970). Such reclassification could not occur under a one-drop rule.

■ Bottom of the Ladder

By a third rule, persons of mixed race are assigned a status lower than that of either parent group. Not accepted on equal terms by either of the parent race groups, such people are defined as a separate and lowly people, as outcasts. In East Africa, mulattoes among the Ganda peoples of Uganda are regarded with condescension and contempt by the Ganda and not accepted by the English or other whites. For a time there was discussion of a plan to remove all the mulattoes to an island in Lake Victoria where they could be completely isolated (Berry 1965). A similar position is occupied by the métis in Canada, the Anglo-Indians in India, Korean Americans in Korea, and Vietnamese Americans in Vietnam.

The métis population originated in the seventeenth century from unions in the Canadian wilderness between Indian women and French and Scottish trappers. At first, the children were called métis if they spoke French, or "half-breeds" if they spoke English, but eventually all racial hybrids were known as métis. They were regarded as neither white nor Indian. They felt superior to the Indians and would not marry them. They became valued middlemen—buffalo hunters, interpreters, and transporters of supplies and furs by canoe or carts. They plummeted from middle to bottom-of-the-ladder status when white settlement and the coming of the railroads in the latter half of the nineteenth century ended the need for their special occupations.

After the métis rebelled against the Canadian government in 1879 and 1884, they dispersed throughout the Canadian West, despised by whites and Indians alike. Some managed to get accepted on Indian reservations, but most lived as outcasts in poor, isolated areas or moved to towns and cities to become an urban underclass. There may be as many as 750,000 métis now in Canada, more than the number of full Indians. They remain a broken, desperately poor people.

Similarly, the mixed Anglo-Indian population in India went from a relatively secure middle minority status under British colonial rule to a precarious and lowly position, especially after India became independent in 1947 (Gist and Dean 1973). Anthropologists classify South Asians as "Hindu Caucasoids," but the British consider all dark-skinned "native peoples" to be nonwhite, and race is what people believe it to be. There is no place for "mixed-blood" people in the Hindu caste tradition (Ballhatchet 1980). Many Anglo-Indians fled to Australia or England as Indian nationalism grew (Berry 1965), but around a quarter of a million remain in India. Caste has been legally abolished, but the traditions still have force, and the Eurasians remain a despised out-group.

Thousands of Korean American children were born to women in Korea during the Korean War, some fathered by white servicemen and some by African Americans, and many more have been born since. Mixed children face extreme difficulties in Korea, where there is a strong prejudice against marrying someone of a different racial or ethnic group. Citizenship there is paternal, so the mixed children have been defined not as Koreans but as Americans. Children of American males are not granted US citizenship if born out of wedlock outside the United States. The great majority of the children thus have had no country and have been denied the rights of Korean citizens. These children are seen as debased and polluted, and some Korean families have refused to accept them. Mixed children under fifteen years of age can be adopted if the mothers give them up and register them with the Korean government as orphans.

The 80,000 or so mixed children fathered in Vietnam by white and black American military personnel during the war there are called the "dust of life" and treated with contempt. They are virtual outcasts in their own society, where, as in Korea, the child's identity and citizenship rights derive from the father. The US approach to this contrasts sharply with that of the French, who took 25,000 mixed children with them when they left in 1954 and offered them French citizenship. In 1982, the United States began allowing the mixed children to emigrate, provided that Americans adopt the younger ones and sponsor the older ones. Although many of these mixed children in both Vietnam and Korea have been adopted in the United States in recent years, most of them and their descendants remain lowly outcasts (Valverde 1992).

■ Top of the Ladder

Sometimes racially mixed people have achieved a higher status than that of either parent group, as experienced by the mulattoes of Haiti, Liberia, and Namibia, and the mestizos of Mexico (Nicholls 1981; Stoddard 1973). The two examples discussed here required a successful political revolution. In the wealthy French colony on Saint Domingue (Hispaniola), later called Haiti, a slave named Toussaint L'Ouverture began a revolution in 1791 that ended slavery. Previously there had been some 30,000 whites exercising extremely harsh control over half a million black slaves, with about 24,000 free blacks and mulattoes occupying an in-between status. After the rebels achieved independence in 1804, the mulattoes emerged as the economically and politically dominant elites and retained their ascendancy for more than a century and a half. They maintained tight kinship ties among mulatto families, preventing intermarriage with both whites and African blacks. They looked down on both unmixed Africans and the small white population, although the Lebanese, Syrians, and other whites performed valuable middle minority commercial functions (Nicholls 1981). The mulattoes lost control to the Duvalier regime in 1957, later regained it, and lost it again, and the volatile struggle for political power goes on.

The Spanish ruled Mexico for three centuries. During the long colonial period, there was massive miscegenation between the Spanish and Indian populations and some that involved African blacks. At first the term "mestizo" meant half-Spanish and half-Indian, but it came to refer to the entire mixed population, regardless of the degree of mixture. Under Spanish rule, mestizos occupied a middle status position, with Indians on the bottom. The mestizos took pride in their Spanish ancestry and played down their Indian backgrounds (Stoddard 1973). Mestizos became the rulers when Spanish control was overthrown in 1821, and today they are by far the largest group in Mexico. Some Spanish and other whites have retained considerable wealth and influence, but political power remains chiefly in mestizo hands. The overwhelming size of the mestizo group would appear to be a major factor in its political dominance, yet in Haiti the mulatto elites retained control for a long time with relatively small numbers.

■ Highly Variable Status: Latin America

Under a fourth rule, mixed-race persons are assigned a status that may vary from quite low to very high, depending more on education and wealth than on color or other racial traits. In Brazil and lowland Latin America generally, the upper class is called white, but it also includes light mulattoes and mestizos. The middle class is a long ladder with many rungs and is composed mainly of mulattoes, although in some countries it also includes many mestizos. The lower class includes most of the unmixed blacks and Indians, along with a few whites and some mulattoes and mestizos.

Race influences class placement, but it is only one factor, and it may be overcome by wealth and education. A plethora of terms is used for the innumerable gradations of racial mixture, but the color designations depend more on the place on the class ladder than on actual racial traits. As people use educational and economic success to climb the class ladder, their racial designations often change. No secrecy is needed to "pass" to another racial identity (Wagley 1963).

Latin Americans can accept light mulattoes and mestizos as whites, referring to any visible traces of African traits in such euphemistic terms as "brunette" or "a little mulatto" (Solaun and Kronus 1973). In Brazil it is class rather than racial discrimination that is pervasive, sharp, and persistent, even involving class-segregated public facilities and a class-based master-servant etiquette (Harris 1964). The expression "money whitens" indicates that class can have more weight than physical traits in determining racial classification. Census estimates of the number of people in different racial categories can be very misleading when compared with the estimates in the United States or other nations.

In Puerto Rico, as in Latin America generally, miscegenation of whites, native Indians, and African blacks has produced the entire range of skin color and other racial features. A substantial proportion of the mixed population is considered white, including many who are quite dark. Individuals are allowed some choice and room to negotiate for a racial identity (Domínguez 1986). Around 10 percent of Puerto Rican migrants to the United States are unmixed blacks, and half or more of the remainder have some African ancestry. Therefore, some three-fifths of the migrants are perceived as black in the United States, whereas on the island most of them were known either as whites or by one of the many color designations other than black. It comes as a shock to the majority of the migrants to be defined as black in the United States. Some manage to become known as Hispanic whites by emphasizing their Spanish language and heritage, but others fail. Parents in the Puerto Rican immigrant community pressure their young to "whiten" the family in order to succeed, which puts them in conflict with the African American community.

On the Caribbean islands colonized by the Spanish and Portuguese, Iberian whites have readily married lighter mulattoes with visible African traits. Iberian colonists brought with them an ideal image of beauty known as Morena (meaning Moorish) and the acceptance of marriage with mulattoes. By contrast, whites on the Caribbean islands colonized by the English, French, and Dutch have accepted intermarriage only with those mulattoes who look white (Hoetink 1967). It is appearance that counts, however, not known African ancestry, so there is no one-drop rule. The Iberian approach seems to be the general rule in southern Europe and the Near and Middle East. The intermarriage rule on the English, French, and Dutch islands was brought from northern Europe. The one-drop rule is not inherent in British culture, then, or in northwestern Europe generally. It emerged on US soil.

■ Egalitarian Pluralism for the Racially Mixed: Hawai'i

As in Latin America, the status of mixed-race people in Hawai'i can range from quite low to very high, depending on educational and economic achievement. However, color and other racial traits do not affect the class placement in Hawai'i as they do to some extent in Latin America. There is no preoccupation with race in Hawai'i and no color ladder with a preferred hue at the top. Hawai'i has a long tradition of treating the racially mixed in an egalitarian manner that contrasts sharply with the hypodescent status on the US mainland. Despite the eventual wresting of political and economic power from the original Hawaiians by US economic interests in the 1890s, the competitive struggles and occasional conflicts have essentially been those of class and ethnicity, not race.

The Polynesian settlers in the Hawaiian Islands some 1,500 years ago were probably a racial blend of Mongoloid peoples from Southeast Asia and Caucasoid stocks from Indonesia and South Asia (Howard 1980). Further miscegenation with many different peoples began when the first *haoles* (non-Polynesians) came. Captain Cook found in 1778 that Hawaiian hospitality included openness to sexual relations and marriage with outsiders. The haoles never stopped coming, first for a way station for the fur trade; next for sandalwood; then for whales; then for sugarcane, pineapples, and other agricultural products; and finally as tourists. Many white traders and planters took Hawaiian wives, and eventually some of the children of Congregational missionaries from New England took native Hawaiian wives.

The demand for sugarcane workers escalated in the 1850s, and large numbers were brought from China and later from Portugal, other European countries, and Japan. By 1900 the Japanese were the largest ethnic group in Hawai'i. Migrants then came from Puerto Rico, Korea, and the Philippines. Still later, more came from South and East Asia, other Pacific Islands, Mexico, the Middle East, Europe, the United States, and elsewhere. Miscegenation never stopped. By 1930 there were more part-Hawaiians than unmixed ones, and by 1960 nine times as many. By the 1970s, Hawaiians and part-Hawaiians (one-eighth or more) were not quite one-fifth of the population, behind whites and Japanese (Howard 1980: 449–451). Native chiefs had made overly generous trade concessions and had lost much of their land. Revival of traditional culture began in the 1970s, along with charges of past and present discrimination against Hawaiians and part-Hawaiians by wealthy whites and other haole groups (see Chapter 5, this volume). This has been an ethnic and class protest, not a racial one. Clearly the native Hawaiians have been badly exploited, but the basis for it has been greed, not racism. The rhetoric of racist ideology is absent.

There has been no systematic racial segregation and discrimination, either de jure or de facto, and the various peoples in Hawai'i generally are scornful of anyone who exhibits racial prejudice. Many of the Pacific Island peoples are relatively dark-skinned, and the class status of the mixed people in Hawai'i seems to be unaffected by color or other racial traits. Ethnic and racial intermarriages are common, and many people can identify ancestry in several groups. It is considered bad manners to express disapproval of miscegenation. The tolerant, egalitarian balance of pluralism and assimilation extends to racially mixed persons, whose status is no lower or higher than that of the parent groups involved. The first racial hybrids in Hawai'i were highly respected, and this model has had a lasting impact (Adams 1969; Berry 1965).

■ Assimilating Minority Status

The seventh rule accounts for the status of persons in the United States who are partly descended from racial minorities other than African American. The children of the first generation of miscegenation may experience ambiguity or be identified as members of the minority group. However, when the proportion of minority ancestry becomes one-fourth or less in the next generation of mixture, the children are accepted unambiguously as assimilating Americans. There is no need for them to "pass" in order to hide the minority background. In fact, they can be proud of having ancestry that is part Native American, Mexican, Chinese, Japanese, Filipino, Vietnamese, or other Asian, and they find little opposition to intermarriage with whites. There is no one-drop rule to deter their further miscegenation and full assimilation into the dominant Anglo-American community.

For many decades, Chinese immigrants in the United States were despised and did not have the benefit of the status of an assimilating minority. Neither did the earlier Japanese Americans, especially during the days of their relocation to prison camps as enemy aliens during World War II. The operating rule was that everyone with one-eighth or more Japanese ancestry was to be removed to the camps. Since the Japanese had been immigrating to the United States only since 1885, this one-eighth criterion was a sure way to intern everyone with any known Japanese ancestry (Williams 1996). During the war years, then, what was in effect a one-drop rule was used for Japanese Americans.

The foregoing comparative discussion dramatizes the uniqueness of America's one-drop rule. It also shows that the status occupied by mixed-race people in a society can change in response to major shifts in racial group power relations. Experiences in other societies can provide valuable perspective on current issues about racial identity and the one-drop rule. They also suggest the need for caution in extrapolating to other societies the findings on the dynamics of the personal identity of mixed-race people in the United States.

■ The Multiracial Identity Movement

In recent years, new challenges to the one-drop rule have emerged. In the 1980s and 1990s, a movement to allow mixed-race persons to adopt a biracial or multiracial identity rapidly gained momentum. Campus groups were organized at many colleges and universities. A national organization called the Association of Multiethnic Americans (AMEA) was created to coordinate groups in thirty or more cities (Grosz 1989). The emphasis, rather than a frontal attack on the one-drop rule, has been on the freedom to acknowledge all of one's ancestries, including black (Nakashima 1992). The movement includes all racial blends, not just those with African black ancestry.

Mixed-race people with no black ancestry, although not subject to a one-drop rule, have been well aware that the rule for blacks has been responsible for the "check only one" instruction. Until the 2000 census, this rendered persons with Native American, Mexican, Asian, or Pacific Islander forebears unable to acknowledge two or more ancestries. Mexican Americans, the majority of whom are mestizos, had to check "black," "white," or "other." In 1990, 48 percent of them checked "other," and 97 percent of all Americans who checked "other" were Hispanics, who may be of any race or blend.

The marked increase in interracial marriages, although still a small proportion of all marriages, is one argument for recognizing the multiracial identity. The trend that began in the 1960s has accelerated, especially since the *Loving* case, in which the US Supreme Court in 1967 held the Virginia statute prohibiting interracial marriage to be unconstitutional. From 1970 to 1991, mixed-race marriages in the United States tripled. During this same period, births for one black and one white parent increased more than fivefold, and increases almost this large occurred in marriages involving one white and one Asian-American parent (Page 1996).

The vast majority of black/white sexual unions over 350 years have not had the benefit of marriage and have involved white males and black females. By contrast, a large majority of black/white marriages in recent decades have been between a black man and a white woman. One estimate is that at least 30 percent of these couples want to identify their children as biracial or multiracial. Many of these wives do not want their children to have to deny their mother's ancestry.

The multiracial identity movement has faced determined opposition. Many blacks fear that persons who want to affirm their European, Native

American, or Asian ancestry want to deny their African roots (Bates 1993). There is also fear that the movement will divide the black community, reduce its numbers, weaken black political power, and undermine civil rights remedies (Daniel 1992). Some fear that whites want to create a buffer class with a status above that of blacks or a system of "colorism" like the one in lowland Latin America.

Despite the opposition, the movement has had some successes. PROJECT RACE (Reclassify All Children Equally) has persuaded a number of states to require the multiracial option on some official forms, and school districts in several states have added the option (Graham 1995). In 1993, both PROJECT RACE and the AMEA testified in favor of the multiracial option before the Subcommittee on Census, Statistics, and Postal Personnel of the US House of Representatives. These organizations later gave similar testimony to the US Office of Management and Budget (OMB), which defines racial categories for all levels of government in the country, including the public schools (Fernandez 1995).

The policy debate centered mainly on the possible use of the multiracial category on the Census Bureau forms for 2000, an option strongly opposed by the NAACP and other black leaders (Daniel 2000b). The OMB decided to reject the multiracial category but to change the traditional instruction, "check only one," to "check one or more." This compromise was approved by the NAACP, the Urban League, the Congressional Black Caucus, and other black groups (Daniel 2000b). Although it was only a partial victory for the multiracial identity movement, the federal government had finally acknowledged the reality of multiple racial ancestries. To counter the fears of civil rights leaders, the OMB instruction was that persons who check "white" and any minority race are to be counted as members of that minority for the purpose of enforcing civil rights laws. Also, the term "multiracial" was not to be used in interpreting the responses. The plan received unanimous support from thirty federal agencies and was adopted for the collection of all governmental data on race, not just census data (Lew 2000).

The percentage of Americans who checked more than one race in the 2000 census was 2.3. That percentage varies according to age group, however. Among African Americans over the age of fifty, 2.3 percent checked more than one race. However, for blacks eighteen years of age or younger, the percentage was 8.3. This age difference is probably due in part to the increase in the number of young interracial parents, in part to the multiracial identity movement, but also to the public rejection of the one-drop rule by a number of black celebrities. These rejections have been a prominent part of the increased publicity about mixed-race experiences in the past two decades. Issues of identity have been featured in books, articles, films, and newscasts and on talk shows.

One of the most dramatic news stories of the 1990s was the DNA testing that showed the high likelihood that Thomas Jefferson was the father of the last son of his slave Sally Hemmings (Foster 1998). Alex Haley's 1976 book *Roots* and the television series based on it had demonstrated how fully both African Americans and whites accept the one-drop rule. It seemed perfectly natural for Haley to pursue his African roots. In his 1993 book *Queen,* however, Haley focused on his white-appearing grandmother, played by Halle Berry in the television series. In 1990, when Renee Tenison was hailed as the first black woman to be Playboy's "Playmate of the Year," she protested that it was unfair for her to have to deny her white mother (Russell, Wilson, and Hall 1992). When Chelsi Smith was portrayed as the first black winner of the Miss USA pageant in 1995, she insisted that she is both black and white. (The first black winner was actually Carole Gist, in 1990.) It seems unlikely that such celebrities would so publicly reject the one-drop rule without the encouragement of the multiracial identity movement and the heightened awareness in the media.

Shirley Haizlip and her book *The Sweeter the Juice* (1994) were featured on the Oprah Show in 1994. The family members on the show all looked white, but some had passed while others had not. The author appeared on the show to explain how this can happen. In subsequent years, there have been other Oprah shows featuring similar experiences with the color line.

When Tiger Woods won the Masters Championship in 1997 and sports reporters asked how it felt to be the first black winner, he replied that he is not only black. He pointed out that his mother is from Thailand. Evidently he is one-fourth Thai, one-fourth Chinese, one-fourth black, one-eighth Native American, and one-eighth white. In the fall of 2003 in South Africa, US television reporters repeatedly referred to both Tiger and Vijay Singh as blacks. Tiger says he checks "Asian" on forms calling for race, and Singh is from India, not Africa. In South Africa, Tiger would be defined as Coloured, Singh as Asian, and neither one as black.

■ Whither the One-Drop Rule?

Do the successes of the multiracial identity movement, along with the increased media attention, foreshadow the end of the one-drop rule? Or will they join the several patterned deviations that point to the rule and reinforce it? Some states that have passed statutes to legitimate a multiracial category are finding them difficult to implement. It remains to be seen how much the states will follow the OMB's instruction to "check one or more" in collecting governmental data. Evidently it will take a lot to convince most African Americans that they have more to gain than to lose by backing away from the one-drop rule, especially in the face of continuing prejudice and discrimination.

Exceptions can become so blatant, however, that a rule becomes conspicuously obsolete. Significant further changes might be a long time coming, yet the fall of the apartheid system in South Africa in 1994 shows that momentum sometimes builds to a point at which major change can occur very fast. Increasing global awareness puts a spotlight on the US one-drop rule and its uniqueness in the world. Since national origins immigration quotas were abolished in the 1960s, the United States has increasingly become a multiracial, multiethnic society. How rapidly might the view grow that persons with partly black ancestry have a human right to have both or all of their racial backgrounds recognized?

If and when the one-drop rule loses its hold, what then? Of the six other status positions for mixed-race people discussed here, which one might incur the least opposition from most whites and most blacks? Is there one that would be accompanied by problems that are less serious than those resulting from the one-drop rule? Some of the six alternatives could not possibly fit conditions in the United States, especially the bottom-of-the-ladder and the top-of-the-ladder statuses. The idea of a return to the in-between, buffer status would arouse intense hostility in the black community. Light mulatto leaders are highly valued and are held tightly in the embrace of black pride. African Americans also disdain the "colorism" of the Latin American pattern, and most whites would abhor very frequent intermarriage between whites and persons with visibly African traits.

The northern European status for mixed-race people would appear to be the closest alternative to the US hypodescent position. To some whites, marriage with persons with known black ancestry but who look white might seem but a limited and beneficial exception to the one-drop rule. After all, "white blacks" carry very few genes from African ancestors, and many common beliefs about miscegenation are false and racist. Other whites, however, would be dominated by irrational fears of massive miscegenation, widespread passing, and "invisible blackness." As for the black community, few would likely consider it a good thing that those wishing to be assimilated could do so without having to pass secretly and abandon their black families and community. It would require the belief that very few persons would be lost to the white community and that black unity would not be impaired. This leap of faith seems highly unlikely so long as fully equal treatment of blacks is still an elusive goal.

Opposition to the assimilating minority status for the racially mixed would no doubt be very strong. That alternative would require acceptance of widespread intermarriage between whites and persons with one-fourth or less African ancestry. This process has helped visible minorities other than blacks to climb the class ladder and achieve equal treatment. To many, if not most, whites, it would probably seem to be an extreme departure from the one-drop rule, which has been designed to prevent total assimilation of persons with invisible as well as visible black ancestry.

Most blacks want equal treatment and economic and political integration, not total assimilation. Some barriers to opportunities have been lowered, but there is still considerable opposition by both whites and blacks to more informal contacts. Churches are as segregated as ever, urban housing segregation has been increasing, and pressures for black unity have limited social contacts between blacks and whites. Neither the black nor the white community exhibits any enthusiasm for complete assimilation.

Unlikely as it may now seem, the mainland United States might someday move toward the Hawaiian approach as most feasible. Mainlanders who move to Hawai'i have seemed able to accept the island pattern, different though it is, within a few months (Adams 1969). The implicit rule for mixed-race status in Hawai'i is consistent with egalitarian pluralism, an outcome that African Americans and Hispanics generally prefer to full assimilation (Davis 1995). Although that may not be the road taken sooner or even later, we have seen that the status of racially mixed people can be changed by shifts in group power relations. Deeply rooted as it has been, then, the one-drop rule may not be perpetuated forever.

3

Black, Honorary White, White: The Future of Race in the United States?

Eduardo Bonilla-Silva and David G. Embrick

"We are all Americans!"[1] That, we contend, will be the racial mantra of the United States in years to come. Because of the deep history of racial divisions in the United States, many analysts believe this prospect implausible, but nationalist statements denying the salience of race are the norm all over the world. Yet this new "E Pluribus Unum" cry ("Out of Many, One") will not signify the beginning of true racial democracy in the United States. Instead, it will signify, as we hint in the title of the chapter, the reshuffling of racial matters in a way that preserves white supremacy by other means.

Our overall claim is that racial stratification in general and the rules of racial (re)cognition in the United States in particular are slowly coming to resemble those in Latin America. By this statement we mean two things: first, that the biracial system typical of the United States, which was the exception in the world-racial system (see Balibar and Wallerstein 1991; Mills 1997; Winant 2002), is evolving into a complex racial order.[2] Specifically, we argue the United States is developing a loose triracial stratification system with *whites* at the top, an intermediary group of *honorary whites* (similar to the middle racial strata in Latin America and the Caribbean), and a nonwhite group, or the *collective black*,[3] at the bottom. As we suggest in Figure 3.1, the white group will include "traditional" whites; new "white" immigrants; and in the near future, assimilated Latinos, some multiracials (light-skinned ones), and individual members of other groups (some Asian Americans, etc.). We predict the intermediate racial group will comprise most light-skinned Latinos (e.g., most Cubans and segments of the Mexican and Puerto Rican communities) (Rodríguez 1999), Japanese Americans, Korean Americans, Asian Indians, Chinese Americans, the bulk of multiracials (see Rockquemore and Arend 2004), and most Middle Eastern

Figure 3.1 Preliminary Map of the Triracial System in the United States

Whites
  Whites
  New Whites (Russians, Albanians, etc.)
  Assimilated white Latinos
  Some multiracials (white-looking ones)
  Assimilated (urban) Native Americans
  A few Asian-origin people

Honorary Whites
  Light-skinned Latinos
  Japanese Americans
  Korean Americans
  Asian Indians
  Chinese Americans
  Middle Eastern Americans
  Most multiracials

Collective Black
  Filipinos
  Vietnamese
  Hmong
  Laotians
  Dark-skinned Latinos
  Blacks
  New West Indian and
    African immigrants
  Reservation-bound
    Native Americans

Americans. Finally, the collective black will include blacks, dark-skinned Latinos, Vietnamese, Cambodians, Laotians, and maybe Filipinos.

Our racial cartography is heuristic rather than definitive and thus we include it as a guide of how we think the various ethnic groups will line up in the emerging racial order. We acknowledge, however, that (1) the position of some groups may change (e.g., many Chinese Americans, Asian Indians, and Arab Americans may end up in the collective black); (2) the map is not inclusive of all the groups in the United States (for instance, Samoans, Micronesians, and other groups are not in the map); and (3) at this early stage of our project and given some serious data limitations, some groups may end up in a different racial strata altogether (e.g., Filipinos may become "honorary whites" rather than another group in the collective black strata).

The second component of our Latin Americanization thesis is that color will increase in significance in a host of social transactions and interactions (Herring, Keith, and Horton 2004; Hochschild 2003). This shift will involve categorical porosity as well as "pigmentocracy," making the map useful for group- rather than individual-level predictions. The term "categorical porosity" refers to individual members of a racial strata moving up (or down) the stratification system (e.g., a light-skinned, middle-class black person marrying a white woman and moving to the "honorary white" strata), and pigmentocracy refers to the rank ordering of groups and members of groups according to phenotype and cultural characteristics (e.g., Filipinos being at the top of the "collective black" group, given their high level of education and income as well as high rate of marriage with whites).

We recognize that our thesis is broad (attempting to classify where everyone will fit in the racial order) and hard to verify empirically with the available data (there is not a single data set that includes systematic data on the skin tone of all Americans). Nevertheless, it is paramount to begin pushing for a paradigm shift in the field of race relations, and we consider this chapter as a preliminary effort in that direction.

■ Alternative Racial Scenarios to Latin Americanization

We are not alone in making predictions about the racial future of this country. There are at least four alternative readings of what may happen in the future. First are racial optimists who argue that the United States is slowly moving toward a more perfect racial democracy. I have addressed the problems with this claim elsewhere (Bonilla-Silva 2001). Second come those who contend that the increasing racial diversity in the United States will lead to balkanization and cultural bastardization (Huntington 2004a). This argument is predicated on outdated Anglo-Saxon arguments and empirically flawed (the United States has always had racial and ethnic balkanization). Third are those who postulate that the various racial minorities will secure their own place in the US racial pentagram. Cedric Herring (2002), for instance, proposed the niche as a model to better capture US racial dynamics in a recent symposium on my thesis in *Race and Society;* many other analysts agree with him (e.g., Vaca 2004). This argument has some similarities to ours, but as we shall see, ours includes the possibility of cross-racial and ethnic solidarities and even identities (but see Bonilla-Silva 2004a). Last come those who argue that the biracial stratification order will remain in place because Asians and Latinos will join the white group. Because this is the subject of Chapter 4 in this volume, we take some time here to discuss that claim and why we do not think it will materialize.

The argument of our colleagues George Yancey, Tukufu Zuberi (2001/ 2003), and Herbert Gans (1999) deserve full consideration as a plausible alternative to ours. It is true that many Latinos and Asians self-identify as white. It is also true that historically many "non-yet-white" Europeans (Roediger 1999) who were viewed as unworthy candidates for assimilation and citizenship were later incorporated into the white family. Hence, if the aforementioned groups become white, the old "black/nonblack divide" will be maintained (Yancey 2003c).

Although the arguments of our colleagues are meritorious and we agree with them on many points (we too believe that many Latinos and Asians will become white), we contend that their overall claim is unlikely for the following four reasons:

1. Latinos and Asians are not "new immigrants." They have been in the United States since at least the nineteenth century! Therefore, if they were going to become white, that process should have started in the 1830s (for Mexican Americans) and 1840s for (Chinese Americans). The fact that it has not happened (we acknowledge that some Asians and Latinos, like

light-skinned blacks in the past, became white through passing) suggests that the racialization of these groups is different from that of people of European descent. It is possible that a new racialization is occurring, making all these groups white, but the available data do not suggest it.

2. All racial categories are historico-political constructions and therefore always exhibit malleability and porosity. However, the incorporation of groups into the US white category has shown, so far, to have some epidermic boundaries; that is, groups and individuals added to the category have looked European. Hence, groups lacking epidermic capital (such as Latinos and Asians) will have more trouble getting admission into whiteness. Yet, the fact that Armenians and Iranians were incorporated into the white category in the past suggests that the boundaries of US whiteness may be more flexible than one thinks.

3. The kind of assimilation process experienced by some groups (e.g., Mexican Americans, Dominicans, Puerto Ricans, Filipinos, etc.) seems different from that of European immigrants in the early part of the twentieth century. Thus, analysts now use the term "segmented assimilation" to refer to the variety of outcomes of these groups (Rumbaut and Portes 2001b).

4. The class and cultural distance between the masses of Mexican, Central American, and some Asian immigrants and whites is such that it is unlikely that most of them will be able to become white. The Mexican, Puerto Rican, and Dominican barrios and the Chinese, Korean, and Vietnamese towns across the nation differ from the temporary ethnic ghettos of the past. Some of these neighborhoods boast more than 100 years of existence, a very long time to be regarded as "transition neighborhoods."

We repeat that many of these new immigrants, as well as many from older minority groups, will either become white or near-white (honorary white). Our main difference with Yancey and others is that we believe that most of these people will not become white and will join blacks in a large, loose group at the bottom of the racial hierarchy (hence, blacks will not be alone at the bottom).

■ Why Latin Americanization Now?

The reasons for the Latin Americanization of race and race relations in the United States are multiple. First, the demography of the nation is changing. Racial minorities comprise up to 30 percent of the population today and, as population projections suggest, may become a numeric majority in the year 2050 (Bean and Stevens 2003; Saenz and Morales 2005; US Bureau of the Census 1996). And these projections may be slightly off: data from the 2000 Census suggest that the Latino population was about 12.5 percent of the population, almost 1 percentage point higher than the highest projection, and the proportion of whites (77.1 percent white or in combination) was slightly lower than originally expected (Grieco and Cassidy 2001).

The rapid darkening of the United States is creating a situation similar to that of Puerto Rico, Cuba, or Venezuela in the sixteenth and seventeenth centuries or Argentina, Chile, and Uruguay in the late eighteenth and early nineteenth centuries. In both historical periods, the elites realized their countries were becoming "black" (or "nonwhite") and devised a number of strategies (unsuccessful in the former and successful in the latter) to whiten their population (Helg 1990). Although whitening the population through immigration or by classifying many newcomers as white (Gans 1999; Warren and Twine 1997) is a possible solution to the new US demography, for reasons discussed below, we do not think such a solution is likely. Hence, a more plausible accommodation to the new racial reality is to (1) create an intermediate racial group to buffer racial conflict; (2) allow some newcomers into the white racial strata; and (3) incorporate most immigrants into the collective black strata.

Second, as part of the tremendous reorganization that transpired in the United States in the post–civil rights era, a new kinder and gentler white supremacy emerged, which Bonilla-Silva has labeled elsewhere as the "new racism" (Bonilla-Silva 2001; Bonilla-Silva and Lewis 1999; Smith 1995). In the post–civil rights United States, the maintenance of systemic white privilege is accomplished socially, economically, psychologically, and politically through institutional, covert, and apparently nonracial practices. Whether in banks or universities, in stores or housing markets, "smiling discrimination" (Brooks 1990) tends to be the order of the day. This new white supremacy has produced an accompanying ideology that rings Latin America all over: the ideology of color-blind racism. This ideology denies the salience of race, scorns those who talk about race, and increasingly proclaims that "We are all Americans" (see Bonilla-Silva 2001).

Third, race relations have become globalized (Lusane 1997). The once almost all-white Western nations have now "interiorized the other" (Miles 1993). The new world-systemic need for capital accumulation has led to the incorporation of "dark" foreigners as "guest workers" and even as permanent workers (Schoenbaum and Pond 1996). Thus today, European nations have racial minorities in their midst who are progressively becoming an underclass (Castles and Miller 1993; Cohen 1997), have developed an internal "racial structure" (Bonilla-Silva 1997) to maintain white power, and have a curious racial ideology that combines ethnonationalism with a race-blind ideology similar to the color-blind racism of the contemporary United States (Bonilla-Silva 2000).

This new global racial reality, we believe, will reinforce the Latin Americanization trend in the United States, as versions of color-blind racism will become prevalent in most Western nations. Furthermore, as many formerly almost-all-white Western countries (e.g., Germany, France, England, etc.) become more and more diverse, the Latin American model of racial stratification may surface in these societies too.

Fourth, the convergence of the political and ideological actions of the Republican Party, conservative commentators and activists, and the so-called multiracial movement (Rockquemore and Brunsma 2002a) has created the space for the radical transformation of the way we gather racial data in the United States. One possible outcome of the Census Bureau's categorical back-and-forth on racial and ethnic classifications is either the dilution of racial data or the elimination of race as an official category (for more on the multiracial "movement" and its implications, see Chapter 11 in this volume). At this point, Ward Connerly (president and founder of the American Civil Rights Institute, a member of the University of California Board of Regents, and one of the most strident opponents of affirmative action) and his cronies lost the first round in California's Racial Privacy Initiative (see Chapter 9 in this volume), but we believe that they may be successful in other states.

Last, the attack on affirmative action, which is part of what Stephen Steinberg (1995) has labeled as the "racial retreat," is the clarion call signaling the end of race-based social policy in the United States. The 2003 Supreme Court decision *Grutter vs. Bollinger,* hailed by some observers as a victory, is at best a weak victory because it allows for a "narrowly tailored" employment of race in college admissions, imposes an artificial twenty-five-year deadline for the program, and encourages a monumental case-by-case analysis for admitting students that is likely to create chaos and push institutions into making admissions decisions based on test scores. Again, this trend reinforces our Latin Americanization thesis because the elimination of race-based social policy is, among other things, predicated on the notion that race no longer affects minorities' status. Nevertheless, as in Latin America, we may eliminate race by decree and maintain—or even increase—the level of racial inequality.

■ Objective Standing of "Whites," "Honorary Whites," and "Blacks"

If Latin Americanization is happening in the United States, gaps in income, poverty rates, and occupational standing between whites, honorary whites, and the collective black should be developing. The available data suggest that is the case. In terms of income, as Table 3.1 shows, "white" Latinos (Argentines, Chileans, Costa Ricans, and Cubans) are doing much better than dark-skinned Latinos (Mexicans, Puerto Ricans, etc.). The apparent exceptions in Table 3.1 (Bolivians and Panamanians) are examples of self-selection among these immigrant groups. For example, four of the largest

Table 3.1 Mean Per Capita Income[a] ($) of Selected Latino and Asian Ethnic Groups Versus That of Whites and Blacks, 2000

Latino Mean Income	
Mexicans	9,467.30
Guatemalans	11,178.60
Puerto Ricans	11,314.95
Salvadorans	11,371.92
Costa Ricans	14,226.92
Panamanians	16,181.20
Bolivians	16,322.53
Cubans	16,741.89
Chileans	18,272.04
Argentines	23,589.99
Asian American Mean Income	
Hmong	5,175.34
Cambodians	8,680.48
Laotians	10,375.57
Vietnamese	14,306.74
Koreans	16,976.19
Filipinos	19,051.53
Chinese	20,728.54
Taiwanese	22,998.05
Japanese	23,786.13
Asian Indians	25,682.15
White Mean Income	17,968.87
Black Mean Income	11,366.74

Source: US Bureau of the Census 2003.
Note: a. We use per capita income. Using family income distorts the status of some groups (particularly Asians and whites) because some groups have more people than others contributing toward the family income.

ten concentrations of Bolivians in the United States are in Virginia, a state where just 7.2 percent of the population identifies as Latino (US Bureau of the Census 2001b).[4]

Table 3.1 also shows that Asians exhibit a pattern similar to that of Latinos. Hence, a severe income gap is emerging between honorary white Asians (Japanese, Koreans, Filipinos, and Chinese) and those Asians we contend belong to the collective black (Vietnamese, Cambodian, Hmong, and Laotians). Substantial group differences fitting our thesis are also evident in the occupational status, poverty rates, and wealth of the groups (see Bonilla-Silva and Glover 2004).

■ Subjective Standing of Racial Strata

Social psychologists have amply demonstrated that it takes very little for groups to form, to develop a common view, and to adjudicate status positions to nominal characteristics (Ridgeway 1991; Tajfel 1970). Thus, it should not be surprising if gaps in income, occupational status, and education among these various strata contribute to group formation and consciousness. That is, honorary whites may be classifying themselves as "white" and believing they are different (better) than those in the collective black category. If that is happening, this group should also be in the process of developing "white" racial attitudes befitting their new social position and differentiating (distancing) themselves from the collective black.

In line with our thesis, we expect whites to be making distinctions between honorary whites and the collective black, specifically exhibiting a more positive outlook toward honorary whites than toward members of the collective black. Finally, if Latin Americanization is happening, we speculate that the collective black should exhibit a diffused and contradictory racial consciousness, as blacks and Indians do throughout Latin America and the Caribbean (Hanchard 1994).

Social Identity of Honorary Whites

Self-reports on race: The case of Latinos. Historically, most Latinos have classified themselves as "white," but the proportion of Latinos who self-classify as such varies tremendously by group. Hence, as Table 3.2 shows, 60 percent or more of the members of the Latino groups we regard as honorary white self-classify as white, but less than 50 percent of the members of the groups we regard as belonging to the collective black do so. As a case in point, Mexicans, Dominicans, and Central Americans are very likely to report "Other" as their preferred "racial" classification, whereas

Table 3.2 Racial Self-Classification by Selected Latin America Origin (percentage), 2000

	White	Black	Other	Native American	Asian
Latino Ethnic Groups					
Dominicans	28.21	10.93	59.21	1.07	0.57
Salvadorans	41.01	0.82	56.95	0.81	0.41
Guatemalans	42.95	1.24	53.43	2.09	0.28
Hondurans	48.51	6.56	43.41	1.24	0.29
Mexicans	50.47	0.92	46.73	1.42	0.45
Puerto Ricans	52.42	7.32	38.85	0.64	0.77
Costa Ricans	64.83	5.91	28.18	0.56	0.53
Bolivians	65.52	0.32	32.79	1.32	0.05
Colombians	69.01	1.53	28.54	0.49	0.44
Venezuelans	75.89	2.58	20.56	0.36	0.60
Chileans	77.04	0.68	21.27	0.44	0.56
Cubans	88.26	4.02	7.26	0.17	0.29
Argentines	88.70	0.33	10.54	0.08	0.35

Source: US Bureau of the Census 2003.

most Costa Ricans, Cubans, Chileans, and Argentines choose the "white" descriptor. These Census 2000 data mirror the results of the 1988 Latino National Political Survey (de la Garza et al. 1993).[5]

"Racial" distinctions among Asians. Although for political matters, Asians tend to vote panethnically (Espiritu 1992), distinctions between native-born and foreign-born (e.g., US-born Chinese and foreign-born Chinese) and between economically successful and unsuccessful Asians are developing. In fact, according to various analysts, given the tremendous diversity of experiences among Asian Americans "all talk of Asian panethnicity should now be abandoned as useless speculation" (San Juan 2000: 10). Leland Saito (1998), in *Race and Politics,* points out that many Asians have reacted to the "Asian flack" they are experiencing with the rise in Asian immigration by fleeing the cities of immigration, disassociating themselves from new Asians, and invoking the image of the "good immigrant." In some communities, this practice has pushed older, assimilated segments of a community to dissociate from recent migrants.

To be clear, our point is not that Asian Americans have not engaged in coalition politics and, in various locations, engaged in concerted efforts to elect Asian American candidates (Saito 1998). Our aim is to point out that the group labeled "Asian Americans" is divided along many axes and to forecast that many of those already existing divisions will be racialized by whites (e.g., sexploitation of Asian women by lonely white men in the "Oriental bride" market) (Kitano and Daniels 1995) as well as by Asian American themselves (e.g., intra-Asian preferences seem to follow a racialized hierarchy of desire) (see Tuan 1998).

Racial Attitudes of Various Racial Strata

Latinos' racial attitudes. Although researchers have shown that Latinos tend to hold negative views of blacks and positive views of whites (Mindiola, Rodríguez, and Niemann 1996; Niemann et al. 1994; Yoon 1995), the picture is actually more complex. Immigrant Latinos tend to have more negative views about blacks than native-born Latinos. For instance, a study of Latinos in Houston, Texas, found that 38 percent of native-born Latinos, compared to 47 percent of the foreign-born, held negative stereotypes of blacks (Mindiola, Rodríguez, and Niemann 1996). This may explain why 63 percent of native-born Latinos versus 34 percent of foreign-born report frequent contact with blacks.

But the incorporation of the majority of Latinos as "colonial subjects" (Puerto Ricans), refugees from wars (Central Americans), or illegal migrant workers (Mexicans) has foreshadowed subsequent patterns of integration into the racial order. In a similar vein, the incorporation of a minority of Latinos as "political refugees" (Cubans, Chileans, and Argentines) or as "neutral" immigrants trying to better their economic situation (Costa Ricans, Colombians) has allowed them a more comfortable ride in the US racial boat (Pedraza 1985). Therefore, although the incorporation of most Latinos into the United States has meant becoming "nonwhite," for a few it has meant becoming almost white.

Nevertheless, given that most Latinos experience discrimination in labor and housing markets as well as in schools, they quickly realize their "nonwhite" status. This experience leads them, as Nilda Flores-Gonzales (1999) and Suzanne Oboler (1995) have shown, to adopt a plurality of identities that signify "otherness." Thus, dark-skinned Latinos are even calling themselves "black" or "Afro-Dominicans" or "Afro-Puerto Rican" (Howard 2001). For example, José Ali, a Latino interviewed by Clara Rodríguez (2000: 56), stated, "By inheritance I am Hispanic. However, I identify more with blacks because to white America, if you are my color, you are a nigger. I can't change my color, and I do not wish to do so." When asked, "Why do you see yourself as black?" he said, "Because when I was jumped by whites, I was not called 'spic,' but I was called a 'nigger.'"

The identification of most Latinos as "racial others" has made them more likely to be pro-black than pro-white. Table 3.3, for example, indicates that the proportion of Mexicans and Puerto Ricans who feel very warmly toward blacks is much higher (about 12 percent for Mexicans and 14 percent for Puerto Ricans) than the proportion of those groups who feel warmly toward Asians (the readings in the "thermometer" range from 0 to 100, and the higher the "temperature" is, the more positive are the feelings toward the group in question). In contrast, the proportion of Cubans who feel very warmly toward blacks is 10 to 14 percentage points *lower* than the same for Mexicans and Puerto Ricans. Cubans are also more likely to feel very warmly toward Asians than toward blacks. More fitting for our thesis, Latinos who identify as "white" express similar empathy toward blacks and

Table 3.3 Proportion of Latinos Who Express High Affect Toward Blacks and Asians

Degrees of Feeling Thermometer	Blacks (%)	Asians (%)
Mexicans		
warm (51–74)	11.9	11.8
very warm (75–100)	34.3	22.2
Puerto Ricans		
warm (51–74)	11.8	9.0
very warm (75–100)	39.5	25.3
Cubans		
warm (51–74)	14.5	9.9
very warm (75–100)	25.1	29.9

Source: Forman, Martinez, and Bonilla-Silva n.d.

Asians, whereas those who identify as "black" express the most positive affect toward blacks (about 20 degrees warmer toward blacks than toward Asians) (see Bonilla-Silva and Glover 2004).

Asians' racial attitudes. Various studies have documented that Asians tend to hold antiblack and anti-Latino attitudes. For instance, Bobo et al. (1995) found that Chinese residents of Los Angeles expressed negative racial attitudes toward blacks. One Chinese resident stated, "Blacks in general seem to be overly lazy," and another asserted, "Blacks have a definite attitude problem" (Bobo et al. 1995: 78; see also Bobo and Johnson 2000). Studies on Korean shopkeepers in various locales have found that over 70 percent of them hold antiblack attitudes (Min 1996; Weitzer 1997; Yoon 1997).

These general findings are confirmed in Table 3.4. This table contains data on the degree (on a scale running from 1 to 7) to which various racial groups subscribe to stereotypes about the intelligence and welfare dependency of other groups. The table clearly shows that Asians (in this study, Koreans, Chinese, and Japanese) are more likely than even whites to hold antiblack and anti-Latino views (for example, whites score 3.79 and 3.96 for blacks and Latinos, respectively, whereas Asians score 4.39 and 4.46). In line with this finding, they hold, comparatively speaking, more positive views about whites than Latinos and blacks (for a more thorough analysis, see Bobo and Johnson 2000). Thus, as in many Latin American and Caribbean societies, members of the intermediate racial strata buffer racial matters by holding more pro-white attitudes than whites themselves.

Table 3.4 Relationship Between Race/Ethnicity and Racial Stereotypes of Intelligence and Welfare Dependency of Blacks, Latinos, Asians, and Whites in Los Angeles, 1993–1994

	Group Stereotyped			
Group Stereotyping	Blacks	Latinos	Asians	Whites
Unintelligent				
White	3.79	3.96	2.90	3.09
Asians	4.39	4.46	2.90	3.25
Latinos	3.93	3.57	2.74	2.87
Blacks	3.31	3.96	3.21	3.32
F-ratio	***	***	***	***
Prefer Welfare				
White	4.22	4.08	2.30	2.48
Asians	5.10	5.08	2.52	2.93
Latinos	5.57	4.49	2.77	2.77
Blacks	4.12	4.29	2.67	2.77
F-ratio	***	***	***	***

Source: Forman, Martinez, and Bonilla-Silva n.d.

Notes: Responses were made on a scale of 1 to 7, where 1 is low stereotyping and 7 is high stereotyping.

*** F-ratios were all significant at p ≤ .001 level.

The collective black and whites' racial attitudes. After a protracted conflict over the meaning of whites' racial attitudes (see Bonilla-Silva and Lewis 1999), survey researchers seem to have reached an agreement: "a hierarchical racial order continues to shape all aspects of American life" (Dawson 2000: 344). Whites express and defend their social position on issues such as affirmative action and reparations, school integration and busing, neighborhood integration, welfare reform, and even the death penalty (see Bonilla-Silva 2001; Sears et al. 2000; Tuch and Martin 1997). Regarding how whites think about Latinos and Asians, not many researchers have separated the groups that comprise "Latinos" and "Asians" to assess if whites are making distinctions. However, the available evidence suggests whites regard Asians highly and are significantly less likely to hold Latinos in high regard (Bobo and Johnson 2000). Thus, when judged on a host of racial stereotypes, whites rate themselves and Asians almost identically (favorable stereotype rating) and rate negatively (at an almost equal level) both blacks and Latinos.

Bobo and Johnson also show that Latinos tend to rate blacks negatively and that blacks tend to do the same regarding Latinos. They also found that Latinos, irrespective of national ancestry, self-rate lower than whites and Asians (blacks, however, self-rate at the same level with whites and as better than Asians). This pattern seems to confirm Latin Americanization in the United States because those at the bottom in Latin America tend to have a diffused racial consciousness. Our contention seems further bolstered by their findings that "blacks give themselves ratings that tilt in an unfavorable dimension on the traits of welfare dependency and involvement with gangs" and that "for Latinos three of the dimensions tilt in the direction of negative in-group ratings" (Bobo and Johnson 2000: 103).

■ Social Interaction Among Members of the Three Racial Strata

If Latin Americanization is happening, one would expect more social (e.g., friendship, associations as neighbors, etc.) and intimate (e.g., marriage) contact between whites and honorary whites than between whites and members of the collective black. A cursory analysis of the data suggests that is in fact the case.

Interracial Marriage

Although most marriages in the United States are still intraracial, the rates vary substantially by group: 93 percent of whites and blacks marry within their own group, but 70 percent of Latinos and Asians do so, and only 33 percent of Native Americans marry Native Americans (Moran 2001). More significantly, when one disentangles the generic terms "Asians" and "Latinos," the data fit the Latin Americanization thesis even more closely. Although the

Asian American outmarriage pattern is very complex (groups such as Filipinos and Vietnamese have higher than expected rates, in part due to the Vietnam War and the military bases in the Philippines), it is worthwhile to point out that the highest rate belongs to Japanese Americans and Chinese (Kitano and Daniels 1995) and the lowest to Southeast Asians.

Furthermore, racial assimilation through marriage ("whitening") is significantly more likely for the children of Asian-white and Latino-white unions than for those of black/white unions, a fact that bolsters our Latin Americanization thesis. Only 22 percent of the children of black fathers and white mothers are classified as white, whereas the children of similar unions among Asians are twice as likely to be classified as white (Waters 1997). For Latinos, the data fit our thesis even more closely: Latinos of Cuban, Mexican, and South American origin have high rates of exogamy compared to Puerto Ricans and Dominicans (Gilbertson, Fitzpatrick, Yang 1996). We concur with Rachel Moran's (2001) speculation that because Puerto Ricans and Dominicans have far more dark-skinned members (see Table 3.2), they have restricted chances for outmarriage to whites in a highly racialized marriage market.

In analyses not presented in this chapter, we found that "Latinos" (there is no systematic data by groups and by phenotype) are more likely than "Asians" to experience residential segregation. Moreover, the Latinos who experience the highest degree of segregation are Dominicans and Puerto Ricans, the darkest of all Latinos in the United States (Massey and Denton 1987; Zubrinsky 2003). These findings mostly fit our Latin Americanization thesis.

■ Latin Americanization and Racial Justice in America

We have presented a broad and bold thesis about the future of racial stratification in the United States (see also Matsuda 1996; Oboler 2000; Okihiro 1994; Spears 1999). However, at this early stage of the analysis and given the serious limitations of the data on "Latinos" and "Asians" (most data are not parceled out by subgroups, and hardly any are separated by skin tone), it is hard to make a conclusive case. It is plausible that factors such as nativity or other socioeconomic characteristics explain some of the patterns we have documented.[6] Nevertheless, almost all the objective, subjective, and social interaction indicators we reviewed fit our thesis. For example, the objective data show substantive gaps between the groups we labeled "white," "honorary white," and the "collective black." In terms of income and education, whites tend to be slightly better off than honorary whites, who tend to be significantly better off than the collective black. Not surprisingly, a variety of subjective indicators signal the emergence of *internal* stratification among racial minorities. For example, some Latinos living in the United States (e.g., Cubans, Argentines, Chileans, etc.) are very likely to self-classify as whites, but others are not (e.g., Dominicans and Puerto Ricans). These "white" Latinos have therefore developed a racial attitudinal profile similar to that of whites. Finally, the objective and subjective indicators have an interactional correlate. Data on interracial marriage and residential segregation show that whites are significantly more likely to live near honorary whites and intermarry with them than with members of the collective black.

If our predictions are right, what will be the consequences of Latin Americanization for racial justice in the United States? First, political mobilization along racial lines will be harder to accomplish as "honorary whites" grow in size and social importance. They are likely to buffer racial conflict—or derail it—as intermediate groups do in Latin American and Caribbean countries.

Second, the ideology of color-blind racism will become even more salient among whites and honorary whites and will also affect members of the collective black. Color-blind racism (Bonilla-Silva 2001), an ideology similar to that prevalent in Latin American societies, will help glue the new social system and further buffer racial conflict.

Third, if the states decide to stop gathering racial statistics, the struggle to document the impact of race in a variety of social venues will become monumental. More significantly, because state actions always influence civil society, if the states decide to disregard race at their level, the *social* recognition of "races" in the polity may become harder. We may develop a Latin American–like "disgust" for even mentioning anything that is race-related.

Fourth, the deep history of black/white divisions in the United States has been such that the centrality of the black identity will not dissipate. Even the "black elite" exhibits racial attitudes in line with their racial group rather than with their potential class/race trajectory (Dawson 1994). That identity, as we argued in this chapter, may be taken up by dark-skinned Latinos (and maybe some Asian Americans) and is being rapidly taken up by most West Indians.

However, we predict some important changes even in the black community. Blacks' racial consciousness will become more diffuse. For example, blacks will be more likely to accept many stereotypes about themselves (e.g., "We are lazier than whites") and have a "blunted oppositional consciousness" (see Bonilla-Silva 2001). Furthermore, the external pressure of "multiracials" in white contexts (Rockquemore and Brunsma 2002a) and the internal pressure of "ethnic" blacks may change the notion of "blackness" and even the position of some "blacks" in the system. Colorism may become an even more important factor as a way of making social distinctions among "blacks" (Keith and Herring 1991).

Fifth, the new racial stratification system will be more effective in maintaining "white supremacy" (Mills 1997). Whites will still be at the top of the social structure but will face fewer race-based challenges. And to avoid confusion about our claim regarding "honorary whites," let us clarify that their standing and status will depend upon whites' wishes and practices. "Honorary" means that they will remain secondary, will still face discrimination, and will not receive equal treatment in society. For example, although we regard Arab Americans as "honorary whites," their treatment in the post–September 11 era suggests their status as "white" and "American" is very tenuous. Similarly, Asian Americans, regardless of their views and their high level of interaction with whites, are still deemed to be "perpetual foreigners."

But not everything has to be gloomy in a Latin America–like America. All systems of racial domination create fractures and subjects who are likely to fight the system. In a Latin Americanized US, the fracture will be the large contingent of people at the new bottom: the collective black. They constitute the potential "historic bloc" to fight back and, if they solidify as a social group, could be the majority in the country for the first time in history. Even those in the honorary white category exhibit vulnerabilities that, if properly politicized, can be exploited to increase the size of those opposing the new white supremacy order.

Yet, the above scenario of resistance implies systematic politicization, organization, and work, processes that have not been part of the US landscape since the civil rights era. If passivity reigns or if we do not understand adequately what is transpiring, Latin America–like race relations will crystallize, and the United States will become a society with more rather than less racial inequality but with a reduced forum for racial contestation. The apparent blessing of "not seeing race" will become a curse for those struggling for racial justice in years to come. We may become "all Americans," as commercials in recent times suggest, but paraphrasing George Orwell, "some will be more American than others."

■ Notes

1. Since September 11, 2001, the United States has embarked on what we regard as temporary "social peace," and the motto, "We are all Americans," has become quite commonplace. Popular parading of the multiracial capture of the country, while continuing to circumvent interracial unions, suggests that "We (may be) all Americans," but we do have our own subnational or racial primary associations. Meanwhile, the inequalities between minorities and whites, men and women, and workers and capitalists remain. In short, this new Americanism, like the old Americanism, is a *herrenvolk* nationalism (Lipsitz 1998; Winant 1994).

2. Our contention is *not* that the black/white dynamic ordained race relations throughout the United States. Instead, our argument is that at the national macro-level, race relations have been organized in the United States along a white/nonwhite divide. This large divide, depending on context, included various racial groups (whites, blacks, and Indians or whites, Mexicans, Indians, and blacks, etc.), but under the white/nonwhite racial order, "whites" were often treated as superior and "nonwhites" as inferiors. For a few exceptions to this pattern, see Daniel's (2000b) discussion of "triracial isolates."

3. We are adapting Antonio Negri's idea of the "collective worker" to the situation of all those at the bottom of the racial stratification system (see Fleming 1984).

4. The Bolivian Census of 2001 reports that 71 percent of Bolivians self-identify as Indian, less than 20 percent have more than a high school diploma, and 58.6 percent live below the poverty line; in contrast, 66 percent of Bolivians in the United States self-identify as white and 64 percent have twelve or more years of education, and have a per capita income comparable to that of whites (Censo Nacional de Población y Vivienda 2002). Thus, the situation of Bolivians in the United States seems like a case of self-selection, that is, they do not represent Bolivians in Bolivia.

5. Survey experiments have shown that if the question on Hispanic origin is asked first, the proportion of Latinos report themselves as "white" increases from 25 to 39 percent (Martin, Demaio, and Campanelli 1990). The same research also shows that when Latinos report belonging to the "Other" category, they are not mistaken, that is, they do want to signify they are neither black nor white. Unfortunately, we do not have results by national groups, but we think this finding does not alter the direction of the overall findings on the self-identification of various Latino groups.

6. Is it color, nativity, education, or class that determines where groups fit in our scheme? It is an empirical question. An alternative explanation of our findings is that "honorary whites" come with high levels of human capital *before* they achieve honorary white status in the United States—thus, class background is key. However, some available data suggest that race/color has an impact on the success of immigrants in the United States. For example, the case of West Indians—who come to the United States with class advantages (e.g., an education) and yet "fade to black" in a few generations—suggests that the "racial" status of the group is independent and also key (Kasinitz, Battle, and Miyares 2001; Model 1991). Also, although some of these groups may do "well" objectively, they often get very little return for what they bring to the fore (Butcher 1994). And, as Mary Waters and Karl Eschbach (1995: 442) stated, "the evidence indicates that direct discrimination is still an important factor for all minority subgroups except very highly educated Asians." Even highly educated and acculturated Asians, such as Filipinos, report high levels of racial discrimination in the labor market. Not surprisingly, second- and third-generation Filipinos self-identity as Filipino-American rather than as white or "American" (Espiritu and Wolf 2001). For a similar finding on the Vietnamese, see Min Zhou (2001) and for a discussion on the indeterminate relation between education and income among many other groups, see Alejandro Portes and Ruben Rumbaut (1990).

4

Racial Justice in a Black/Nonblack Society

George Yancey

When the Irish came to the United States to escape the great potato famines of the mid-1840s, they enjoyed little respect and prestige in American society. They were not part of the majority but instead were thought of as "niggers turned inside out" (Ignatiev 1995; Waters 2000). Racist stereotyping, residential segregation, and occupational discrimination were common experiences for the Irish. However, over time this ethnic group has become one of the best examples of the dynamic nature of racial identity. Later generation Irish escaped the minority status that plagued early Irish immigrants. As documented by Noel Ignatiev (1995) the Irish began a journey that eventually led to their acceptance into mainstream society and to gaining dominant group status. With the election of John F. Kennedy, the Irish—a group that started out reviled and excluded from "respectable society"—had finally reached the highest levels of prestige in the United States. Today most Americans perceive the Irish as just another group of whites.

Because racial identity changes over time, social scientists have struggled to understand the possible new permutations of race in the United States, creating a very important debate among race/ethnicity scholars. This debate focuses on the fate of nonblack racial minorities. On the one hand, some argue that the transformation of white ethnic minority groups into dominant group members does not predict what will happen to contemporary nonblack racial groups. These theorists argue that contemporary racial barriers are qualitatively different from the ethnic hurdles of yesteryear. They assume that the basic white/nonwhite divide that has characterized race relations in the past will continue to be our society's dominant divide. On the other hand, some argue that the changing nature of race relations will result in the merging of nonblack racial minorities into the dominant culture. They essentially contend that the processes of assimilation that characterize European

49

ethnic groups are the same social forces that influence nonblack racial minorities today. If these theorists are correct, then we may eventually see the development of a society in which blacks are separated from all, or at least most, other racial groups—or a black/nonblack society.

I have argued in previous work (Yancey 2003c) that the latter prediction is more accurate than the former. I first explore both arguments and briefly recap why I favor the second argument more than the first. Then, I look into the implications a black/nonblack society has for racial justice. The development of a black/nonblack society challenges the notion, implied within a white/nonwhite assumption, that our future racial reality will include a multiracial community that fights for racial justice (see Wilson 1999). Rather, in the coming years we are likely to see a tendency of certain nonblack minority groups to support the dominant group perspective and to have less concern for racial justice. I argue that as a result of this tendency, African Americans will soon find themselves relatively alone in their struggle for racial justice.[1] In this chapter I explore the racial justice repercussions of the possible black/nonblack society.

■ White/Nonwhite or Black/Nonblack?

A White/Nonwhite World

Milton Gordon (1964) defines structural assimilation as the entrance of minority groups into primary groups and cliques with dominant group members, and marital assimilation as the intermarriage of minority group members with dominant group members without facing any social stigma. He argues that members of a social group must experience structural assimilation before they can experience marital assimilation and that marital assimilation must occur before members of racial minority groups can identify with dominant group status. Afterward, complete assimilation becomes possible, and former minority group members become full-fledged majority group participants.

This "straight-line" process of assimilation has recently been criticized. One of the most important disputes of the straight-line assimilation has developed from Alejandro Portes and Min Zhou's (1993) argument about segmented assimilation. They contend that how first-generation immigrants are incorporated into the society helps determine contrasting ways that later generations accept the culture and values of the dominant society. Thus, Portes and Zhou argue that there are profound differences in the immigration experiences of older European immigrants and the newer non-European immigrants. Considering the various paths that immigrant groups have taken into this country, later arriving immigrant groups may be more likely to succeed *without* assimilation. With this argument, there is no need for these non-European immigrant groups to undergo marital and identificational assimilation in order to gain economic and social success.

Beyond the critique of segmented assimilation, other schools of thought have risen to criticize the notion of straight-line assimilation. The first school of thought is primordialism (Geertz 1963; Issacs 1975; Shils 1957). Advocates of this perspective contend that racial/ethnic identity is fixed and cannot be altered by interaction with members of other racial/ethnic groups. Harold Issacs (1975) argues that ethnic identity must be treated as a form of group identity and that such an identity develops from birth. These identities are then ingrained into the larger community that ethnic groups are attached to, which makes ethnic identities immune to further challenges from other forms of social identity (Grosby 1994). Therefore, racial/ethnic identity is static and not malleable to the changing culture. Assimilation is not possible because our racial/ethnic identity is innate. Minority groups will not lose their identity to become part of a dominant group, and thus identificational assimilation cannot take place.

Circumstantialism is a seemingly contradictory perspective (Anderson 2001; Barth 1969; Cornell and Hartmann 1997). This perspective contends that racial/ethnic groups are interest groups and that members of these groups use their racial identities to pursue their collective concerns. To this end, under the proper circumstances, members of distinct groups may adapt some of the elements within their collective identities to gain benefits for the group. Individuals may seem to lose their racial/ethnic identity for a time, but merely because the circumstances are right for them to act contrary to their traditional racial/ethnic identity. If those circumstances change, then they will accept their previous racial/ethnic identity. With such a perspective, racial identity survives because it is useful for gaining resources and because such identity is flexible enough to adapt to the changing societal circumstances.

Stephen Cornell and Douglass Hartmann (1997) offer a promising compromise to the theoretical contradictions between primordialists and circumstantialists. They argue that racial/ethnic actors can manipulate their identity to gain what they desire but that this identity does not go away. Instead it can become "thicker" or "thinner." Thickness and thinness denote the degree of comprehensiveness of the identity. Therefore, it is possible that the primordial argument is correct in that identity never goes away and the circumstantial contention is accurate in that the identity is flexible enough to change as circumstances warrant. If the situation is right, then racial/ethnic identity loses its superficial saliency and is thin, or not very comprehensive; however, if conditions change, then it can become thick, or very comprehensive. Assimilation can never really take place because minority groups will never completely lose their ethnic identity. Gordon's scheme requires that identificational assimilation occurs before minority groups can be totally incorporated

into mainstream society; thus these critiques resist Gordon's ideas by showing the stability of minority group racial/ethnic identity.

However, it is doubtful that most contemporary European ethnic groups
have maintained a thin ethnic identity that can become thick if the conditions warranted it. It is more likely that these groups have undergone identificational assimilation and that their ethnic identities are gone for good,
with the members of these groups completely accepting their position in the
majority (see Waters 1998). If the primordialists and circumstantialists are
correct, then why did the former European ethnic groups eventually become
part of the majority? One reason can be that European ethnic group members are still European. They could eventually be accepted into a dominant
society that was defined in Eurocentric terms.[2] It can be argued that the
identity of the Europeans never really changed but merely adapted itself to
dominant group status. However, non-Europeans' racial identities can survive in a minority status despite the increasing educational, residential, and
vocational interracial interactions in the United States. The basic racial
divide in our society has been, and will continue to be, between the dominant European Americans and all other racial groups. Over time, some racial
minority groups may draw closer to dominant status, but none will achieve
a completely egalitarian social position with dominant group members. In
such a racial world all minority groups have vested interests, to varying
degrees, to continue to fight for racial justice since all minority groups will
desire to obtain an elusive egalitarian status with the dominant group. This
position can be fairly classified as a white/nonwhite perception of future
race relations.

A Black/Nonblack Reality

The perception of a black/nonblack racial future contrasts with the above
arguments. In previous work (Yancey 2003c), I assert that the evidence of a
black/nonblack perspective can be seen in the differential residential segregation and marital exogamy experienced by African Americans relative to
other racial minorities. The greater tendency of blacks to face residential
and marital rejection from other groups is indicative of the high degree of
alienation that African Americans encounter in the United States. I argue
that since nonblack minority groups do not experience the degree of alienation that blacks face, it becomes easier for them to accept the racial perspectives of dominant group members. In my previous work I provided
empirical evidence suggesting that nonblack minority groups are beginning
to adopt social attitudes reflecting the racial identity of dominant group
members more than racial minorities. Although I was limited by static data,
I argued that the alienation of African Americans—both in the reluctance of
whites to live among (Emerson, Yancey, and Chai 2001; Massey and Denton 1993/1995) and to marry blacks (Herring and Amissah 1997; Spickard
1989)—would prevent them from following the path of societal acceptance

enjoyed by most nonblack racial minorities. Instead of a racial future in which whites remain on top of the racial structure and all other groups lag behind them, I predict that the defining reality of our racial future is one whereby blacks remain at the bottom of the racial hierarchy in the United States, while nonblack racial groups are able to obtain dominant status. Quite simply, I argue that a black/nonblack racial reality will soon replace the current white/nonwhite one.

I am not alone in forwarding this argument. Joel Perlmann and Roger Waldinger (1997) contend that there are important parallels between Asians and Hispanics and earlier European ethnic groups. They stop short of arguing that these nonblack racial groups will be able to use the same "ethnic" card that European ethnic groups were able to apply to incorporate themselves into the dominant group; however, they do contend that these groups are likely to differentiate themselves from the lower racial strata occupied by African Americans. Furthermore, Alba and Nee (1997) point out that although Asians and light-skinned Hispanics may lose some of their racial distinctiveness with the dominant group, the racial boundary between whites and blacks remains the most intractable barrier between racial groups. Finally, although other scholarly work falls short of actually predicting a concrete black/nonblack reality, the possibility of such a future is considered at least as likely as other types of potential racial formations (Alba 1999; Sanjek 1996).

There may be alternate ways that one can conceptualize the future racial reality in the United States than either a white/nonwhite or black/nonblack racial structure. For example, Eduardo Bonilla-Silva (2004b) contends that we have not a dichotomous but a trichotomous racial structure in our society, with the three groups being whites, honorary whites, and the collective black (see Chapter 3, this volume). But I would argue that many of the groups he labels "honorary whites" generally share the same racial perspective of the dominant group and thus are in the process of becoming white. Furthermore, since they are not encumbered by the one-drop rule, I would hasten to point out that the high outmarriage rate of many who are labeled "honorary whites" has important implications for the children of these individuals. Hispanic and Asian Americans who have children with European Americans are not systematically forced to ignore the dominant heritage of their children. Given this history, there is reason to believe that future generations of the honorary whites will continue to move closer to dominant status. Thus, I tend to believe that although the "Latinization of race" that Bonilla-Silva discusses may be an accurate way to perceive race relations today, its ability to predict future race relations is doubtful. What is more likely is that the children and grandchildren of those in the honorary white category will experience a relatively high acceptance into the dominant culture and eventually escape minority group status. However, since future possibilities cannot be predicted with precision,[3] it would be a

mistake to ignore the possibility of the emergence of a possible buffer group between whites and blacks.

But that is an argument for another time. What neither Bonilla-Silva nor I foresee is the typical white/nonwhite paradigm so often accepted today. This paradigm begins with a prediction of whites becoming a numerical minority within our society and ends with a vision of the future in which there is a multiracial, multicultural movement that challenges Eurocentric hegemony (Daniel 1996b; Garcia 1995; Hall 1997; Lee 1998; Martinez 1993). Oh, if that were to come true! But what if this prediction is wrong and the white/nonwhite paradigm fails to explain future race relations? In that case, even those who hold on to the ideal of an emerging multiracial progressive social movement would do well to anticipate possible alternatives to our contemporary racial structure. It is vital to look at the implications of how a black/nonblack[4] reality would differ from a white/nonwhite one and what those differences mean for issues of racial justice.

■ Racial Justice in a Black/Nonblack World

In 1984 Jessie Jackson ran for president, touting what he called his "Rainbow Coalition." He believed that he could bring together various disenfranchised groups who would support his effort to bring about social justice. His vision never materialized, but the hope still exists among progressives that a multiracial, multicultural movement will eventually overcome traditionalist Eurocentric structures in our society (see Bates 1994; Crass n.d.; Lind 1997; Houston 1996; Spencer 1994; Yamamoto et al. 2001). Yet, such a vision assumes that intermarriage will not take place or that when it does, the children of such unions will value the racial perspective of their minority parents more than their white parents. There is evidence that children of white and nonblack minorities are very likely to experience some degree of identificational assimilation.[5]

Interracial marriages provide racial minority spouses and multiracial children an opportunity to adopt the racial perspective of the dominant group. It is possible that these multiracial families develop a biracial identity and that their children will not identify with either the majority or minority race. However, even if children of biracial unions develop a biracial identity instead of a dominant group identity, these children will still possess a racial identity different from that of the minority parent and may be less likely than the parent of color to see issues of racial justice as important. It remains to be seen whether a multiracial identity is a step on the path toward assimilation into the dominant culture or whether multiracial people will form a separate subculture from both majority and minority groups. It is reasonable to assert that individuals with a multiracial identity will at least partially identify with the dominant group and thus will be less supportive of issues of racial justice.

In a white/nonwhite world it is expected that all minorities will join a "Rainbow Coalition" to fight against the dominant group. But in a black/nonblack reality, nonblack multiracials and nonblack minorities may not side with the most disenfranchised group since there is much to gain by adopting dominant group identity. Furthermore, former minority individuals who adopt dominant group identity will be less likely to be motivated by appeals to white guilt since they can use their ancestral minority status to legitimate their own social status—much as European ethnic minorities have done (Waters 1990).

To comprehend what the future struggle for racial justice can look like in a black/nonblack society, it is vital to evaluate the consequences of gaining dominant status for nonblack racial minorities. The best way to assess what can happen as nonblack groups adopt a dominant group identity is to look at what has happened historically when a minority group gains dominant group status. Ignatiev (1995) provides such an example with the Irish. According to his work, the early Irish immigrants supported the abolitionist movement. This support was plausibly linked to their understanding of economic and social oppression. Yet over time the Irish assimilated into the dominant group. Ignatiev argues that the Irish achieved assimilation in part because of their willingness to reject their former support of abolitionism and to adopt an antiblack stance. The acceptance of the ideology of the dominant group does not happen overnight. By the latter part of the nineteenth century, ideological distinctions between the Irish and dominant group members still existed. The Irish were a big part of a labor movement that was consistently more progressive than the political ideology of dominant group members in general. Yet, they had already moved closer to having a dominant group position in society, and over time the Irish lost their distinctive ethnic identity and much of their desire for racial and economic justice. Today, the social and racial attitudes of the Irish do not seem to differ from that of other dominant group members.

If the path of the Irish becomes the path of the nonblack minority groups, then important implications of this process can be predicted. The transition of Hispanics and Asian Americans into dominant status will not be immediate, and the results of that transition will not happen overnight. However, eventually Hispanic and Asian Americans will lose much of their interest in dealing with issues of racial justice. As this occurs African Americans will lose valuable allies in their struggle to escape racial oppression. Racial minority groups who previously aided blacks will increasingly perceive themselves as being "white," as opposed to having minority status. Their natural inclination will be to work to uphold the benefits associated with that status rather than to work for issues of racial justice.

If Hispanic and Asian Americans start to fully accept the racialized attitudes of dominant group members, then conflicts between these groups and African Americans will develop as Hispanic and Asian Americans obtain more social power and attempt to distance themselves from African Americans. Documenting the alliances that may develop between Hispanic and Asian Americans and dominant group members will provide additional evidence of the assimilation of these nonblack minority groups and help researchers understand the dynamic nature of intergroup racial relations in the United States. If the paths of European ethnic groups are followed completely, then these nonblack minorities will eventually lose their racial identity completely and their ability to gain back a minority perspective.

There is already evidence of conflict between African Americans and Asian Americans in many larger US metropolitan areas. Kim (2000–2001) and Anderson (1992) provide examples of this conflict. In the middle of this conflict African Americans often complain that Asian Americans invade their neighborhoods and steal their jobs. Asian Americans often complain that African Americans do not have the initiative to lift themselves out of poverty, are lazy, and exhibit racism and jealousy toward them (Martha 1992; Palumbo-Liu 1999). The concerns of Asian Americans resemble the general concerns of dominant group members about racial minorities. This type of complaint should be expected from a minority group, in this case Asian Americans, who live among African Americans but accept the perspectives of the dominant racial group.

As a result of the distance that Hispanic and Asian Americans have put between themselves and African Americans, another profound implication of the black/nonblack social world is likely to develop. African Americans will find themselves unable to rely upon these racial minority groups as allies who will fight to resist the enduring, oppressive, racialized structures. I have documented several instances in which the racial perspectives of Hispanic and Asian Americans were generally closer to those of the dominant group than to African Americans (Yancey 2003c). However, these differences dealt with variations in abstract concepts between these racial groups.[6] Nevertheless, there are important political and social realities behind these attitudinal contrasts.

For example, those who hope to hold on to the possibility of a rainbow coalition for social justice would surely envision Hispanic Americans as part of that coalition. Hispanic Americans are only slightly better off economically than African Americans (see Yetman 1999), and they want to work to bring their people out of the underclass. Yet, it is a mistake to automatically link the fate of African and Hispanic Americans, since middle-class African Americans tend to live in segregated neighborhoods, even as they move up the economic class ladder, and tend to remain trapped near disenfranchised communities (Massey and Denton 1993/1995). The black ghetto becomes a permanent home for African Americans. Middle-class Hispanic Americans, however, tend to leave their disenfranchised barrios. The barrios become way stations on the path to the American dream for Hispanic Americans. This difference makes it easier for Hispanic Americans to identify with dominant group members since they can envision one day being part of the dominant culture.

Perhaps it is the tendency of middle-class Hispanic Americans to identify with whites that explains a recent newspaper article in Florida (Padilla 2000) that documents the reluctance of Hispanic Americans to support the efforts of African Americans to fight Florida governor Jeb Bush's and University of California Board of Regents member Ward Connerly's attempt to end affirmative action. Perhaps we should not be surprised at the lack of support among Hispanic Americans since a large percentage of that population are Cuban Republicans. The recent arrival of Cubans,[7] combined with their relative economic success, is linked to their belief that affirmative action will not help them. The lack of Cuban American support can be a mere anomaly because of the economic opportunities they have relative to other Hispanic groups. But that is precisely the point. As Hispanic Americans move into the middle class, they do not identify with the aims of the minority underclass. Instead, they identify with the concerns of the dominant group. There is no evidence that middle-class status leads to such identification among African Americans. The Florida example indicates that a move into dominant group identity and away from the concerns of racial minorities is possible among Cuban Americans. Time will tell whether other Hispanic groups will follow suit.

Affirmative action is a more complicated issue for Asian Americans. On the one hand, Asian Americans have experienced the type of racial discrimination that affects their economic and social opportunities. On the other hand, Asian Americans currently are overrepresented on college campuses and are unlikely to directly benefit from affirmative action. These countervailing forces have led to an ideological split among Asian Americans (Lim 2001; Zhou 2003). During the recent University of Michigan case, groups representing Asian Americans filed briefs on both sides of the case.[8] This ideological division makes Asian American support for issues that exclusively aid racial minorities, at best, unstable. Needless to say, African Americans would do well not to count upon the assistance of Asian Americans when it comes to race-based preference programs.

These implications should be of particular importance to activists for racial justice. If these implications are correct, then African Americans will increasingly find themselves alone in their fight for racial justice. Progressive social activists would do well to monitor the "whitening" of Hispanic and Asian Americans and the persistent alienation that blacks suffer, since these twin developments can indicate a need for activists to redouble their efforts in advocating for African Americans. As African Americans become more isolated from other racial groups, they will need support from individuals in the dominant group to deal with enduring institutional racism. Some of these dominant group individuals will include progressive Hispanic and Asian Americans who have dominant group status but are still willing to advocate for African Americans. As they gain more benefits from white privilege, the number of Hispanic and Asian Americans who support the empowerment of racial minorities will decline—since these groups will have a stake in protecting dominant group privilege. And as more nonblack minorities are recruited into the dominant group and start to work toward protecting the racial status quo, a racialized society that continues to deprive certain racial groups of full participation, that status quo seems destined to persist.

▪ Is There Anything We Can Do?

If my assumptions are accurate, then how can we deal with the emerging racial reality of a black/nonblack world and the consequences that arise from it? I am pessimistic that we can ever fully alter these consequences. However, it is important that we assess how we can best escape the potential pitfalls that lie ahead.

African Americans experience an alienation that eludes most other racial groups. Solutions to the emerging black/nonblack society must recognize the distinct needs that blacks have. For example, Charles Moskos and John Butler (1996) have argued that affirmative action programs should concentrate upon aiding African Americans. They do not contend that other minority groups should be excluded from affirmative action aid but argue that the unique history and predicament of blacks justify a special emphasis. I generally agree with them that a special emphasis should be placed upon the needs of African Americans, but affirmative action has come under attack lately (e.g., Connerly 2002; Eastland 1997; Lynch 1989; Sowell 1985). It can be questioned whether a program that treats African Americans differently from other racial groups can survive this political assault. The justification for affirmative action must be retooled, away from notions of historical justice and toward an understanding of the likely future of blacks—which is one of racial alienation. We must construct an argument that because of this alienation, African Americans do not have the same access to the benefits in the dominant culture as other racial minorities. Therefore, public programs designed to aid African Americans must prepare to deliver long-term assistance rather than act as a short-term fix.

Making this distinction is important, because in the coming years Hispanic and Asian Americans will likely improve their economic situation relative to African Americans. If that occurs, then many members of these nonblack minority groups will begin to justify their higher status by adopting the concepts of white privilege, just as many European ethnic group members have done before them (Waters 1990). Even if Hispanic and Asian Americans do not fully adopt white privilege, it is still likely that dominant group members will use the relative success of nonblack minorities to justify their superior social position (Hurk and Kim 1989; Palumbo-Liu 1999;

Woo 2000). It is important for the proponents of affirmative action pro-grams to clarify a different design to address the long-term alienation of African Americans, as opposed to the relatively short-term needs of non-black minority group members. Since research has demonstrated that, once they reach middle-class status (Massey and Denton 1987, 1988), most non-black minority groups can integrate into dominant group neighborhoods and educational institutions, an effective way to serve Hispanic and Asian Amer-icans can be through class-based economic programs. Economic equality can lead to a great deal less hostility between dominant group members and Hispanic and Asian Americans. For African Americans, such programs will not, by themselves, dramatically improve their social and economic position, since even middle-class blacks find themselves alienated from the dominant group (Feagin 1991; Oliver and Shapiro 1997). Thus, even improving the economic condition of blacks will not alleviate the social divide between African Americans and dominant group members.

Dealing with the racial alienation of African Americans will require efforts beyond integration in secondary organizations. Institutions where primary relationships are developed, such as churches and social clubs, must also become multiracial. These primary organizations hold important keys for helping dominant group members to become more accepting of African Americans and to challenge notions of white privilege. For example, pre-vious research has found that Americans who attend multiracial churches are more likely to have integrated social networks (Emerson, Kimbro, and Yancey 2002), and to accept racial exogamy (Yancey 2001). Furthermore, there is evidence that being part of a multiracial church is one of the strongest predictors of whether a person has an integrated social network.[9] Integra-tion into primary institutions can have more of a qualitatively distinct effect upon the attitudes of Americans than integration into secondary institutions (Yancey 2003a). Nonblacks who attend interracial churches may be more accepting of the presence of African Americans in their intimate social spheres, which allows for the possibility that racial alienation will lessen. Since there is at least some evidence that racial attitudes supportive of the maintenance of the racial status quo, or white privilege, are inversely re-lated to the presence of African Americans in multiracial churches (Yancey 1999, 2001), it is plausible to argue that these interracial organizations are part of the solution to racial alienation.

If such interracial organizations are part of the solution, then an impor-tant question is, what can the public sector do to encourage such organiza-tions? Once again Charles Moskos and John Butler provide insight (1996), suggesting that the military can break down walls of racial misunderstand-ing in ways that have not occurred in educational institutions.[10] Since most Americans will not enter the military, Moskos and Butler suggest that a National Service Corps can serve the same purpose. Even after September 11, 2001, I am still skeptical about the need to encourage a larger military, but I do concur with much of their argument concerning the importance of such a corps and believe that it is one of the ways that the US government could encourage fruitful interracial contact. However, beyond this corps and the military there is little the public sector can do, since the voluntary nature of primary integrated organizations is part of what makes them effective. The public sector can support these organizations through applied research,[11] publicly encouraging these groups, and highlighting successful multiracial primary organizations.

Beneath all these measures is a very fundamental question: how important is it for African Americans to maintain a distinctive racial identity and to retain their cultural uniqueness? The philosophy of cultural pluralism can be justified as a way of protecting African Americans from rejection by the dominant society. We can assert that since we are not going to be accepted in the dominant society, we should make sure that we receive maximum support from our own culture. Yet, advocates for cultural pluralism sometimes discourage any actions or practices that might lead to assimilation. An unfortunate side effect of this discouragement is that African Americans can unknowingly help keep themselves estranged from the social power structure in the United States. For example, except for white separatists, the group most strident in its defense of the one-drop rule is African American activists. Blacks often police this rule by pressuring biracial individuals into identifying themselves as fully black (Korgen 1998–1999; Rockquemore and Brunsma 2002a and 2002b; Twine 1997). Considering the ominous history of the one-drop rule (Davis 1991; see also Chapter 2, this volume), it can be argued that such pressure can reinforce the separation of blacks from other racial groups. When the desire to maintain the uniqueness of black culture encourages self-defeating actions, then we must question certain applications of an Afrocentric paradigm. Rather than blindly overvaluing the maintenance of black distinction, we must contemplate when we should participate with the dominant group and when we should fight for our cultural uniqueness. A careful questioning of how we can balance the advantages of cultural accommodation and cultural pluralism is an important task for future academic work.

Because this is a controversial subject, let me be clear. I believe that all attempts by blacks to become incorporated are likely to fail due to the powerful forces of alienation. But resistance to these forces of alienation by African Americans is still necessary, if only so that African Americans do not fool themselves into believing that the black/nonblack society is of their own choosing. African Americans need a more nuanced support of cultural pluralism, whereby at times we use that philosophy to advance our goals but at other times we question cultural pluralism when it exacerbates black disenfranchisement. Although the maintenance of black culture is important, it cannot be allowed to override all other concerns. If certain types of dominant group cultural accommodation can provide African Americans with other racial allies and gain social capital for our communities, then we must consider how and when that accommodation can take place. I, for one, will not seek to maintain a mythical "pure" black culture if it costs us an opportunity to improve the plight of African Americans.

As we become more aware of the coming black/nonblack society, we must continue to search for solutions that overcome the alienation of blacks. There may be little that can immediately slow the movement toward a black/nonblack society. Yet this pessimism does not absolve us of the responsibility of doing all we can to reduce the alienation that African Americans continue to experience.

■ Notes

1. It is always dangerous to discuss racially based tendencies since no racial group is monolithic. Throughout this chapter I will discuss the higher propensity of African Americans to desire racial justice relative to majority group members (Emerson and Smith 2000; Kinder and Sanders 1996; Schuman et al. 1997; Sears et al. 2000). Yet, clearly there are some African Americans for whom racial justice issues are unimportant and European Americans who are constantly fighting for racial justice. However, it is safe to assert that on average, African Americans have more concern about racial justice than European Americans. The fact that some blacks pay little attention to racial issues and some whites care a great deal about them does not eliminate the overall tendency of whites to dismiss such issues and of blacks to care about them. Likewise, accepting the caveat that there are many exceptions to this rule, my previous explorations (2003c) of the attitudes of Hispanic Americans and Asian Americans indicate that their racial attitudes more closely align with those of the majority group than do African American attitudes. The racial justice implications of this tendency are this chapter's focus.

2. It can be argued that there never has been a racial difference between former minority European groups and the majority, only an ethnic distinction. Yet, I would contend that for all practical purposes, Europeans from southern and eastern Europe were treated as if they were racially inferior to the majority group and suffered many of the same types of discrimination that other racial minorities faced. Thus, making a racial versus ethnic distinction is irrelevant. The key fact is that these groups have been able to escape the social stigma they once suffered to become full-fledged members of the majority.

3. It is worth noting that the racial reality that both Bonilla-Silva and I observe is the same but that we have produced different conclusions from this observation. Both of us have noted a mostly black underclass, an elite white racial group, and a fluid in-between racial group in our contemporary racial hierarchy. We part intellectual company when he argues that this middle will not be able to join the dominant elite and I contend that over time that they will be part of that elite. Only future racial developments will ultimately determine which of us is correct.

4. Of course, part of the challenge of understanding this new black/nonblack reality will be defining who is black. Clearly, not all Hispanic and Asian ethnic groups will be able to assimilate into the dominant culture with identical ease. Some groups, such as the Hmong, are new immigrants who will remain alienated from the dominant culture for some time to come. Other groups, such as Puerto Ricans, may have a harder time assimilating because of their close association with African Americans and their African origin (Massey and Denton 1988). Finally, the fate of

Middle Easterners is still up for grabs. The recent antagonism between the United States and Middle Eastern nations and the threat of terrorism produces a definite potential for the demotion of Middle Easterners into an alienated status. Although I discuss only African Americans as part of the perpetually alienated racial group, there are clearly circumstances that may lead other groups to join them in this status.

5. This position is supported by evidence that indicates that white/Hispanic children (Gallagher 2004b; Waters 1998), white/Indian (Harris 2002), and white/Asian children (Harris 2002; Moran 2001: 107; Waters 1998; Wu 2001) are relatively more likely to identify as white or multiracial than black/white children. Furthermore, research with census data has indicated that black/white couples who do not identify their children as multiracial tend to identify them as black, whereas Asian/white and Hispanic/white couples who do not identify their children as multiracial tend to identify them as white (Tafoya, Johnson, and Hill 2004). Thus, it is unlikely that the offspring of whites and nonblack minorities are more likely to accept a minority-based social perspective than one that is grounded in their potential majority position.

6. The use of attitudinal surveys has come under criticism of late (e.g., Bonilla-Silva 2001), but, as I argued in my book (2003c), such quantitative work is necessary if we are going to make generalizable arguments about distinct racial groups.

7. Padilla (2000) argues that the recent arrival of Cubans is important since it deprives this group of experiencing the civil rights struggle that resulted in the development of affirmative action. Thus, Cuban Americans may devalue the worth of a program that they did not have to fight for.

8. The National Asian Pacific American Legal Consortium filed a brief in support of affirmative action, whereas the Asian American Legal Foundation filed a brief to oppose it.

9. Personal communication with Michael Emerson.

10. It is insightful that Moskos and Butler compare the military to educational institutions because there have been many overt attempts to use educational organizations to enhance racial diversity and many scholars have envisioned that education is an important solution for racism (Jackman and Mahu 1984; Kluegel and Smith 1986; Selznick and Steinberg 1969). To the degree that military institutions may be more successful in accomplishing these goals than educational organizations, it is valuable to examine why the military may be relatively successful.

11. For example, I recently finished a book (2003b) aimed at helping religious organizations to racially integrate. In this book I outline several principles used by successful racially integrated churches to maintain their multiracial nature. Although this book is targeted at religious congregations, these principles may be useful for nonreligious organizations supporting multiracial primary relationships.

5

Carving Out a Middle Ground: The Case of Hawai'i

Jeffrey Moniz and Paul Spickard

Hawai'i has long been linked to ideas and images about race and particularly about multiraciality. Those ideas and images have in turn been linked to a racial hierarchy that has sustained racial injustice in the islands. For several generations, the hierarchy has meant racial injustice, primarily for Native Hawaiians (Kanaka Maoli)[1] and less for other peoples of color, masked by a tourist discourse celebrating happy, docile Polynesians and a genial multicultural society. Late in the twentieth century and early in the twenty-first, a new racial discourse championing Native Hawaiian sovereignty began to change some of the implications imputed to the local racial hierarchy. Those changes have the potential to affect racial justice in ways both positive and negative for Hawai'i's people. This new racial discourse incited our critique and inspired our further development of a conceptual cultural space, a middle space that we call the midaltern. We introduce the concept of the midaltern as a more precise and inclusive way to describe the identities of those ignored or erased by the current discourse.

◼ Colonial Thinking in Hawai'i

Captain James Cook and nineteenth-century Euro-American missionaries saw Hawaiians as a race apart from themselves, physically different and characterologically inferior (Green 2002). European-derived outsiders emphasized the strangeness and the strange attractiveness of Hawai'i and Hawaiians. They wrote about the natural wonders of the Hawaiian landscape—volcanoes, gleaming sands, teeming reefs, deep jungles, and tall waterfalls—and set those images alongside descriptions of Native Hawaiian people, portraying them as part of the landscape too, as childlike, primitive, violent, irresponsible,

63

gloriously sexual, and in need of benevolent colonial rule by such people as themselves (Porteus 1945).

By the final third of the nineteenth century, European diseases had reduced the Kanaka Maoli population by 95 percent. Entrepreneurs, mainly Euro-Americans, brought in tens of thousands of Chinese and then Japanese, Filipinos, Koreans, and others to work the islands' growing sugar plantations (Beechert 1985; Osorio 2002b; Stannard 1989; Takaki 1983). Thus the population of the islands quickly came to include substantial numbers of people from many parts of the Pacific, from Asia, and from North America. In short order, the white *(haole)* minority seized control of most of Hawai'i's agricultural land, overthrew the Native Hawaiian monarchy, made Hawai'i a formal US colony, and set about marketing the islands abroad (Allen 1982; Dougherty 1992; Kame'eleihiwa 1992; Kent 1983; Lili'Uokalani 1898/1964; Osorio 2002b; for comic relief, Twigg-Smith 1998).

A central theme in the haole attempt to market Hawai'i was to characterize it as "the melting pot of the Pacific" and "the meeting place of East and West." The theme of multiracial harmony was a crucial support for the haole attempt to take over and make over the islands. Lori Pierce, a historian of territorial-era Hawai'i, characterizes it this way:

> Racial tensions lay just beneath the surface of daily life in Hawai'i, but race as a source of conflict or distress was rarely if ever discussed publicly. Instead, the haole ruling class constantly depicted Hawai'i as a racial paradise, a place where the Hawaiians, haole, Japanese, and Chinese lived cooperatively. Civic celebrations such as Balboa Day that featured all of the ethnic groups of Hawai'i were typical. These parades, pageants, and public celebrations were a way of depicting life in Hawai'i to tourists, residents, and mainland audiences, who read about them in *Paradise of the Pacific* and *Mid-Pacific Magazine*. The message being communicated was that ethnic diversity was not a threat to the haole ruling class. In fact, Euro-Americans were firmly in control and turning Hawai'i into a thoroughly American territory. (2004: 127)

Pierce (2005) links this celebration of harmony to Americanization campaigns in the continental United States and to uses of social science to subjugate Asian and Pacific peoples.

The haole elite that created the story of intercultural harmony as a mask for its own racial privilege then sold that image abroad, in the United States and elsewhere, as a way to bring tourists and money into the islands. Hawai'i was marketed, in the 1910s as in the 2000s, as a place of warm, conflict-free interaction among peoples where tourists would be welcome to come and spend their dollars and yen. Outrigger Hotels (2004), in marketing Hawai'i, completely erases Kanaka Maoli from their literature, naturalizes Euro-Americans as if they were native to Hawai'i, and assumes the inevitability and superiority of "modern" Euro-American culture in what they characterize as the "Melting Pot of the Pacific."

Multiraciality in Hawai'i

Some of the most influential books about Hawai'i stress multiraciality. Sidney Gulick, an American missionary to Japan born in the Marshall Islands to missionary parents, lived his later years in Hawai'i and wrote *Mixing the Races in Hawaii* in 1937. The book's first several pages, prior to even a title or paragraph of text, consist of pictures of twenty-eight high school and college students, most of them racially mixed. Each of them is labeled racially, and many are fractionated—"6/8 Hawaiian, 1/16 French, 1/16 Hindu, 1/16 Negro, 1/16 Arabian"—but none is given a name. What was important, apparently, was not their persons but the pseudoscientific racial categories that could be laid on them. Gulick began the written portion of his rhapsody to multiraciality and American triumphalism with this paean to harmonious blending:

> Here a poly-racial, poly-chrome, poly-linguistic, poly-religious and thoroughly heterogeneous population is being transformed into a homogeneous people, speaking a common language—English—holding common political, ethical, social and religious ideas and ideals, putting into practice with remarkable success the principles of racial equality, and maintaining a highly effective, democratic form of government. The races are actually growing together—fusing biologically. (1937: v)

The most widely read book about Hawai'i in the territorial period was University of Hawaiian sociologist Romanzo Adams's magnum opus, *Interracial Marriage in Hawaii* (1937). Although it was more scholarly than Gulick's, it also had the racially labeled pictures, and it celebrated racial mixing and told a story of interracial harmony. So, it appears, what was important about Hawai'i was race—specifically, racial harmony—and intermarriage and multiracial people were the emblems of that harmony.

As the territory slipped toward statehood, James Michener wrote the novel *Hawaii,* a thousand-page tribute to "those Golden Men who see both the West and the East, who cherish the glowing past and who apprehend the obscure future" (1959: 937) that would necessarily be framed by Euro-American cultural imperatives. This was a variation on the melting pot theme that stressed not racial blending so much as Hawai'i's location as the place where the peoples of Asia met the peoples of Europe and America in harmony and mutual understanding. The meeting place theme is the very raison d'être for the East-West Center, Hawai'i's most prominent intellectual factory. It is behind the location of a major Baha'i temple nearby, along with the headquarters of innumerable East-West internationalist societies. The center's mission statement (1999) praises East-West harmony, but Hawai'i and Hawaiians are not mentioned. They are subsumed under Asia, and the United States is assumed to be the leader and the agenda setter of the dialogue with Asia the center is designed to foster.

Some parts of this picture are accurate. There are in fact a lot of people in Hawai'i whose ancestors came, or who came themselves, from different countries. Hawai'i's identity as a land of many different kinds of immigrants reflects demography as well as haole propaganda. Hawai'i is in fact the only state where whites have never constituted a numerical majority of the population despite their disproportionate power, and the only one with an Asian and Pacific Islander majority (Gibson and Jung 2002). A higher percentage of people in Hawai'i acknowledge multiple racial ancestries than in any other US state, perhaps more than anywhere else in the world. Hawai'i is the only US state or territory that has long kept statistics that record racial multiplicity. For many years, people of mixed Kanaka Maoli and haole parentage constituted something of a distinct social group, and their numbers were recorded separately in state records (Schmitt 1968, 1977).

In 2000, 21.4 percent of Hawai'i's residents voluntarily checked more than one racial box on US Census forms, compared to a national rate of 2.4 percent. Far more than that could have qualified: many mixed people checked only one box, and others had mixed ancestry that fell within one of the census's "racial" categories ("New Multiracial Classification" 2001). Hawaiians and other islanders are especially mixed. A survey in the mid-1990s found that 69 percent of Pacific Islanders who lived in Hawai'i and 86 percent of Native Hawaiians recognized they possessed multiple ancestries. Despite substantial social pressure to identify with their island ancestries only, 53 percent of Pacific Islanders and 49 percent of Native Hawaiians identified with another ancestry as well (Spickard 1995). One accompaniment of all this actual mixing has been the rise and celebration of a mixed culture and identity called "local," including local food, local styles of dress, local modes of human relationship (Grant and Ogawa 1993; Okamura 1994; Yamamoto 1979), and a local language, Pidgin (Pak 1992; Sakoda and Siegel 2003; Tonouchi 2001, 2002).

So the motif of racial mixture in Hawai'i is not just a tourist marketer's myth; it is also a social fact. Yet the multiracial characterization does run the risk of glamorizing multiplicity and ignoring the harder racial realities of colonial domination in the islands, not just in the past but currently. What Pierce (2004) calls "the discourse of aloha" makes the islands seem an attractive tourist paradise. At the same time, it obscures the racial domination by haoles over other island residents and the hierarchies among those peoples of color. Insofar as it treats non-native peoples of color in Hawai'i, the discourse of aloha speaks of them in heroic terms of Asian immigrant uplift from plantation near-slavery to middle-class achievement by way of virtuous behavior, hard work, and not openly challenging haole domination. Eiko Kosasa (2000) describes

the immigrant ideological perspectives Nisei [second-generation Japanese] settlers wanted to pass on to the Sansei and Yonsei [their children and grandchildren]. . . . the Japanese response to U.S. nationalism, representing the Japanese experience as *willingly traveling* on the American "immigrant"

journey—beginning in poverty and ending in riches, moving from a simple, rural culture on the plantation to the sophistication of Western urban
culture. (78; emphasis author's)

Dorothy Hazama and Jane Komeiji cast their community's history as the
"story about the struggles and successes of the Japanese in Hawaii," which
was achieved by "belief in strong family ties, hard work, and perseverance,
. . . education, and sensitivity and humility" (Hazama and Komeiji 1986:
255; see also Glick 1980; Kimura 1988; Lind 1946; Ogawa 1978).

The discourse of aloha ignores Native Hawaiians almost completely,
treating them as museum curiosities, tourist entertainers, and a dying breed.
This is true even in so fine a book as Ronald Takaki's *Pau Hana: Plantation Life and Labor in Hawaii* (1983). After the first chapter, Kanaka Maoli
are all but invisible; the plantation laborers are almost all Asians of one sort
or another, and no questions are asked about the status of Hawaiians. The
standard histories of Hawai'i attend to the radical decline of the Hawaiian
population, and then, after the 1898 annexation by the United States, they
act as if Native Hawaiians all but ceased to exist and turn their attention
almost exclusively to haoles and Asians (Daws 1968; Fuchs 1961). Ralph
S. Kuykendall and A. Grove Day lament what they regard as the inevitable
"native population . . . extinction" (1961: 127; but see Noyes 2003). In the
"modern Hawai'i" celebrated by Outrigger Hotels, Native Hawaiians have
ceded the islands to entrepreneurial Asians and Euro-Americans. They contribute culture that others then get to perform and from which others take the
profit, but they are no longer actors in their own land. The action has been
taken over by other racial groups.

■ Kanaka Maoli Sovereignty

In recent years, Native Hawaiians have created a political movement to
reestablish Kanaka Maoli political and cultural sovereignty. A cultural
renaissance of Hawaiian music, dance, and language use in the 1970s and
1980s led to increasingly insistent demands for restoration to the Hawaiian
people of the independence that was taken away in the nineteenth century
(Kanahele 1986). There are as many strategies for sovereignty as there are
groups of Hawaiians active in the strident public debate. Some organizations, like Ka Lāhui Hawai'i, advocate creation of a self-governing Hawaiian nation within the nation that is the United States, in a relationship roughly
analogous to that of federally recognized Native American tribes on the
North American continent. Such an arrangement would involve creation of a
Hawaiian government from within the Kanaka Maoli population and the
transfer to that government of substantial public lands. Others advocate a
greater degree of autonomy in a compact of free association with the United
States like that employed by the Federated State of Micronesia. Some call

for full independence (Dudley and Agard 1993; Laenui 1994; McGregor 2002; Osorio 2002a; Trask 1999, 2000).

The push for Native Hawaiian sovereignty is a movement with which both authors of this chapter are in sympathy. At its heart, the sovereignty movement is a quest for racial justice. Haunani-Kay Trask describes the situation in Hawai'i and the Pacific this way:

> We in the Pacific have been pawns in the power games of the "master" races since colonialism first brought Euro-Americans into our vast ocean home. After Western contact destroyed millions of us through introduced diseases, conversion to Christianity occurred in the chaos of physical and spiritual dismemberment. Economic and political incorporation into foreign countries (Britain, France, the Netherlands, the United States) followed upon mass death. Since the Second World War, we Pacific Islander survivors have been witnesses to nuclear nightmare.

She decries "militarization and increasing nuclearization of the Pacific . . . toxic dumping . . . commidification of island cultures . . . economic penetration and land takeovers . . . and forced outmigration." She concludes:

> Hawaiians have been agitating for federal recognition of the following:
>   1. our unique status as Native people;
>   2. the injury done by the United States at the overthrow, including the loss of lands and sovereignty;
>   3. the necessity of reparation of that injury through acknowledgment of our claim to sovereignty, recognition of some form of autonomous Native government, the return of traditional lands and waters, and a package of compensatory resources, including monies. (1999: 58, 27)

■ Problems with the New Racialized Discourse

One unfortunate feature of the sovereignty movement, however, at least among certain of its advocates, has been a racial essentialism that fails to account for the dominant fact of multiplicity in the population of Hawai'i and, by that failure, threatens at least rhetorically to create another kind of racial injustice (but see Laenui 1994; McGregor 2002). That is, the rhetoric of certain prominent sovereignty advocates ignores the multiraciality of nearly all Native Hawaiians, at the same time that it lumps together all non-ethnic-Hawaiians as "settler colonialists" (Kauanui 1998, 2000, 2002). The argument is advanced by Candace Fujikane, who ranks herself among the Asian settler colonialists:

> Our presence as local Asians in Hawai'i was established through a colonial process, and Hawai'i's history, like that of Native Americans, is a violent one of genocide and land theft. . . . In 1954, the Democratic Party "Revolution" ushered in a new era of local Asian political ascendancy. Although Asians in Hawai'i and on the continent are settlers, Hawai'i has

become a white and Asian settler colony in which Asian settlers, particularly Japanese settlers, now dominate state institutions and apparatuses. (2000: xvi)

Fujikane repudiates the "master narrative of hard work and triumph that has been adopted by a new 'democratically' elected Asian ruling class." She charges that "local Asians' efforts to differentiate themselves from *haole* or whites in Hawai'i mask Native struggles against Asian settler colonialism. In a colonial situation, *haole* and Asian settlers actively participate in the continued dispossession of Native Hawaiians" (xvii).

What, in such a schema, is the place of people who are native to the Hawaiian islands but who are not Native Hawaiians? Granted that Asians who came on labor contracts to work in sugar and pineapple fields were taking part in a colonial process, it is not the case that they came on the same terms as haoles who seized the lands and government. One may criticize the self-glorification of their descendants and those descendants' habit of erasing Native Hawaiians from their historical narrative (as we have criticized them in this chapter), without dismissing all non–Kanaka Maoli as foreign to the islands and illegitimate usurpers of places there. In particular, this extreme, essentialist version of sovereignty racializes all non–Kanaka Maoli together and blurs pertinent distinctions among some of the settler peoples who live in the islands. Any survey, scholarly or popular, of Hawai'i's current social structure would put three ethnic groups at the top in terms of wealth, education, status, and access to power: haoles, Chinese, and Japanese (in that order). But such a survey would put these three groups at the bottom: Hawaiians, Samoans, and Filipinos (in that order). Samoans, by the definition of Fujikane and others, are settler colonialists, and Filipinos are Asian settler colonialists. But if they are settler colonialists, then their colonialism is of rather another sort than that of Chinese, haoles, or Japanese.

Further, the advocates of this particular, racialized version of Kanaka Maoli sovereignty ignore the multiracial lineage of many people in Hawai'i. Nearly all the advocates of Native Hawaiian sovereignty are themselves ancestrally mixed. That does not make them less Hawaiian or less able to represent the aspirations of the Hawaiian people. But the discourse of Hawaiian sovereignty, at least in the extreme racialist form advocated by Fujikane and others, does tend to mask that multiraciality and to set up extreme oppositions between native people and others.

■ The Midaltern

As a way out of the current impasse of essentialism and opposition in Hawaiian racial politics, we propose the concept of the "midaltern." We have coined "the midaltern" and its associated state of "midalternity" in reference to subaltern studies as postcolonial criticism. They are useful notions for moving beyond a dominant-dominated dichotomy toward a deeper understanding of the complex and dynamic interplay of social identities in Hawai'i. Although efforts to essentialize and dichotomize may seem useful for simplifying arguments aimed at critiquing colonial domination, thinking only in terms of a settler colonialist–Kanaka Maoli binary fails to acknowledge those who do not fit neatly into those categories. Three examples germane to the Hawai'i context challenge the binary and necessitate the further conceptual understanding made available through the concepts of the midaltern and midalternity.

First, the settler colonialist–Kanaka Maoli binary fails to acknowledge the multiraciality that is so ubiquitous in Hawai'i. According to the 2000 census, over 20 percent of Hawai'i's population chose to report being more than one race. Most of them include Kanaka Maoli in their ancestry. If the rule of hypodescent applies in cases of determining Kanaka Maoli ancestry, what becomes of the other, often unacknowledged, aspects of their identities? Midalternity readily permits one the possibility to claim membership in more than one social group.

Second, binary thinking obscures the status of those in Hawai'i who are from groups who were also directly colonized by the United States. For example, Filipinos, Puerto Ricans, Chamorros, and Samoans were colonized as part of the same US colonial expansion that occurred at the time of the Spanish American War (see *Amerasia Journal* 26(2); and Wei and Kamel 1998). Focusing on the plight of Kanaka Maoli as a colonized people but ignoring or discounting others whose homelands were also colonized only serves further to oppress members of these other groups who also live in Hawai'i. The midaltern provides a more pertinent conceptual space for the colonized in Hawai'i who are not Kanaka Maoli. Although they are not indigenous to the islands, they too are subjugated peoples who should not simply be branded as oppressors.

Third, binary thinking does not allow us to understand and conceptualize beyond the dominant-dominated, colonizer-colonized relationship, especially with regard to those whose personal cultural values are not consistent with those typically ascribed to their particular racial identities. What about Native Hawaiians who espouse Euro-American cultural values more than Kanaka Maoli values? Or consider a Native Hawaiian who acts haole in public but lives as a Kanaka Maoli at home? They are examples of people who do not fit neatly into the binary but who instead would be suited to a midaltern understanding of their identities.

The midaltern is a middle space that allows for the inclusion of and a richer understanding of these kinds of phenomena. Although the midaltern was named in relation to the subaltern and the superaltern, the concept is actually based on a kind of worldview common to Hawai'i and much of the Pacific. In Hawai'i, this kind of worldview clearly manifests itself in the culture, language, and identity known simply as "local." Local identity,[2] frequently characterized by the use of Pidgin[3] and the celebration of mixedness, is a viable and often salient identity choice available to multiracial people in Hawai'i. Although this midaltern identity provides for hybridity, it is also a conceptual space for fluidity, ambiguity, and contradiction. Local midaltern identities include those formed between and among particular, indigenous ways of being and dominant, Western, colonial, and even so-called global ways. Other terms that reflect this midalternity include duality, multiplicity, multiple identities, and strange compromises—language that commonly describes the social identities of many navigating race in Hawai'i.

■ The Local as Midaltern: The Emergence of the Local from the Old Racial Discourse

Although the older racialized discourse of aloha is merely being replaced by a newer, racialized, settler–Kanaka Maoli discourse, it is important to take stock of the most significant contribution of the old discourse. The unexpected consequence of promoting aloha and celebrating diversity is the multiethnic identity commonly referred to in Hawai'i as local. A clear dichotomy existed that divided the population during the plantation period in Hawaiian history. Haoles held most of the positions of power as plantation owners, managers, supervisors, financiers, and merchants. Non-haoles did the backbreaking work at meager wages as plantation laborers, service workers, and domestics. The roots of local identity developed out of this shared class experience, but the egalitarian attitudes toward other ethnic groups also grew out of familiarity facilitated by the passage of time and expedited by living and working in close proximity. Most importantly, nonnative and non-haole residents took up the prevailing attitude of aloha, from both the authentic native source and the haole discourse. Non-haoles embraced the melting pot ideal promoted by the haole oligarchy and readily bought into the myth. The discourse of aloha that Pierce described was easy to buy into, simply because it was based on truth and because the social conditions of the islands were ripe for panethnic alliances among its working class. Indeed, aloha was the glue that facilitated the formation of alliances that crossed ethnic boundaries.

Non-haoles forged alliances that reflected their common subordinate status to the dominant haole group (Okamura 1980). An alliance evidently appeared during the sugar strike of 1920. Although it was not the first strike against plantation ownership and management, the 1920 strike was significant because it was the first interethnic strike in Hawai'i (Okamura 1980; Takaki 1983). Workers, mainly Filipinos and Japanese, cooperated with each other, but as soon as Filipinos struck, large numbers of Spanish, Portuguese, and Chinese joined in. Their solidarity prevented the planters from effectively pitting ethnic groups against each other as strikebreakers, which had previously been the planters' prevailing strategy. Although the planters claimed victory after weathering the six-month strike, in hindsight strikers considered the strike of 1920 a success because three months later, the planters quietly met the strikers' demands. The time was marked by a sense of cooperation and unity that transcended ethnic boundaries (Takaki 1983).

More evidence of this interethnic unity exploded onto the public landscape through sentiment surrounding the Massie case of 1931–1932. The sensationalized case, which made national headlines, concerned a haole woman, the wife of a naval officer, who was allegedly raped by a group of five young men. Two of the men were Native Hawaiian, two were Japanese, and one was Native Hawaiian–Chinese. The rape case ended in a mistrial. The husband and mother of Thalia Massie, the alleged victim, with the help of two naval midshipmen, took matters into their own hands and lynched Joseph Kahahawai, one of the accused five. The haole vigilantes were found guilty of manslaughter. They were sentenced to ten years of hard labor, only to have their sentence commuted to one day served in the territorial governor's office. Hawai'i residents were outraged with the inequitable handling of the case by haole leadership. The case was an insult to non-haoles, who overwhelmingly identified with the "local boys." Discussions of the Massie case, whether in the print media or on the lips of gossips, are often cited as the first time that the term "local" was used with any salience (Rosa 2000; Yamamoto 1979).

This unity further solidified during World War II, when the distinction between non-haoles and the hordes of haole servicemen stationed in the islands became even more apparent. Solidarity manifested itself once again during the large-scale sugar strikes of 1946. Workers of all the various ethnic groups drew on their shared experiences of mistreatment by American haoles and combined together in one labor organization—the Congress of Industrial Organizations–International Longshore and Warehouse Union (Rademaker 1947). This alliance, nurtured by harmonious race relations reinforced by the discourse of aloha, developed into a common identity.

This common identity coalesced over time as a result of social interactions among different ethnic groups at work, school, and church and in the community, leisure activities, and the home, most notably through intermarriage. Various character traits are associated with a local identity. They include being "easygoing, friendly, open, trusting, humble, generous, loyal to family and friends, and indifferent to achieved status distinctions" (Okamura 1998: 268). These attributes characterize the positive perceptions of Hawaiians and are in opposition to conventional haole values that emphasize "directness, competition, individualism, achievement of status, and the necessity for impersonal, contractual relationships." Jonathan Okamura provided this description of local: "Local has come to represent the common identity of the people of Hawai'i and their appreciation of the inherent value of the land, peoples, and cultures of the islands" (Okamura 1980).

Local identity transcends ethnicity but does not assume that being local guarantees equal status between ethnic groups. Okamura pointed out that differences between groups tend to be ignored in certain situations, especially when nonlocals are involved. Locals often emphasize their links of class and racial solidarity (Chang 1996). Differences arise in situations in which disparate access to positions of status is at issue. For example, Okamura described the contention from Kanaka Maoli and Filipino groups that the public school system, at the hands of mostly Japanese administrators and teachers, does not provide equal educational opportunities or attend to the special educational needs of Kanaka Maoli and Filipino students (Okamura 1980).

Jeff Chang addressed these differences within local identity when he wrote: "From the social, political and economic margins, Filipino and native Hawaiian activists often speak of how the privileged local elite (most often, Japanese and Chinese) have forgotten the memory of their oppression at the hands of haoles" (1996: 22). Chang sees local consciousness as split, "sometimes mimicking and other times resisting colonial narratives" (Chang 1996). His notion of local consciousness accurately describes the fluid nature of local identity that depends so heavily on context. Sometimes Hawaiian locals reflect more Euro-American values, and sometimes they exhibit more Hawaiian values. Due to the range of fluidity between value systems that are often polar opposites, localness can be difficult to pin down—that is, unless multiplicity and fluidity are considered as key descriptors of local identity.

■ Local Types

There are many kinds of locals in Hawai'i. The scope of local diversity depends on one's definition of local. Providing concrete examples may help to define what counts as a local in Hawai'i. An important part of our argument is that midalternity allows for fluidity—namely, the shifting of identities depending on context—and we argue against essentializing identities, but a typology can be a useful heuristic tool for beginning a closer examination of different kinds of locals. The typology presented in Table 5.1 represents a starting point for further understanding the complexity involved with constructing racialized identities in Hawai'i.

The table illustrates the interactions of two variables, racialized identity and worldview. The identity categories used here include those consistent with both the old and the new racialized discourses. For instance, the non-haole and *hapa* (someone of partial Native Hawaiian ancestry, but see Table 5.1) categories from the old discourse are both subdivided to reflect the further distinction from the new discourse categories of Kanaka Maoli and settler. Four basic types of worldview categories represent the multitude of diverse ideologies held by those living in Hawai'i. Again, they correspond to categories drawn from the old and new racialized discourses. A

Table 5.1 Types of Midaltern Expressions in Hawai'i (shaded), Racialized Identity by Worldview (including indications of local identity)

	Haole	Hapa		Non-Haole	
		Part-Hawaiian	No Kanaka Maoli Ancestry (settler)	Settler	Kanaka Maoli
Euro-American worldview	The most *haole kine* haole (one-dimensional); *not local*	Part-Hawaiian who internalized haole values; *can be local*	Hapa who lives as haole; *can be local*	"Coconut," "Banana," or even "Katonk"; *doesn't feel local, but can be local*	Hawaiian who lives by haole values; *can be local*
Local worldview	Haole who performs localness; *may be local*	Hawaiian; *local*	*Local*	*Local*	Hawaiian; *local*
Monocultural settler/immigrant/non-haole/non-Hawaiian worldview	Haole who lives Japanese-style; *may be local*	*Local*	*May not feel local but may be treated as local*	Operates solely by culture of origin; *may be local*	*Local*
Indigenous Kanaka Maoli worldview	Haole who is *hanaid* (adopted) into a Hawaiian family and adopts Hawaiian worldview (like the park ranger at Volcanoes National Park); *local*	Part-Hawaiian who rejects his or her haole ancestry and wholly embraces a Kanaka Maoli worldview; *can choose to identify as local*	Hapa who lives with a Hawaiian family and adopts Hawaiian worldview; *local*	Settler or settler's descendant who lives with a Hawaiian family and adopts Hawaiian worldview; *local*	"Pureblood" who lives "da Hawaiian way"; *can choose to identify as local*

Note: The unshaded areas of the table indicate those who are typically more unidimensional in character. They ordinarily identify, or are identified, with the cultural worldview usually attached to their identity. We also argue, of course, that these identities are not necessarily fixed.

Euro-American worldview is most associated with haole identity. Although a local worldview is associated with non-haole identities in general, a Kanaka Maoli worldview specifically represents indigenous perspectives mostly reserved for Native Hawaiians. And the monocultural settler/immigrant/non-haole/non-Hawaiian worldview category serves as a catchall for all other monolithically defined settler worldviews (e.g., Japanese, Chinese, Filipino, etc.). The intersections of these identity and worldview categories begin to depict the kinds of diverse possibilities for identity that actually exist in Hawai'i.

Each cell provides a description or example of a type of potential identity, based on the interaction of one's racialized identity and one's personal worldview. For example, note that the identity of a person racialized as haole and possessing a Euro-American worldview is not considered local. The identity represented in that particular cell is prototypically haole. In this example, the visual physical cues linked with the haole racialized identity are directly paired with the views and behaviors most associated with a Euro-American, or haole, worldview. In contrast, consider someone racialized as haole who actually possesses an indigenous Kanaka Maoli worldview. An example of this is someone who was adopted or married into a Kanaka Maoli family and who may have internalized a Kanaka Maoli worldview while being embraced by their Kanaka Maoli family. In this case, someone whose racialized appearance is haole may actually be considered local, possibly even as Kanaka Maoli. So this typology makes it possible to distinguish differences in identity that go beyond superficial classification based on physiognomy or ancestry. This typology also considers the ideological perspectives of an individual in the construction of her or his identity.

The typology presented here also includes an indication of the degree to which each particular interaction of racialized identity and worldview can be considered local. All but one of the cells in this table represent identities that can potentially be regarded as local. Some have more claim to local identity than others. For instance, a Kanaka Maoli who possesses an indigenous worldview may choose to identify as local. This choice would not be contested because Kanaka Maoli are usually considered the most authentically local identity associated with Hawai'i. By contrast, a haole possessing a Kanaka Maoli or local worldview is not automatically granted local status, due to his or her appearance. In order to prove one's localness, that person would have to perform localness or Hawaiian-ness by practicing language or cultural expressions associated with being local or Kanaka Maoli. This can often be accomplished through speaking Pidgin or Hawaiian or adopting Hawaiian cultural practices like surfing, performing hula, or any of a number of traditions associated with local culture in Hawai'i.

Multiraciality, though not expressly mentioned in the local-haole and Kanaka Maoli–settler dichotomies, was an undeniable aspect of localness in the old discourse but is totally obscured in the new. This virtual erasure of hapa in the new discourse further masks the undeniable diversity among those of mixed backgrounds. What is apparent in the new discourse is the inclusion of part-Hawaiians in the Kanaka Maoli category, regardless of their personal worldviews. In terms of localness, a hapa person, whether or not that person has Kanaka Maoli ancestry, is prototypically local. In fact, next to being Kanaka Maoli, being multiracial in Hawai'i is considered the next most quintessentially local marker. Hapa represents the value of sharing and mixing linked with local culture built on aloha. This valuing of multiplicity, essential to being local, is nowhere to be found in the new discourse.

Although the indigenous Kanaka Maoli, who are the original people of this locality, are logically the most local, two characteristics help to define the concept of being local. Multiplicity, whether it be a multiplicity of racial backgrounds, possessing a syncretic worldview, or owning a worldview different than the one usually associated with one's racialized identity, is an essential characteristic of being local.

Fluidity, the other essential characteristic, is not easily represented in the typology table. The dashed lines separating the cells attempt to portray the permeability of these boundaries, which allows for the fluidity of identity—the fluidity that accounts for the perception of locals possessing split consciousnesses that vary depending on context. A visual model created to represent local identity was conceived as a more helpful heuristic device for showing this fluidity.

■ Local Identity Models

Imagine a blob that has the consistency of the lava in a lava lamp. The blob represents everyone living in Hawai'i. The blob morphs into a form shaped like an hourglass and eventually pulls apart and separates in the middle. This image indicates the current direction that identity politics in Hawai'i are heading. It describes the effect of the change in racialized discourse and the corresponding decrease in the salience of local identity. The dwindling salience of the local is due to a number of factors, including the diminution of Pidgin, the language of local culture, and the increasing influence of American popular culture, especially MTV and hip-hop. It is also an effect of the ever-increasing number of people of Kanaka Maoli ancestry who identify more strongly with the Hawaiian sovereignty movement, focusing primarily on their identity as indigenous people instead of their local identity. This is, of course, consistent with the new shift in discourse.

In Figure 5.1, the local part of each model pictured, bounded by dashed lines, represents the middle space that includes both haole and Hawaiian portions. Local identity, which includes elements of haole and Hawaiian cultures in addition to major contributions from other settler cultures, is the space that allows for fluid movement between the poles, depending on context. Although local identity emerged as a directly resistant response to colonial domination, it also encompasses resistant and compliant responses that have incorporated and internalized the values of the colonizer. In other words, local includes both those who resist and those who mimic dominant colonial narratives, consciously or unconsciously. In midaltern terms, the local midaltern identity represents an inclusive middle positioned between superaltern and subaltern identities.

In the first model, pictured on the left, local identity is shown as encompassing most people in Hawai'i, excluding dominant haoles. In the second model, note the clumping at the poles, resulting in a shrinking middle space. Most people are grouped in the dominant settler category, with indigenous Kanaka Maoli clearly separate. Local identity is portrayed as shrinking and fading, reflecting its dwindling significance.

The process of supplanting the colonial resistance narrative with a postcolonial indigenous rights narrative will certainly contribute to the diminution of local as a salient identity. This change is already being reflected in observable trends indicating a continuing cultural shift. Of the three major languages spoken in Hawai'i—English, Hawaiian, and Pidgin—Pidgin is the only language not taught in Hawai'i's schools. Rampant consumerism and materialism, the pervasiveness of mainstream US media (e.g., the aforementioned hip-hop culture on MTV), and the indigenous movements of

Figure 5.1 Local Identity Models: Old Versus New

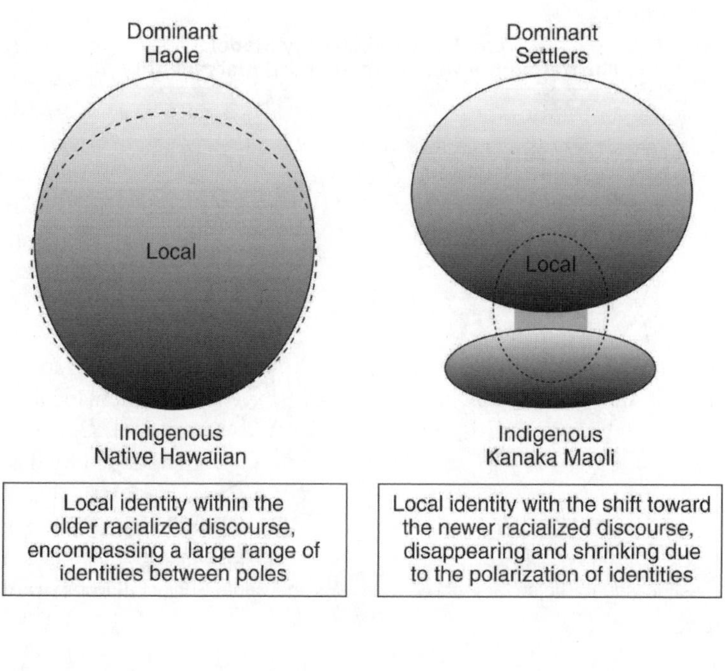

| Local identity within the older racialized discourse, encompassing a large range of identities between poles | Local identity with the shift toward the newer racialized discourse, disappearing and shrinking due to the polarization of identities |

Native Hawaiian sovereignty and nationalism combine simultaneously to give Hawaiian and English currency and prestige at the expense of Hawaiian Pidgin. This analogue is significant because it considers the forces that are diminishing Hawai'i Pidgin and the local identity it represents. While the once-dying language of Hawaiian is experiencing a resurgence, Pidgin is gradually losing its status as the primary language of most non-haoles. Codified into law as official languages of the state of Hawai'i, English and Hawaiian continue to increase in prominence, but the use of Pidgin is frowned upon in schools and is mostly utilized in public discourse for comic relief and the telling of ethnic jokes. Even as the decline of Pidgin and local identity is becoming increasingly noticeable, so are efforts to maintain and preserve it. The recent publication of a Pidgin translation of the New Testament and a growing body of local literature written in Pidgin contribute to its legitimization as a language and help to perpetuate the cultures to which Pidgin is tied. Plays written and performed in Pidgin continue to gain in popularity, resulting in a strong enough following to support performing arts dedicated to local culture.

Just as these local identity models are useful for understanding phenomena at the societal level, they can also illuminate the fluidity that occurs at an individual level. The model represents the identity of a single individual, and the details depicted by the figure represent aspects of that individual. Consider the example of a Native Hawaiian who acts haole in public but lives as a Kanaka Maoli in the privacy of his own home. Imagine that both models pictured in Figure 5.2 represent this same person in two different contexts.

**Figure 5.2 Local Identity Model
Illustrating the Fluidity of an Individual's Identity**

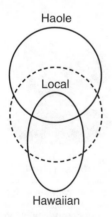

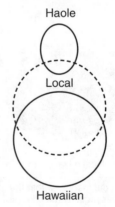

Identity Shape of an
Individual Subject at Work

Identity Shape of an
Individual Subject at Home

The first one represents our subject's apparent identity at work, and the second one represents him or her at home.

In the first model, on the left, note the large haole portion and the smaller Hawaiian portion. Imagine that our subject works in a business office in Honolulu, a context primarily governed by haole values. To act more haole would likely be advantageous in this situation. Once our subject leaves the workplace and retreats to the sanctuary of home, the model transforms into a different shape. In the version of the model pictured on the right, note the small haole portion and the larger Hawaiian portion. Away from the haole-dominated workplace, our subject is able more fully to assert the Kanaka Maoli portion of his or her identity. The presence of the local part of the model, the middle space that includes both haole and Hawaiian portions, represents a salient identity in which all this operates.

Multiplicity and fluidity are the hallmarks of local identity. Various kinds of identities in Hawai'i fall under the local umbrella, making it a diverse and dynamic identity that defies strict categorization. Local identity is Hawai'i's organic manifestation of midalternity. It is akin to *mestizaje* (i.e., "the mixing of races," but see Anzaldúa 1999) and borderland theoretical projects in how it constructs a sanctioned space devoted to conceptualizing identities for those left out or pushed out by dominant paradigms, especially dichotomies. The local cases described here were presented to help define midalternity and the midaltern. Although it would be impossible to describe the potentially limitless ways that local identities play out, it is apparent that local identity challenges dichotomous thinking, creates more possibilities, and allows for more precise identification.

■ Midaltern Theory

In midaltern terms, the local midaltern identity represents the center between superaltern and subaltern identities. Theories of middle or third spaces may not be new, but the introduction of the midaltern to postcolonial discourse about the subaltern provides an additional dimension to the discussion. Just as asserting local identity as midaltern proposes a way out of the current impasse of essentialism and opposition in Hawai'i racial politics—hence, a move in favor of racial justice—the concept of the midaltern can also be useful for understanding colonial and postcolonial situations in other places besides Hawai'i. Applying the concept elsewhere, however, would involve rethinking the notion of the subaltern.

The concept of the subaltern comes from Antonio Gramsci's writings about fascism in post–World War I Italy (Gramsci 1971; Hall 2000). Subaltern refers to subordination in the context of dominant-dominated relationships in history (Gramsci 1971; Prakash 2000). This subordination can be in terms of class, caste, gender, race, language, or culture. Although subaltern studies have witnessed differences and shifts in the use of the concept of subalternity, the idea of subordination has remained central. The effort to rethink history from the perspective of the subordinated, or the subaltern, has also remained a consistent goal of subaltern studies (Prakash 2000). This "history from below" (Hall 2000; Prakash 2000), focusing primarily on critiques of colonialism and Western domination, prompted the question, "What about a history from the middle approach?" Again, thinking only in terms of a dominant-dominated dichotomy fails to recognize those who reside, figuratively, somewhere in the middle. Subaltern scholars seem to relegate persons in the middle simply to the subaltern. Those meandering somewhere between and throughout dominant and dominated spaces are simply thought of as a kind of subaltern expression. In other words, the subaltern would subsume all those who, somewhere, in some way, reside in the middle. In our opinion, distinguishing the midaltern from the subaltern is an important distinction with valuable implications.

We propose the midaltern because it allows the conceptualization of a wider range of possibilities than does the subaltern. Rather than assigning people into static, essentialized, either/or categories, midalternity recognizes the existence and importance of multiplicity, thus creating the possibility for a more precise accounting of identities. The fluidity of the midaltern also allows us to take context and worldview into consideration. The performance of one's identity can shift dramatically between contexts. Midalternity provides the conceptual space to consider shifts, depending on the situation. Midalternity's recognition of the contextual nature of identity allows the potential for one's identity to broaden beyond just one dimension.

This conceptualization provides the potential for more inclusive coalition building in the quest for racial justice. Although local identity is endemic to Hawai'i and midaltern-type identities are not unique just to the islands, the United States, in general, needs a midaltern discourse. Hawai'i's midaltern identities may be neither applicable nor directly generalizable to all contexts in the United States, but that does not rule out the utility of midalternity for transforming the way that Americans consider identity. After all, the dichotomous terms of the current racial discourse in Hawai'i, pitting Kanaka Maoli versus settlers, directly resemble the classic American binary of a color line separating whites and nonwhites. Many who are engaged in the struggle for social and racial equality, in their fervent quest for justice, tend to employ the same kind of limiting discourse that originally helped construct and maintain racial inequality. Even though this kind of rhetoric may seem effective in the short term for bringing matters of injustice to the fore, it in fact mimics or replicates the same kind of dominant discourse that their struggle seeks to contest (Spickard and Daniel 2004). For example, multiculturalists and multicultural educators, in their struggle against white male supremacist hegemony, often assert their diverse perspectives in essentialized, monolithic terms. Their radical discourses actually reinscribe the very kind of power relations that they seek to challenge. When multiculturalists assert their respective agendas as members of groups who define themselves in mono-lithic, essentialized, and categorical terms, they in turn actually ignore or marginalize those of mixed ancestry. Thus, they have replicated the same kind of inequitable power relations that they had sought to challenge. Mid-alternity offers the promise of ending this kind of divisiveness. It does so by providing a more comprehensive metaphor than the color line.

In Hawai'i, this quest for racial justice would not be only for Native Hawaiians, but also for all local multiracial people and settler people who have not shared fully in the blessings of settler colonialism. For example, non–Kanaka Maoli locals who feel threatened by the rhetoric of some sovereignty activists would not be as defensive if they did not also feel under attack. In fact, many of these locals may turn out to be the best allies for Kanaka Maoli and their quest for sovereignty. For those faced with the extermination of cultures, whether they be indigenous or midaltern cultures, employing all the available assistance instead of alienating potential allies would seem to better the chance of preserving those threatened cultures.

A shift toward a more inclusive and thoughtful discourse may assist locals who feel threatened by the sovereignty movement. They may finally realize that it is actually in the best interests of all locals to support whole-heartedly all efforts at achieving Kanaka Maoli sovereignty in Hawai'i. As the original inhabitants of Hawai'i, with a history of experience in the islands stretching back for many hundreds of years, Kanaka Maoli possess indige-nous cultural values that are almost certainly the best suited for living in Hawai'i. Local culture is heavily interconnected with Kanaka Maoli culture. If protection and active support are not given to Kanaka Maoli efforts at sovereignty, there will be a greater chance of both Kanaka Maoli and non-Hawaiian locals being engulfed and extinguished by those whose worldviews emphasize economic exploitation over the preservation of Hawai'i's limited and valuable resources—which include, most notably, its people.

■ Notes

1. We use "Kanaka Maoli" and "Native Hawaiians" interchangeably to refer to those people who are descended from those who inhabited the islands before Euro-peans first arrived. For islanders' modes of reckoning identity and inclusion, see Spickard (1995).

2. Throughout this chapter we use the term *local identity* as a unitary cover term for what are actually local identities (emphasizing plurality). In the same respect, local culture can arguably be viewed as a unitary panethnic culture within which are nested various local subcultures (e.g., local Japanese, local Filipino, Hawai-ian, etc.).

3. Pidgin here refers to the vernacular associated with local identity and culture in Hawai'i. Hawai'i Pidgin is a Creole language based primarily on Hawaiian and English, with significant contributions from the languages of other ethnic groups that settled in Hawai'i.

6

New Racial Identities, Old Arguments: Continuing Biological Reification

Rainier Spencer

And now, I said, let me show in a figure how far our nature is enlightened or unenlightened:—Behold! human beings living in an underground den, which has a mouth open towards the light and reaching all along the den; here they have been from their childhood, and have their legs and necks chained so that they cannot move, and can only see before them, being prevented by the chains from turning round their heads. Above and behind them a fire is blazing at a distance, and between the fire and the prisoners there is a raised way; and you will see, if you look, a low wall built along the way, like the screen which marionette players have in front of them, over which they show the puppets.

I see.

—Plato, *The Republic,* Book VII

As Americans move into a new millennium, a strange and unsettling phenomenon has become more and more evident. Although most people have failed to notice its pervasiveness and (importantly) its inconsistency, it is there and growing nonetheless. The phenomenon to which I am referring is the conflicting and double-sided coincidence of (1) increasingly ubiquitous assertions that the concept of race is supposedly unraveling before our eyes, especially in the form of multiracial identity, and (2) the distinct reality that racial blackness is actually being reinscribed more and more deeply all the while.[1] The tension existing between these two opposed propositions is relieved, wrongly, by the fact that virtually all commentators carelessly, if not desperately, accept the first proposition while ignoring the second.

From sources as diverse as popular magazines and the federal government, we are told that racial distinctions are breaking down and that a new multiracial population is rising in our midst. This is particularly true of the popular media, which, since the 1990s, has adopted a clear tendency toward uncritical, trendy, and overly sentimental treatments of race and multiracialism (for example, Clemetson 2000; Leland and Beals 1997; White 1997). As Danzy Senna points out satirically in her brief but biting essay "The Mulatto Millennium," "And just last month, two established magazines, both bastions of liberal thought, had cover stories predicting 'the end of blackness.' Not too long ago, *Newsweek* officially declared it 'hip' to be multiracial" (Senna 1998: 27).

The authors whom Senna lampoons have not developed this information entirely by themselves but have instead relied partly on the federal government as a source. Entities such as the US Bureau of the Census regularly issue statements and reports indicating that multiracial Americans are a new and growing population. Figures are offered for the numbers of blacks and whites engaging in interracial marriage as well as for the ostensibly multiracial children such couples produce (US Department of Commerce 1997). Armed with this federal data—data that takes on an unquestioned aura of truth—magazine writers then wax prophetic concerning the declining significance of race, the hipness of multiracial identity, and the coming of a new racial order.

It is imperative, however, to question these claims and the assumptions upon which they are based. Is the concept of race in the United States suddenly under assault from a recent and continuing biracial baby boom? Does this ostensibly new generation of multiracial children represent a biological phenomenon that is unique in US history? And, very importantly, is it the case that race and especially blackness (the most pervasive racial essence in US history) are diminishing, blurring, or otherwise fading away? In this chapter I explore crucial but overlooked questions concerning race and multiraciality by examining the assumptions that underlie the above claims, subjecting them to a level of critical analysis they do not normally encounter. Through this examination it will become clear that these assertions are hopelessly misguided, philosophically invalid, and complicit with rather than subversive of the hegemony of the US racial hierarchy.

The general argument that the above claims are mistaken and inaccurate shall proceed along two axes. The first of these is a historically contextualized evaluation of the assertion that the United States has been in the midst of a biracial baby boom since 1967. The focus of this first line of argument is that what is taken today to be interracial sex has in fact been going on for centuries in North America and has produced millions upon millions of children during that time. Thus, the so-called black/white multiracial children of today are no different biologically than the average Afro-American child (who possesses a significant African, European, and Native American admixture in his or her ancestry). By calling attention to the historical facts of the "true" biracial baby boom of the seventeenth century (Joel Williamson's 1980 book *New People* remains the classic text here) as well as the ensuing and still continuing phenomenon of internal miscegenation, I problematize the notion of post-1967 black/white multiracial persons as being distinct from Afro-Americans.

This historical context will facilitate the interrogation of what has become an unquestioned premise of the multiracial movement, namely that since the *Loving v. Commonwealth of Virginia* Supreme Court decision of 1967, a new and documentable multiracial population that is biologically distinct from the general Afro-American population has arisen as a result. My argument will not contest the notion that persons who have considered themselves to be of different races have intermarried in greater numbers since the *Loving* decision. Rather, the argument will center on the assertion that the resulting children of these unions are distinct biologically from Afro-Americans in general, said assertion being the centerpiece of the multiracial identity thesis. In this regard, Kathleen Korgen's *From Black to Biracial* (1998–1999) serves as a convenient example of how claims for contemporary multiracial identity have become entangled both by a necessary reliance on biological race and by the impossibility of demonstrating a distinction between Afro-Americans and black/white multiracial persons.

The second axis builds on the above conclusions by casting a critical eye toward the categorization of Afro-Americans as the black partners in interracial marriages. Such categorization is of course nonproblematic for many Americans; however, it is here especially that people's claims of eschewing race are shown to be anything but sincere. Even given the proven fallaciousness of biological race, Americans cling to the concept ever more tenaciously. It is vital to acknowledge the quite simple truth that it is only possible to posit the existence of black/white multiracial children by claiming that one of the respective parents is black. Yet, as already noted, this would be a black parent with extensive population mixture in her or his family history.

Indeed, given that multiracial ideology is premised on the idea of population mixture, Afro-Americans must, if multiracial advocates are to take their own ideology seriously, be considered quintessentially multiracial. The fact that they are not considered multiracial brings into focus the philosophical dissonance between the necessary biological foundation of multiracial ideology and what appears to be the selective agenda of its most vocal leaders (see Spencer 1999).[2] We are therefore left with the ironic and inconsistent coincidence that current projections of multiracial identity as representing the end of race are based precisely on the continual reproduction of Afro-American parents as monoracially black through the selective application of hypo-descent, or, the "one-drop rule" (see Chapter 2, this volume).

Interestingly then, black people find themselves ever so necessary for most expressions of multiracial identity in the United States. Americans can thus hardly be said to be moving away from the idea of race when the very vehicle providing that alleged movement—multiracial identity—reinscribes and reproduces blackness in an essentialized and overtly biological way.

This is precisely what the Bureau of the Census as well as popular magazines do when they produce figures representing multiracial births and interracial marriages. Afro-Americans, the most genetically diverse people in the United States, are effectively placed together in a single biological black box in order to provide half the ingredients for creating multiracial children—children who are in fact no more the result of population mixture than they themselves are. Far from dismantling the race concept, it is cemented all the more firmly in place through multiracial ideology and the relentlessly uncritical coverage granted by the popular media.

Having presented these two lines of argument, the remainder of the chapter questions the premise that the concept of race in the United States is presently breaking down in the wake of the multiracial identity movement. Precisely what does the growing public attention to light-appearing multiracial persons imply about changes to the racial superstructure? Are such persons overtly accepted as white, or are they accepted only if their full ancestries remain veiled—by passing, in other words? If the borders of whiteness were truly widening, it would be an extremely important event, even if still open to criticism in terms of being race-based thinking. But is that really happening now? In the United States it seems that whiteness has always allowed for the admixture of Native American ancestry, and it may also be the case that Asian ancestry is assimilable to whiteness over time. But what of African ancestry? Are white-appearing Afro-Americans currently being accepted fully as whites, even if their African ancestry is known? The answer here is still a clear and resounding "no," and we haven't any reason to suspect that it will change any time soon. Rather than a challenge to the American racial paradigm, the multiracial movement comes closer to representing the reincarnation of the nineteenth-century mulatto, sans her overtly tragic trappings.

Instead of multiraciality being used in an abstract sense to discredit the idea of race, it is deployed in such a way that it reinforces racial boundaries. The assertion of a multiracial class as the product of mixture between whites and Afro-Americans creates the theoretical space for whiteness to maintain its mythical purity and for blackness to retain its essentially impure quality. Multiracial ideology serves this particular function well in that it provides a phantom buffer against the reality of what thousands of years of population mixture have made plain—the fact that race does not exist. And even though the application of hypo-descent may be waived selectively by some multiracial advocates in their own cases, it is nonetheless thereby reinscribed all the more deeply for their Afro-American parents and for all other Afro-Americans who do not subscribe personally to the goals of the multiracial identity movement.

In this chapter I go beyond the simplistic and trendy attention usually given to race in general and to multiracial ideology in particular. Through historical context and philosophical analysis, the disjunction between popular assertions regarding the supposed decline of race and the reality of an ever more deeply entrenched racial consciousness will be made clear. It remains vital to challenge and problematize those popular understandings, for they serve to disguise the unchanging reality of the American racial paradigm.

■ Forgotten Reality: Historical Population Mixture in North America

> And do you see, I said, men passing along the wall carrying all sorts of vessels, and statues and figures of animals made of wood and stone and various materials, which appear over the wall? Some of them are talking, others silent.
> You have shown me a strange image, and they are strange prisoners.
> —Plato, *The Republic,* Book VII

The proposition that the race concept in the United States is becoming unstable due to a rising population of multiracial individuals depends on accepting the continued repetition of a single scenario—an explicit mixture of biological racial essences resulting in the birth of a multiracial child. The child in question, the multiracial individual, is categorized as such because she or he is presumed to have parents of different biological racial groups. The general argument is that such individuals have become increasingly common since the 1967 *Loving* Supreme Court decision. Kathleen Korgen identifies the *Loving* decision as the primary stimulus of an increase in interracial marriages and multiracial births: "The first and foremost legal influence is the 1967 Supreme Court decision to overturn the *Loving v. Commonwealth of Virginia* verdict and invalidate laws that made interracial marriage a crime. . . . An increase in interracial marriages followed the *Loving* verdict that repealed this legislation. A 'biracial baby boom' began shortly thereafter" (Korgen 1998–1999: 20).

Korgen here provides the typical rationale for asserting the existence of a modern biracial baby boom. The basic premise of this position is that the two parents are racially distinct from each other (making their union an interracial one), and that their child is a mixture of both parents but is racially distinct from either of them (making the child multiracial). The fundamental idea is that the multiracial child is the product of two distinct and exclusive biological racial groups. Presumably neither two white parents nor two Afro-American parents produce a multiracial child.[3] Appeals to socially constructed race notwithstanding, the operative dynamic in this scenario can only be biological mixture. If, after all, socially constructed race were actually being invoked by multiracial advocates, then the resulting child's being multiracial would not depend as it does on an act of biological mating.

The issue I intend to raise here is whether, in the case of presumed black/white mixture, such children are in fact distinct from their Afro-American parents. I want to be very careful in what I am suggesting via this challenge. I am very specifically not saying that persons who believe they are black/white multiracials are really black and should "just get over it," as so many who are invested in black racial identity have argued. Race, to be sure, is a fiction. What I am going to suggest is that persons who believe they are black/white multiracials cannot in any meaningful way distinguish themselves from the millions upon millions of persons of African and European descent (and Native American descent as well) who have lived in British North America and the United States since the seventeenth century. The fundamental question is not "Are they black?" but "Are they distinct?"

The philosophical linchpin of my argument is the fact that one cannot claim a legitimate distinction between two things that are not distinct. The two things in question here are, on the one hand, the person who believes herself or himself to be a black/white multiracial, and, on the other, that person's Afro-American parent. One of the principal foundations of multiracial ideology is a claimed alterity between black/white multiracials and Afro-Americans. For some of the more vocal supporters of multiracial identity, establishing and defending this alterity is the raison d'être of the multiracial movement. Many multiracial advocates, but most especially some white mothers of so-called multiracial children, have gone to near-heroic lengths to prevent black/white multiracials from being categorized, labeled, or otherwise associated in any way with Afro-Americans (interestingly, no such energy is expended to disclaim the whiteness of the same individuals).

Susan Graham, executive director of the multiracial advocacy organization Project RACE (Reclassify All Children Equally) provides an illustration of this attitude. As the self-identified white mother of several children she has had with her Afro-American husband, Graham has held consistently that black/white multiracials are not black. Indeed, when the conversation on a radio talk show on which she was a guest turned to the subject of her children's racial ancestry, "Graham responded ardently, 'My daughter is not black; my daughter is multiracial'" (Spencer 1997: 80). Two connected points are of particular interest here. First, Graham appears to be rejecting the concept of hypodescent by declaring that her part-black daughter should not be considered black, and second, Graham draws a clear distinction between the child (who has both African and European ancestry) and the father (who presumably does not). Yet, as is the case with virtually all Afro-Americans, Graham's husband must himself be the product of extensive population mixture.

Both of these points arise in a particularly insightful story Graham tells regarding the pair:

> My husband, who is Black, went to our local Recreation and Parks Department to enroll our five-year-old daughter in a gymnastics program. . . . Our daughter was not with him. A clerk checked off "Black" [on the

registration form]. In other words, the clerk looked at the father and made the assumption that the child was Black. . . . The point is: she was mistaken. My husband has a Multiracial child and the clerk had no way of knowing. . . . The problem here is . . . the old rule of hypo-descent. (Spencer 1997: 80)

Yet, while unequivocally rejecting hypodescent for her daughter, Graham shows no hesitation whatsoever in looking at the girl's father—an Afro-American of mixed heritage—and using "the old rule of hypodescent" to label him monoracially black. Both Gordon Graham and his daughter have African and European ancestry. To label the daughter multiracial and the father black is to engage both in a profound suspension of critical thought and, importantly, selective hypodescent. Unfortunately, this kind of suspension, and the selective hypodescent that is coextensive with it, is undertaken daily in the United States, from the federal government to the popular media. It seems that Americans have forgotten, if in fact they ever really knew, the long history of population mixture on this continent.

Indeed, this mixture was ongoing even prior to African slaves arriving on American shores. One of the racial myths Americans cherish is the idea that the West and Central African slaves who were transported to the Americans via the transatlantic slave trade were *unmixed* blacks. As Gunnar Myrdal describes the situation, however:

The slaves imported from Africa by no means represented "pure Negro races." Of the original tribal stocks many had an admixture of Caucasoid genes from crosses with Mediterranean peoples. During the slave trade more white genes were added. The Portuguese who settled on the Guinea Coast had relations with the natives. The slave traders themselves were known frequently to have had promiscuous intercourse with their female merchandise. (Myrdal, Sterner, and Rose 1944: 123)

Writing of slave-trading centers on the West African coast, Ira Berlin reports of a growing mulatto population, some of whom no doubt found themselves enslaved and bound for the Americas:[4]

The peoples of the enclaves—both long-term residents and wayfarers—soon joined together, geographically and genetically. European men took wives and mistresses (sometimes by arrangement) among the African women, and before long the children born of these unions helped populate the enclave. Elmina sprouted a substantial cadre of Euro-Africans (most of them Luso-Africans, that is, of Portuguese and African descent)—men and women of African birth but shared African and European parentage, whose swarthy skin, European dress and deportment, acquaintance with local norms, and multilingualism gave them an insider's knowledge of both African and European ways but denied them full acceptance in either culture. By the eighteenth century, they numbered several hundred in Elmina. Along the Angolan coast they may have been even more numerous. (Berlin 1998: 145)

In a similar vein, while considering the islands off the West African coast such as São Tomé and O Principe, Hugh Thomas reports that "all these territories, like the Cape Verde Islands, had, as a result of continual contact between the Portuguese and the Africans, a thoroughly mulatto population" (Thomas 1997: 365). When one adds to these facts the mixture that occurred on the other side of the Atlantic—in the Caribbean, for instance, some of whose slaves and free blacks were subsequently transported to North America—the notion of an essentializing racial blackness being invoked in the present day becomes even more hopelessly tenuous.

As the work of Joel Williamson and others demonstrates, talk of a post-1967 biracial baby boom is misinformed and inaccurate historically. If one is to speak of a biracial baby boom it occurred some 300 years ago, principally in the Chesapeake colonies, as European indentured servants and Africans (indentured servant, slave, and free) procreated together and established what might be termed the original mulatto stock of British North America, which was followed by later surges in the mixed-race population:

> The ultimate result of early colonial mixing was that in the upper South in the years around 1700 a strong beginning was made in the creation of a mulatto population, both slave and free. It built upon the earlier beginning that was made by the mulattoes who lived through the seventeenth century. The mulatto population reached that "critical mass," that "take-off point," whence over the next century and a half it grew into a wellspring of mulattoes, a "mulatto pool" that not only supplied slaves to the Southwest and emigrants to the Northwest but also greatly increased the numbers of those who stayed at home. (Williamson 1980: 56–57)

Berlin also points to the mixed origins of many of the Chesapeake's early Afro-Americans: "In 1755 about 80 percent of [free people of African descent] in Maryland were of mixed racial origins. Like white Marylanders, about half of the free colored population was under sixteen years of age, and of these, almost nine out of ten were of mixed ancestry. In other words, Chesapeake free blacks were becoming progressively light-skinned" (Berlin 1998: 124).

The coinciding of the international slave trade's end with the surge in cotton production in the early nineteenth century, as well as the concurrent overabundance of slaves in the Chesapeake, opened the doors of an internal slave trade in which thousands upon thousands of mulatto slaves were transported south and west. According to Williamson, the Chesapeake's original mulatto stock "served most significantly to lighten the great mass of black Americans, and especially those in the lower South, the black belt, as thousands of mulatto slaves were dumped onto the plantation frontier" (Williamson 1980: 59). At the very least, present-day attempts to distinguish black/white multiracials from Afro-Americans in general fly in the face of the history of African-descended people in North America.

Although there was a general decrease in black/white sexual activity after emancipation, the process of internal miscegenation (in this case, sexual activity in which at least one partner had both African and European ancestry) continued its work of diminishing the distinctions between the lighter and darker members of the Afro-American community, in what Williamson refers to as the "Browning of America" (Williamson 1980: chap. 3). Although it might have been possible to speak of blacks (Africans) and mulattoes in the seventeenth and eighteenth centuries, it became increasingly difficult to do so as darker and lighter people of African descent mixed with each other. Williamson argues that "probably in late slavery and certainly with emancipation, mulattoes and blacks commenced to mix at a high rate. By 1918 this miscegenation between blacks and mulattoes was rapidly generating a large Negro population and eroding the line between mulatto and black. Just as America was working as a melting pot for whites, so was it working as a melting pot for Negroes" (Williamson 1980: 113).

Writing more than a half-century ago, Myrdal came to the same conclusion: "*Internal miscegenation* within the Negro group between individuals with a varying degree of white ancestry is, and will in the future be, going on. The result is a tendency toward a slow but continuous equalization of Negro and white genes in the Negro people, decreasing the relative numbers at both the black and white extremes and concentrating the individuals ever closer to the average" (Myrdal, Sterner, and Rose 1944: 135). This is of course why Afro-Americans (with the possible exception of isolated Sea Island pockets) do not look like their West and Central African ancestors of 200 to 400 years ago. Indeed, even if one were to pretend for an instant that biological race existed, the history of population mixture in the United States would force one to conclude that sub-Saharan West and Central Africans on the one hand and Afro-Americans on the other constitute different racial groups.

A serious examination of historical population mixture brings to light a critical issue that no one, it seems, gives much thought to. Three or four hundred years ago, when there was less total population mixture between the peoples on the North American continent than there is now, when the extremes for the most part were more polarized, it would not have been very difficult to tell a mulatto from either his African or European parent. Whereas today people tend to use very light skin, straight hair, or green eyes as cues of mixture, in the seventeenth century the brown-skinned child of a West African freeman and a female English indentured servant would not have been mistaken for either a presumably unmixed African or European. Unawareness of this important fact causes people today to mistakenly believe that racial cues have remained static over the past four hundred years, when in fact they have moved along a temporally modulated sliding scale that tends increasingly to make the threshold of blackness lighter and lighter still as the years go by—whiteness remains unchallenged and unchanged.

Commentators and social scientists of the early- to mid-twentieth century would doubtless be profoundly skeptical of the current conception of black/white multiracials as somehow comprising a biological category distinct from a much larger, general Afro-American population. Myrdal, for instance, argued that:

> Thus, while we cannot say that existing research permits a definitive answer to the question as to how many Negroes have some white blood, the best available evidence and expert opinion point to a figure around 70 percent. This figure must tend to increase with time, if for no other reason than that full-blooded Negroes intermarry with mixed bloods and their offspring become mixed bloods. (Myrdal, Sterner, and Rose 1944: 133)

Today's scientists and intellectuals are in general agreement with Myrdal. According to Audrey Smedley, principal author of the American Anthropological Association's 1998 *Statement on Race:*

> From a purely biogenetic perspective, most black Americans, and probably most Native Americans, can claim to be of "mixed" ancestry. It has been estimated that the genetic ancestry of the average African American is from one-quarter to about one-third non-African. Indeed, there is a greater range of skin colors, hair textures, body sizes, nose and lip shapes, and other physical features among black Americans than almost any other people identified as a distinct population, attesting to this mixed ancestry. (Smedley 1993/1999: 332)

F. James Davis adds that "at least three-fourths of all people defined as American blacks have some white ancestry, and some estimates run well above 90 percent. . . . In terms of gene frequencies, apparently somewhere between one-fifth and one-fourth of the genes of the American black population are from white ancestors" (Davis 1991: 21). Yet, in spite of the very clear historical fact that Afro-Americans are the products of large-scale and continuing population mixture, many commentators nonetheless unquestioningly accept the premise that a distinction between black/white multiracials and Afro-Americans is possible biologically.

This tendency is illustrated by multiracial identity advocate Charles Byrd, who departs somewhat from the usual practice by allowing that persons of mixed ancestry did exist in the United States in significant numbers prior to 1967. Byrd, however, posits Afro-Americans and mulattoes as comprising two continuous, distinct, and isolated groups through the decades:

> No one has kept track of our collective numbers since shortly after the turn of the century. As a result, no one knows exactly how many multiracials there are in the United States. . . . The Census Bureau kept tabs on "mulattoes" until the early 1900's when the agency stopped that practice.

Then, "mulattoes" represented approximately 20–25% of the total "Negro" or "colored" population. Twenty percent of today's black population would yield a mixed-race figure of around 6,000,000. (Byrd 1996)

There are at least two fundamental difficulties with Byrd's overly simplistic estimate. First, there is no reason to believe that censuses counting mulattoes did so with any degree of accuracy beyond the enumerator's judgment of the person's phenotype. Williamson's analysis of the Census Bureau's decision to eliminate a separate mulatto count in the early twentieth century is instructive here:

> No one could be very certain what the numbers meant. Those persons who had been counted as mulattoes were people whom the census takers perceived as mulattoes. They had been counting mulattoes "visible" to themselves. Moreover, "visibility" probably changed over the generations. A person whom the census taker in 1850 might have judged as a mulatto in 1920 might be judged as black. In brief, as the entire Negro population became lighter, both what was thought to be black and what was thought to be mulatto became lighter and mulattoes were counted as black in increasing numbers. (Williamson 1980: 114)

Second, even if there had been a reliable count of mulattoes as a separate population in the early twentieth century, which is highly doubtful, there is no evidence that in the intervening decades these persons procreated only with other similarly designated mulattoes, as they would have been required to do in order to justify Byrd's estimate and still be distinguishable today from some mythically pure, essentially African, US black population.[5] If anything, historical analysis illustrates that internal miscegenation among people of African descent in the United States has negated the possibility of any distinction being drawn between Afro-Americans and multiracial individuals of European and African heritage.

Finally, we might attain a measure of utility in considering the interesting case of Edward Reuter, one of the first sociologists of the early twentieth century. As a social scientist of his time, Reuter was of course aware of the population mixture in US history and focused some of his early work on that area. Attempting to use sociology as a tool of continued white supremacy, Reuter argued that American mulattoes were the natural leaders of a permanently subordinate Negro population and should accept that role in lieu of agitating for equal civil and political rights. In a bizarre exercise devised to prove this point, Reuter sought to demonstrate that the vast majority of Negroes who had made anything of themselves were of mixed racial ancestry. Canvassing each of the various professions, he compiled what he considered a generous, contemporary list of all the successful Negroes in the United States: "The list of 4267 Negroes before us includes every member of the race who has made any marked success in life" (Reuter 1969 [1918]: 310).

As in the case of the other scholars we have considered, Reuter also understood the extent to which the American Negro population possessed European ancestry:

> Many questionable and border-line cases were placed with and counted as Negroes of full blood. Consequently, in the full-blooded group, there are doubtless many individuals of mixed blood; probably a goodly percentage of them are in some degree of mixed ancestry; possibly there are in this so-called full-blooded group more individuals of mixed than of pure blood. A stricter definition of the terms *full-blooded* and *mixed-blood* would decrease the number classified as full-blooded and increase the mixed-blood group by an equal number. (Reuter 1969 [1918]: 311)

Reuter determined that of his list of 4,267 successful Negroes, "447 names fall into the full-blooded group and 3820 names fall into the group of mulattoes. . . . The ratio of eight and one-half to one is thus the ratio prevailing between the mulattoes and blacks in a list of about four thousand of the most prominent individuals of the race" (Reuter 1969 [1918]: 312, 313). Reuter's conclusion was that practical leadership for US Negroes could only come from the mulatto class, which he called the "aristocracy" of the race (Reuter 1969 [1918]: 389).

To be sure, Edward Reuter's work is more useful in terms of what it tells us about thoughts and attitudes in his day than in terms of its lasting value to the field of sociology. What Reuter does provide, however, is yet another affirmation that population mixture is nothing new and that persons of African and European ancestry are certainly not the sudden result of a postulated post-1967 biracial baby boom. Indeed, the Afro-American parents of today's misnamed biracial boomers are themselves the products of an extensive history of African and European mixture in North America. Reuter was aware of that historical mixture and even recognized that it was likely wider than his study allowed for.

Having established the necessary historical context—including the presence of population mixture in Africa, slave-era miscegenation in British North America and in the United States, and internal miscegenation that continues to this day—we are now in a position to assess the current and widespread practice of transforming Afro-Americans of mixed ancestry into monoracial blacks and then serving them up as producers of mixed-race children who are somehow distinct from them in terms of possessing mixed ancestry. Undertaking this examination will make clear the extent to which multiracial identity advocates invoke the concept of hypodescent in an inconsistent and selective way for Afro-American parents while rejecting hypodescent in the case of purported multiracial children.

■ Passing for Black: The Alchemy of Interracial Sex

> Like ourselves, I replied; and they see only their own shadows, or the shadows of one another, which the fire throws on the opposite wall of the cave?
>   True, he said; how could they see anything but the shadows if they were never allowed to move their heads?
>   And of the objects which are being carried in like manner they would only see the shadows?
>   Yes, he said.
>
> —Plato, *The Republic*, Book VII

The title of Kathleen Korgen's *From Black to Biracial: Transforming Racial Identity Among Americans* is a fascinating example of the general confusion attending multiracial ideology.[6] In fact, the book's title represents the inverse of reality. The actual transformation that is being effected continually by multiracial advocates (and Americans generally) is not from *black to biracial* but rather from *biracial to black*. By this I mean that in order for the assertion of black/white biracial identity to be made for a specific child, that child's Afro-American parent must first be transformed from someone who possesses mixed ancestry to someone who is monoracially black.

One might be tempted here to object that what I am suggesting is not necessary after all. In other words, the case could be made that an Afro-American parent who is herself or himself mixed may still serve as the producer of a multiracial child, thereby obviating the need to cast that parent as monoracially black. In fact, one could argue that the child of such a person will always be multiracial, regardless of who the other parent is. However, if this path is chosen, the chimerical framework of multiracial distinctiveness falls in upon itself, for there would then be no basis for distinguishing between the purported black/white multiracial individual and the average Afro-American since both are the result of population mixture. Multiracial ideology's fundamental condition that there be a distinction drawn between black/white multiracial individuals and Afro-Americans logically requires that black parents be monoracially black. To allow otherwise would be tantamount to an admission that all 30 million Afro-Americans in the United States are already multiracial and that no further distinction is either necessary or possible.

I have been arguing this position throughout the chapter, and it is no small point. Although multiracial advocates often attempt to avoid this criticism, such evasions prove inadequate. One such defense occurred while I was participating on a scholarly panel concerned with multiracial identity and changes to federal racial classification. A fellow panelist, one of the more highly regarded multiracial advocates, asserted that multiracial ideology did not involve race at all but rather was based on ancestry (Daniel 2000b). In explaining this he said that multiracial advocates do not take biological race to be a reality, but that they are merely addressing questions of ancestry. Even as he said this, however, I wondered what the difference could possibly be between race and ancestry as he was using the latter term.

Indeed, there is no difference. We are not, after all, referring to multinational identity, multicultural identity, or multiethnic identity. The issue here is multiracial or biracial identity, and it is unalterably based on the notion of biological race. The seat of multiracial or biracial identity is interracial sex between persons of supposed distinct and exclusive racial groups. For my purposes in this chapter, that sexual contact is between ostensible white and black partners.

According to *Newsweek* writer Lynette Clemetson, "Thirty years ago, only one in every 100 children born in the United States was of mixed race. Today that number is one in 19" (Clemetson 2000: 70). It is critical to take notice of what commentators such as Clemetson achieve via these naive and typically unchallenged assertions. Clemetson's reckoning here is precisely the kind of facile calculus that reinscribes blackness while ostensibly creating a mythical and new multiracial population. If one were to give credence to the notion of race and mixed race, the fact is that (excepting recent immigrants) thirty years ago, *every* Afro-American child born in the United States would have been of mixed race, and the same would be true today. The exclusionary mechanism that determines which Afro-Americans of mixed ancestry are multiracial and which Afro-Americans of mixed ancestry are merely black depends upon the selective deployment of hypodescent.

As I have argued throughout this chapter, such a selective hypodescent effectively *creates* multiracial individuals who are in fact no more racially mixed than the Afro-American halves of their respective parent sets. That this is so is made evident by the fact that advocates of multiracial identity ignore the massive mixing of European, African, and Native American genes that literally defines the Afro-American population, preferring instead to assert that Afro-Americans are a monoracial group that is properly distinguished from black/white multiracial individuals.

Nor is this mechanism difficult to understand from the perspective of the proponents of multiracial identity. The distinctive cachet of biracial identity can only be maintained if there are differently raced monoracial parents who engage in interracial sex in order to produce that biracial child. On the Afro-American side, then, this fiction requires monoracial black parents—even if those black parents have light skin, green eyes, and naturally straight hair. Part of what takes place here is that biology is confounded with personal identity politics when convenient. Thus, proponents of multiracial identity will assert that they are not talking about biology, but rather about ancestry. Or they will assert that the question does not revolve around one's biological inheritance, but instead around one's personal identity preference.

Therefore, a particular Afro-American woman who is extremely light-skinned, with a straight nose and thin lips can—if she identifies personally as black—stand as the black parent of a multiracial child. Through this confounding of biological race and personal identity politics, a human signifier of blackness may in fact appear to be very nearly, although not quite, white. Clearly, however, this moves the entire enterprise to the level of extreme absurdity. The redefinition of such a woman as monoracially black—and similar redefinitions occur daily—reinscribes the notion that there are distinct and exclusive separate races, even when the evidence before our very eyes literally screams to us that there are not.

This is no small matter, for it is the very foundation of multiracial identity politics in the United States. Afro-Americans (who are virtually all of mixed ancestry) are continually reinscribed as monoracially black in order that the fiction of multiracial persons and the fiction of a biracial baby boom may be propounded. What we witness in this exercise is not the deconstruction of race but rather the reinscription of racial blackness. The great irony, of course, is that the supposedly progressive and hip (but decidedly exclusionary) status of multiracial identity is not possible unless it stands on the back of a variety of biological race thinking that US scientists consigned to the trash heap of myth some fifty years ago. Yet, from *Time* and *Newsweek* to the Office of Management and Budget, we find Americans paying dutiful homage to the myth while ignoring the reality.

■ **Running in Place:**
Deconstructing Race, Reinscribing Blackness

> And if they were able to converse with one another, would they not suppose that they were naming what was actually before them?
> Very true.
> And suppose further that the prison had an echo which came from the other side, would they not be sure to fancy when one of the passers-by spoke that the voice which they heard came from the passing shadow?
> No question, he replied.
> —Plato, *The Republic,* Book VII

It is a particularly dangerous practice to allow these sources to convince us that we are currently engaged in the process of deconstructing race. It is dangerous because a false conviction that the race concept is falling apart can lead to a premature relaxing of our guard, an unwarranted erosion of still-necessary vigilance, and a potentially disastrous self-delusion that the antiracist project has been accomplished. Incorrect assumptions that race is being deconstructed may lead to efforts (beyond those already in action) aimed at dismantling the federal government's civil rights compliance monitoring structure.

The interesting thing in this regard is to observe what is actually happening in terms of race. Racial blackness is becoming so reinscribed that we may be moving toward a future where the critical distinction is not between white and black but between white, black, and nonblack. The essential barometer of whether race is breaking down in the United States is the status of racial whiteness. Here, however, we find no evidence of deconstruction, fading, erosion, or other significant alteration.

Whiteness remains a mythically pure and unchallenged racial essence, even (or indeed, especially) in the context of multiracial identity politics. Whereas racial blackness is reinscribed through the production of multiracial children, racial whiteness is reaffirmed via the same paradigm. As Abby Ferber puts it: "It is through the construction and maintenance of racial boundaries, and the demarcation of 'whiteness' as a racially pure identity, that the white subject is constructed" (Ferber 1998: 112). The project of multiracial identity politics therefore aids the convergent projects of white racial identity, hypodescent, and white racial superiority by validating the idea of monoracial white purity.

In fact, close examination reveals reality to be far more complicated and far more ominous than *Time, Newsweek,* or multiracial proponents would have us believe. Indeed, rather than perception being constituted by the shadows of true forms thrown imperfectly on a cave wall, in this case perception is reality stood on its head. Far from multiracial identity deconstructing race, we find that whiteness—the determinative element of the US racial paradigm—is itself dependent upon the idea of racial mixture. Ferber lays out the critical and largely unrecognized relationship between race and mixed race when she argues that "the construction of stable racial identities can only occur in relation to the production and regulation of the impure" (Ferber 1998: 112). In other words, not only does multiracial identity depend upon the maintenance of fallaciously pure monoracial identities, but those monoracial constructs themselves depend upon representations of racial impurity (i.e., racial mixture) for the preservation of the very boundaries that make them possible conceptually.

Ferber goes on to state:

> While those who are discovered to be of mixed black/white ancestry are usually defined as black in the United States, they nevertheless represent a potential threat to the construction of racial identity based on the illusion of white racial purity. More importantly, mixed-race people signal the instability and permeability of racial boundaries; the regulation of interracial sexuality is required in order to secure the borders. Blackness, as long as it is carefully separated and subordinated to whiteness, poses no threat to the existence of a white identity; in fact, blackness is necessary to the definition of whiteness. White and black form a binary opposition, and white identity requires its relationship to blackness. Those who are mixed-race, however, threaten the white/black binary; they signify the instability of

that opposition. Recently mixed-race people have increasingly organized under the banner of mixed-race identity, refusing to accept the predominant system of single-race categorizations. This development is particularly troublesome for white supremacists. Mixed-race people announce that the boundaries are permeable and put at risk the possibility of a racially pure identity. (Ferber 1998: 112–113)

Here, however, I would part with Ferber and argue the opposite case. Before doing that, though, I should say that in a purely theoretical sense, she is correct that mixed-race identity suggests the impossibility of monoracial identities as fixed essences since the mixed person would represent a racially composite being. Given the theoretical possibility of racially composite beings, the racial paradigm's entire foundation of purity is then at once undermined. Moreover, once this line of analysis is begun, mixed-race identity would then work to invalidate itself given that it would have already demonstrated the invalidity of the monoracial essences upon which it is based. As a theoretical concept, then, multiracial identity has the subversive effect Ferber mentions.

However, something very significant and very different would occur were mixed-race identity to be instantiated, especially in the form of the federal multiracial category the activists Ferber describes are seeking. Were multiracial identity to become an explicit choice on federal forms, taking its place alongside the already existing monoracial categories, in that very moment it would lose all the subversive power it possesses in its theoretical incarnation. A federal multiracial category would pose no danger at all to white supremacists since it would represent an official, state-sanctioned racial identity distinct from racial whiteness. In that sense it would serve as merely another nonwhite option in a hypodescent-framed racial hierarchy in which whiteness was the only pure essence. The US racial paradigm and white supremacists could both easily accept an official expression of multiracial identity as the signifier of yet another nonwhite group. Stripped of its theoretical power to disrupt the racial paradigm, the instantiated multiracial option would act as, and in effect become, merely another monoracial category.

Understood in this way, it is apparent that mixed-race people do not in fact "announce that the boundaries are permeable and put at risk the possibility of a racially pure identity." What they instead announce is that they intend to occupy a distinct and separate racial space alongside the already existing racial options. This is what I mean by an instantiated multiracial identity acting essentially as a monoracial identity. Rather than deconstructing race, this approach reinforces and is reinforced by the same biological constructions that underlie the racial paradigm in the United States. In this regard I believe it possible to reformulate Ferber's point so as to assert that "multiraciality, as long as it is carefully separated and subordinated to whiteness, poses no threat to the existence of a white identity; in fact, multiraciality is necessary to the definition of whiteness."

All the same, the success of multiracial ideology in the popular realm has led to blind acceptance of the notion of mixed-race identity as a destabilizing force. As a result, statements asserting, for example, that some presumed "morphing demographics give many teens a chance to challenge old notions of race" receive little in the way of critical questioning when in fact those old notions remain as strong and as deeply entrenched as ever (Clemetson 2000: 70). Indeed, how much of a challenge is it if all that is meant is that some teens may now be able to distance themselves from blackness while those who are less ambiguous cannot? Given that racism depends necessarily on the idea of race, this supposed destabilization is no more than a shell game, a mere reshuffling of the deck of race.

In general, what we find is that racially ambiguous persons are not destabilizing race at all. Most commentators make the mistake of viewing this alleged racial deconstruction only through the dark end of the continuum. By doing so, they fail to see that the other end of the continuum—the white end—remains as fixed, stable, and pure as always. In other words, when people assert that some particular black/white person is racially ambiguous, they typically mean that the person is not confidently categorizable as black. Rarely do they mean that the person is not confidently categorizable as white. To be sure, the doors to whiteness may be breached occasionally, but in the main they stand as closely guarded as ever.

What we are therefore witnessing is not the destabilization of race per se but rather the fracturing of blackness without an attendant fracturing of whiteness. What this means is that Afro-Americans may be fracturing into at least two groups: black nonwhites and seeming nonblack nonwhites, with so-called racially ambiguous black/white multiracials beginning to move toward that seeming nonblack nonwhite status. Of course, the critical point is that the latter are still nonwhites, albeit with a higher status in the racial hierarchy than blacks. But this is merely a false fracturing of race itself, for, as I have indicated, whiteness remains mythically pure and at the top of the hierarchy. One thousand instances of wondering if the racially ambiguous person is black fail to equal even one instance of wondering if the racially ambiguous person is white. Most people do not even realize that what they think is the deconstruction of race is really and merely the fracturing of blackness—along with the reinscription of blackness for those who are unambiguous either physically or ideologically and a coextensive reaffirmation of whiteness. As such, this is a conceptual block that complements the hegemony of the racial paradigm in perfect fashion.

This is a function, it seems to me, of a little-considered aspect of hypodescent. Most people see hypodescent as meaning that any known or detectable sub-Saharan African ancestry makes an individual black, but there is a corollary meaning as well. The corollary meaning is that any known or detectable sub-Saharan African ancestry also makes an individual nonwhite, and it is this latter sense that is operative in the case of multiracial identity and its failure to destabilize race. Persons who see themselves as black/white multiracials are not breaking down any aspects of the US racial paradigm. They may have lighter skin, and they may have features marking them as ambiguously black or as just ambiguous in general, but they are in no sense accepted as whites as long as their African ancestry is known. And this is the critical point, for minor alterations to the paradigm are insignificant as long as the pure and hierarchical status of whiteness remains unchallenged and unchanged.

An increased distance from traditional conceptions of blackness is not currently being met with an equivalent increased nearness to traditional conceptions of whiteness. Thus, from popular entertainers and sports figures to the ubiquitous ambiguous females who populate so many television commercials, some black/white mixed-race persons may move away from blackness in some degree or other but they do not really move toward whiteness. As has been the case for centuries, African-descended people are accepted as white only by traveling the road of racial passing.

■ Conclusion

> To them, I said, the truth would be literally nothing but the shadows of the images.
> That is certain.
>
> —Plato, *The Republic,* Book VII

The US racial paradigm, with its hegemony and its hierarchy, is a strong and flexible structure. Its strength lies in its ability to persuade millions that race (whether in biological or social reality form, for they are the same thing) is real and that people should base their identities on it and organize their lives around it. Its flexibility lies in its long-standing genius at adapting to challenges. Even though most people would not admit to a nineteenth-century sort of belief in race, people today nonetheless continue to believe in a watered-down and less explicitly racist version of the same.

Viewed in the context of the history of race in America, it is naive indeed to suppose that the racial paradigm is suddenly dissolving in the present day due to something as inconsistent, as faddish, and as dependent on biological race as is multiracial ideology. The US racial paradigm, its foundation of white purity, and the personal and institutional racism that have been the result have withstood a great many challenges over the past several hundred years, and it is clear that it will take something much more formidable than today's multiracial movement to undermine it, especially when that movement is in fact complicit with the paradigm. Race in the United States will not be undermined by movements that collaborate with the race concept, but rather by uncompromising assaults on the belief in race itself, whether biological or social, and by deliberate and unceasing deconstructions of whiteness. As long as only a white woman can give birth to a white child, and as long as any woman can give birth to a black child, we can rest assured that there has not been the slightest real unraveling of the race concept in American society.

■ Notes

1. Race terms in this chapter are always a reference to people's misguided belief in the biologically fallacious US racial paradigm. Race is a social construction, but I part with many colleagues in my refusing to label it a social reality, which I see as implying something very different. Racism, like the former Roman Inquisition, does exist; however, race, like the geocentric universe, does not. Given that my arguments here concern the notions of racially distinct and racially mixed people in the United States, my use of such terms in some instances is necessary as I endeavor to chart the intersections of multiracial ideology with the current racial paradigm. Race terms in this chapter—including *multiracial* and *biracial*—should always be read as if preceded by the words "so-called."

2. Assertions that multiracial identity is socially based rather than racially based are without merit. At its most basic level, multiracial ideology revolves absolutely around the sexual mixing of supposedly racially distinct persons.

3. The question of whether one or two multiracial parents can produce a multiracial child is an unsettled one, with some multiracial advocates insisting that only so-called first-generation births are truly multiracial. This position is especially prominent among those multiracial advocates who particularly seek to distance themselves or their children from being associated with the Afro-American population.

4. I want here to make explicit reference to my use of the term "mulatto" in this chapter. One example of the numerous inaccuracies surrounding the multiracial identity debate is the fact that many multiracial activists object to the word "mulatto" because, they say, it is derived from the Spanish word *mulo* (for "little mule"), and is therefore a derogatory term. This complaint is inaccurate, however. As Jack Forbes has shown, "mulatto" is derived from the Arabic word *muwallad,* meaning someone of partial Arab ancestry. Forbes demonstrates that the root of mulatto has nothing to do with mules but rather "has the special meaning of being born among Arabs and covers all persons (mixed-bloods included) who are not perceived as being originally of 'old' Arab ancestry" (Forbes 1993: 145).

5. One might respond to this point by making the case that of course these mulattoes did not self-segregate but instead mixed with the general Afro-American population. However, Byrd cannot take this avenue and then still claim a distinction between so-called multiracials and the general Afro-American population. Indeed, that is precisely what I have been arguing.

6. What is particularly astonishing in this regard is Korgen's aforementioned claim of a biracial baby boom, since Korgen herself cites Williamson in her text. Given that Korgen accepts and even relies on Williamson's extensive account of population mixture in North America, her assertion of a modern-day biracial baby boom is surprising. Indeed it is mystifying, since in to order propose such a baby boom, she must first erase both the direct and internal miscegenation she cites Williamson for and then recast present-day Afro-Americans as monoracially black (Korgen 1998–1999: 15–17).

7

Color Blindness:
An Obstacle to Racial Justice?

Charles A. Gallagher

Most Americans subscribe, at least in principle, to William Graham Sumner's dictum that "stateways cannot change folkways." The idea that government should not be in the business of creating and imposing new societal norms on the population is not, however, supported by a number of historic events of the twentieth century. From 1917 to 1920 the United States was locked in a vicious cultural war concerning the women's suffrage movement. The "commonsense" argument made by male and mostly white leaders at the time was that women lacked the intellectual capacity to understand the complexities of politics or were too emotional, and hence too irrational, to be given the awesome responsibility and privilege of voting. Once the Nineteenth Amendment became the law of the land, no serious systematic backlash ever emerged that threatened to repeal a women's right to vote.

After World War II, in a rare display of regional unity, whites in both the north and the south supported legislation to keep their children in race-segregated schools. After the Supreme Court's *Brown v. Board of Education of Topeka* ruling in 1954, attitudes toward racial segregation in public schools started to change (Schuman, Steeh, Bobo, and Krysan 1997). Resistance to integrating public schools was initially fierce, and progress was slow, but now there is near unanimity among whites in support for integrated schools (Meyer 2000). Public schools continue to be racially segregated, but the belief that the state should sort students by skin color as a matter of policy is absent from public dialogue.

In 1958, Richard Loving, a white man, and Mildred Jeter, a black woman, traveled to Washington, D.C., to get married because their home state of Virginia forbade interracial marriage. Their honeymoon almost turned into a jail sentence, however. Upon arrival back in Virginia, their options were to face prison for violating antimiscegenation laws or leave the state. After moving to

Washington, D.C., they appealed their conviction, and the case wound its way up to the Supreme Court. In 1967 in *Loving v. Commonwealth of Virginia,* the Supreme Court ruled that state laws banning interracial marriages were unconstitutional (Kennedy 2003). National polling data now tell us that most Americans, particularly young Americans, believe they should be able to marry whomever they want (Kaiser 2001). A small but growing number of individuals marry across the color line, and although these unions do raise eyebrows in some circles, general acceptance of these relationships is becoming more common (Dalmage 2000).

Each of these laws violated core ideological beliefs that undergird what it means to be an "American," namely Gunnar Myrdal's assertion that the United States is a society that endorses the "American Creed of liberty, equality, justice and fair opportunity for everybody" (Myrdal, Sterner, and Rose 1944: xviii). These examples of how basic civil rights were eventually afforded to marginalized or disenfranchised groups is not meant to be a Panglossian endorsement that US jurisprudence is always self-correcting or that in the long run the US government always drifts toward socioeconomic justice. There was, however, in each of these examples, denial of fundamental civil rights: the right to vote, the right to public schooling, and the right to intimate associations of one's choosing. In each case there was no mistaking what rights were denied to each group. Sisters, mothers and daughters were disenfranchised merely because of their sex. Black children were forced to attend schools that were racially separate and wholly unequal in resources. Consenting adults were denied the social and economic benefits of marriage because of state-mandated endogamy. Debate was vigorous on both sides of the ideological aisle about how these seismic social events would shape American culture, but over time a tacit and grudgingly accepted understanding formed that core tenets of the American creed had been violated. In the end the state did, at least over the course of several generations, change folkways.

In 1944, Myrdal, R. Sterner, and A. M. Rose's *An American Dilemma* framed the "Negro problem" as a "moral struggle" concerning the treatment of blacks by whites in a society organized around white supremacy. Unlike the court cases mentioned above, violation of the American creed as it relates to racial justice has not evoked the same type of moral outrage or ethical obligation to rectify what continues to be a social problem of enormous proportions. Racial inequality, far from being recognized as an "American dilemma" that is attacked by the government, debated nightly on the national news, or made a constant topic in our nation's pulpits, has been rendered invisible. In a relatively short amount of time, the public dialogue shifted from acknowledging the "race problem" as a moral dilemma as reflected in the *Brown* Supreme Court ruling and the Great Society programs to one in which many in the dominant group have come to genuinely believe institutional and individual racism has been eradicated, thus ending the need

for race-targeted programs. As many whites now see it, little difference separates the life chances, opportunities, or fortunes of most blacks and whites.

How did this happen? How is it possible that 71 percent of the white
population believe African Americans have "more" or "about the same
opportunities in life" as whites (Kaiser 2001), when black unemployment is
almost three times that of whites? How is it possible that a Gallup poll
could find that eight in ten whites believe that there is no difference in educational opportunities between blacks and whites (Gallup 2001), when
blacks graduate from high school or finish college at rates significantly
below those of whites (Blank 2001)? How is it possible that a majority of
whites perceive the "race problem" has been solved at a time when every
quality of life indicator shows persistent and in some cases growing racial
disparities (Brown et al. 2003)?

In this chapter I examine how recent changes in representations of race
and race relations have made racial inequality invisible to most whites
while simultaneously transforming race from an unequal power relation to
one perceived as merely a style, symbol, or purchasable commodity that
has been stripped of any coercive or institutional power. I argue that this
process has created a narrative of race in which the desired goal of racial
equality has been acknowledged, addressed, and achieved. As many whites
now see it, the war on racial inequality is a mission accomplished.

In this chapter I examine four overlapping and interrelated shifts in
perceptions of racism and racial group standing to explain how a narrative
of racial equity could come to be the frame through which many whites
view contemporary race relations. First, I argue that laissez-faire racism
and color-blind racism as theoretical models oversimplify how race, racial
equity and racial justice are understood by a sizable part of the white population. While making extremely important contributions to our understanding of how racism and white privilege are maintained and reproduced,
these theories do not adequately tell the story of how whites have come to
truly believe they are part of a society where color no longer shapes life
chances. These models clearly map how Jim Crow racism has mutated in
response to changing social, economic, and political circumstances while a
sizable part of the white population has come to believe racial equality is
now the norm. Second, the media have created the perception of a racially
inclusive society. The near ubiquitousness of nonwhite, particularly black
celebrities in the media has created the perception that with increased media
representation comes social parity. Third, the promise inherent in assimilation theory that "large-scale intermarriage" will necessarily improve race
relations assumes a linear and near monolithic trajectory that integrates and
assimilates mixed-race couples and their children in the same way. Research suggests we are moving away from the rigidity of a "one-drop rule"
framed by a black/white dichotomy of racial sorting and self-identification
to one I would characterize as a "which drop rule" in which certain white

and nonblack racial pairings are significantly privileged over others. Finally, there is a growing body of research that suggests an inchoate "new white nationalism" is starting to congeal around issues of immigration, affirmative action, bilingualism, welfare reform, and identity politics. Whiteness as an unapologetic frame of cultural and political reference may congeal as whites perceive their race privileges as eroding, but given contemporary race politics it is very unlikely a large mainstream white nationalist movement will materialize.

Together these trends create an understanding of race relations and relative group position in which *acknowledging* racial inequality is extremely difficult because many whites are not only oblivious to the depths of racial inequality but have been convinced by media accounts that little difference exits between the socioeconomic outcomes of whites and racial minorities. This process is circular and self-reinforcing; a virtual reality of racial harmony is constructed and presented as fact in popular culture, politics, and the media. This view supports many whites' desire to imagine racial equality as the lens through which they can frame contemporary race relations. The result is that many whites start their conversation of race relations with the false premise that racial socioeconomic parity has been achieved.

■ The Need for New Theoretical Starting Points

As sociological theories, laissez-faire and color-blind racism (herein LF/CB racism) argue that whites have embraced a vision of contemporary race relations in which the socioeconomic playing field is now level, cultural stereotypes are deployed by whites to explain racial inequality, and non-discriminatory market forces, rather than racist government actions, now allocate resources. These theories examine the relational and normative expectations of existing racialized hierarchies and how group-level relationships adapt to new social, political, and cultural circumstances (Blumer 2003; Bobo and Smith 1998; Bobo 2001; Bonilla-Silva 2001). Laissez-faire racism is grounded in demographic and ideological shifts that occurred as the United States moved from an economy based on agriculture to one based on industrial production: the resulting economic restructuring of the black laboring class, the ensuing internal black south-to-north migration, and the emergence of the modern civil rights movement. These changing social circumstances necessitated a dismantling of Jim Crow racism and the adoption of a more flexible system of oppression that could maintain white privilege, subordinate blacks, and accomplish all that in the name of post–World War II liberal democracy (Bobo and Smith 1998; Bobo 2001).

Following the *Brown* decision and the civil rights acts of the 1960s, the state shifted from an overtly racist caste system to one in which classic liberalism and free market forces could provide the ostensibly race-neutral state with the mechanisms through which racial hierarchy could be maintained.

Rather than drawing on the notions of biological inferiority that character-ized Jim Crow racism, LF/CB racism focuses on how perceived cultural in-feriority has led to "the tendency to blame blacks themselves for the black/ white gap in socioeconomic standing" (Bobo, Kluegel, and Smith 1997: 16). These perceived deficiencies become the basis for whites' rejection of "structural accounts of racial inequality" (Bobo 2001: 292), and the end result is that "blacks are blamed [by whites] as the cultural architects of their own disadvantage" (Bobo and Smith 1998: 212). In a similar way color-blind racism explains the way "whites rationalize minorities' contem-porary status as the product of market dynamics, naturally occurring phe-nomena, and blacks' imputed cultural limitations" (Bonilla-Silva 2003: 2).

Lawrence Bobo argues that "the tenacious institutionalized disadvan-tages and inequalities created by the long slavery and Jim Crow eras are now popularly condoned under modern free-market or laissez-faire racist ideology" (Bobo and Smith 1998: 186). Both these models point out that most whites now view the cumulative effects of slavery and Jim Crow racism as tragic yet distant and irrelevant background information. These theories argue that whites view institutional racism and discrimination as having been eradicated and replaced with a reward structure in which one's qualifi-cations, not one's color, are the means by which upward mobility is achieved. These theories suggest white privilege is maintained in a seemingly non-racist manner by the use of cultural stereotypes and the negation of how the recent past has shaped contemporary views on racial inequality.

These models make an unwarranted assumption about whites' views of race that minimizes contemporary racism, however. What has been excluded from any analysis of white racism are the various factors that reproduce and reinforce a narrative in which racial equality is perceived to be the norm. LF/CB racism implies that whites (to draw on Bobo's language) understand their "socioeconomic standing" relative to blacks, fully comprehend "struc-tural accounts" of racial disparity, comprehend the huge racial socioeconomic chasm that separates their experiences from blacks, and in spite of this infor-mation willfully choose to ignore such disparities or embrace government policies that would ameliorate racial inequality. Worse than benign neglect, there is an implied racist intent in LF/CB racism because whites are assumed to know that racial disparities are widespread, understand how their whiteness privileges them in almost every social situation, and yet do nothing to re-nounce these unearned privileges or agitate for racial equality. LF/CB racism presupposes that whites know the racial socioeconomic scorecard, and their collective inaction becomes proof of white racism. This is a dangerous assumption to make politically and, most importantly, is not an accurate account of the view a sizable number of whites hold about racial inequality in the United States.

As a white researcher who has spent an extensive amount of time inter-viewing whites around the country (and living and teaching undercover among them), I have found that what is missing from LF/CB accounts of contemporary racism is an acknowledgment that many whites are under the false impression that the socioeconomic playing field *is* now level. My own research (Gallagher 2004a, 2004b, 2003a, 2003b, 1997), as well as that of others who research how whites construct their understanding of race, has found that many whites know very little about the relative socioeconomic standing of other racial groups (Bonilla-Silva 2003; DiTomaso, Parks-Yancy, and Post 2003; Pierce 2003; Feagin and O'Brien 2003; Frankenberg 2001). What makes whites' overly optimistic view of racial equality so insidious is that the perception of racial equality is constantly reinforced through exaggerated depictions of racial harmony in popular culture, the common racial ground found in consumerism, and the norm of color-blindness so embedded in twenty-first-century classic liberalism. Representations of upward mobility, intergenerational transfers of wealth, and a society now free of institutional racism are viewed by many whites as the rule rather than the exception. Ignorance is not bliss in the case of whites not seeing the depths of intergroup racial inequality but becomes a form of hegemony that serves to maintain white privilege.

It is a very small step from falsely believing that race no longer shapes life chances to being able to argue that blacks "are doing at least as well or better than most whites in income and educational attainment" (Gallup 2001). These whites' accounts of racial equity are not (necessarily) a self-interested dodge or an evasive strategy to minimize their own white privilege. Color blindness as a nascent political principle has matured into a belief that "equality of opportunity" has finally, once and for all, been replaced with "equality of results." We have moved to the next level of race discourse, where many whites truly believe that whites and blacks are socioeconomic equals. With racial equality as the "commonsense" starting point for many whites, the consequences and obstacles to racial justice are clear; it can now be argued on ostensibly nonracist grounds that the state should not advance any solutions to racial inequality because these problems have been rectified. Any such unnecessary government involvement in which race was made to be a social issue after this dilemma had been rectified would constitute, as whites have responded over and over again in numerous studies, reverse discrimination (Bonilla-Silva 2001; Gallagher 2004a; Pinkus 2003). Convinced that all things are now equal, whites are then able to argue that blacks are, as Bobo and Smith so eloquently put it, "the cultural architects of their own disadvantage" (Bobo and Smith 1998: 212).

My aim here is not to be an apologist for whites who are "blissfully unaware" of their own privileged social location. In the end the "sincere fictions" (Feagin and Vera 1995: xi) whites believe about their own enlightened and often-delusional views on how equitable a society we have become reproduce racial inequality, maintain white privilege, and re-create systemic racism.

There are dire consequences of ignoring, underestimating, or misunderstanding whites' perceptions of racial inequality. The faulty and biased information many whites use to construct a narrative that portrays the opportunity structure in the United States as being free of any racial bias allows whites to delegitimate federal programs attempting to ameliorate racial inequality while validating their belief that their own successes had nothing to do with white privilege (see DiTomaso, Parks-Yancy, and Post 2003 for a brilliant account of this process). This new frame of reference, in which racial equality is viewed as a universal norm, also serves to confirm deeply held stereotypes by whites about blacks who remain mired in poverty. If we wish to understand how whites reconcile these schizophrenic positions in which racial stereotypes and delusions of racial equity coexist with growing racial inequality, we need to recognize that many whites enter conversations knowing very little about the extent to which race continues to shape life chances. Recognizing this blind spot and how this perspective came to be the dominant frame through which whites see race relations needs to be the starting point for future research on racial relations.

▓ The Media's Narrative of Racial Equity

Since the mid-1990s there has been a change in the way race, race relations, and racial hierarchy have been depicted in the mass media. Super Bowl 38 provides a partial glimpse into how the racial hierarchy in the United States has increasingly been leveled by popular culture. During the Super Bowl half-time show, Janet Jackson had a "wardrobe malfunction" when a dance routine she was doing with pop singer Justin Timberlake resulted in her breast being exposed to over 600 million viewers worldwide. The incident resulted in a flood of media stories about the effect her exposed breast would have on children, the need for greater federal oversight of television content, and a general agreement that television had become too crude and risqué for most Americans. The US Federal Communications Commission recommended that CBS be fined $550,000 for the incident, arguing that had a tape-delay system been in place countless children around the country would have been spared exposure to Janet Jackson's pierced nipple and breast. In a Lexus/Nexus search following this event, nowhere was I able to find any discussion concerning the racial significance of a black woman and a white man gyrating and groping one another in front of one of the most widely watched spectacles in human history. It is hard to imagine this ribald interracial duet happening in the 1980s. Interracial dance routines, even ones that are sexually explicit, are now quite unremarkable. The sheer banality of this event, which would have quickly been forgotten had no wardrobe malfunction occurred, characterizes how the media now provides Americans with an almost endless supply of overt and coded depictions of a multiracial, multicultural society that has finally transcended the problem of race. The mainstreaming of rap music into a corporate vehicle to sell, among other things, fast foods and soft drinks; the explosion of music videos on cable networks; and the general trend to appropriate and repackage racialized, counterculture styles (rap, tattoos, dreadlocks, piercing, retro-afros) into bankable commodities has blurred the color line, especially for the generation who were just approaching their teens when the 1992 Los Angeles riots took place.

The American racial "presentation of self," at least on television, in the multiplex, and in magazines, is overwhelmingly depicted as an integrated, multiracial environment where individuals consume products in a postrace, color-blind world. Mainstream magazines like *Time, Newsweek,* the *New Yorker, Vibe,* and *Bon Appetite* routinely present advertisements in which whites, blacks, Asians, and Latinos gather together to shop, eat, work, and interact in spaces where race is meaningless. In this carefully manufactured racial utopia, television commercials depict actors of different races inhabiting race-neutral environments like Chili's or Applebee's or show middle-class living rooms where men of varying races bond over football, Coors beer, and Domino's Pizza.

An example of how color, consumption, and a constructed cultural "common ground" conspire to create the impression of a level playing field is demonstrated in many fast-food marketing campaigns. Church's Chicken (a division of AFC, which owns Popeye's, Seattle's Best Coffee, and Cinnabon) recently started an advertising campaign in fifty US markets that includes forty-two English and Spanish thirty-second commercials in which the 1970s hit "We Got the Funk" by George Clinton's band Parliament has been resurrected as "We Got The Crunch" to promote Church's new line of crunchy chicken products. Chief Marketing Officer Melinda Ennis-Roughton explains the racial crossover appeal of these ads this way: "Walk into a Church's restaurant and you'll generally see a cross-section of America. Be it Latinos, African Americans or Caucasians, our customers have varied backgrounds and languages. Yet, our new 'Crunch' campaign is about finding common ground" (Church's Chicken Press Release 2004). The media construct a narrative of racial equality, a racial "common ground," through these market transactions in which consumption of commodities and racial parity become synonymous. It is these shared and observed acts of consuming products in the interracial setting of television, the ubiquity of such advertisements, and the sheer repetition of such commercials that creates the impression that racial equality is the norm. If whites and blacks are shown sharing the same desire for Church's chicken, Nike sneakers, or flat screen televisions, how different, at least socioeconomically, could each group be?

Manufacturing racially integrated settings in advertisements is a cost-effective way to reach larger national markets because each racial group will see themselves represented in the commercial and identify with the product on a personal level. But although these staged integrated settings may be an effective way to tap different racial markets, they also reframe how groups come to view one another. Herbert Blumer suggests that "the building of the image of the abstract group takes place in the area of the remote and not of the near. It is not the experience with concrete individuals in daily associations" (Blumer 2003: 116) that determines how racial groups will be defined. Hernan Vera and Andrew Gordon suggest as well "that much of what we know about people we consider to be 'others' we learn through the movies" (2003: 9), but I would argue that in addition to a virtual understanding of the "other" constructed by the media, whites use the image of the "other" to measure their socioeconomic success relative to other groups. The process of redefining a "sense of group position" is currently going through yet another racial rearticulation as this account of racial equality emerges as the dominant ideological frame of reference for whites. If non-whites, relative to whites, appear to be doing well, as demonstrated by the way racial minorities are depicted in movies, television dramas, sports, music, or majority-minority city politics, then polling data in which whites believe blacks have it "good or better than whites" start to become comprehensible, even if those beliefs are not supported by fact.

■ From the "One-Drop Rule" to a "Which Drop Rule"

In his classic statement in *Assimilation in American Life,* Milton Gordon observed, "once structural assimilation has occurred, either simultaneously with or subsequent to acculturation, all of the other types of assimilation will naturally follow" (1964: 81). According to Gordon, marital assimilation would signal a point in the assimilation process at which a minority group "loses its ethnic identity in the larger host or core society, and identificational assimilation takes place" (80). The purported benefits of widespread interracial marriage in reducing group-level conflict are many and have been a central claim of assimilation theory. Multiracial unions would blur the color line, resulting in a leveling of racial hierarchies. Interracial marriage would forge new and mutually beneficial relationships between different racial communities, resulting in intergenerational upward mobility for racial minorities as they gain access to new social, political, and economic networks. The need, desire, and support for pluralistic communities would erode as marital assimilation brings full civic incorporation into the dominant culture. "Prejudice and discrimination are no longer a problem" as widespread interracial marriage occurs because, explains Gordon, "the descendants of the original minority group become indistinguishable" from the dominant group (80). These multicolor unions will result in a reduction of social distance between groups, and a decline in racial conflict will follow, at least in theory, bringing about a reduction in racial inequality. It is no wonder that interracial marriage is "generally regarded, with justification, as the litmus test of assimilation" (Alba and Nee 2003: 90).

Unfortunately, current trends in interracial marriages reflect a reshuffling rather than a razing of existing racial hierarchies. Herbert Gans observes that "about half of all Asian-Americans and light skinned Hispanics now marry whites, and at that rate, they may be defined as near white in a few decades" (Gans 2004: 44). In one of the most extensive and thorough contemporary treatments of assimilation to date, Richard Alba and Victor Nee point out that almost 70 percent of young Japanese born in the United States marry individuals who are not Asian, mostly to whites. They also note that as of 1997, 20 percent of all Asians in the United States had non-Asian partners who had "produced about 750,000 mixed-race children under eighteen years of age" (Alba and Nee 2003: 94). Research has found that when one parent is white, which is very likely among Asians, there is a very strong possibility that the child will be identified as white. The tendency to push children toward the white end of the racial identity spectrum is true for white/Latino and white–American Indian mixed-race children as well (Waters 1998).

Expanding the boundaries of whiteness to include the children from some interracial pairings (white with Asian, Latino, or American Indian) but not others (whites with dark-skinned partners) points to the need to further complicate the one-drop rule. The one-drop rule, or the law of hypodescent, means that "one drop" of black blood defines any individual with African ancestry as black (Davis 1991). The law operated to keep the white/black color line rigidly in place and police any white and nonwhite romantic transgressions. Continued policing and stigmatization of black/white unions is common, but what is different now is a growing acceptance of white and nonblack couples and the assimilation of their mixed-race children. The one-drop rule still confers status or stigma based on the tastes and prerogatives of the dominant group, but it seems not all "drops of blood" carry the same stigma. Perhaps it may be more accurate to conceptualize this process as a "which drop rule" in which certain racial pairings will be privileged, whereas others will be relegated to the bottom of the racial pecking order. If the crucial litmus test of assimilation is interracial marriage, then at least in the media's presentation of this trend, the test has been passed with flying (nonblack) colors. The media has seized upon these "hip" pairings as a way to sell products, further cementing a vision of the United States as a postrace society. Randall Kennedy points out that "interracial couples are being deployed as enticements to shop at Nordstrom's, Club Monaco or Wal-Mart, or to purchase furniture from IKEA, jeans from Guess, sweaters from Tommy Hilfiger, cologne from Calvin Klein, shampoo from Proctor and Gamble, or watches from Gucci" (Kennedy 2003: 128). The film and television industries have also done much to influence the perception that interracial couples are, like Janet and Justin singing a duet at the Super Bowl, so commonplace that such interactions no longer warrant commentary. If there is mention of an interracial relationship, it is to point out how little race now matters, as evidenced by conservative pundits Stephen and Abigail Thernstrom's comments that "black basketball star Charles Barkley, who has a blond wife, talks of running for governor of Alabama when he retires from the NBA" (Thernstrom and Thernstrom 1999: 523). It was more noteworthy that Cablinasian (Caucasian/black/Indian/Asian) golf sensation Tiger Woods spent $3 million on his wedding than the interracial union he was forming with his white, supermodel Swedish bride. Within the narrative where racial equity is defined as normative, mate selection gets bracketed as a consumer choice in which anyone from any racial or ethnic group can choose whomever they wish to marry. If blacks' rates of exogamy are low relative to other groups at a time when mate selection is viewed as being like any other consumer preference, the free market response would be that blacks choose not to assimilate through intermarriage.

The problem with this account of free-market principles now defining mate selection is that it only tells part of the story. In a national study of marriage preferences, George Yancey found that "nonblack racial groups are more likely to reject African Americans as potential partners than any other group (Yancey 2003c: 71). Lawrence Bobo and Ryan Smith found an "unambiguously greater average level of hostility to contact with blacks among nonblacks than occurs in reference to any other group" (1998: 201). In a national survey on racial attitudes, whites, Asians, and Hispanics had the greatest resistance to a member of their racial or ethnic group marrying someone who was black (Herring and Amissah 1997). The result of continued high levels of residential segregation, social distance, and racial stereotyping of blacks by nonblacks will lead to a racial hierarchy where some pairing of white, Asian, and Latino populations will enjoy the prerogatives of the dominant group while dark-skinned groups (African American, Afro-Caribbean, black Latinos) will experience continued socioeconomic stagnation and continued pariah status (Gans 1999).

The high rates of interracial marriage between Asians and whites and the general acceptance of such pairings suggest, as some race scholars have explained, that "Asians are becoming 'white'" (Omi 2001: 259; see also Gallagher 2004b; Gans 1999). But these observations do not capture what these selective interracial pairings imply and how these developments pose an obstacle to racial justice. If Asians, whites, American Indians, and Latinos are intermarrying, having mixed-race children, and blending quietly into the American mainstream, one could argue that race place plays little or no role in contemporary race relations. Depictions of the color line disappearing through interracial marriage may be a cause for celebration, but the inaccurate and selective depictions in the media and the popular press about this trend reframes the idea of race as no longer being about power and privilege. Within this framework where freedom of mate selection is proof of racial equality, racism can be dismissed as a force that continues to shapes life chances.

■ One Nation, Not White Nationalism

In her book *The New White Nationalism in America,* political science professor Carol Swain explains that using "frames associated with black civil rights movement and multiculturalism, some ordinary white Americans are making a case for increased white solidarity and white consciousness by employing the same brand of identity politics that minorities have successfully used in the past to further their own group interests and group identities" (Swain 2002: 5). The idea of a reactionary "undifferentiated mass of white people" (5) is also a theme discussed by Samuel P. Huntington in recent scholarship in which he warns that the United States will lose its core Anglo-Saxon identity because Latinos, in stark contrast to every other immigrant group in this nation's history, will not assimilate. Agreeing with Swain's contention that white nationalism is the "next logical stage for identity politics in America," Huntington poses this question: "Today, white nativists could well ask: If blacks and Hispanics organize and lobby for special privileges, why not whites? If the National Association for the Advancement of Colored People and the National Council of La Raza are legitimate organizations, why not a national organization promoting white interests?" (Huntington 2004b: 41). These authors suggest whites will develop racial solidarity around cultural, social, and economic issues that threaten white privilege. Divisive issues like immigration, crime, affirmative action, bilingual education, and multiculturalism will bring an extremely diverse population of 200 million whites under the umbrella of their shared claim of victimization.

It is unlikely that many Americans will embrace a reactionary social identity framed around race or immigration in the way these issues were packaged by Patrick Buchanan in his failed bids for the presidency in 1992 and 1996. Nor are we likely to see the emergence of the kind of organized white nationalism Swain describes as being a "repackaged, relabeled and transformed white supremacy that is aiming its appeal at a broader and better-educated audience" (Swain and Nieli 2003: 16). Swain believes that average Americans will be drawn to the white nationalist movement because it provides the "only forums" where white Americans can lament race policies without being labeled racists. Her claims miss an important venue for redress of whites' grievances, however. To appease white constituents, both major political parties have sacrificed the meager protections afforded to racial minorities, as evidenced in just these two of many examples: President Bill Clinton dismantled social welfare programs, and President George W. Bush's attacked affirmative action. There are most certainly forums for whites to be heard about their perception of racial slights and allegations of reverse discrimination; they are the Democratic and Republican parties.

White nationalism is not likely to be embraced by white middle-Americans because group claims of racial victimization violate a deeply held belief in the individual over group rights and the conviction that the government should always be race-neutral, at least outwardly so, in its actions. Although it may be possible to rally whites around a particular single issue like a state referendum ending the use of race in government data collection, race-based grievances are too disparate and often too locally specific to create the kind of solidarity or master status around which a cohesive white racial identity can form or be maintained. It is not the rise of white nationalism that will be an obstacle to racial justice but the endless stream of racial equality story lines delivered from politicians, television dramas, music videos, sporting events, and advertisements, all of which suggest to, tell, or imply to Americans that racial equality, equal opportunity, and upward mobility are now available to all.

■ New Obstacles to Racial Justice

In my interviews with whites on race, my respondents would ask rhetorically if there were "any clubs, like a white pre-law society," that were specifically for whites or if a "white college fund" existed to help them through college or would lament that whites "can't have anything for ourselves anymore that says exclusively white or anything like that. But everyone else can." These comments may appear to support the contention that conditions are ripe for the emergence of a "new white nationalist" movement. I would argue, however, that this is not the case. My respondents' comments above, quite representative of whites I interviewed around the country, were more typically the starting point for a conversation about why racial minorities seemed fixated on race and racism when it was their understanding that racial equality now defined the opportunity structure in the United States. Since they were not racist, how could it be that racism still played a role in achieving the American dream?

White America has been utterly saturated with images of black middle- and upper-middle-class couples living a life quite similar to their own. Watching television depictions of well-off, successful black Americans has the effect of convincing white Americans that blacks and whites share the same socioeconomic opportunities (Lewis and Jhally 2004). The media shape these perceptions of racial equality because most whites in metropolitan areas in the United States live in neighborhoods where blacks account for less than 5 percent of the population (Farley 2000). The black success stories they see in situation comedies and television dramas, much like the day-to-day experiences of most whites, are told in a society free of institutional racism or discrimination. The ease with which individuals dance, date, love, and marry across the color line in the media is further evidence that race has been defanged. Within this account, interracial assimilation, like race itself, is redefined as being a set of cultural choices one can slip on or off with little or no social cost. The great challenge to racial justice will not be the impending race war from white nationalists but from white Americans who truly believe the war on racial inequality, institutional racism, and discrimination has been fought and won. If the starting point for a national discussion about racial equality is that there is no problem, racial justice in the era of color blindness is highly unlikely.

8

Racism, Whitespace, and the Rise of the Neo-Mulattoes

Hayward Derrick Horton

In this chapter, I wish to reflect on the function of "multiracials" as an emerging group in the social structure of the United States. At the center of the argument advanced here is the persistence of racism. In this context, racism specifically refers to a multilevel and multidimensional system of dominant group oppression that scapegoats the race and/or ethnicity of one or more subordinate groups (Horton 2002). Racism has not disappeared. Instead, it has mutated, changing its appearance and manifestations. One such manifestation is the emergence of the multiracial phenomenon. Hence, in a structural sense, the mixed-raced population functions as a neo-mulatto class that has been provided with access to what is termed "whitespace." I maintain that whitespace becomes not only a conceptual tool that facilitates the interpretation of the role of neo-mulattoes in contemporary American society, but also a means of identifying and operationalizing indicators of racism as well.

■ The Critical Demography Paradigm and Contemporary Racism

I introduced the critical demography paradigm in 1999 as a means of creating a safe place for the development of concepts, theories, and methods that do not readily fit what has become, by default, conventional demography. Critical demography has four characteristics that distinguish it from its conventional counterpart. It is (1) explanatory and predictive; (2) theory-driven; 3) a challenge to the status quo; and 4) reflexive (Horton 1999). Thus with critical demography, as opposed to the euphemism "race," we can forthrightly speak of racism, population power, and population control. Critical demography provides a new lens with which to view the topic of the mixed-race population and places it within a broader sociohistorical and sociocultural context. The paradigm likewise provides concepts that facilitate the identification of linkages in the various manifestations of racism that bear directly on the presence of the neo-mulatto population. One such concept is whitespace.

■ Whitespace and the Rise of the Neo-Mulattoes

Whitespace refers to those physical and social places that have been culturally defined as being designated primarily as being appropriate for the dominant population.[1] As a manifestation of racism itself, whitespace becomes a multilevel, conceptual, and empirical tool for the identification and measurement of other indicators of the same. Each of these indicators is based upon one or more of the dimensions of inequality: wealth, status, and power.

For instance, residential segregation can be viewed as an indicator of racism because it is the result of the preservation of whitespace. Occupational discrimination can likewise be viewed in this vein because certain positions in this society, particularly the most prestigious and lucrative, tend to be preserved for dominant group members. The oft-cited glass ceiling is indicative of this fact. Again, these lofty positions in the occupational structure represent whitespace. Elected positions, political appointments, and political participation itself represent another form of whitespace. Recent efforts to suppress the votes of disadvantaged minorities and the poor underscore the importance of this social place that the dominant group considers its exclusive preserve.

Finally, interracial relationships likewise represent a form of whitespace. Indeed, in times past an intimate relationship with an individual of the dominant group was the most sacred of whitespaces. In general, this was particularly the case with a black man and white woman. Indeed, this black/white combination continues to be the more typical despite its likewise being the most feared union. It is important to note that greater access to whitespace in the form of these interracial relationships does not necessarily imply a decline in racism. Instead, it is maintained here that black/white relationships are no longer a threat to the power structure because of the growing influence and independence of white women. In short, white women are no longer a primary symbol of the white man's power (Horton and Sykes 2004).

Thus, the emergence of the neo-mulatto population should not be viewed as an indicator of the declining significance of racism. Nor is it simply a matter of self-awareness and group identification of the "mixed-race population." Again, the crucial issue is whitespace. The neo-mulattoes have simply returned to their antebellum role as a buffer between blacks and whites.[2] Thus, they have greater access to whitespace, but the essential racist nature of the social structure can be maintained because these neo-mulattoes are defined as other than black.

As noted above, the utility of the term "whitespace" transcends the ability to understand the rise of the neo-mulattoes. The concept represents a means by which sociologists and other social scientists might unify strands of research that have little apparent commonality. It is to this issue that I now turn.

■ Implications for Future Research

The potential for the concept of whitespace is considerable. In the context of the rise of the neo-mulattoes, let us return to the aforementioned examples of residential segregation, occupational discrimination, political participation, and interracial relationships. Each represents a unique opportunity for a bold and exciting research agenda heretofore unrealized.

In the case of residential segregation, one might inquire about the extent to which neo-mulattoes have access to white neighborhoods relative to the general black population. One would hypothesize that the former would have a greater level of access to these neighborhoods than the latter. However, under what conditions is this most likely to be true? What factors explain the differentials in the neo-mulatto/black gap? Are there instances or specific locales where blacks have levels of access to whitespace that are comparable to or greater than that for neo-mulattoes? Generally speaking, could we not argue that a better indicator of a declining significance of racism would be a decline in the neo-mulatto/black whitespace access differential?

Similarly, in the case of occupational discrimination, it would be expected that neo-mulattoes would have lower levels of occupational discrimination than the general black population. Two interesting subtopics emerge here. First, do neo-mulattoes have greater access to whitespace than other light-complexioned blacks? This is particularly the case with the corporate structure where promotion to a great extent is predicated upon the extent to which one fits into the prevailing organizational subculture. In turn, do light-complexioned blacks have greater whitespace access than medium brown and dark-complexioned blacks? In essence, this scenario tests a typology of four categories of blacks relative to access to whitespace and could provide considerable insight into the nature of racism within modern organizations.

The second subtopic relative to occupational discrimination and neo-mulattoes centers upon the extent and nature of their differences with other blacks external to the formal organizational or corporate structure. It is argued that although neo-mulattoes may have higher occupational status than other blacks within the corporate structure, that would not be the case among entrepreneurs—the logic being that without white sponsorship, ambitious and talented blacks are not as likely as neo-mulattoes to break the glass ceiling.

Thus, these individuals are probably more likely than their neo-mulatto counterparts to leave those structures (or to avoid them altogether). External to these structures, these blacks are probably more likely to thrive. Anecdotal examples abound of the most successful black entrepreneurs (e.g., Reginald Lewis, Oprah, Bob Johnson, John Johnson) clearly not being neo-mulattoes. Ironically, this scenario is quite analogous to the house slave (neo-mulatto) and field slave (other blacks) dichotomy that prevailed during the antebellum era that spawned the original mulatto category. Once again, the concept of whitespace makes this very exciting line of research possible.

Neo-mulatto political participation represents a particularly intriguing area of research. At this writing, the 2004 presidential (and lesser position) elections are under way. Of particular interest here is the candidacy of Barack Obama for the senate seat from the state of Illinois. Obama identifies as a black man in the United States, although he has gained access to whitespace because his father was an African immigrant and his mother was white. Thus, he is perceived as acceptable as a neo-mulatto. Obama's circumstance underscores the difference between the concepts of "mixed race" and neo-mulatto: access to whitespace. However, more generally, one could logically argue that Obama represents the first of many future neo-mulattoes who will run for political office. From a research perspective, one would argue that neo-mulattoes would be expected to hold office disproportionately relative to their numbers in the general black population.

Finally, the issue of marital preferences of neo-mulattoes would be an exciting way to explore the impact of access to whitespace. One could logically argue that neo-mulattoes are expected to be more likely than other blacks to marry whites. Indeed, one could go further. It would likewise be expected that access to whitespace was independent of neo-mulatto status in affecting the likelihood of marrying a white individual. In other words, neo-mulattoes who had greater access to whitespace were more likely to marry white than those who had lower levels of the same, which implies an interaction effect in which access to whitespace moderated the impact of neo-mulatto status on the likelihood of marrying a white individual. This line of research would in turn have to consider the impact of access to whitespace and interracial marriage on the social, political, and cultural fragmentation of the black community.

■ Conclusion

The purpose of this chapter was to reflect on the issue of the mixed-race population and to add insight on the broader sociostructural issues related thereto. I employed the new critical demography paradigm to advance the argument that this population is more appropriately termed "neo-mulattoes" because of their function in the US social structure. A discussion of the nature of whitespace was followed by the delineation of four broad areas of future research related to how this concept is likely to affect the neo-mulatto population on a broad range of topics. At the heart and soul of this analysis is the acknowledgment that racism continues to play a role in the functioning of the social structure in the United States and that the concept of whitespace only has meaning as a manifestation thereof.

It is important to note that I have only scratched the surface relative to the potential for research on neo-mulattoes. In the future, my critical demography project will explore many more dimensions on this topic. Nevertheless, it is important to note that the rise of the neo-mulatto population is not likely to signal the twilight of the black community. Although it is quite conceivable that neo-mulattoes might ultimately become a separate and distinct racial and ethnic category in reality, rather than simply by the statistical accounting of the U.S. Bureau of the Census, this would not be altogether a disastrous development. Why? Because it brings clarity. Persons who distance themselves from or deny the black community were not likely to have been of much value to its further social and economic development in the first place. Let them go. According to the critical demography paradigm (as well as historical evidence), access to whitespace is neither an absolute nor permanent condition. Indeed, it is subject to change based upon the manner in which population and structural changes shape the lifestyles and livelihoods of the dominant population. In the antebellum era, in times of crisis, the old mulattoes discovered that they were not as special as the white man led them to believe. "Masa" looked after his own and demonstrated that to him the mulattoes were just another form of slave. In all likelihood, the "new mulattoes" will have to learn the same painful lesson.

▓ Notes

1. The concept "whitespace" bears some apparent similarity to Emory Borgardus's social distance. However, it should be pointed out that social distance is a subjective, microlevel measure of racial/ethnic prejudice, as opposed to an objective and multilevel measure of racism.

2. It should be noted that other groups, specifically quasi-whites, honorary whites, and black ethnics, also serve this function. Once again, the key distinction is greater access to whitespace than the black population. See Horton (2002) for an elaboration on these groups.

Part 2

Manipulating Multiracial Identities

9

Race, Multiraciality, and the Neoconservative Agenda

G. Reginald Daniel and
Josef Manuel Castañeda-Liles

■ "Metaracism" and the Color-Blind Society

"Doing Race" in the Post–Civil Rights Era

The debate in the 1990s surrounding census racial categories, along with the Racial Privacy Initiative (RPI), or Proposition 54—which was placed on the October 7, 2003, California recall ballot—provide excellent case studies of "doing race" in an era in which color blindness has become the dominant racial discourse. In both cases, neoconservatives have made a strategic link between the rhetoric of color blindness and the multiracial phenomenon, using the latter as an indication of racial justice while denying continuing inequities and undercutting the tools necessary to pursue racial justice.

The US racial order that emerged after the dismantling of Jim Crow segregation and the implementation of civil rights legislation during the 1950s and 1960s included the removal of the last laws against racial intermarriage in the 1967 Supreme Court case *Loving v. Commonwealth of Virginia*. This decision, along with the comparatively more fluid social relations that followed, led to a growth in the number of interracial marriages and multiracial births. Increasingly, many interracial couples have socialized their offspring to embrace a "multiracial" identity. This "new" identity seeks to transform traditional racial categories and boundaries, as well as challenge racial hierarchies, by dismantling the rule of hypodescent (see Chapter 2, this volume).[1]

The liberalization of the US racial order also expanded educational opportunities to working-class communities of color. The ensuing growth of the middle class among communities of color, as well as their increased overall participation in business and politics, has prompted some to argue

125

that the United States increasingly rewards education and technological expertise largely independent of race, indicating that racial discrimination itself has declined in significance (Boston 1988; Lacayo 1989; Small 1994; Wilkerson 1998). Beginning in the 1980s, the belief that the United States has transcended racism, also referred to as "metaracism" (Kovel 1970: 211), became the cornerstone of United States racial etiquette—and a key tenet of neoconservative ideology. This belief, which informs the dominant racial ideology of "color blindness" (Bonilla-Silva 2003; Omi and Winant 1994; Ringer and Lawless 1989; see also Chapters 3 and 7, this volume), has helped perpetuate the grand illusion that racial comity and egalitarian integration are imminent. This in turn obscures the fact that real egalitarianism remains unattainable for most racial "minorities," particularly African Americans and Latinas/os (Steinhorn and Diggs-Brown 2000).

During the same period, organizations representing the interests of interracial families and multiracial individuals became part of a multiracial movement that sought revisions in federal racial categorization so that multiracial-identified individuals could be acknowledged and tabulated. The resulting national debate has led proponents of neoconservative discourse to frame increased intermarriage and the growing numbers of multiracial-identified people as a reaffirmation of color-blind ideology and the realization of an egalitarian racial order. This in turn has been used to justify the elimination of race-conscious policies, antidiscrimination legislation, and even racial categories themselves, as well as the collection of data on race.

Indeed, one of the recent attempts by neoconservatives to undermine the legal apparatus necessary for addressing racial inequality, the RPI, has furthered this association between the multiracial movement, color-blind ideology, and the neoconservative agenda. Generally speaking, however, the multiracial movement should not be considered complicit with the neoconservative agenda. We argue, rather, that the mutual alignment between highly visible and influential segments of the movement and prominent neoconservatives has overshadowed other organizations that have acknowledged the concerns of traditional communities of color as well as the importance of race-conscious policies. However, we argue that multiracial organizations need to formulate a more effective, yet uniquely multiracial, response to color-blind ideology as part of the larger antiracist struggle.

Naive Egalitarianism and the Neoconservative Agenda

In *An American Dilemma* (1944), Gunnar Myrdal, R. Sterner, and A. M. Rose argued that the racist attitudes and practices that systematically prevented equality between African Americans and European Americans comprised a "racial creed" that was a flagrant breach of what he defined as the "American creed." The latter was based on the principles of egalitarianism and individual rights enshrined in the Declaration of Independence, the US

Constitution, and the Bill of Rights. By contrast, the racial creed was based on the goal of excluding individuals on the basis of racial group membership. Though Myrdal may have recognized the contrast between the ideals of the American creed and the reality of the racial creed, his analysis nevertheless operated on the false premise that the racial creed was an aberration that did not represent the nation's core values.

Many contemporary analyses (and the dominant color-blind racial ideology) reflect this long-standing tradition of naive egalitarianism, or the belief that the egalitarian tenets of the American creed, reflected in the ideal of individual meritocracy, were intended to include people of color. However, this belief elides the fact that the racial creed was inscribed in the Constitution and ultimately elaborated into a distinctive legal-normative code that sanctified racial domination and discrimination (Blauner 1972; Ringer and Lawless 1989; Steinberg 1995).

During the Johnson and Nixon administrations of the late 1960s and early 1970s, civil rights mandates, as well as affirmative action and other compensatory programs, were perceived as a means of rectifying the inequalities fostered by the racial creed (Bonacich 1995; Omi and Winant 1994; Steinberg 1995).[2] However, during the Reagan and Bush administrations in the 1980s, many whites and some privileged blacks and other individuals of color began to assert that white racism and white supremacist ideology had been repudiated with the dismantling of Jim Crow segregation and the implementation of civil rights legislation. Accordingly, the growth of the middle classes among communities of color (especially the example provided by Asian Americans) reaffirmed the values of individual merit and excellence upon which the American creed rests.

Neoconservatives (and Republican Party politics) that emerged during this period thus used the ideals of "individualism" and "fairness" embodied in the American creed to dismantle the very policies that were implemented to fulfill those principles (Laham 1998; Myers 1997; Omi and Winant 1994; Pinkney 1984). They gained support for this agenda by claiming that "unfair preferences" had been given to racial minorities, preying on the fears of those working-class European Americans who felt themselves somewhat disenfranchised and occupied an already tenuous position in the economy. However, neoconservatives have avoided overt appeals to white racism and supremacy, deploying instead a rhetorical sleight of hand, or "semantic infiltration" (Steinberg 1995: 116), to further their agenda. Specifically, they have "rearticulated" (Omi and Winant 1994: 99, 131) civil rights discourse by framing affirmative action and other programs as a betrayal of the egalitarian virtues of the civil rights movement. This was vividly illustrated in the 1996 campaign supporting California's Proposition 209. Deceptively titled the "California Civil Rights Initiative," its proponents skillfully employed color-blind rhetoric and civil rights iconography (particularly images of Martin Luther King, Jr., and excerpts of his "I Have a Dream" speech in television advertisements) to advance the notion that affirmative action had tipped the scales of racial justice.

By framing affirmative action and other policies as "reverse discrimination" against European Americans, neoconservatives have successfully positioned themselves as the harbingers of an egalitarian society based on individual rights, as opposed to "group rights" (Daniel 2000b; Gelman et al. 1988; Omi and Winant 1994). Yet, this discourse has effectively masked pervasive structural inequality, in which the masses of color remain disproportionately represented in the secondary labor force of service and blue-collar employment, and among the ranks of the underemployed and unemployed (Bobo, Kluegel, and Smith 1997; Farley and Allen 1987; Feagin and Sikes 1994). It has also obscured the selective nature of racial integration, in which a few individuals of color—particularly from the middle class—have been allowed to gain access to wealth, power, privilege, and prestige, provided that they do not challenge the racial status quo (Bonacich 1995; Daniel 2000b).

■ Race Counts:
Multiraciality and the Decennial Census

The Foundations of the Multiracial Movement

Given that neoconservatives have articulated an "egalitarian" vision of American society based on individual opportunity and free from the constraints of race-based policy, it is not surprising that some have questioned the utility of racial categorization and data collection. It was not until the 1990s, however, that neoconservatives made a major attempt to link color blindness with the multiracial phenomenon. This strategy became most apparent in their response to the emergence of a movement composed of multiracial activists and organizations that called upon the state to allow a multiracial identification on census forms and other forms that collect data on race (Daniel 2000b; Omi and Winant 1994). This initiative was reflected in a series of oppositional projects at local, state, and federal levels and was pursued most vigorously with respect to the decennial census.

The multiracial movement originated in the growing numbers of individuals in the United States that identify with more than one racial background. From the outset, activists embarked on various projects that have challenged the mutually exclusive construction of race dominant in the United States, though its impact has been most evident in its challenges to official racial classifications. Its earliest success came in 1979 in Berkeley, California, when members of the recently formed organization Interracial/Intercultural Pride (I-Pride) succeeded in petitioning the local school board to add an "interracial" designator to school forms—the first such designator in US history. However, California state education officials restricted it to internal district uses only, citing federal reporting requirements that did not allow such a category (Daniel 2000b).

Within a decade after the founding of I-Pride, similar locally based support organizations for interracial families and multiracial-identified individuals had formed in various regions of the United States. By the 1990s, more than forty grassroots organizations forged a coalition that began pressuring the federal government to revise its racial data collection standards, particularly with regard to the decennial census. Fourteen support groups, including Multiracial Americans of Southern California (MASC) in Los Angeles, the Biracial Family Network (BFN) in Chicago, the Interracial Family Alliance (IFA) in Atlanta, and the Interracial Family Circle (IFC) in Washington, D.C., joined to form a national umbrella organization called the Association of Multiethnic Americans (AMEA). In addition, the coalition included A Place for Us/National (APUN), a nondenominational religious support network for interracial families; Project RACE (Reclassify All Children Equally), an activist, informational, and educational organization currently based in Florida; and *Interracial Voice* (www.interracial voice.com, hereafter *IV*), an Internet advocacy journal (Brown and Douglass 1996, 2003; Daniel 2000b).

The drive to implement changes in federal racial categorization began in 1988. On January 20, the Office of Management and Budget (OMB), the branch of government responsible for implementing changes in federal statistical surveys, solicited public comment on potential revisions of Directive No. 15. This directive was implemented in May 1978 as the federal standard for collecting and presenting data on race and ethnicity, particularly for the monitoring and enforcement of civil rights mandates and legislation. It provided a minimum set of racial categories (black, white, Asian/Pacific Islander, and American Indian or Alaska Native) and a separate ethnic category (Hispanic or not of Hispanic origin). The revisions permitted individuals to identify themselves as "other" if they believed they did not fall into just one of the four basic racial categories established by Directive No. 15. Although an "other" category has been provided on each census since 1910, write-in responses in the "other" category have been reassigned to one of the traditional racial categories (Daniel 2000b).

Many interracial couples and multiracial-identified individuals requested that a multiracial or biracial identifier, instead of "other," be added to the five categories. However, the OMB received overwhelmingly negative responses from various federal agencies, as well as the public, to the addition of a multiracial identifier. The most significant opposition came from various African American leaders and organizations. Acknowledging that most, if not all, African Americans have some European and, in many cases, Native American ancestry, they feared that many individuals would designate themselves as "multiracial" in order to escape the continuing negative social stigma associated with blackness. This, in turn, would reduce the number of individuals who would be counted as black, which would affect the ability to track historical and contemporary patterns of discrimination and enforce civil rights initiatives. Similar concerns were expressed by representatives from other communities of color.

On November 12, 1988, the AMEA was formed in Berkeley, California, to serve as a national agent to coordinate strategies for gaining official recognition of multiracial-identified individuals. At the founding meeting and in subsequent discussions, much attention focused on the concerns—particularly in the African American community—regarding the impact a multiracial identifier would have on affirmative action and other race-based government programs. There was no general agreement on how the organization should deal with these concerns, nor could consensus be reached on how to characterize multiracial individuals. Furthermore, members debated whether a multiracial designator would apply to everyone who identified as such or whether the term should be restricted to the first-generation offspring of interracial marriages (Daniel 2000b).

The formats that might be used to collect data were also discussed. They included having a separate multiracial identifier (the "pluralistic format"); checking more than one box (the "integrative format"); or having a separate multiracial identifier in conjunction with some means of acknowledging more than one group, either through writing in a race, filling in blanks, or checking all applicable boxes (the "combined format"). Although no national consensus as to format existed, the AMEA leadership recommended the combined format. The general public and the media, however, typically framed the discussion as if the movement supported only a stand-alone multiracial category (the pluralistic format), which informed later negotiations with traditional civil rights organizations (Daniel 2000b).

In the months after the founding of the AMEA, support groups held public education forums to discuss the complexities and controversy surrounding multiracial identity, particularly in relation to the upcoming 1990 census. A flurry of phone calls and correspondence between OMB and Census Bureau officials, the AMEA leadership, and affiliated groups ultimately culminated in a small but significant reform in official policy. Though the Census Bureau announced that there would be no multiracial identifier on the 1990 census, officials quietly notified support groups that the government would accept "biracial," "multiracial," or similar designations as write-in responses to the "other" category. These responses would help the OMB determine what, if any, changes should be made to include a multiracial identifier on the year 2000 census. However, the OMB did not announce this policy to the general public. Consequently, most individuals who would have potentially identified as multiracial remained unaware of the new census policy (Daniel 2000b).

The 2000 Census

The efforts of the AMEA and its affiliates to make "multiracial" an acceptable means of official self-identification failed for the 1990 census. Meanwhile, quite apart from the efforts of the AMEA, Project RACE had begun to strategize at the municipal and state levels using the combined format, ultimately gaining support for a stand-alone multiracial identifier in several states.[3] From December 1996 to July 1997, APUN attempted to garner support for a ballot initiative to add a multiracial category on California state forms but did not gather the necessary number of signatures. Though most universities resisted making changes on admissions forms, Williams College in Williamston, Massachusetts (among other universities), included a multiracial identifier on its official forms.[4] Nevertheless, these data were necessarily reassigned at the federal level to one of the four official racial categories (and the ethnic category, when given as an option), so that numbers for historically underrepresented group(s) could be obtained for the purposes of affirmative action (Daniel 2000b).

In 1993, the OMB began a comprehensive review process to discuss possible changes for the 2000 census. Meanwhile, the AMEA and Project RACE joined forces, testifying at government hearings between 1993 and 1997. Both groups mounted letter-writing campaigns during the public comment period on each *Federal Register,* recommending that the combined format be used at the federal level, though they advocated that federal agencies be able to break down that information when necessary. Officials in Washington, however, as well as others in traditional communities of color, seemed to believe that the stand-alone category was the movement's only goal, perhaps in part because Project RACE gave this impression on several occasions, including congressional testimony.

By the time the May 1997 congressional subcommittee hearings began, the results of federal field testing showed that the integrative format was more likely to be approved at the federal level than the combined format. Shortly after the hearings, the AMEA and Project RACE called a Third Multiracial Leadership Summit to discuss the hearings and a possible compromise. The meeting was held on June 7, 1997, in Oakland, California, and sponsored by I-Pride. The summit included AMEA and Project RACE representatives; legal experts; representatives of other educational and support organizations, including Hapa Issues Forum (a national organization for individuals of partial Asian descent, hereafter referred to as HIF); and a representative of the Census Advisory Committee, who was also part of the National Coalition on the Accurate Count of Asian and Pacific Islanders.[5]

A consensus emerged that a separate multiracial box without multiple checkoffs was unacceptable. Participants knew that even the combined format was unlikely to gain support from the OMB and that traditional civil rights groups would reject it simply due to the presence of a multiracial box. In spite of a general preference for the combined format, the summit leadership settled instead on a revised model presented by Project RACE that recommended an integrative format. It was argued, nevertheless, that the movement's goals could be achieved in part by incorporating the word "multiracial" only in the instructions to the race question, but not as one of the boxes. This compromise format was drafted after eight hours of intense and heated discussion (Daniel 2000b).

This proposal, which has been called the "Oakland Compromise," was endorsed by many individuals and support groups (Douglass 1997a, 1997b). However, strong opposition came from individuals (including Charles Michael Byrd, the editor of *IV*) who wanted a stand-alone multiracial identifier or a multiracial identifier in which checking or writing in all the applicable racial groups was optional (Byrd 1997a, 1997b, 1997c, 1997d, 1997e, 1998; Douglas 1997a, 1997b, 1998a, 1998b). In addition, the leadership of Project RACE—perhaps under pressure from its constituents—retracted support of its own revised model (Graham 1997f). Consequently, the "Oakland Compromise" caused a rift between hard-liners who continued to support the combined format and moderates who supported the integrative format. The former more or less coincided with Project RACE and its supporters and the latter with the AMEA and its affiliates.

Among other things, the leadership of Project RACE criticized the insistence by multiracial adults—who were disproportionately represented at the summit—that the proposal emphatically reject a stand-alone identifier. Unlike the executive director of Project RACE, Susan Graham, who is a European American partner in an interracial marriage, these multiracial individuals saw themselves as people of color. Consequently, they rejected any racial/ethnic data collection format that might be interpreted as insensitive to the concerns of traditional communities of color about the potential loss of numbers.[6] However, from Project RACE's perspective, this rejection not only dismissed but also potentially jeopardized its work at the state and municipal levels, where a stand-alone multiracial identifier had been approved for use on official forms. It also jeopardized federal legislation (H.R. 830, or the Petri Bill) that supported a stand-alone identifier and was pending congressional approval (Daniel 2000b). Introduced by Representative Thomas E. Petri (R-Wisconsin), and named in honor of golfer Tiger Woods, H.R. 830 was intended as a last resort if the OMB failed to enact changes on its own.[7]

On July 9, 1997, the OMB announced its recommendations, unequivocally rejecting a stand-alone multiracial identifier, as well as the combined format or any mention of the word "multiracial" in the race question (Daniel 2000b). Instead, it recommended that federal data collection forms be

changed so that individuals could check off one or more racial identifications (the integrative format). This format was chosen partially in response
to the various federal agencies that require data on race and ethnicity. They
argued that the "mark one or more" alternative—unlike the combined format—would require fewer changes on existing forms and allow for data continuity. Furthermore, the data could be retrofitted in each of the existing official single-racial categories with which multiracial individuals identified,
facilitating the continued enforcement of civil rights legislation.

In response to these recommendations, HIF and the AMEA actively
sought the support of traditional civil rights organizations such as the National Association for the Advancement of Colored People (NAACP), the
Japanese Americans Citizens League (JACL), which played a key role for
the defense in *Loving v. Commonwealth of Virginia,* and the Mexican American Legal Defense and Education Fund (MALDEF). The NAACP and
other African American leaders had previously announced that they would
oppose a stand-alone multiracial identifier, which they erroneously (though
perhaps understandably) assumed was the only option acceptable to the
multiracial movement (Daniel 2000b). Perhaps what was most disconcerting to traditional civil rights groups and activists about the multiracial identifier was the considerable Republican support it received, whereas Democrats were either neutral or strongly opposed (undoubtedly out of fear of
alienating their constituents in communities of color and black elected officials).[8] For example, Speaker of the House Newt Gingrich challenged the
Democrats' lukewarm response to the multiracial identifier when he
charged that "many Americans cannot fill out their census because they are
an amalgam of races" (Graham 1997c, 1997d, 1997e). He also criticized
Clinton's Advisory Committee on Race (Gingrich and Connerly 1997) and
wrote the director of the OMB a letter supporting the multiracial identifier
(Gingrich 1997).

Though ostensibly sympathetic toward the multiracial movement's goal
of challenging the oppressive rule of hypodescent, Gingrich and other
prominent neoconservatives in fact seized upon this controversy to further
their agenda of dismantling affirmative action and other race-conscious
mandates. They argued that a multiracial category would help to dilute racial
consciousness, thereby undermining the obsession with race and ethnicity
that fuels identity politics. They applauded the fact that a "multiracial" category did not denote a protected class under the law and thus served no
statutory purpose. Consequently, they viewed gathering data on those individuals who identify as "multiracial" as a step toward dismantling what they
called the "racial spoils system" (Sousa 1996; Will 1997a, 1997b).

Thus, Republican support for a multiracial identifier led many individuals
to view the multiracial movement—particularly the stand-alone identifier—
as part of a right-wing "conspiracy." The movement's goals were seen as

countering civil rights claims and efforts aimed at addressing social and economic inequity. Despite this guilt by association, some activists felt that the Republican majority in the House made their support essential, particularly if it became necessary to pursue this struggle through legislative channels. In other words, the move to join with Republicans had more to do with political opportunism than actual support of the neoconservative agenda (Daniel 2000b). Nevertheless, when Project RACE proposed an alliance with Gingrich during the Third Multiracial Leadership Summit, none of the other representatives expressed support for this alliance (Brown and Douglass 2003). However, particular segments of the multiracial movement, including APUN and especially Byrd of *IV,* began to actively foster ties with neoconservatives and converge with their ideological position on race, prior to and after the OMB's final decision in October 1997.

Ultimately, intense lobbying efforts by AMEA and HIF convinced a host of traditional civil rights organizations, including the NAACP, MALDEF, the Urban League, and the National Council of La Raza to lend their support to the integrative format. Although they felt this format addressed their concerns about the loss of numbers, they voiced concerns about how the data would be tabulated for voter districting and other purposes related to tracking and addressing continuing racial inequality. Meanwhile, Project RACE and its supporters, as well as Byrd and other commentators in *IV,* continued to speak out against the OMB recommendations and support the combined format. They also criticized the AMEA and HIF for cutting a "behind-closed-doors deal" with the NAACP (Byrd 1997a, 1997b, 1997c, 1997d, 1998; Douglas 1997a, 1997b, 1998a, 1998b). Ultimately, the OMB's final decision on October 31, 1997, did in fact support the check-one-or-more format, though "multiracial" terminology was not incorporated on official forms.

The Aftermath of the 2000 Census

Once the general contours of state reformism were clear, the movement's internal divisions intensified even further. The format for collecting data on multiracial-identified individuals was the site of the most intense and acrimonious conflict. One segment of the movement, the AMEA and its affiliates and supporters, advocated the new state policy; its leadership was eventually incorporated in an oversight committee related to the census.[9]

However, Project RACE and commentators on *IV* argued that there was no assurance federal agencies would tabulate data on those who checked more than one box. They balked at the OMB's March 9, 2000, announcement that individuals who checked more than one race on the census would be reassigned to one racial category for the purpose of monitoring discrimination and enforcing civil rights laws.[10] Consequently, the opposition did not consider the OMB's recommendations to be a significant advance over previous methods of data collection and tabulation (Douglas 1998a, 1998b; Graham 1997a, 1997b; Graham and Landrith 1999). Project RACE and its supporters continued to demand either a stand-alone multiracial identifier (with or without multiple checkoffs) or at least the retention of the term "multiracial" in the wording of the instructions on the race question.

Meanwhile, another segment of the movement, represented by the Multiracial Leadership Conference, met on March 31, 2000, in Washington. D.C. (sponsored by APUN), and publicly supported the elimination of official racial designations altogether (C-SPAN 2000; Landrith 2001a; Sample 2000). Those attending included Steve and Ruth White of APUN, Byrd of *IV*, and James Landrith, editor of the website The Multiracial Activist (TMA) and the online journal the *Abolitionist Examiner*. Also in attendance was Ward Connerly, the neoconservative University of California regent who rose to prominence as one of the architects behind California's Proposition 209. Connerly's organization, the American Civil Rights Institute, wrote a commentary criticizing the rejection of a multiracial identifier by the OMB (Nelson 1997). In addition, he had been interviewed by Byrd for *IV* (Byrd 1999), and was inducted into APUN's "Racial Harmony Hall of Fame" at the conference (C-SPAN 2000).

The rift in the multiracial movement over the OMB recommendations thus led to a more sustained collaboration between neoconservatives and particular leaders of the movement. Particularly significant was the growing collaboration between the two website editors, Byrd and Landrith, and Connerly. Interestingly, Byrd and Landrith did not necessarily identify themselves as "conservatives." Byrd had been a registered Democrat (at least up until 1997), and although he consistently criticized black intellectuals and civil rights organizations (especially the NAACP) for what he perceived as embracing the one-drop rule and racial separatism (Byrd 1996, 1997d), he initially opposed the conservative agenda of abolishing affirmative action and other race-based programs (Byrd 1995, 1997c). Landrith has featured a "Hall of Shame" on his website, focusing on public figures and organizations across the racial and political spectrum who have "demonstrated a repugnant view of multiracial identity/interracial relationships" (www.multiracial.com/projects/hallofshame.html).

However, Byrd and Landrith were both frustrated with the objections of traditional civil rights organizations to multiracial identifiers, resulting in what they perceived as the continuation of hypodescent under a different guise (Byrd 1998, 2000b; Landrith 2001b). Both saw as irreconcilable and hypocritical the calls of civil rights groups to dismantle racism while supporting the maintenance of racial categories, which were originally established to perpetuate racism (Byrd 2000a; Landrith 2001b). Ultimately, both editors shared a self-professed "libertarian" approach to race.[11] This approach viewed government-imposed racial classifications, along with race-based policies and indeed all forms of race consciousness, as not only impinging upon individual freedom and choice (particularly with regard to identity) but also perpetuating false divisions among humanity (Byrd 1997b; Landrith 2000,

2001b). Therefore, they perceived the elimination of racial categories as the only assured way of dismantling racism (Byrd 2000a, 2000b; Landrith 2001b).

Meanwhile, Connerly had already embarked on plans to make the elimination of racial categories a reality. In the aforementioned 1999 interview with Byrd, Connerly revealed his intention of introducing a bill in the California state legislature as a pilot test for the ballot measure he later planned on submitting to voters. In later guest commentaries for *IV*, Connerly discussed the need for the United States to get rid of "those silly little boxes" (Connerly 2000, 2001a, 2001c). By April 2001, Connerly, along with his organization, the American Civil Rights Institute, had launched a statewide campaign to submit the Racial Privacy Initiative (RPI) to voters; both Byrd and Landrith accepted the invitation to participate in the steering committee for the initiative (Landrith 2001b).

■ The Racial Privacy Initiative, or the "Son of Proposition 209"

The RPI and the Rhetoric of Race

The RPI represents an unprecedented event in the history of US race relations, the significance of which should not be overlooked. On one level, the RPI illustrates the transformation of the construction of race in the United States initiated by the civil rights movement and furthered in part by the challenge posed by multiracial-identified people to the mutually exclusive, "check-one-only" format of racial categorization. In other words, the RPI rests on the now largely accepted premise that race is socially constructed and that racial categories do not reflect fixed biological entities. Yet on another level the RPI represents the new and more complicated challenge potentially facing advocates of racial justice. In other words, advocates increasingly confront a racial climate in which neoconservatives strategically link color-blind ideology with the progressive veneer of "dismantling" or "deconstructing" race in order to promote an agenda that actually seeks to undermine race-based compensatory programs. Consequently, this strategy not only undercuts the tools necessary to pursue racial justice but also deflects attention away from continuing patterns of racial inequality, which remain largely hidden from view.

Briefly, the Racial Privacy Initiative, which ultimately qualified and was placed on the October 7, 2003, special California recall election ballot as Proposition 54, would have banned the state of California from classifying individuals on the basis of race, ethnicity, color, or national origin, effective January 1, 2005. In other words, it would have prevented most state agencies from collecting data on race and ethnicity. However, the initiative identified a series of exemptions, or areas in which the collection of racial and ethnic data were perceived as necessary and permissible. They included the classification of medical research subjects and patients, as well as exemptions for law enforcement officers in conducting their duties, and the assignment of prisoners. The Department of Fair Employment and Housing was also exempted from the RPI, though only for ten years after the effective date of the initiative. Yet, exemptions were not provided for the areas of public education, public contracting, or public employment—they were, in fact, the areas identified in the first paragraph of the initiative as subject to the ban on racial/ethnic data collection. This provision led many civil rights organizations to view the RPI as the "Son of 209" that would deal the final blow to any state policies oriented toward ameliorating racial inequality (Khimm 2003).

For his part, Connerly did not deny that the RPI was designed to undermine any attempts to resurrect affirmative action policies under a different guise. Connerly was quoted as saying that the RPI "would be an express prohibition in the areas of public education, public contracting, and public employment, which are banned for purposes of preferential treatment anyway in California as a result of Proposition 209" (Rossomando 2001). Indeed, like Proposition 209, the RPI was yet another neoconservative attempt to undermine race-based policies through the skilled use of color-blind rhetoric and the masterful "rearticulation" (Omi and Winant 1994) of civil rights discourse and iconography.[12] However, the rhetoric surrounding the RPI also selectively incorporated concerns raised by individuals and organizations in the multiracial movement throughout the previous decade. The phenomena of increasing intermarriage and the growing numbers of multi-racial-identified individuals (and by extension the multiracial movement itself) were co-opted as the centerpiece of the rhetorical strategy for the RPI, symbolizing the color-blind ideal that should be reflected in state policy.

This strategy is evident in Connerly's introduction to the Reader's Guide for the RPI, featured as a guest editorial in the November–December 2001 edition of *IV* (Connerly 2001b). Connerly begins this piece by referring to previous commentaries by Byrd and other contributors to *IV* about the need to "deconstruct 'race'" and offers the RPI as an opportunity to implement this goal. Later, Connerly cites a 2000 report by Sonya Tafoya of the Public Policy Institute of California, which documents the substantial percentage of multiracial births in California (14 percent of all births in 1997). Engaging in a rhetorical sleight of hand, he then associates "the remarkable blurring of racial lines in California" with the rise in University of California applicants declining to state their race. Though Connerly could hardly have proven this association, he nevertheless concludes "the state needs to catch up and recognize that Californians increasingly no longer see themselves in racial boxes" (Connerly 2001b). The RPI would thus serve to "create a colorblind state for our children and grandchildren, one that is more respectful of the inherently private and complex nature of racial identity" (Connerly 2001b).

The Public Response to the RPI

Though the logic and language of the RPI were framed within the dominant racial ideology of color blindness that was likely to resonate with many voters, California voters across the racial spectrum overwhelmingly rejected this proposition by a 64–36 margin. Indeed, exit polls indicated that three-quarters of African Americans and Latinas/os voted against the initiative, as well as a majority of European Americans (Khimm 2003; MSNBC 2003). The RPI's failure can be attributed in part to the broad range of organizations and individuals that joined in opposition to this initiative. Though the RPI was predictably opposed by traditional civil rights groups, the coalition against it also included the California Medical Association and the American Heart Association and prominent figures such as former surgeon general C. Everett Koop. The strategy sought to kill the initiative by focusing more on the ambiguous medical exemption that might have prevented physicians and other public health officials from tracking the impact of diseases on different populations, rather than highlighting the detrimental impact of the initiative on efforts to address structural racial inequality in public education and other areas (Chemerensky 2003; Khimm 2003; Sen 2003–2004).[13]

Opponents of the RPI also staged a far more visible campaign than Connerly and his coalition, which included television and radio advertisements, as well as grassroots mobilization by students and community-based organizations. By contrast, the pro-RPI coalition waged a relatively low-profile campaign, marked by a few radio advertisements and some public appearances (including a few debates over the initiative) by Connerly himself. This may have reflected a strategy of relying on voter ignorance of the initiative to work to its advantage, but it most likely reflected the limited amount of funding received by the proponents. By August 2003, the "Yes on 54" campaign had received a total of $1.87 million, most of which was used to organize and gather signatures. From January to August 2003, the pro-RPI campaign received less than $45,000, whereas the anti-RPI campaign received over $500,000 in contributions within the same period (Sanders 2003). The anti-RPI campaign received an even bigger contribution from Democratic lieutenant governor Cruz Bustamante when he channeled funds from his gubernatorial campaign to defeat Proposition 54.

The Multiracial Response to the RPI

The RPI's message may have resonated with some interracial families and multiracial individuals, particularly those who have had negative experiences with being classified monoracially by school administrators or other officials. That said, the debate over the RPI continued to reflect the cleavages in the multiracial movement that emerged after the OMB decision in 1997. Byrd and Landrith enthusiastically promoted the RPI as the ultimate progressive step toward the elimination of racism. Landrith argued that the RPI would

help complete the work of the abolitionist project, by eliminating those categories that were originally used as a tool to maintain the institution of
slavery. He stated, "It is my steadfast belief that until these categories are
gone, we will not be able to begin to give 'racism' the proper burial it
deserves. These categories, created for the sole purpose of ensuring state
political power at our nation's birth, are not the solution to racism. . . . It's
time to let the deconstruction begin" (Landrith 2001b). Similarly, Charles
Michael Byrd envisioned the RPI as part of a larger "jihad" against race
consciousness (Byrd 2000a) and as engaging "in the final battle of deconstructing the race notion" that traditional civil rights leaders had abandoned
(Byrd 2003).

Meanwhile, a number of other multiracial organizations and public
forums came out against the RPI. HIF endorsed the campaign to defeat
Proposition 54. Dubbing the RPI the "Racial Ignorance Initiative," they
argued that the RPI was "in direct opposition to the needs of the mixed-
heritage Asian Pacific Islander community," as well as those of other communities of color (Hapa Issues Forum 2003). The AMEA also endorsed the
anti-RPI campaign, after a discussion involving representatives from the
board of directors and advisory board (including the authors of this chapter).
Earlier, Ramona Douglass, a former president of the AMEA, had debated
Connerly on the need for census racial categories on the television program
"Uncommon Knowledge," which is sponsored by the conservative Hoover
Institution at Stanford University and aired on some PBS affiliates.[14]

In addition to HIF and the AMEA, the recently formed MAVIN Foundation voiced its opposition to the RPI. The MAVIN Foundation is a non-
profit organization founded by Matt Kelley, which started with the creation
of MAVIN magazine, a publication devoted to examining and celebrating
the experiences of multiracial people. Currently, the MAVIN Foundation
produces the above magazine, sponsors a program to enroll multiracial bone
marrow donors, and produces the Multiracial Child Resource Book, to educate parents and professionals about the needs of multiracial youth, among
other projects. The MAVIN Foundation issued a joint statement with HIF
and the AMEA, in which the RPI was framed as rolling back the hard-won
gains of the multiracial movement to implement changes in racial data
collection so that multiracial people could be officially recognized (www
.mavin.net/pr100703.html; Khanna 2004).

Meanwhile, Susan Graham of Project RACE expressed misgivings
about the RPI but affirmed that she was "not against the spirit of Prop. 54"
(Graham 2003). Her criticism focused on the ambiguous medical exemption,
which she argued could have a detrimental impact on providing health care
for multiracial patients. Ultimately, she felt the defeat of the RPI signaled a
window of opportunity to push for a separate multiracial category, due to
the lack of information about the medical needs of the multiracial population. Finally, Swirl, a New York–based organization founded in 2000 by Jen

Chau (with chapters in seven major metropolitan areas throughout the United States and Japan), declined to take a position on the RPI. However, Swirl provided links on its website to online resources (pro and con) discussing the initiative and advertised some anti-RPI rallies and forums (www.swirlinc.org).

■ Epilogue: Multiraciality and Racial Justice

Neoconservatism, Antiracism, and the Multiracial Movement

This most recent strategic link between the multiracial phenomenon and the rhetoric of color blindness raises questions about the role of the multiracial movement in perpetuating color-blind rhetoric and, more importantly, its role as part of a larger sustained movement for racial justice. Some critics have argued that the multiracial movement is detached from the antiracist struggle. Their critique hinges on the conflation of the entire movement with the project of advocating for multiracial identifiers, particularly with regard to the 2000 census. In part, they focus on the perceived lack of consideration among multiracial activists for the impact such a revision in racial categorization could have on efforts to monitor compliance with civil rights mandates and to track structural inequalities among communities of color. These critics also focus on how some multiracial movement activists and leaders (specifically Byrd and Graham) sought neoconservative support for a multiracial identifier (Dalmage 2000; J. Spencer 1997; R. Spencer 2003; Texeira 2003).

Indeed, the above discussion of the debates surrounding changes to the 2000 census and the Racial Privacy Initiative validates, to a degree, some of these criticisms of the multiracial movement. Both controversies highlight how some leaders and organizations within the movement (i.e., Graham and Project RACE, Byrd and *IV,* Landrith and TMA, Steve and Ruth White and APUN) have willingly allied themselves with neoconservatives in the pursuit of a multiracial category or the elimination of all racial categories on government forms. These same leaders have often been dismissive of, if not outright hostile to, the concerns of traditional civil rights organizations. At the same time, these controversies reveal how other organizations (AMEA, HIF, the MAVIN Foundation) have not only refused to ally themselves with neoconservatives but also have resisted the wholesale co-optation of the multiracial movement. Thus, it is inaccurate to characterize the multiracial movement as generally complicit with the neoconservative agenda, even as the highly organized and visible coalition between *Interracial Voice,* The Multiracial Activist, and Ward Connerly may tend to overshadow other segments of the movement.

Although it is important to recognize that the multiracial movement comprises several factions that vary in their complicity with the neoconservative agenda, questions remain about the role of the multiracial movement as part of the larger antiracist struggle. Indeed, some critics accuse the movement of lacking an antiracist agenda, which they construct as being synonymous with a political initiative that addresses continuing structural inequalities. However, part of the struggle to dismantle racism also entails cultural initiatives that seek to increase the understanding of race as a social construction, in contrast to the construction of race as biology. The latter phenomenon underpinned the US racial order, justifying slavery, de jure segregation, and antimiscegenation legislation. Though biological constructions of race have been largely discredited, they continue to hamper efforts to promote greater racial integration in relationships, education, work, and politics (Omi and Winant 1994).

In particular, interracial couples and multiracial individuals are still confronted with discrimination based on these "essentialist" (Frankenberg 1993; Omi and Winant 1994) constructions of race.[15] Through cultural initiatives, multiracial organizations (regardless of their political alliance) have attempted to challenge these lingering notions by sponsoring educational forums for the general public, organizing petition drives, providing resource materials, and providing support for interracial couples and families and multiracial individuals. In addition, although the advocacy activity of Byrd and Landrith may actually detract from the antiracist struggle, their commentaries have nevertheless highlighted how traditional civil rights organizations, leaders, and intellectuals may uncritically embrace identities and politics that have essentialist underpinnings (such as the one-drop rule). Thus, it can be argued that the primary contribution of multiracial movement as a "racial project" (Daniel 2000b); Omi and Winant 1994) to the larger anti-racist struggle has been in challenging biological notions of race, especially rules of hypodescent (although some critics may disagree with this assessment; see R. Spencer 1999; and Chapter 6, this volume).

That said, many of the organizations and individuals involved in the multiracial movement have failed to mount political initiatives that address the issue of lingering structural inequality. Indeed, the leaders of *IV*, TMA, APUN, and Project RACE have variously lent support to an agenda that would severely undermine efforts to track (and thus address) persistent racial disparities in educational attainment, health, income, and other areas. Their advocacy, informed by an uncritical acceptance of the dominant ideology of color blindness, reflects a naive egalitarianism that views all forms of race consciousness as detrimental to societal progress, thus ignoring the context of sustained racial inequality that requires the collection of racial data and race-based policy. Paradoxically, to the extent that the above organizations reproduce color-blind ideology and support policies that would inhibit the tracking of continued structural inequalities, they also hinder the goals of individual and collective racial transcendence these activists profess to advocate.

In contrast, organizations such as the AMEA, HIF, and the MAVIN Foundation have been sensitive to the needs of communities of color and objected to initiatives that could have a detrimental effect on efforts to ameliorate structural inequality. However, it is unclear how far these organizations have gone in developing their own projects that address structural racism (see Chapter 11, this volume; Williams 2003), notwithstanding the commitment of individual members to such concerns. Moreover, these organizations have not been particularly adroit and aggressive at challenging color-blind ideology. Instead, they have focused almost exclusively on challenging dysfunctional and pathological images of interracial couples and multiracial individuals by promoting images of these individuals as stable, "normal," and potential "racial bridges." Accordingly, the rhetoric of AMEA, HIF, and the MAVIN Foundation in some ways parallels that of *IV*, TMA, APUN, and Project RACE. This similarity in turn serves to further conflate the different agendas of factions of the multiracial movement with the neoconservative agenda.

Consequently, the AMEA, HIF, and the MAVIN Foundation face a formidable challenge, as the coalition between *IV*, TMA, and Ward Connerly advances a multiracial political initiative that perpetuates an association between the multiracial movement, color blindness, and the neoconservative agenda.[16] Yet, the defeat of the RPI signals an opening whereby the AMEA, HIF, and the MAVIN Foundation (and other organizations) can join forces and deploy an oppositional political initiative premised on an incisive critique of the ideology of color blindness. Doing so would necessarily involve decoupling that ideology from its automatic association with interracial marriage and multiracial identity. It would also mean questioning the naive egalitarianism employed by neoconservatives, in which more freedom in interpersonal relationships (the primary structural sphere) is equated with political, educational, occupational, and income parity (the secondary structural sphere), although in fact significant inequality remains.

Confronting the Future of Racial (In)Justice

The defeat of the Racial Privacy Initiative hardly signifies the defeat of the neoconservative agenda or the retreat of Ward Connerly from the political scene. As it became apparent that the RPI would be defeated, Connerly indicated that he would work with the head of the California Medical Association to draft language that would clarify the Achilles' heel of the initiative—the ambiguous medical exemption (Pritchard 2003). Following the recall election, Connerly shifted from advocating the elimination of racial categories to recommending the addition of a stand-alone multiracial identifier to University of California admissions and other university forms that report data on race and ethnicity (Maitre 2004).

Connerly was perhaps hoping to elicit support from those sectors of the multiracial movement that opposed the RPI, but would support the collection of data on multiracial-identified individuals. However, HIF, the MAVIN Foundation, and AMEA organized an online petition drive opposing his recommendations, which was submitted to the University of California Regents.[17] Connerly's proposal was defeated (Locke 2005), and his primary focus has shifted to dismantling affirmative action policy in Michigan with a ballot initiative similar to California's Proposition 209.[18] It is doubtful, however, that he will abandon the deployment of multiraciality as part of his rhetorical strategy. Thus, it is incumbent upon multiracial organizations and individuals that oppose this wholesale co-optation to be vocal and organize oppositional projects that highlight the persistence of racism, including its impact upon multiracial-identified individuals.

The controversy surrounding the census and the Racial Privacy Initiative have highlighted the role of interracial families and multiracial individuals in shaping the future of race relations in the United States. As traditional, binary (and biological) constructions of race become increasingly discredited, multiracial-identified people will increasingly play a central role in reifying or deconstructing the racial status quo. The challenge facing advocates of racial justice involves subverting the seductive and persuasive racial ideology of color blindness; multiracial organizations must help dismantle this ideology as part of the antiracist struggle.

Yet, it remains to be seen whether a greater coalition can be built between multiracial and traditional civil rights organizations. Such a coalition could combine a cultural initiative that seeks to dismantle rigid, essentialist, and socially imposed group boundaries with a political initiative that addresses inequalities of opportunity and life chances (see Chapter 11, this volume). However, it is clear that the achievement of a genuinely "colorblind" social order in which race would not determine the distribution of wealth, power, privilege, and prestige requires a unified and concerted effort to address the myriad ways in which racial essentialism, hierarchy, and inequality are maintained. Moreover, it is imperative that all advocates of racial justice be aware of their own potential role in reproducing these phenomena. It is only through our collective attention to racial inequality that true liberation can be achieved.

■ Notes

1. The configuration of and impetus behind the new multiracial identity is not synonymous with previous multiracial identity projects (e.g., "passing," blue-vein societies, Louisiana Creoles of color, and triracial isolate communities). Generated by racist pressure that has rewarded whiteness and punished blackness, these projects

were inegalitarian. Though they challenged the dichotomization of blackness and whiteness, they left intact the racial hierarchy that maintains white privilege, perpetuating a divisive and pernicious "colorism" among Americans of African descent (Daniel 2000b).

2. However, note that Richard Nixon's support of affirmative action and other civil rights mandates was not aimed at achieving deep structural change and redistribution. Rather, the aim was to create the illusion of power sharing without requiring the dominant European American elite to relinquish control (Allen 1990: 221–231; Kotlowski 2002: 120–250; Pauley 2001: 230–250).

3. Georgia, Ohio, Illinois, Michigan, Indiana, and Maryland made this option available on all official state forms, and Florida and North Carolina included this option on all school forms (Daniel 2000b).

4. Likewise, the University of Michigan's Rackham School of Graduate Studies and alumni associations at the University of California at Los Angeles and Tufts have included a multiracial identifier on official forms (Daniel 2000b).

5. Participant observation of public behavior by G. Reginald Daniel at the Third Multiracial Leadership Summit, June 7, 1997, Oakland, California.

6. Participant observation of public behavior by G. Reginald Daniel at the Third Multiracial Leadership Summit, June 7, 1997, Oakland, California.

7. Susan Graham, personal communication with G. Reginald Daniel, May 25, 1997. Personal correspondence between G. Reginald Daniel and Ramona Douglass, president, the AMEA, June 19, 1997.

8. For example, when President Bill Clinton was asked for his view regarding the addition of a multiracial identifier at a press conference in 1995, he gave his support, only later to equivocate (Falkerstein-Jordan, 1995). At one point, however, leading Democratic Representative John Conyers of Michigan broke rank with other members of the Congressional Black Caucus by publicly supporting the "combined format." Statement of Congressman John Conyers Before the Subcommittee on Government Management, Information and Technology of the House Committee on Government Reform and Oversight, Hearing on Federal Measures of Race and Ethnicity and the Implications for the 2000 Census (July 25, 1997), p. 535. Furthermore, at the state level, more Democrats have sponsored legislation supporting a multiracial category than Republicans. In most cases, such legislation has received bipartisan support (Williams 2003).

9. Specifically, the AMEA is a member of the Subcommittee on the Census. Ramona Douglass, president of the AMEA from 1994 to 1999, has been a key liaison between the AMEA, its constituency, and the Census Bureau (www.ameasite .org).

10. Individuals who identify with both the white and a racial minority category are counted as members of the minority background when government officials analyze patterns of discrimination. Thus, someone who checked black and white would still be counted solely as black and tabulated with the data on African Americans.

11. Indeed, Landrith refers to his website as a "libertarian-oriented activist journal" (www.multiracial.com).

12. Martin Luther King, Jr., was again invoked in some commentaries supporting the RPI. For instance, Shelby Steele commented that Proposition 54 was the attempt to infuse the California constitution with the spirit of King's dream (Steele 2003).

13. This is not to state that the anti-RPI campaign altogether eschewed discussions about the RPI's impact on efforts to address racial inequality. In fact, online literature provided by the Coalition for an Informed California discussed the threat the RPI posed to civil rights enforcement, school reform, and efforts to track racial

profiling, as well as public health disparities (www.defeat54.org). However, television advertisements focused exclusively on health care and medical concerns. As Rinku Sen (2003–2004) notes, this strategy was not only designed to appeal to voters across racial and ethnic lines, but specifically to avoid alienating European American voters by sidestepping the issue of white culpability in racial discrimination.

14. The program was taped on February 22, 2002, www.uncommonknowledge .org/01-02/638.html.

15. One of the more notable cases in recent years involved ReVonda Bowen, a high school student in Wedowee, Alabama. The principal, Hulond Humphries, threatened to cancel the prom if interracial couples attended and told Bowen (of black/white parentage) that her parents had made a "mistake" (Byrd 1994). APUN helped organize a petition drive to fire the principal (www.aplaceforusnational.com/ experience.html), while Byrd and Landrith decried the incident (Byrd 1994; www .multiracial.com/projects/hallofshame.html).

16. However, *Interracial Voice* went on hiatus in 2003–2004 due in part to the founding editor's shift to "nonracialism" (www.interracialvoice.com). In the interim, Landrith has created a blog to attract interested readers (www.multiracial.com/blog).

17. Correspondence with Alfredo Padilla, project manager, Mavin Foundation Campus Awareness and Compliance Initiative, November 3, 2004.

18. As of January 6, 2005, organizers had completed the signature drive to place the "Michigan Civil Rights Initiative" on the ballot (www.michigancivilrights .org).

10

White Supremacists in the Color-Blind Era: Redefining Multiracial and White Identities

Abby L. Ferber

■ The Changing Racial Landscape

Numerous scholars argue in this book that the dynamics of race are undergoing dramatic changes in the United States. The population is increasingly being segmented into two or three broad racial categories, characterized as either white and black (with whiteness enlarged to incorporate Asian Americans, Latinos, and other nonblack minority groups), or white, brown, and black.

Eduardo Bonilla-Silva and David G. Embrick argue in Chapter 3 that the racial system is moving from a white/nonwhite framework to more of a Latin American triracial model, accompanied by an increase in color-blind racism (see also Bonilla-Silva 2002; Bonilla-Silva and Doane 2003). Exploring similar dynamics, George Yancey argues in Chapter 4 that Americans are moving from a white/nonwhite division to a black/nonblack dual classification. As Rainier Spencer points out in Chapter 6, whiteness has in the past often included Native American ancestry and may in fact be capable of assimilating Asian ancestry as well. As these scholars have observed, Americans are experiencing a change in the definition of whiteness, which represents a transition from the past where white/nonwhite was the essential distinction. Throughout US history, the rules of hypodescent have operated to attempt to keep white "pure." White racial purity has been the operating assumption underlying the construction of racial categories throughout US history.

Although socially constructed definitions of race are never stable, they are increasingly in flux in the United States, and we seem to be witnessing a redrawing of the boundaries around whiteness. Just how the boundaries will be redrawn remains unclear and the subject of much debate. What is clear, however, is that these changes are unsettling to many. As older,

147

accepted notions of whiteness shift, many people grasp more strongly to the seemingly clear rules of the past. For the organized white supremacist movement, concerned primarily with preserving whiteness and white privilege, these changes are particularly disturbing. This movement has always accepted the entrenched US view of race, which defines whiteness by white purity. They hold tight to the one-drop rule, defining whites as those who are racially pure. In fact, their constructions of whiteness are stricter than mainstream definitions of whiteness today in that they define Jews as nonwhites.

Scholars see the white supremacist movement responding to these shifts with a growing emphasis upon racial separation. Many in the movement have increasingly begun calling themselves "white separatists," as have numerous scholars tracing the movement, highlighting the movement's ultimate goal of geographic separation of the white race from all nonwhites, including Jews.

In this chapter, I explore the contemporary white supremacist movement within the context of the construction of race in the United States more generally. Examining white supremacist discourse provides us with an up-close arena for examining conscious and overt efforts to construct race, especially whiteness. I argue in this chapter that to understand the construction of whiteness, not only in white supremacist discourse but broadly speaking, we must examine the absolutely central role of interracial sexuality and why race mixing has always posed the greatest threat to the construction of whiteness. The construction of race cannot be understood apart from an analysis of boundary maintenance and race mixing. They are two sides of the same coin; race depends upon vigilant maintenance of the borders for its existence. Second, I argue that the construction of whiteness is *always* tied to inequality, power, and privilege.

■ The Foundations of White Supremacist Beliefs

Although considered extremist in their beliefs, white supremacists construct identity based on modern Enlightenment conceptions of identity that have been taken for granted by mainstream discourse. White supremacist beliefs are rooted historically in mainstream American beliefs about the significance of race and the necessity of racial segregation.

White supremacist antagonism toward interracial sexuality is also not as extreme as we might expect, especially when viewed within the context of US history. Prior to the 1967 US Supreme Court ruling in *Loving v. Commonwealth of Virginia,* seventeen states had laws against interracial marriage. At one point, forty of the fifty states banned interracial marriage (Young 1995).

Today, interracial marriages constitute less than 3 percent of all marriages, suggesting that strong cultural taboos against intermarriage still exist (DeGenova and Rice 2005). The vast majority of these marriages, however, occur between white and nonblack others. In fact, marriages between whites and nonblack others are three times more likely than marriages between whites and blacks, and respondents to a Knight-Ridder poll were most approving of marriages between "other combinations of races, and were least critical of Asian and Hispanic unions" (Arnett and Pugh 1997). Clearly, black/white relations remain the most problematic. In their recent work, *White Men on Race,* Joe Feagin and Eileen O'Brien interviewed close to 100 elite white males and found that most still harbored fears of interracial marriage, especially when it involved relationships between whites and blacks. As one respondent admitted, "I would rather that my grandchildren be white. I have a tremendous amount invested in my identity as a white person. . . . I would prefer that my lineage be white" (Feagin and O'Brien 2003: 132).

It is imperative, then, that we situate white supremacist constructions of race and interracial sexuality within the broader historical and social context. Examining white supremacist discourse within the context of contemporary color-blind racism leads to a complex picture of a movement both embracing and rebelling against current formations of race and racism. On the one hand, white supremacist discourse is moving further into the mainstream; on the other hand, its narrow definitions of whiteness seem increasingly at odds with a populace willing to expand the borders of whiteness. In *White Man Falling: Race, Gender and White Supremacy,* I explored a number of reasons why white supremacist discourse relied almost exclusively on discussions of blacks and was most vehement in its antiblack imagery, while we less often encounter images of Latinos and hardly ever of Asians. This tactic serves them well in the current climate where antiblack sentiment remains strong, and the mainstream is moving more toward a black/nonblack division. White supremacists still seek to maintain white racial purity and do not wish to expand the boundaries of whiteness to include Latinos and Asians, but they use their focus on socalled black inferiority and criminality and especially their focus on white/black intermarriage to appeal to new recruits.

■ Overview of the Contemporary White Racist Movement

There are approximately 600 white supremacist groups in the United States today, but the movement is not a new phenomenon. The Ku Klux Klan, historically the most influential white supremacist organization in the United States, was founded in 1865. The reach of the movement is expanding as a result of the Internet and the World Wide Web, and far more people read white supremacist publications and websites than actually join the movement. The movement's use of the Internet to reach a wider audience since the 1990s makes it increasingly difficult to measure its audience and influence. The Simon Wiesenthal Center now monitors 4,000 hate sites around the world, and according to the Southern Poverty Law Center, the number of US-based hate websites rose 12 percent in 2003 to 497.

There are a wide variety of white supremacist organizations, ranging from neo-Nazis and Klan groups to Christian Identity adherents and skinheads. Although some organizations attempt to move into the political mainstream, others have become increasingly violent. Members of white supremacist organizations resemble the general population in terms of education levels, occupation, and income. The organizations attract primarily men, but many groups have recently targeted women for recruitment. Despite the growing numbers of women in the movement, it remains centrally concerned with preserving white male privilege. It is not only about hatred of others but about defining identity for its members and maintaining white male power. This movement provides white men with an opportunity to perform and prove their masculinity. The movement has also recently focused efforts on recruiting young people via white power music and the web.

The white supremacist movement draws upon historically mainstream views about race and gender and tends to flourish in communities that are most sympathetic to racist beliefs. Research reveals that many Americans share the views of white supremacists, even if they are not members of the movement. Less than 10 percent of hate crimes are committed by members of white supremacist organizations, and their ideology reaches far beyond their membership. The presence of the movement serves to encourage hate-motivated violence, providing a voice, community, and even a sense of legitimacy for a wider audience. As survey research reveals, the movement articulates the wider concerns shared by many Americans, as well as a comprehensive ideology that enables a broader audience to interpret their own experiences and concerns (Ferber 1998, 2004).

■ Basic Beliefs

The movement is united by a shared system of beliefs. White supremacists believe that racial and gender differences are essential and unchanging, given either by God or biology. Social inequality is seen as a reflection of the natural order. This naturalized hierarchy places white men securely on top. Jews, defined as a nonwhite race, are constructed as the ultimate enemy, trying to race-mix the white race into oblivion. People of color and women are defined as inferior to white men, and it is believed to be white men's duty to protect innocent white women and children from the brainwashing Jews who control the world and the criminal, animal-like blacks and other people of color. For adherents, the only way to secure the future of the white race is through the creation of a racially pure homeland.

Race is naturalized and offered as justification for inequality. These assumptions undergird the movement's critique of the contemporary United

States. As white supremacists explore a myriad of social problems, they blame each one upon American attempts to change people's essential racial nature. White supremacist ideology thus offers itself as the antidote to current social problems in the United States by promising to empower white men to regain control of the nation and solve our social ills. White men are encouraged to become real men by standing up and protecting white women, reasserting their place in the natural hierarchy, and taking over the world. Furthermore, the movement's fear of white genocide leads to an obsession with controlling white women's sexuality and reproduction.

■ Defining Race

Representations of the white supremacist movement traditionally define it as one that attempts to champion white interests while espousing hatred toward blacks and Jews, taking the given reality of race for granted. However, this movement is actively involved in constructing racial identities, for both its members and others. The construction of racial difference is central to racism (Bonilla-Silva and Doane 2003; Ferber 1998; Goldberg 1993; West 1982). Rather than reading white supremacist discourse as one that is *descriptive* of race, I interpret the movement as actively involved in constructing race, and these constructions shift with the changing racial landscape.

The movement spends a great amount of time and effort trying to reify its constructions of race as inner essences, immutable and ordained by nature. They maintain a hierarchy among racial groups, with whites at the top and Asians next, followed by Latinos and then blacks. Jews are seen as a nonwhite race and the ultimate enemy. According to Don Black, publisher of the *Stormfront* website, "Jews are a distinct racial and cultural group" (Swain and Nieli 2003: 159). Even though racial identity is posited as a biological or God-given fact of nature throughout this discourse, the definition of whiteness is in constant flux. For example, there is disagreement among groups and individuals over the characteristics that define whiteness and who is, or is not, white. In some of the discourse, Aryans are defined as strictly northern Europeans, and there is debate over exactly where to draw the line in Europe. As one white supremacist claims in the film *Blood in the Face,* "We're more Nazi than the Nazis were!"

They all agree, however, in their conviction that the white race is superior. Intelligence, morality, character, and culture are all posited as racially determined. As an *NSV Report* (National Socialist Vanguard) article proclaims, "racists believe that values and ideals are a manifestation of race and are thus biologically inherited" (*NSV Report* 1991: 3). Differences in intelligence or brain size, as well as the accomplishments of "Western civilization," are frequently referenced to construct the superiority of whites, and the beauty of white women is invoked to signal the superiority of white aesthetics (Ferber 1998).

David Duke argues that "blacks on average have a higher propensity to crime than whites, and I think it has to do with a number of factors, including brain differences and also including testosterone levels. . . . We know that there is—and this has been confirmed by literally thousands of studies—that there's almost an entire standard deviation of difference in IQ between whites and blacks" (1999: 174). Proffering a religious origin to these differences, he argues, "There's no question that God created different races on this planet. There's also no question that God created those races and he separated those races" (Kaplan 2000: 484).

Jared Taylor, the highly educated chief editor and founder of the more mainstream and intellectual *American Renaissance,* argues, "the different racial groups are different biologically, and they differ on average in their intelligence. . . . it is the unwillingness of America at large to recognize these differences in ability that I think are the cause of a certain very specific set of problems you see in the United States today" (Swain and Nieli 2003: 91–92). Michael Hart, Taylor's associate, agrees: "there is a substantial difference in the average intelligence of the two races, and that difference is partly genetic in origin" (Swain and Nieli 2003: 188). Matt Hale declares, "genetically we *are* the elite" (Swain and Nieli 2003: 240). As these examples illustrate, the construction and definition of race and racial differences are inherently hierarchical. Just as they have always been throughout US history, race and racism are inseparable; race is a justification for inequality.

In response to today's increasingly "color-blind" rhetoric, a wider array of racist organizations and publications are emphasizing and arguing that race *does* matter. An array of new publications and organizations have arisen to emphasize this point, many appealing to a more educated, intellectual audience, including college students. As Taylor argues:

> The United States is scarcely more integrated today than it was in the 1950s and the 1960s, and I think that's because once again race is a salient and significant biological and social fact. I suppose you could say that that is the major assumption that underlies the positions *American Renaissance* takes—race is important and race matters, and its folly to try to build a society on the assumption that it can be made not to matter. (Swain and Nieli 2003: 89)

According to Hart:

> When I speak to people about racial differences in, say, IQ, they seem to understand that those differences exist. Sometimes they argue or quibble a bit, or make some excuses, but most of them seem to understand these differences exist, and they are large. Nevertheless, they feel: "You mustn't talk about this. It will cause disharmony and anger and resentment and embarrassment." (Swain and Nieli 2003: 186)

Acutely aware of the prevailing color-blind discourse, Hart is attempting to redirect white people's attention to what he sees as the biological basis of race and racial inequality.

▪ Preserving the Race and the Threat of Mixing

Inseparable from the agenda of defining racial differences is the goal of preserving those differences. According to the *Aryan Nations Creed,* first and foremost they "BELIEVE in the preservation of Our Race, individually and collectively" (Kaplan 2000: 469), and their one-time leader Richard Butler proclaimed, "That for which we fight is to safeguard the existence and reproduction of our Race," which is believed to be God's plan (Kaplan 2000: 472). According to the sixteen commandments of the Church of the Creator, number one is "the avowed duty and the holy responsibility of each generation to assure and secure for all time the existence of the White Race upon the face of this planet" (Kaplan 2000: 474). Similarly, the famous *14 Words,* penned by the Order's David Lane, declares, "We must secure the existence of our people and a future for White children" (Kaplan 2000: 492).

Of course, whiteness can only be maintained by securing its own boundaries and clearly demarcating who is and is not white. Interracial mixture, therefore, poses a great threat to these efforts. In his *88 Precepts,* Lane wrote, "A People who allow others not of their race to live among them will perish because the inevitable result of racial integration is racial inter-breeding which destroys the characteristics and existence of a race. Forced integration is deliberate and malicious genocide" (Kaplan 2000: 495).

Because race is not grounded in genetics or nature, the project of defining races always involves drawing and maintaining boundaries between those races. Indeed, from the moment the concept of race was invented, interracial sexuality became a concern. Robert Young observes that "the idea of race here shows itself to be profoundly dialectical: it only works when defined against potential intermixture" (Young 1995: 19). Although whiteness has been defined in opposition to blackness, multiracial identity poses the greater threat to the construction of these essential racial classifications; multiracial peoples reveal that the borders between races are permeable and penetrable. Further, the existence of multiracial peoples throws into question the "purity" of white identity, making it difficult to distinguish who is and is not white. For these reasons, interracial sexuality is an obsession in white supremacist discourse. Newsletters, novels, and websites are preoccupied with race mixing.

This obsession mirrors the general obsession with interracial relationships throughout US history in legal, popular, political, and scientific discourses. Conceptions of race have always been linked to the fear of interracial sexuality (Ferber 1998). Louis Agassiz argued for rigid segregation and warned against the dangers of miscegenation:

> Conceive for a moment the difference it would make in future ages, for the prospect of republican institutions and our civilization generally, if instead of the manly population descended from cognate nations the United States should hereafter be inhabited by the effeminate progeny of mixed races. . . . I shudder from the consequences. . . . How shall we eradicate the stigma of a lower race when its blood has once been allowed to flow freely into that of our children. (Gould 1981: 49)

The issue of miscegenation and questions of how to define and identify mulattoes played a central role in early scientific theories of race. Any discussion of the existence of races had to address the question of the mixing of races, and any attempt to define the distinctive characteristics of races also had to address the characteristics of the mulatto, the product of racial mixture.

The construction of biological races and the belief in maintaining the hierarchy and separation of races has led to widespread fears of integration and interracial sexuality. Throughout U.S. history, the fear of black political and economic equality has been rearticulated as the fear of interracial sexuality and guarded against with force. As the racial boundaries become increasingly unclear today, the white supremacist movement appeals to those seeking to maintain the seemingly clear boundaries of the past. They protest against all forms of interracial mixture. Don Black argues that

> we want to see the government get out of the business of race mixing, get out of the business of forcing races together, and of telling employers who they can hire, who they must hire, and who they must promote, telling schools how they have to run their business, and telling people where they have to live or who they have to live with. And I think left to their own devices, members of most races will separate naturally. (Swain and Nieli 2003: 158)

Interracial sexuality is constructed as eliminating difference, making everyone the same inhuman brown. It is a "multicultural movement to turn everybody into one homogenized brown mass," according to Black:

> It's really not diversity, it's antidiversity when one promotes the mixing and homogenization of every race. From that standpoint, we at *Stormfront* are the true promoters of diversity because we want to see our race preserved, as well as every other race, as a distinct cultural entity. Why is there such an imperative to bring everybody together into one society where they are all going to somehow assimilate, where they are going to be equal and the same? (Swain and Nieli 2003: 159, 162)

Mixed-race people make it difficult not only to construct whiteness but to maintain white privilege as well. An article in *New Order* explains, "The 'murder by miscegenation' device works all too well when . . . 'almost Whites' . . . can gain acceptance when a nigger cannot" (*New Order,* March

1979: 2). The existence of "almost whites" poses a threat to the constructed surety of racial identity and symbolizes the insecurity and permeability of racial boundaries, threatening the possibility of racially pure reproduction. It is for this reason that white supremacists see race mixing as the ultimate tool being used against them. They fear genocide of the white race and argue that their ultimate enemy, the Jews, are trying to race-mix whites out of existence. According to Ben Klassen and the Church of the Creator, "Pollution of the White Race is a heinous crime against Nature and against your own race" (Kaplan 2000: 474). Another article argues, "We could never again rebreed the White Race out of interracial mongrels" (*Thunderbolt* 1979: 12). What the movement fears, then, is the disintegration of "whiteness" as they understand it. Because they see the white race as a unique and superior people, threats to the category of whiteness are for them comparable to genocide. According to Lane, "miscegenation, that is race-mixing, is and has always been, the greatest threat to the survival of the Aryan race" (Kaplan 2000: 496).

Popular movement novels also highlight the dangers of race mixing. The number one best-selling white supremacist text, *The Turner Diaries,* was written by the deceased neo-Nazi leader of the National Alliance, William Pierce, and is believed to have provided the blueprint for the Oklahoma City bombing. This futuristic novel about white revolution leads to one of the most grim scenes of the book, where white women who engaged in relationships with nonwhites are strung up from every lamppost and tree in town. In the end, the revolution leads to worldwide white domination. The next best-selling novel, *Hunter,* also by Pierce, describes the lone-wolf tactics of one white man, who begins a murderous spree targeting interracial couples. Indeed, white race traitors are perhaps the ultimate enemy of the movement. After all, according to white supremacist ideology, nonwhites are by nature inferior and have no control over that nature. Whites, however, are defined as superior and must make the conscious choice to join the struggle to preserve the white race; if they do not, they are traitors. Race mixers are seen as the absolute worst traitors, speeding the race toward genocide.

◼ The Goal: Separation

According to Don Black,

> today the people who are attracted to the white nationalist movement want separation. . . . We believe that we as white people, as European Americans, have the right to pursue our destiny without interference from other races. And we feel that other races have that right as well—the right to develop a nation with a government which reflects their interest and their values without domination from whites. . . . the only long-term solution to racial conflict is separation. As long as races are forced together by

government, there will continue to be racial hatred and mutual animosity. (Swain and Nieli 2003: 156–157)

For most white supremacists, their ultimate goal is to create an all-white homeland where whites will be permanently segregated and protected from mixing, and white purity ensured. Black argues, "Our purpose is simply to provide white people with their own territory with defensible borders" (Swain and Nieli 2003: 159).

Plans for separation vary tremendously (Ferber 1998). In 1996, Michael Hart, at an *American Renaissance* conference, proposed a tripartite plan that generated tremendous interest. He argued for the partitioning of the country into three states: a white separatist state, a black separatist state, and an integrated state. In an interview in 2000, he amended the plan, explaining, "by now it is apparent that at least four independent states are needed: A separate Hispanic country" is necessary, and, "if any of the larger Indian reservations would like to constitute themselves as independent nations, I would have no objection" (Swain and Nieli 2003: 193). Hart argues that "a multiracial state hurts all of us, and hurts whites in particular. Whites have to put up with very high crime rates. . . . Because of the presence of so many non-whites, we have to put up with a high incidence of social problems—illegitimacy, for example, and many others. We have to put up with high taxes. We have to put up with declining schools" (Swain and Nieli 2003: 190). Matt Hale argues, "the only way to end the violence and the tension between the races is to have separation" (Swain and Nieli 2003: 239).

Each organization seems to have its own plan for geographic separation. Tom Metzger reflects, "Perhaps the White idea of the Northwest or Southeast solution is more than can be expected. As smaller becomes more beautiful, why not city states with satellite village states? By effective immigration, this is a reachable goal" (Kaplan 2000: 553). Others like Robert Mathews and the Order had a grander vision, however, proclaiming in a *Declaration of War:* "We hereby declare ourselves to be a free and sovereign people. We claim a territorial imperative which will consist of the entire North American continent north of Mexico" (Kaplan 2000: 524).

Yet others, following the lead of *The Turner Diaries,* believe that to secure the white race, only a white world will suffice. Lisa Turner, of World Church of the Creator, explains, "We ask of them [nonwhites] to live their own lives in their own culture, and in their own nations, and let us do the same. But they refuse." Therefore, she argues, an all-white world would be the only real solution. "'Do I want to see an all-white world?' Well, that would be a very beautiful world in my opinion, yes. An all-white world would be a paradise on earth because I know that it would be the highest expression of the human creative potential that I could possibly imagine . . . we would have a much cleaner, more crime-free, more beautiful world.

. . . in the course of asserting our rights, our expansionist rights. . . . if violence comes about, then we're ready for it" (Swain and Nieli 2003: 257).

■ Conclusion: Separatists or Supremacists?
And What Is the Difference, Anyway?

The movement itself has generally shifted to embracing the language of
separatism—calling itself either "white nationalist" or "white separatist."
"Far from being a form of white domination or white supremacy, white
nationalism and white separatism, Black insists, reflect a true respect for
the integrity and autonomy of the world's diverse peoples" (Swain and
Nieli 2003: 154). Movement leaders argue that they are not about hate,
supremacy, or dominance but simply about separation—their ultimate goal
is separation of the races. Reflecting this shift in terminology by the movement itself, some scholars of the far right have adopted the movement's own
language. On the one hand, as we have seen, the movement truly is concerned with separation of the races, no matter how this must be achieved.
They argue that attempts to create integration and allow multiple races to
peacefully coexist have failed miserably (Duke 1999; Ferber 1998, 2004;
Kaplan 2000; Swain and Nieli 2003). Yet, the situation is much more complex than this. First, as even the above brief review of the literature suggests, the movement is willing to resort to extreme violence to separate the
races, and some will not be content until purity can be assured through the
extermination of all nonwhites.

According to David Duke:

> I simply want to have my own country reflect my own values as a mem-
> ber of the majority. So I'm not a supremacist. But, as far as racism is con-
> cerned, I'm not a racist. A racist today is defined as someone who hates
> other people or wants to oppress other races, and that's not my opinion of
> the race problem. If anything, I'm a race realist, and that simply means to
> recognize and understand the fact that there are racial differences and that
> these differences have an impact on society, education, crime, and many
> other aspects of life. (Swain and Nieli 2003: 180)

So Duke is not a supremacist or racist because he hates no one and wants to
suppress no one; he merely wants to live by the laws of nature, which have
preordained the white man to be superior in intelligence and the creators
of civilization. Matt Hale proclaims, "The whole purpose of the World
Church of the Creator is to straighten out the white man's thinking so that
he can become the elite, as he was really destined by nature to be" (Swain
and Nieli 2003: 241). Hale also sees himself as a realist, recognizing the
reality of racial differences and the reality that whites are by nature superior.
These definitions make sense only within the white supremacist framework,
which assumes that racial differences are vast, rooted in nature, immutable,

and hierarchical. The "white separatist" label does not make sense from a sociological perspective, which sees race as a social construct.

Language creates meaning, and this question of labeling the movement is no small matter. These differences in language reflect significant differences in the underlying theoretical perspective of race that is being employed. In *White Man Falling,* I argued that historically scholars have defined the movement as one preoccupied with race, taking the reality of race and races for granted. Instead, reflecting the social constructionist tradition in sociology, as well as the insights of postmodern theory, I have explored the movement as actively *constructing* race and defending white privilege. Scientific advances have revealed that race has no biological existence, and it is now generally accepted among sociologists, anthropologists, and biologists that race is certainly a social fact but not a scientific one.

Once we recognize that race is socially constructed, we can explore the various sites and methods by which the reality of race is constructed. Failing to do so makes us complicit in the reification of race as a biological reality, still so assumed by the general public. Thus, while some scholars note in passing that race is a social construct, they move ahead with research as usual, defining the movement as a group of white people who seek to separate themselves from other races and do not necessarily harbor hatred toward those of other races.

Recognizing that race is socially constructed, however, necessitates doing research differently, I believe. It means that we cannot take race at face value but should explore race-based social movements as actively involved in racial projects, that is, the construction of race and the justification of racial inequality. It is inequality that produces the illusion of natural differences. We can see that historically, the construction of race was not arbitrary. Essential differences are constructed out of power relationships to produce inequality. There are reasons why we separate people based on race, or gender, or sexuality and not height or eye color. The reasons are embedded in historical power struggles and access to resources and wealth. Thus, race, gender, and sexuality have been constructed hierarchically to protect the interests of some at the expense of others. The construction and maintenance of racial differences has always been about relationships of privilege and oppression. For white supremacists, the rationale for separation is that the white race is a given biological/God-given reality, endowed with superior intelligence, potential, and culture. Thus, although it is correct that the white supremacist movement is primarily concerned with separation of the races, this already always assumes a racist construction of race. This more benign label distorts the real extent to which the movement is about the construction of whiteness and the maintenance of white privilege. Defining and defending whiteness only makes sense when seen in the context of maintaining white privilege. It is obvious why the movement itself has increasingly adopted the label of "white separatism," which presents a much kinder, gentler face for the movement. It is troubling, however, to see researchers follow their lead.

In short, relying upon the labels "white separatist" or "white nationalist" reifies race and makes white privilege invisible. The language of "white supremacy" and "organized racism," while perhaps not perfect, brings to the fore the project of maintaining racial inequality. It highlights the inseparability of the construction of race and whiteness with the maintenance of white privilege. In this chapter I have demonstrated that the project of white separatism is part of the broader agenda of constructing and reifying race and securing the boundaries of whiteness to prevent intermixture and dilution and maintain white privilege and power.

This project is being embraced now more than ever before given the broader racial context. When people feel that racial categories are in flux and white privilege is threatened, white folks are more likely to find white supremacist discourse appealing. Looking toward the future, the increasing prevalence of color-blind discourse may also continue to push many white people into the arms of the white supremacist movement. In the United States today, the results of racial inequality are clear: segregation, the wealth gap, the educational gap, and so on. However, the causes of this inequality are not clear to the average person, and the operating color-blind framework makes it seem impolite to discuss such issues. There is one clear exception, however: the white supremacist movement. They are speaking loud and clear about race to anyone who will listen. As color-blind ideology narrows the field of opportunities for public discussion about race, white supremacist organizations often appear to be the only voices speaking out. The danger we face is that the white supremacist movement will increasingly become the only public voice speaking to white people about race, utilizing the Internet to their advantage. For those wondering why racial differences in poverty and unemployment remain, white supremacist groups seem to provide simple answers.

How should we respond to this threat? My students' first inclination is usually to argue that we ban such organizations and limit their speech. But the answer is not censorship. Instead the answer is to struggle *against* the censorship that is *already* in place: the censoring of public discourse on racial privilege and oppression that is currently taking place. As scholars and students, we must do a better job or organizing and reaching the public with our research and knowledge. We need to push the subject of racial inequality *back* into public discourse. We need more dialogue, not less.

11

Defining Racism to Achieve Goals: The Multiracial and Black Reparations Movements

Johanna E. Foster

As I write this in the spring of 2004, communities across the United States are commemorating the fiftieth anniversary of what many consider to be one of the most important judicial decisions, if not the most important, in the history of civil rights, namely *Brown v. Board of Education of Topeka.* Ruling that the racial segregation of public schools was separate and unequal and thus unconstitutional, the US Supreme Court effectively delivered the death knell to roughly sixty years of legalized racial apartheid in the United States. However, along with these commemorations has come a good deal of media attention to data suggesting that even though state-imposed racial segregation is against the law, the United States is, in fact, more racially segregated in 2004 than it was in 1954 (Toppo 2004). At the same time, the media has profiled black people questioning the merits of racial integration and lamenting the loss of strong community ties in black communities as well as the threats to black institutions as the central transmitters of African American culture and history to young people. Indeed, in the spring of 2004, as measured by these indicators alone, it would seem as if the need to mobilize a massive number of American citizens in support of the new wave of the civil rights movement is as great today as it was fifty years ago.

The US multiracial movement and the modern movement for black reparations are two distinct social movements for racial justice that have emerged at the end of the twentieth century. Not only are activists in both the multiracial movement and the black reparations movement organizing around an issue once thought of as "fringe" in struggles for racial justice, both are claiming political space as the "next wave" of the traditional civil rights movement of the 1950s and 1960s. It is likely that readers of this volume are already familiar with the multiracial movement, a movement of self-identified multiracial people and their monoracial allies who have spent over two decades lobbying the federal government and various states to discontinue the use of discrete monoracial categories in the collection of official data on the racial composition of various populations, whether in public schools, health care, or the census (Williams 1998). As is the case in most social movements, not all multiracial movement organizations have been in precise agreement on political strategy, though the most widely profiled organizations have also demanded the institutionalization of a stand-alone "multiracial" identifier on the US Census and in other official data collection operations. Readers of this volume may also be aware of the recent efforts of the modern movement for reparations for slavery. A child of the black nationalist movement of the 1960s and grandchild of the pension movement for former slaves that spanned the latter part of the nineteenth century (Winbush 2003a), the modern black reparations movement demands a full accounting and apology, as well as restitution and compensatory damages, for the crimes of the transatlantic slave trade and the system of racial apartheid in the United States, both de jure and de facto, that has persisted for nearly a hundred and fifty years since slavery was abolished.

What I imagine is less widely known, however, is that each movement contains a vocal group of activists who understand their work as both distinct from that of the "traditional civil rights establishment" and as a kind of work that will bring racial harmony and racial unity to a nation so deeply divided by race, despite the decades that have passed since the modern civil rights movement was at its peak. As contributors in other chapters may also discuss, multiracial movement activists assert that the multiracial movement is the "next logical step in the progression of civil rights" (Daniel 1997: n.p.) and that "the multiracial community [is the one] poised to move this country forward toward racial liberation. . . . We are the best hope for a truly multiracial, multicultural future, because we have already been there. We know what it looks like and how to achieve it" (Douglas 1996, n.p.). At the same time, the reparations movement contends that the United States can best achieve political stability and national unity in a time of such great and persistent social strife between blacks and whites by healing the crimes of the past via reparations for slavery (e.g., Farmer-Paellmann 2003). In this case, advocates contend that "at the head of America's race relations problems are the unresolved issues surrounding the institution of slavery" (Asante 2003: 13), and thus "reparations is an idea whose time has come" (Conyers and Watson 2003: 14). Indeed, for reparations activists, the movement for black reparations "will be the greatest public education effort ever mounted on racism in this nation's history" (Winbush 2003b: 54). Yet, despite these similar claims to be on the forefront of racial justice campaigns, for the most part there is no overlap between either the leadership or the issues of either movement (for a critique, see Chapter 9, this volume).

As a result of previous research I conducted, largely between 1998 and 2000, I had come to understand the multiracial movement as a movement to legitimate a previously denied racial identity and one in which activists deploy deconstructionist claims, however paradoxical, to do so (see Foster 2004). In my more recent thinking, I began to realize in the late 1990s that the "mainstream" multiracial movement was addressing identity classification but not structural redistribution, whereas the black reparations movement was working to collect a massive and multifaceted, though largely economic, debt owed to the descendants of African slaves in the United States. Based on my sociological training in inequalities and my understanding that cultural schemas of identity classification often keep structural inequalities in place, the possibility that these movements may focus on either the politics of classification or the politics of structural advantage in their claims-making both interested and troubled me, analytically and politically. Consequently, in this chapter, I set out to explore whether or not, and to what extent, activists in each movement attend to the relationships between a politics of racial classification and white structural advantage in their claims-making and with what implications for racial justice.

■ Critical Social Theory and the Link Between Identity Classification and Structural Inequality[1]

It was as a doctoral student in sociology in the 1990s that I first became interested in the relationship between the politics of identity classification and structural inequality. Like many other feminist scholars in the social sciences, I was trained to attend to institutional discrimination, particularly the intersections of inequalities. When postmodernism and poststructuralism moved into academia as what Todd Herzog might call the "academic flavor-of-the-day" (1997), I began to appreciate the importance of attending to the cultural politics of identity classification as well. I was not alone in exploring the deconstruction of identity categories. Indeed, as I have argued elsewhere (Foster 2004, 1999), contemporary progressive scholars in both the social sciences and the humanities have devoted considerable attention to the politics of identity classification, given the assumption that in order to deny people basic rights, privileges, and freedoms based on group membership, dominant groups must decide on what grounds people can claim membership in an advantaged class (e.g., Butler 1990; Davis 1991; Fausto-Sterling 1993; Fields 1990; Kessler and McKenna 1978). One's racial classification today constrains or enables the accumulation of a whole host of material advantages. Current practices of racial classifications may constrain one, say, in avoiding incarceration in a time of racial profiling and restriction on civil liberties or finding desirable housing in a time of de facto redlining and racial steering. Although the controversial debates around the politics of racial classification almost never investigate the politics of how we classify sex, gender, and sexuality, the latter classification systems have also been used to constrain and enable. Today, one's access to employment, education, political power, and even leisure time free from the demands of housework and child care are all still directly related to race and gender.

Informed by such a perspective in feminist theory, I began doctoral research on the similarities and differences between multiracial, intersex, and disability rights activism. In a world where persistent structural inequalities are justified by claims to obvious and essential differences between the privileged and the dispossessed, those who cross or blur or allude the boundaries of hierarchical identity categories potentially sabotage the workings of social inequality by exposing hierarchical identity classification systems as social constructions. And in the 1990s, there was much to be said in critical theory about the radical potential of what alternatively has been termed "hybridity," "fluidity," and "liminality" (Foster 2004).

Ultimately, I found myself wondering more seriously if, despite the lessons of social theory that structural inequalities give way to politics of classification that justify these institutional arrangements, this bifurcation between the structural and the cultural in critical analyses of inequality was also happening on the ground in organized political struggles (Anner 1996). Have we indeed come to construct unnecessary distinctions between struggles for redistribution and struggles for recognition in both theory and practice, such that struggles over "who *is* what" have begun to take precedence over struggles over "who *gets* what" (Koopmans and Statham 1999, emphasis in original)? And if the theoretical consequences of not attending to the intertwining of identity classification and structural advantage is that we do not get an accurate picture of the complexity of the intersections of structural inequalities, what are the political consequences? It is these analytical and political concerns that brought me to explore the claims-making of the multiracial and reparations movement.

■ Methods

In order to address these questions about the political consequences of disconnecting moves for cultural change from moves for structural redistribution, I conducted a qualitative comparative case study of the multiracial movement and the modern movement for black reparations. In 1998, as part of my dissertation research on the paradoxes of identity politics, I had purposely selected the multiracial movement as a case in which activists explicitly politicized a particular method of identity classification as a matter of social injustice. As readers of this volume will have learned in previous chapters, the US government does not legally recognize individuals as "multiracial" per se. For the past two decades or so, and more successfully in the mid-1990s, multiracial movement activists have lobbied at the local, state, and federal levels not only for a stand-alone "multiracial" identifier on the US Census and other official forms, but for an attendant list of monoracial categories from which citizens could further choose the racial groups that they feel best constitute their particular multiracial identity (Daniel 1998).[2] As such, public movement documents from the multiracial movement served as my sources of evidence and were selected into the sample based largely on the condition of availability. These social movement documents included congressional testimony; texts used to lobby the state and other relevant bodies such as the Office of Management and Budget (OMB); and additional advocacy and educational materials produced by major social movement organizations, including multiracial movement march speeches, position papers, and website testimonials. I analyzed the data using a combination of interpretative methods. In the earliest stage of my analysis, I relied on the procedures of a modified grounded theory approach, starting with the search for relevant themes and concepts as they emerged from the data. After this initial foray, my subsequent approach involved additional stages, namely initial coding, focused coding, memo writing that enabled me to theorize the properties of codes, and then the integration of these memos into a larger matrix of cases and conceptual categories. This movement from codes to memos to matrices eventually led me to the comparative development of ideal-typical (Weber 1949) notions of ambiguity politics as a heuristic device.

In 2003, I became interested in juxtaposing these previously collected data on the racial identity claims of the multiracial movement against racial justice claims that were likely to deemphasize matters of racial classification. What little I knew about the modern movement for black reparations made it an excellent candidate for such a comparative exploration. Led by three key organizations, namely the National Coalition of Blacks for Reparations in America (N'COBRA), the National Black United Front (NBUF), and the December 12th Movement, the reparations movement emerged in the late 1960s and grew from a much larger movement for reparations for slavery and legal segregation that has spanned over 100 years (Winbush 2003a). The contemporary push for black reparations moved into the national spotlight in 2000 with the publication of Randall Robinson's bestselling book, *The Debt: What America Owes to Blacks,* and gained additional momentum in 2002 when, among other recent developments, a class action lawsuit was filed on behalf of African slave descendants against Fleetboston Financial Corporation, Aetna, and CSX for their various roles in the slave trade. Once again, public social movement documents from this most recent wave of the reparations movement were my sources of evidence, but unlike the evidence from the multiracial movement, the texts I analyzed from the reparations movement were already compiled for me in the form of Raymond A. Winbush's 2003 collection on the reparations movement entitled *Should America Pay? Slavery and the Raging Debate on Reparations.* The collection is the only one of its kind on the reparations movement to date and includes at least twenty separate essays by advocates themselves on the importance of reparations, along with a distinct section on the major historical documents of the movement as activists define them. Here again, I used a modified grounded theory approach to analyze texts. In the final stage of analysis, I developed a larger matrix of claims from both the multiracial and reparations movements that enabled me to compare and contrast the perceived relationships between structure and culture across the two cases.[3]

■ Findings

After this comparative analysis of the claims-making in the multiracial and reparations movements, the pattern was clear: advocates in the multiracial movement do indeed deconstruct racial identity categories to legitimate "multiracial" as a distinct racial identifier. However, the data also show that multiracial movement activists do not explain the connection between racial classification and structural advantage; they simply assume it. Reparations advocates, however, do not address the connection between structural advantage and racial classification at all.

As is the case in much contemporary scholarly analysis of the social construction of race, activists in the multiracial movement deploy an explicit set of claims that (1) deconstruct the boundaries between racial identity categories as inherently discrete, (2) deconstruct the meaning of race as an identity that is essentially biological, and (3) expose, however generally, the use of normative beliefs about racial classification to maintain white supremacy.

For example, as I have documented at length elsewhere (see Foster 2004), multiracial activists directly problematize the view of race as discrete and/or dichotomous categories in their repeated claims that there is a significant and growing portion of the US population that has long existed but has not been accurately counted as distinct, namely that portion of the citizenry who are "more than one race," "both one race and another" simultaneously, or "none of the above." In many places, multiracial movement activists justify the reasonableness of their demands for official recognition of multiracial identities by citing historical, cross-cultural, and subcultural evidence of changing or varied patterns of racial classification that clearly suggest racial categories are not inherently monoracial but socially defined as such (e.g., Root, 1992a, 1996a). As a case in point, many advocates point out the ever-shifting classification of race in the US Census itself, which has failed to use the same racial classification schema twice since the first recorded census in 1790 (Welland 2003). For example, at his speech at the first Multiracial Solidarity March, Vandon Jenerette explained, "In one lifetime—a student who went from Negro to Afro-American to African-American—but has a white grandmother and Indian grandmother—and no one asked him about all these changes—every time he fills out a form he has to lie and deny" (1996).

Not only do activists explicitly reject the definition of race as discrete, immutable identity categories, but they simultaneously reject the essence of race as biological purity. The data are peppered with explicit charges that racial classifications in the United States do not merely reflect the objective reality of race "out there" in the country but are instead reflective of "arbitrary distinctions," "fictions," or "social constructions." Ramona Douglass, president of the Association of Multiethnic Americans (AMEA), highlights the openly articulated movement sentiment that race is not a biological given but a social construct produced in ongoing social interactions when, in at least three separate places in social movement documents, she conceptualizes race as "a conversation" (e.g., Douglass 1997a, 1997b). Similarly, and taking aim—at least on the face of it—at the conceptualization of race as biological, immutable, and self-evident, well-cited and controversial activist Charles Byrd[4] argues:

> Otherwise self-determined individuals should have the ability to self-identify, since Census forms are supposed to be based upon self-identification.[5] There's so much at stake here that goes to the heart of one's self-esteem and to one's basic right to free association. . . . Though there is no factual foundation for race, racial pressures of all kinds—particularly where people have to choose one part of their heritage and deny the other—are harmful to psychological health, especially for children. (Byrd 1997f)

Valerie Wilkins-Godbee, founding president of Multiethnic Women for Media Fairness and representative for A Place for Us/New York, sums up advocates' social constructionist critique succinctly when she argued in her speech at the first Multiracial Solidarity March in Washington, D.C., that "Racial identity is neither simple nor fixed but complex and fluid—always changing across time" (Wilkins-Godbee 1996). By calling into question both the conventional meanings *and* boundaries of racial identity categories, multiracial movement activists send a central message in their claims-making: racial purity is a fiction, as evidenced by the very existence of multiracial people throughout history and across cultures. Hence, if racial purity is a fiction, then the notion of essentially discrete racial identity categories is unfounded and must also be abandoned.

More importantly for ongoing debates in critical theory, however, not only do multiracial movement activists openly deconstruct popular concepts of racial identity, but also they critique the reification of binary and/or discrete identity categories as a mechanism of social injustice. For example, Nathan Douglas, in his speech at the first Multiracial Solidarity March, implied this connection between identity classification and racial inequality when he suggested, "We [should] begin by abolishing that illegitimate 'Black/White' dichotomy which haunts us: The one that incessantly tells us that we are opposites, forever doomed to a self-imposed semantic isolation. We could begin to be true brothers and sisters, joined by one word, no longer portrayed as polar opposites" (Douglas 1996, n.p). The position of academic and activist (and volume contributor) G. Reginald Daniel is more explicit and is shared by many multiracial activists: "the inclusion of a multiracial identifier, along with the 'check all that apply' format . . . would help deconstruct the very means by which racist ideology and racial privilege are enforced in the United States, which is the notion of racial 'purity,' as well as mutually exclusive racial categories" (Daniel 1997, n.p).

However, the most obvious example of advocates connecting identity classification to institutionalized racism is the consistent charge from many advocates that the state's contemporary failure to officially legitimate a distinct multiracial identity merely perpetuates the infamous rule of hypodescent rather than being a part of contemporary efforts to gather racial data for the monitoring and enforcement of civil rights remedies. As others in this volume have already noted, the policy of hypodescent, known colloquially as "the one-drop rule," was instituted in the early twentieth century to further protect white privilege by mandating that individuals with any African ancestry be legally classified as black and thus also legally denied any of the material benefits of whiteness in an apartheid system. Consequently, by challenging the rule of hypodescent, many multiracial movement advocates perceive themselves as raising a serious challenge to racial inequality.

For example, testifying before a House Subcommittee at the 1997 Congressional Hearing on Federal Measures of Race and Ethnicity and the Implications for the 2000 Census, Nathan Douglas argued, "People who continue to uphold the one-drop myth [by not identifying as or recognizing multiracial people], whatever their stated reasons, are major contributors to lingering racism in America" (1997c, n.p.) Again, Wilkins-Godbee helps succinctly illustrate this pattern in the data when she remarked in her speech at the first Multiracial Solidarity March, "This [multiracial identity] is a political act, aimed at undermining complacent racism in our society. . . . The interracial community is making a frontal attack on the makers and guardians of the one drop rule" (1996, n.p.). Making the same point in more detail, advocate Carlos Fernandez also testified before Congress in 1997 and explained, "[The check-one-only rule serves] no compelling state interest and neither does it satisfy the lesser judicial scrutiny of being 'rational' in any discernible way" (Fernandez 1997, n.p.). As Fernandez continued to tell Congress, the only basis for such a monoracial mandate is to protect the policy of hypodescent, which he claimed "consigned multiracial individuals of part African or Native American ancestry to the classification of their nonwhite ancestry despite mixed background. . . . The purpose was to subject these multiracial individuals to the same discrimination laws aimed at their nonwhite parent or ancestor" (Fernandez 1997, n.p.).

Despite the prevalence of these critiques of the importance of the policy of hypodescent in maintaining white supremacy, there is no actual patterned analysis of the problem of structural racism in multiracial movement claims-making. The data suggest, instead, that the central problem for the multiracial movement is not the structure of white privilege but the subsequent violation of individual rights of privacy, choice, and self-determination caused by forcing multiracially identified individuals to identify themselves as monoracial. Moreover, even though the deconstruction of identity takes center stage in multiracial movement advocacy, embedded in these openly deconstructionist claims are interrelated assumptions about multiracialism as true, inherent, ever-present (albeit denied), obvious, fixed identities attached to individuals, with meanings that are consistent across cultural contexts and historical periods. Of course, these same essentialist assumptions about race have justified the construction of discrete, exhaustive, and/or binary categories of identity that foreclose the possibility of multiraciality in the first place. It is in their deployment of the language of truth, accuracy, and denied reality of multiraciality, more specifically, that activists paradoxically reinforce familiar notions of race at the same time that they leave little room for a structural analysis of racism.

For example, one of the most paradoxical discursive effects of multiracial movement activists' claims-making is the production of multiracialism as distinct, "real," and "true" identities naturally given by the body rather than ones made possible by social practices of classification that activists so poignantly argue cause all sorts of physical and psychological harm (see also Spencer 1997). Over and over again, activists assert that multiraciality is a "true identity" in comparison to the "false identity" that multiracial people must claim when they are forced to check only one racial category on various federal and state forms. Multiracial movement activists' repeated use of terms and phrases such as "the reality is," "the truth is," "forced to lie," "we need a true and accurate account," and "forced to commit fraud" expose a more complicated position that there is nothing fictional about *multiracial* identity even if race itself is "a conversation." To be clear, it is not that multiracial activists routinely claim *all* people lie about their true racial identities on official forms, a position that would be more consistent with their deliberate claims that race is a fiction. Rather, the implication is that only multiracial people are forced to be fraudulent when they must choose from a list full of inapplicable identities.

Similarly, multiracial movement activists paradoxically reinscribe racial difference as both obvious and prior to the variable processes of social interaction when they insist that multiracial people are "out there" and thus have the right to be counted like all other racial groups. Suggesting that "biraciality" and "multiraciality" exist beyond the bounds of the very practices of classification they reject, activists consistently argue that the US government needs a valid count of its citizenry, that there are unique health risks associated with being multiracial that demand that multiracial people be documented, and that multiracial people face a unique kind of discrimination based on their "blended status." Again, these appeals illustrate a kind of theoretical tension whereby activists claim that racial distinctions are arbitrary and used to enforce white supremacy, while also claiming that there is a clearly identifiable community of multiracial people that deserves to be enumerated like all other distinct and legitimate racial groups in the United States.

In other places, multiracial movement activists suggest some "truth" about racial identity when they claim that choosing only one racial category on official forms not only forces multiracial children to deny a parent but denies parents the right to pass on race to their kids. Although multiracial movement activists claim that racial purity is a myth, and racial classification a social construct rather than a function of biology, they nonetheless frame the need for a multiracial identifier as an infringement on the rights of children and families to legally recognize genetic ties. For example, testifying before Congress, Susan Graham explained, "The reality is that not all Americans fit neatly into a little box. The reality is that multiracial children who wish to embrace all their heritage should be allowed to do so" (1997a, n.p.). More pointedly, and also before Congress, Nathan Douglas says, "Fifty percent of my son's genes come from me. This means he is neither Black nor White. He is both. And no one should presume to have the authority to tell him or me anything to the contrary" (1997a, n.p.). Taken together, these examples suggest that many activists are in the precarious position of rejecting the one-drop rule by legitimating historically discounted biological ties. And regardless of specific critiques of the rule of hypodescent, in multiracial movement advocacy in general, the races of the parents still determine the race of the child. Consequently, and as I have argued elsewhere, as multiracial movement activists construct the legitimacy of the category "multiracial," they must, out of necessity, reinscribe the essentialism of the very "monoracial" categories they claim are social constructions.

In the end, it would seem that multiracial movement activism shifts the debate to which biological ties are marked rather than fundamentally challenging the use of biology to naturalize identities. By asserting that the very boundaries between conventional racial categories are not as impassable as we would like to believe—because there is a "true" or "real" multirace identity that has been denied—activists deploy a kind of "strategic ambiguity" (Foster 2004), or a set of explicit social constructionist claims about identity that then paradoxically help solidify new boundaries around "clearly" distinct "both-and/or-neither" identities. In contrast, as I will suggest next, the reparations movement relies on seemingly similar claims to rights of self-determination, demand for accuracy, and the recognition of family ties but does so in order to make a case for the material dimensions of institutional racism. Moreover, in doing so, reparations activists make hardly any mention of the cultural politics of identity classification in general and, in the data I reviewed, no explicit mention of the issue of multiracialism in particular.

■ Black Reparations Advocacy:
Lots of Structural Analysis, Little Cultural Analysis

Whereas the multiracial movement places claims to a denied identity at the center of their problem definition, the reparations movement puts an analysis of the cumulative dimensions of structural racism and whites' denial of it at the center of theirs. As I demonstrate in this section, for reparations activists, the current problems of racial stratification are largely material ones that can be traced to slavery, and thus the remedies must be largely focused on the redistribution of wealth rather than the reclassification of racial identities.

In particular, at the core of the claims-making of reparations activists is not demands for an acknowledgment and accurate count of a distinct racial group, but rather demands for an acknowledgment of and accounting for the crime against humanity that was the transatlantic slave trade and its role in the current manifestations of structural racism in the United States. Almost all the reparations texts I examined analyze white structural advantage by framing slavery and its aftermath as crimes against humanity, ones that can no longer be denied as such. For example, expressing a commonly held sentiment in the reparations movement, Winbush argues that the transatlantic slave trade is "the greatest crime in world history" and until "*all* people understand its causes and continuing impact on Africans through the world there will *never* be an honest dialogue about race and racism" (Winbush 2003a: xix, emphasis in original). For reparations activists, the most pressing problem for people of African descent is whites' collective denial that slavery, which began in the American colonies in 1619 and remained legal until 1865 (Van Dyke 2003: 59), was the grossest violation of human rights the world has witnessed to date. Citing the research of W. Michael Byrd and Linda Clayton, supporters of black reparations contend that "Black Africa sacrificed 40 to 100 million souls to the slave trade; 15 to 25 million survived" (as cited in Crawford, Nobles, and Leary 2003: 254).

Advocates draw on the language of declarations from a range of human rights conventions that contend: "No principle of international law is more firmly established than the prohibition on slavery in all its forms" (Van Dyke 2003: 60). For example, activists regularly cite the 2001 Dakar Declaration, which describes the transatlantic slave trade as an *unparalleled* violation of international human rights law, unique in its level of institutionalization in America alone for over two centuries, the transnationalism of sheer barbarism against and profound negation of the humanity of African people around the world, and the intergenerational consequences of this holocaust that black reparations activists call the *Maafa*[6] (Worrill 2003: 207). In other places, advocates call on the principles set forth in the 1948 Universal Declaration of Human Rights and the 1978 American Convention on Human Rights to denounce slavery as a crime integral to European colonialism and imperialism and eventually the hegemony of US capitalism and its white beneficiaries, one that included centuries of white people kidnapping millions of Africans from the African continent into brutal conditions of forced labor around the world; centuries of white people systematically stealing the land, property, and wages of African people and their descendents; centuries of white people torturing and murdering millions of African people; centuries of white men raping and sexually terrorizing African women and men alike; centuries of white people denying the very humanity of African people and their descendants; and the decimation of the very continent of Africa itself at the hands of white imperial powers. Given the nature and magnitude of these crimes, reparations advocates argue that if the United States considers itself a member of the international community bound by agreed-upon principles of human rights, then it has no choice but to agree that "states that pursued or supported these policies should assume full responsibility" (Worrill 2003: 207). In fact, Haunani-Kay Trask expresses a stance shared by many reparations advocates when she argues, "In terms of the international community, the right to obtain *financial* compensation for human rights abuses and to have the perpetrators of such an abuse prosecuted and punished is itself a fundamental human right that can not be taken from a victim or waived by a government" (2003: 4, my emphasis).

Although a detailed accounting of the atrocities of slavery and the slave trade are outside the bounds of this chapter, reparations activists themselves document and demand recognition of the horrors of slavery in movement texts to make clear that these human rights atrocities are largely material in nature and form the very foundation of both past and present structural disadvantages for black people. For example, the position of law professor Robert Westley is commonly found in the data: "the burden of the reparations argument, for which material inequality may serve as a first predicate, is to show that current disparities in material resources are causally linked to unjust and unremedied actions in the past" and that "a key causal element in the maintenance of structural racism [is] the economic determinant of wealth" (2003: 10). Advocates operationalize these unremedied actions in the past, as when Representative John Conyers, Jr., and JoAnn Watson cite Georgetown University professor Richard America's estimation that "the U.S. government owes African Americans $5 trillion to $10 trillion for the enslavement of Africans" (2003: 18). In other places, advocates repeatedly remind readers of the failure of the federal government to deliver on the famous—and sometimes thought of as mythical (Farmer-Paellmann 2003)—promise of "forty acres and a mule" to assist black people in the transition from slavery to freedom.

Not only do activists explicitly analyze the systemic stripping of material benefits from blacks by whites during slavery, but activists also make concrete the ways in which the subsequent system of legal segregation allowed for the continuation of such institutionalized theft. In more than several places, advocates recount the 1921 Tulsa, Oklahoma, and 1923 Rosewood, Florida, massacres[7] in which economically thriving black communities (indeed, the Black Greenwood section of Tulsa was considered the Negro Wall Street) were gutted and hundreds of black people murdered (e.g., Winbush 2003a; Van Dyke 2003). In his own essay in his edited collection, Winbush documents "white-capping" by the Klan and other white mobs as a kind of systematic land theft that occurred in the latter part of the nineteenth century. According to James R. Grossman's research on the confiscation of black land by whites, "At least 239 instances of whitecapping were recorded during the two decades beginning in the late 1880s with Mississippi being the most common site. The term seems to have originated in Indiana, where night riders invading a small community or threatening an individual African American resident would wear white caps as part of their disguise" (cited in Winbush 2003b: 49). Winbush calls this "issue of land-taking from African-Americans . . . the greatest unpunished crime in U.S. history" (2003a: xv).

Reparations movement activists are equally clear that these enormous material losses for black people were, of course, material gains for whites. As is the case with the related themes above, this critique of whites' "unjust enrichment" (e.g., Westley 2003) at the expense of Africans permeates the pro-reparations pieces in the Winbush collection in ways that are entirely absent from the multiracial movement data I examined. Not only has the white-controlled federal government been directly and unjustly enriched by slavery and segregation, say activists, but so have white-controlled individual states and private enterprises. And when these entities have not directly benefited, argue reparations supporters, they have indirectly benefited from slavery and segregation, as have all individual white people. For example, law professor Kevin Outterson provides an analysis of how the federal government and individual states profited from the tax on slave commodities, as well as slaves and servants themselves, and concludes that "from Colonial times to the Civil War, American governments derived more revenue from slave taxes than from any other source" (2003: 135). The collection also includes analyses of how the cotton and tobacco industries, as well as the shipping, railroad, and insurance industries and their individual shareholders, made their very fortunes from the torture, enslavement, and murder of African people (e.g., Winbush 2003b). Along with these kinds of illustrations, activists also refer to whites' use of profits derived from the slave trade or slave labor to finance some of the nation's premier institutions of higher education, such as Yale and Brown Universities, thus allowing generations of elite white people to accrue educational and cultural capital at the cost of African people's fundamental human rights (e.g., Fagan et al., 2002: 355). The data also include analyses by individual white supporters of reparations (e.g., Wise 2003; Secours 2003) who conceptualize their own current material advantage as literally inherited from white ancestors who, as slave owners, slave trade financiers, or the beneficiaries of state-sponsored white-only "investment opportunity structures" (Oliver and Shapiro 1997), accumulated land and income at the expense of black people that they could pass on to their white descendants.

As this last data point suggests, advocates' central claim is that slavery and segregation were crimes against humanity that are in no way crimes of the past alone. As Westley argues, "because racism, in addition to its psychological aspects, is a structural feature of the U.S. political economy, it produces intergenerational effects" (2003: 110). Again and again, reparations advocates contend that the current system of white supremacy, as indicated by persistent and enormous racial gaps in wealth, health care and education, entrenched racial divisions of labor, and residential segregation, is a structural one made possible by the *intergenerational transmission* of material advantages accumulated by whites at the expense of black people, assets not only stolen from black people but then passed down to whites during the 250 years of slavery and the six decades of legal racial apartheid that followed (e.g., Crawford, Nobles, and Leary 2003; Nzingha 2003).

In another sense then, multiracial and reparations activists are similar in their articulation of the problem as the denial of family and biological ties. However, many activists in the multiracial movement frame the problem as one in which multiracial children, when forced to identify as monoracial, are prevented from sharing a similar racial identity with a parent. This particular anxiety appears to be the most pronounced among activists when the rule of hypodescent demands that a child with a white parent and a black parent identify monoracially as a person of color, thus removing the right of a child with white ancestry to claim white heritage. By contrast, when reparations advocates lament the profound lack of respect for ancestral ties, the claims are of a different sort. In this case, advocates protest the denial of access to the material advantages stolen by whites and passed on unfairly to white heirs—land and money that activists attempt to show rightfully belong to Africans and now to the descendants of African people. Aside from the creation and enforcement of unequal opportunity investment structures that have made the intergenerational transmission of wealth next to impossible for black people, reparations advocates also lament the denial of ancestral ties manifested in slavery's attacks on the transmission of African culture and language and religion from one generation to the next, not to mention the torture, rape, and murder of millions of African ancestors, an estimated 25 to 75 million killed in the Middle Passage alone (Crawford, Nobles, and Leary 2003: 255). As such, these crimes against humanity not only set in motion the intergenerational transmission of asset poverty but a kind of "intergenerational grief" (Pewewardy 2004).

For multiracial movement activists, a major theme in their claims-making is that current official racial classification schemas are ghosts of the past that should be put to rest. Vandon Jenerette implied this interpretation of the importance of past policy when he said, "The government is using definitions of the past . . . long dead . . . to define the future of our children . . . that is the problem" (Jenerette 1996). By contrast, then, reparations activists see this ghost of the past as certainly one that continues to haunt, not because it cannot be forgotten, but because it has never been acknowledged and thus continues to do harm. For reparations activists, part of the very crime of slavery and segregation is that the state and individual white people alike deny the impact of slavery and segregation on the rise of the United States as an economic world power, as well as whites' disproportionate control of all valuable social resources in the modern period. For example, as Winbush argues, for white people, "a connection is made between slavery and poverty among Africans in America, but rarely is it associated with wealth and privilege in white America, but only recently have we seen serious research connecting slavery to what Peggy McIntosh refers to as white privilege" (2003b: 50). In this way, while multiracial movement advocates claim that multiracial people are forced to lie and deny and commit fraud themselves, reparations activists talk about denial and fraud in terms of the centuries of denial of whites' theft of wages and land from people of African descent, the systemic destruction and falsification of records that would document or account for these crimes, the denial of the centrality of slavery in the history of US wealth accumulation, and its intergenerational material consequences.

Although I, myself, feel compelled to try to document the history of entrenched asset poverty made possible by these crimes of slavery and segregation, that history is a story too big to tell here. The point is that it is precisely this explication of the history of wealth stripping and its intergenerational effects that shows up in patterned ways in reparations movement documents. It is from this central position that advocates like Van Dyke can then argue that "because of the property losses that are so evident, economic development should probably be highest on the list of targets [for reparations]. Low-interest loans, sources of venture capital, mortgage money, and the other infrastructure revenues that are so central to economic growth are examples of appropriate destinations" (2003: 74). Westley is even more direct about the enormous material consequences of structural racism when he states that "compensation must first and foremost be about money . . . as well as free provisions of goods and services [to all black people] throughout the country. . . . The guiding principle of reparations must be self-determination in every sphere of life in which Blacks are currently dependent" (2003: 129).

Despite the keen analysis of the intergenerational transmission of white advantage as a result of slavery and the slave trade, however, the data show no deconstruction of racial categories in the claims-making of reparations activists, and I could find only two vague references (e.g., Trask 2003: 42; Westley 2003: 117) to the use of racial classification as it relates to the distribution of structural advantages among the pro-reparations advocates selections in Winbush's collection. Unlike the multiracial movement, nowhere in the movement literature is there a critique of race as dichotomous or discrete or essential identity categories based erroneously on notions of essential biological difference. Inspiring black supporters of reparations to recognize the strength and the moral righteousness of the movement, for example, founding N'COBRA member Adjoa Aiyetoro notes that "those who share common blood relation will never break apart" (2003: 215). Once again, then, one's race is the race of one's biological ancestors.

To make this critique more illustrative, discussions of how we might decide who counts as the beneficiaries of reparations appear in several places in the texts, and without disagreement, advocates define those who are among the class of people deserving redress as black people who are descendants of Africans held as slaves in the United States. In the case of *Farmer-Paellman vs. FleetBoston, Aetna Inc., CSX,* for instance, the "Plaintiffs and the plaintiff class are slave descendants whose ancestors were forced into slavery from which the defendants unjustly profited" (Fagan et al. 2003: 357). Given that records accounting for these very crimes against Africans and their descendants were frequently falsified or destroyed (Winbush 2003b), finding documentation of one's status as a slave descendant may prove impossible, as might documentation of property ownership. For many reparations advocates, then, the beneficiaries of reparations in the United States are best defined practically as all African American people (e.g., Westley 2003: 129). In stark contrast to the claims-making in the multiracial movement, however, there is no discussion of what defines one as a black,[8] and readers are left to assume that anyone who has an African ancestor would be among the class of people deserving of reparations.

Moreover, for reparations advocates, the class of people clearly deserving of reparations is without a doubt an *international* community. Even though the modern reparations movement in the United States focuses its energy on winning reparations for African Americans, advocates understand the reparations struggle in the United States as deeply connected to the movement for liberation of all black people in the *Maafa*. In this way, the movement's reliance on human rights discourse and international law as a primary mechanism to justify reparations demands converges with the equally central discourse of pan-Africanism in a larger struggle against global white supremacy (e.g., Asante 2003). The convergence of these two political philosophies in the reparations movement emerges, for example, in advocates' references to the legacy of Malcolm X, who, when speaking to the Organization of African Unity in 1964, proclaimed, "Our problem is your problem. It is not a Negro Problem, nor an American problem. This is a world problem for humanity. It is not a problem of civil rights, it is a problem of human rights" (as cited in Wareham 2003: 227). In another place, Deadria Farmer-Paellman reminds readers of Malcolm X's 1963 interview by Alex Haley in *Playboy* when he proposed "that in return for the economic wealth that enslaved Africans brought the United States, . . . the government should give their descendants land and resources" (2003: 23).

Given the convergence already mentioned, some of the most salient politics of identity in movement texts address the role of antiracist white people in struggles for racial justice, thus begging familiar debates in racial politics regarding the purported separatist and essentialist strains in black nationalist discourses. In the tradition of Marcus Garvey and Elijah Muhammad, reparations movement advocates agree that although the cause of reparations will ultimately need the backing of some white people to succeed, the movement itself has always been and should remain a movement led by African people of the *Maafa* for African people of the *Maafa* (see also Wise 2003). Unlike the multiracial movement in which activists claim to actively represent people of all racial identities and in which white people or multiracial people with white ancestry play central leadership roles, the reparations movement thus provides opportunities for white allies to be supportive of the movement but demands that whites hold no active participation and certainly no leadership positions (Aiyetoro 2003: 214).

Overall, then, my analysis suggests that the problems of racial injustice for reparations activists are structural ones, and where there is attention to the nonmaterial in any patterned way, it is given to the importance of human rights discourse in laying the groundwork for a global reparations claim. For multiracial movement activists, the problem of racial injustice is largely cultural, and where there is attention to the structural elements of race, such attention is not sustained. Neither the multiracial movement nor the reparations movement has as central to their claims-making a clear explication of the interdependence of the cultural and structural components of racial inequality. Not surprisingly, these different understandings of the problem have led to different goals for each movement. Whereas mainstream multiracial movement advocacy demands identity recognition, the modern reparations movement demands redistribution. In the end, in their definitions of the problem and thus the remedies to which advocates in each movement have decided to devote their energy, competing conceptualizations of racism emerge: For multiracial movement activists, it would appear from their key claims and political strategies that racial classification largely fuels racial stratification. For reparations advocates, however, who have argued that the economic structures of global white supremacy are at the root of the problem of racism, the opposite is implied: racial stratification fuels the process of racial classification.

■ Implications for Racial Justice

At the close of this project, it seems to me that the problem of racial inequality lies not in a racial classification system in and of itself, but in the use of ideas about difference to justify various crimes against humanity. It also seems to me that such crimes against humanity are both structural and cultural, yet persist largely because white people, well-meaning and bigoted alike, routinely cash in on their white privileges at the expense of all people who are racial and ethnic minorities. As others in sociology have already argued (e.g., Bonilla-Silva 2003; Johnson 2001; Oliver and Shapiro 1997; Wellman 1993), until both prejudiced and well-intentioned white people are forced to give up a range of unearned structural advantages that they have knowingly and unknowingly stripped from people of color, much will remain the same for multiracial and monoracial people of color alike.

If these premises are true, than we cannot afford to lose focus on struggles that demand that hegemonic social groups stop taking their unfair share of jobs, land, housing, natural resources, wages, leisure time, education, health care, and what have you. In the end, then, I find myself, a white biological mother of sometimes black, sometimes brown, sometimes African American, sometimes multiracial, sometimes multiracial black children, with more confidence in the movement for black reparations than the movement to officially recognize a multiracial identity category. Nonetheless, as it stands, each of these movements will fall short—in different ways—of the goal of bringing racial harmony and political unity to a nation literally built by institutionalized racism, unless the agenda in each case is broadened.

The multiracial movement, with its primary focus on the right of people to choose freely how to name themselves, still lacks a complementary focus on the redistribution of a range of material resources so much so that, *by itself alone,* the movement seems an unlikely threat to the entrenchment of structural inequality in the United States. In fact, as volume contributor Eduardo Bonilla-Silva has warned, "by focusing on the instability of race as a category, [progressives] miss its continuity and social role in shaping everyday dynamics. . . . The elimination of race from above without changing the material conditions that makes race a *socially* real category would just add another layer of defense to white supremacy" (2003: 21, emphasis in original). In any case, if we are to heed the advice of Frederick Douglass that "power concedes nothing without demand" (1857/1985), then the massive redistribution of economic, social, and political power by race seems unlikely to happen without making specific demands for precisely that. And it is here that the movement for black reparations, in their particular demands for material redistribution, emerges as a more serious challenge to racial oppression. Indeed, it seems to me that a full accounting of the unjust enrichment of generations of white people of all social classes, combined with an actual redistribution of wealth based on this acknowledgment, would fundamentally transform the very meaning of the national collectively and the material positions of millions of people within it.

If the multiracial movement could broaden its agenda to include a frontal attack on the material dimensions of institutionalized racism, the reparations movement could stand a more nuanced discussion of the intended beneficiaries of redistributive efforts. Whether those on the right or left are ready for it, there is no doubt that more and more people are embracing multiracial identities. How, then, will the reparations movement understand the role of multiracial people—some of whom have African ancestry, some of whom have both African and white ancestry, and some of whom have neither African nor white ancestry—in political struggles for reparations? Are black reparations activists prepared to argue that these persons of color are not entitled to reparations for what amounts to global white supremacy? Certainly, it would be difficult to deny that global white supremacy sets up many racial and ethnic minority groups as targets, and reparations activists themselves suggest as much.

In the end, if global white supremacy is the problem, the answer is neither simply the recognition of multiracial identity nor a singular focus on Africans in the *Maafa* but rather broad-based multiracial coalitions at the level of the collective, one that prioritizes solidarity among all people who do not have the full benefits of whiteness. Movements like this already exist (see Anner 1996; Moore 2004). Although there may be contingents of the multiracial and reparations movement that have formed such broad-based multiracial coalitions against structural racism, the major themes that emerge in the claims-making in each case do not suggest that these contingents are setting the agenda. And perhaps most telling, these movements do not work in coalition with one another, and each has been in conflict to some extent with the traditional civil rights establishment. Those of us who *do* have the full or even some of the benefits of whiteness, either because we are white people, we have the benefits of white ancestry, or we are perceived as white, must actively work to give up what we earn unfairly and join in solidarity with large-scale movements to redistribute white privilege. In fact, we might all make a commitment, regardless of our racial identity category, to align ourselves with those groups most disenfranchised by white privilege (see Bonilla-Silva 2003).

Movements like this one do not preclude struggles to identify freely as multiracial or monoracial or neither. Nor do they preclude racial and ethnic minority groups from demanding safe spaces free of both white supremacist influences and the influences of well-meaning white antiracist activists. And for both white allies and multiracial people with white ancestry, a movement to disavow white privilege does not require them to disavow individual white people they love. In the same way that I myself feel no need to honor my white heritage as such, I take no offense should my own multiracial children decide to identify monoracially as black people. What would distress me, however, is if my children grew up without a critique of white privilege, including the ways in which my own whiteness, in some contexts, has afforded them advantages that other children of color do not have. Nonetheless, a unified struggle to understand, actively give up, and/or take back what has been lost to white privilege must be at the heart of the "next wave" of the civil rights movement—a program where all antiracist advocates can meet, regardless of whether they are people of color or white people, monoracial people or multiracial people, with or without African ancestry, or with or without white ancestry—and a program in which the compounding effects of racism, classism, and hetero/sexism are taken seriously. It is also this kind of battle against the intersections of structural inequalities, not monoracialism per se, that I believe has the greatest promise of bringing relief for multiracial people and multiracial families.

▨ Notes

1. A much longer version of this theoretical discussion, as well as a longer version of my findings from the multiracial movement, appear in my work, "Strategic Ambiguity Meets Strategic Essentialism: Multiracial, Intersex, and Disability Rights Activism and the Paradoxes of Identity Politics," in *Research in Political Sociology,* Volume 13, 2004. Thanks to Elsevier Science for permission to incorporate these segments here.

2. Multiracial movement organizations and activists have not been unified in their demands for recognition. Some organizations have promoted a stand-alone multiracial identifier *with* the option to "check all that apply," but other organizations have resisted that option (Daniel 1998). Some individual activists are very vocal in their position that racial classification must end entirely. "Mainstream" multiracial organizations, however, do not reject the use of racial classification in and of itself but rather object to the use of monoracial identifiers only.

3. Although the concept of "culture" in sociology refers to both material and nonmaterial elements of social systems, I use the term here to refer to the nonmaterial components of social systems such as symbols, language, shared values, beliefs, norms, and cultural attitudes. By "structure," I mean not only the patterned relationships among status positions within social systems but the institutionalized, unequal distribution of social rewards (see Johnson 1997).

4. Given my sources, there is the danger that the most well-circulated claims, such as those of Charles Byrd, may not represent the most widely held positions among activists themselves. For example, as Sandra Welland explains, "Multiracial people with anti-racist politics express frustration with media reports that conflate all multiracial politics with the 'colorblind,' anti-affirmative action opinions on websites like [Byrd's] *Interracial Voice* and libertarian *Multiracial Activist.* While the editors of these online journals support Ward Connerly's Racial Privacy Initiative, a California Ballot measure proposing to end all racial classification, several membership-based multiracial organizations have issued counterstatements. Groups including the Association of Multiethnic Americans, the Hapa Issues Forum, and the MAVIN Foundation have called Connerly's initiative a setback to racial justice and misguided in the way it uses multiracial families as proof that race is an illegitimate category" (Welland 2003: 33).

5. As volume editor David Brunsma points out, several authors in this text alone have demonstrated that the census was never intended for self-identification.

6. *Maafa* is a Kiswahili word meaning "disaster" and is used by advocates "to describe over five hundred years of warfare and genocide experienced by African people under enslavement and colonialism and their continued impact on African people throughout the world. Until now, words such as 'diaspora' and 'holocaust' had been appropriated from outside African culture and therefore do not embody the experience of the African reality" (Winbush 2003a: 9).

7. According to Robert Westley (2003: 119), the state of Florida paid reparations to the survivors of the Rosewood massacre.

8. There is a debate, however, over which black people in the United States would count as materially disadvantaged enough to claim reparations. Some supporters expressed concern over including as beneficiaries elite black people who may be considered by other blacks as too elite to deserve reparations. Here, other advocates for reparations point out that *all* black people, regardless of economic class, should be eligible since reparations is not a need-based remedy but an entitlement. All black people share the same risks of institutionalized racism and should not be penalized for doing well financially, despite historical and present-day structural barriers (*Harper's* 2003: 87).

12

Selling Mixedness: Marketing with Multiracial Identities

Kimberly McClain DaCosta

Strange to wake up and realize you're in style.
—Danzy Senna (1998: 12)

Since the mid-1990s, social scientists have spent a considerable amount of time speculating about the meaning of and impact on group boundaries of the growing numbers of interracial families and multiracial-identified people in the United States. Most of that analysis has centered on the state. What would it mean, researchers have asked, if the state allowed and enumerated multiple race responses? How would such responses affect civil rights enforcement, and what do patterns of intermarriage between groups say about which racial boundaries matter most? (see Chapter 4, this volume; Gans 1999; Perlmann and Waters 2002; Sanjek 1996).

In our attempts to understand the social implications of new racial categories and increased interracial intimacy, however, we have ignored one of the most far-reaching and consequential institutions likely to shape new racial identifications and their meanings in the years to come—the marketplace. When the Census 2000 multirace data was released to the public, marketing industry professionals wasted no time in accessing and interpreting it. In 2001, the marketing magazine *American Demographics* began a series of articles examining and interpreting the new multirace numbers. Marketers are eager to understand the significance of a range of characteristics that delineate this demographic, most notably its largely urban and coastal geographic dispersal, its ethnic patterning, and its relatively young age.

Not surprisingly, marketers are also interested in the buying power of multiracials. According to a report by the Selig Center for Economic Growth, at $148 billion, the buying power of multiracials is about one-quarter that of African Americans but over three times that of Native Americans. Multiracial buying power is expected to increase at a faster rate than that of blacks or whites in the next few years (projected growths of 32.7 percent, 30 percent, and 26.5 percent, respectively, by 2007; see Humphreys 2002).

Currently marketers know only the broadest demographic characteristics of the multiracial population. What they seek to find out is who "the multiracial consumer" is—her tastes, habits, and beliefs—in order to market to her. According to one marketing analyst, "the growth of multiracial America . . . means that the time to figure out what multiracial means to today's consumers, whether it creates specific consumer marketing or communication needs, and exactly how to tap into the market was about five minutes ago, and it's time to catch up fast" (Wellner 2002).

Not only have corporate marketers been devising strategies to identify and target messages at "the multiracial consumer," but entrepreneurs have also begun to develop products designed to appeal to multiracials.[1] These entrepreneurs are largely of mixed descent or live in interracial families. They sell items like shampoo and greeting cards, each tailored to the specific "needs" of multiracial consumers. This marketing *by* multiracials, like the marketing *to* multiracials by mainstream companies, is about selling for profit. It is also motivated by—according to its purveyors—a desire for social recognition.

The creation of products for and the development of consumer profiles about multiracials is a new phenomenon. A relationship between marketing and multiracials, however, predates the ability to count this population. During the 1990s, racially ambiguous people and even interracially intimate scenes began to appear in advertisements designed to appeal to a broad, ethnically nonspecific audience. The construction of such images requires no knowledge about multiracials and their putatively unique habits and needs. Rather, their impact and advertisers' motivation for using such images lie in their symbolism—the ability to evoke for a viewer positive qualities, feelings, or desires. Of course, multiracialism's capacity to invoke such desirable qualities and even what is considered "desirable" are historically and context-specific.

Danzy Senna is right. Multiracials are definitely in style. But *why* are they "in style"? Moreover, what does the marketing of multiraciality imply about contemporary modes of racial formation and racial justice? Despite the fact that social scientists have long looked at consumption as a major means through which Americans define their identities and compete for social status (Bourdieu 1984; DiMaggio 1994), researchers have only just begun to explore the relationship between consumer culture and ethnic identity formation. Marilyn Halter (2000) demonstrates marketers' increasing reliance on ethnicity as a hook to stimulate demand for their product and develop brand loyalty. Moreover, she argues that the marketplace is a site through which people learn representations of ethnic groups (their own and others) and through which they can participate and enact culture. Arlene

Davila (2001) argues that marketers shape public perceptions of the culture as well as the relevance and influence of racial groups by determining the kinds of racialized images we see.

■ Marketing Multiraciality in the Age of Target Marketing

Mass marketing—crafting one-size-fits-all messages—reached its peak at midcentury. Since the 1940s, segmented marketing has steadily supplanted it. The difference between the two strategies, simply put, is that mass marketing approaches differentiate between products, while market segmentation differentiates between consumers.[2]

Segmentation by race and ethnicity did not begin to gather momentum in the industry until the late 1960s. As early as the 1940s, however, companies began to recognize the money to be made by getting African Americans to buy their products. To capture black dollars, they began to advertise their products in black-owned and consumed media outlets. Lizabeth Cohen (2003) dubs these early attempts to reach African Americans "colorblind advertising" because the ads used were largely the same as those featured in mainstream media outlets. Many African Americans saw the mere fact that companies were advertising in black media outlets as a symbol of greater social acceptance. Gradually, African Americans called for advertisements that included black people and reflected their culture. In response, companies began to craft messages specifically designed to reach African American consumers (and later Latinos and Asian Americans). By the late 1990s, we began to see the creation of advertisements with all-black casts that appeared in mainstream media outlets and which appealed to a mass audience. Budweiser's "Whassup?!!" campaign is perhaps the most successful example of this phenomenon. Despite its success, the use of all-nonwhite casts to reach ethnically nonspecific consumers is still a rare event (Walker 2003, Wynter 2002).

From one vantage point, marketers' interest in multiracials looks like just another manifestation of the ethnic target marketing in which they have engaged for years. Recognizing a growing multiracial population with purchasing power, marketers seek to attract their dollars and so begin to market to that population. From another point of view, the marketing of multiraciality appears different than marketing toward other ethnic groups. When marketers began to court African American dollars, African Americans were already defined as a distinct social group with distinctive values and ways of thinking and acting. Multiracials are not yet so clearly defined. The category "multiracial" encompasses people of a broad range of racial and ethnic ancestry combinations. One could argue that this situation is no different from the construction of Latinos and Asian Americans as racialized groups in which diverse immigrant populations are lumped into overarching categories on the basis of language difference (e.g., Spanish) or the logic of racial sameness (e.g., Asian). The "lumping" of a diverse group of multiracials, however, is predicated on the logic of *multi*raciality, within which language, tradition, *and* racial identification vary.

Such variability poses a challenge for marketers figuring out just who "the multiracial consumer" is. The challenge, however, is not insurmountable. To a considerable degree, when marketers recognize and cater to market segments, they have contributed to reinforcing those divisions (Davila 2001, Cohen 2003). As a sort of self-fulfilling prophecy, they create what they appear to only reflect and feed back to consumers an image of what they are supposed to be (Frank 2000). In this respect as well, however, multiracial marketing may prove to work differently. As I discuss in more detail later, some marketers do indeed emphasize the commonalities among multiracials and their collective *difference from* "monoracials." This will likely strengthen some segment of the population's sense that multiracials are a distinct class of people. Much of the marketing of multiraciality, however, emphasizes an ideal of racial harmony and the transcendence of racial division through racial blending and cultural hybridity.

■ Defining the Multiracial Consumer and Identifying Her Needs

Despite the diversity of the multiracial population, marketers appear to be developing a profile of just who the multiracial consumer is. Much of that profile is driven by demographic data (see Table 12.1). In an early article on the multirace data published in *Forecast,* the concentration of multiracials in Hawaii is highlighted. Hawaii, we are told, "is home to the nation's largest share of multiracial consumers." The author goes on to characterize the Hawaii data as the "first look at the multiracial market" and informs us that multiracials in Hawaii are "more likely to live with family than average" (Wellner 2001). In subsequent articles in *American Demographics,* researchers pay more attention to the racial breakdown of this population and delineate multiracial buying power by ethnic subgroup (the greatest of which, according to industry analyses, is that of Asian-white biracials; see Whelan 2001). They are particularly attuned to the age of multiracials, who are disproportionately young. Of the two or more races population, 42 percent is under age eighteen, compared to 25 percent of those who indicated one race only (US Bureau of the Census 2001c).

Demographics, however, merely sketch the contours of a multiracial market, alerting marketers to its statistical existence and general characteristics. They do not by themselves constitute markets. The creation of a market requires some interpretation of what those numbers mean—of what makes this demographic different from others. To get a better sense of how a multiracial market is being constructed, a good place to look is at the

Table 12.1 Selected Population and Economic Characteristics by Race

	Multiracial[a]	Black	Asian	White
2000 population (in millions)	6.8	34.7	10.2	211.5
US population (percentage)	2.4	12.3	3.6	75.1
Under 18 years old (percentage)	41.9	31.4	—[b]	23.5
Geographic dominance (percentage)	40.0	54.8	48.8	34.4
	West	South	West	South
Buying power (in billions of dollars)[c]	148.1	588.7	254.6	5,800

Source: US Bureau of the Census 2001c, 2002; Humphreys 2002.

Notes: a. "Multiracial" refers to those who marked more than one race on the census. All other race figures are for those who chose single-race responses.

b. No data available.

c. Buying power is another term for disposable personal income, defined as "the share of total personal income that is available for spending on personal consumption, personal interest payments, and savings" (Humphreys 2002: 8).

companies developing products specifically for multiracial consumers. Curls is one such company. Curls bills itself as "a premium, ethnic hair care company whose purpose is to deliver quality products that cater to the unique needs of today's multi-ethnic market." The company tagline reads "Curls. . . . Because your curly hair is different from the rest" (www.curls.biz).

Purveyors of the various products developed specifically for multiracial consumers—be they books, conditioners, or cards—emphasize a special need that they claim multiracial consumers share. The owners of Melting Pot Gifts, for example, have developed a line of interracially themed greeting cards. They assert that the need for such cards arises from the "substantial number of interracial families and couples," many of whom, they claim, "want cards that look like them. Children of these couples are reassured by cards with pictures of children that reflect their identity" (www.meltingpotgifts.com).

"Need" is a highly malleable and manipulable concept. Making decisions about what we buy often involves distinguishing between our need for the thing purchased and our desire for it. In some cases, like clean water and food, most of us can agree we need such things, for without them we will die. In other cases, such as when a child claims he "needs" the latest electronic game, most of us would agree that is not a need but rather a desire. Needs and desires, however, are not always so clearly distinguishable. What we strongly desire, we often feel we desperately need. Moreover, different people define needs and desires differently (Baudrillard 2000).

It is standard operating procedure in the marketing arena to make desires feel like needs. The rationale of need serves a twofold purpose. First, claiming people need a particular item is intended to make the case that the product performs a service. Second, claiming that a group has needs to be met reinforces the idea that the group is distinctive from others as it stimulates demand. In the world of advertising, the delineation of needs goes hand in hand with the construction of a market.[3]

The promotions for Curls delineate a market of "bi/multi racial women and girls with naturally curly hair" for whom Curls was "truly created." According to Curls, *Women's Wear Daily* was set to focus a "spotlight" on the company in the December 2003 issue that would have discussed "the needs of multi ethnic hair care, and how CURLS is fulfilling an unfulfilled need in an overlooked market."[4] In an example of even more specific market segmentation, Curls has created a line of products marketed specifically to "racially mixed *girls* with naturally curly hair" (my emphasis). It is called "Curly Q's."

What, then, are the needs of multiracial women and girls as seen through the marketing department at Curls? Although the supposedly unique needs of racially mixed girls and women are not explicitly stated in the ad copy, a set of "needs" are delineated nonetheless through the vehicle of "customer reviews." The most often repeated "need" is for a way to control, make shiny, and moisturize one's curls.

A common advertising strategy is to establish (or make claims about) the superiority of one's product—why this shampoo and not others, for example, will do the job. In the testimonials used and company claims made by Curls, however, seldom are the particular ingredients in Curls or Curly Q's discussed. Instead, the market at which the products are pitched serves as endorsement enough for the product itself. That is why in almost every testimonial, the customer's relationship to multiracialism is communicated. Sometimes this relationship to multiracialism is conveyed subtly, as in the following testimonials.

> I can't tell you how happy I am with your products. They "understand" my hair. After trying product after product for as long as I can remember, I was thrilled to find Curls. Curls products bring out the best in my biracial hair without weighing my curls down or leaving my hair greasy or "heavy" feeling. . . . Curls lets my hair retain it's [*sic*] own "happy spirit" without taking a [*sic*] time out of my busy schedule. . . . Thanks so much for developing a product that knows my hair! (C. Donnow, www.curls.biz)
>
> I absolutely LOVE the products! My hair is moisturized without feeling greasy, and it's soft and swingy—yet the curls and waves are defined. I'm thrilled. Thanks for thinking outside of the box. It's refreshing to be able to use products that are more specific to my biracial hair type, instead of my constant experimental mix-n-match routine. (H. Holliman, www.curls.biz)

These descriptions accomplish several tasks at once. First, they establish that mixed-race women share a common dilemma in finding the right products for their hair type. Moreover, the statement that the company "understands" a customer's hair implies that the company—whose president, Mahisha Dellinger, is of mixed descent—has an insider's knowledge of that presumably unique experience that allowed her to develop the products. At the same time, such descriptions conjure up an image of the characteristics that typify "mixed hair" (defined, shiny curls and waves, not coarse, dull kinks or frizz)—if only the right products are used.

Finally, in these testimonials, racially mixed women's hair is implicitly, and sometimes explicitly, contrasted to that of African American women. About Curly Q's, one couple writes:

> we are amazed at the difference the products have made in the texture of our daughter's hair. We have tried just about every African-American hair care product in the market place for children. We have a bi-racial (Black/Caucasian) child and this is the first product in the market place that we have come across that unequivocally has made it easier to maintain our child's hair. . . . We highly recommend the Curly Q's products to all parents of bi-racial children. (www.curls.biz)

The delineation of this market has, in my opinion, disconcerting race-making capacities. In order to buy into the rationale that mixed-race women have unique hair care needs, one must believe that the kind of curly hair such women have is different *in a generalizable way* from the curly hair of racially unmixed women and girls. As we know, however, lots of women (including African American women) have curly hair and have managed to "care" for it all these years without Curls or the statistics necessary to identify a multiracial market. Such a claim relies for its impact on the folk belief that there is an inherent bodily difference between the races that expresses itself in *predictable* ways when the races mix (without ever needing to say so directly).[5] Although it may be true that many people of partial African descent have corkscrew curls, it is also true that many do not. Moreover, the universe of racially mixed women and girls is far larger than the population of people of partial African descent.

I assume that that the intention of Curls' founder is not to reinscribe biological notions of race, but rather to delineate a characteristic fairly widespread among people of partial African descent (curly hair), package it as a point of cultural uniqueness that unites the racially mixed together, and use that to sell them hair care products. Curls is also capitalizing on the desire of those who purchase it to believe that they are part of a definable, knowable group of women.

■ Multiracials as Branding Tool

Even before the 2000 Census reported multirace statistics, images of multiracials were used to sell things. Although certainly not ubiquitous,[6] depictions of multiracials *as such* began to appear with some regularity during the 1990s. Advertisements for items like jeans, sneakers, laundry detergent, and pain reliever depicted mixed-race people both well known and anonymous.

Multiraciality itself is becoming a branding tool. Unlike target marketing, in which a message or product is created to appeal to a particular demographic, this kind of marketing uses multiracialism to appeal to a mass audience. By definition, such images, created before there were statistics and industry research reports on multiracials, rely on stereotypes, clichés, and dominant ideas of racial mixedness. That is not to suggest that the market research currently proceeding (in large part because statistical data on multiracials are now readily available) will result in more "accurate" depictions of multi-racials. Rather, without any empirical information about the basic demo-graphic characteristics of this "group," the image of multiracials *can only be* based on culturally dominant or resonant ideas about this population.

In the United States, the multiracial body has often served as a resonant symbol for Americans' racial anxieties. At times multiracials have been vili-fied as harbingers of the death of particular cultural communities or depicted as manifestations of the degeneracy of human populations or as evidence of their parents' traitorous disloyalties. They have also been celebrated as "bridges" of racial harmony and unity, possessors of an inherent disposition against prejudice, and a maverick, new people.[7] It probably will surprise no one to learn that advertisements depicting multiracials nearly always em-ploy the latter symbolism. To do the former would be unwise, to say the least, in trying to appeal to a mass audience that includes a near majority nonwhite population. But the growing use of such multiracial images has more to do with convergences between trends in advertising generally and the cultural and social position of multiracials.

Multiracial demographics and the symbolism of racial mixedness fit very nicely into an advertising model that has dominated the industry since the 1970s. "Hip consumerism," as cultural critic Thomas Frank dubs it, is defined by advertising that draws from the symbols of 1960s counterculture and offers to "help consumers overcome their alienation, to facilitate their nonconformity and . . . celebrate[s] rule breaking and insurrection." As a commercial style, he argues, hip is everywhere—"a staple of advertising that promises to deliver the consumer from the dreary nightmare of square consumerism" (Frank 1997: 28, 32).

Much of the content of this "hip" consumerism draws from and seeks to appeal to youth. Since the mid-1940s, when the teenage demographic began to be recognized as a unique stage of life "with its own language, customs, and emotional traumas" (Cohen 2003: 319), marketing to teens has expanded exponentially (Linn 2004). Other forms of segmented mar-keting, not only by race and ethnicity but also age and gender, have as well. For an industry whose modus operandi is to craft "hip" messages, target ethnic audiences, and appeal to the young, multiracialism must seem a tailor-made marketing vehicle. First, as industry reports always point out, multiracials are disproportionately young. Forty-two percent of multiracials were born after 1982. In some regions, like parts of Hawaii and the San

Francisco Bay area, they make up a substantial proportion of the local population. The overall growth in interracial births suggests that younger audiences may have more familiarity and comfort with multiracials, particularly in those areas where they are a significant demographic presence.

■ Packaged Rebellion

One of the earliest ad campaigns to use interracialism to craft a hip brand image was Benetton. Seeking to associate its brand with a fight against racism, this late 1980s campaign featured a racially mixed cast of models—a relatively rare phenomenon in fashion advertising at the time.[8] The models were often arranged in ways to visually heighten their physical differences—very dark skin, hair, and eyes next to very light. Their attack on social convention was made in the form of posing models in interracially intimate scenes. The campaign garnered the company praise and criticism. The most controversial ad featured a bare-chested black woman breastfeeding a naked white baby. From one perspective the image depicts crossracial nurturance, caring, and bonding. From another it recalls African American women's use as wet nurses to white children under slavery.

The Benetton campaign pushed the limits of the public's tolerance for interracially intimate imagery back in 1988 (Blum 2000). Given the debate it stirred back then, it might be surprising to learn that two decades earlier, Mattel had created a mixed-race doll and marketed her as Barbie's cousin. "Colored Francie" was at once ahead of and behind her time, as her name (outdated even thirty-seven years ago) makes clear. When they brought her to market in 1967, company officials misread the demand for such a doll. She was discontinued after poor sales and concerns that she promoted interracialism (DuCille 1996, Halter 2000). Ironically, her unpopularity thirty-seven years ago has resulted in her being a very hot (and pricey) collectors item among doll enthusiasts.[9] Currently there is no Barbie explicitly marketed as a multiracial doll, but Mattel has developed a line of racially ambiguous friends of Barbie (that's *friends,* not cousins).

A decade after the Benetton campaign, Levi Strauss began a new campaign to bolster flagging sales of Levi's jeans. To do so, they sought to appeal to young consumers by crafting a campaign that centered on "assertions of the brand's authenticity" and that used images that were "familiar yet utterly surprising" (Kane 1998a). As part of that effort, the creative people at TBWA Chiat/Day in San Francisco (Levi Strauss's ad firm) published an ad showing a brown-skinned woman with a golden afro holding a sign that read, "I can't be prejudice [*sic*], I'm mulatto." The ad uses discursively familiar elements of racial mixedness. Decked out in flared low-riding (or is that "hip-hugging") jeans, her image recalls the 1960s counterculture.

According to its creators, the campaign of which this ad was a part sought to craft an "unconventional, streetwise attitude . . . to take fashion

ads from the catwalk to the sidewalk" (Kane 1998b). Mixed ethnicity symbolized this "attitude," as many of the ads, some illustrations, "blend ethnicities and blur racial definitions." According to the ad manager on the
project, the campaign is "a virtual melting pot of cultures and races linked
by similar interests and diversity." Although the "mulatto" ad is supposed
to be streetwise, authentic, and hip, the mixed-race character's use of an
outdated, even offensive, term to refer to herself belies such assertions. The
notion that multiracials cannot be prejudiced is a recurring (if absurd) con-
ceit about multiracialism. Finally, the misspelling of "prejudiced" is, I suspect, included for an added dose of "streetwise authenticity." According to
a marketer working on a related Levi's campaign at the time, the creators of
the ad seemed unaware of what she called the "ridiculous" and "offensive"
nature of the ad. The creators, she said, "didn't get it." She attributed their
lack of sensitivity to the fact that all of them were white. Whether or not
their whiteness explains the content of the ad, I do not know. Neither do I
know if the Levi's marketers "didn't get it." But maybe they did not have
to. Advertisements sell fantasy, not necessarily reality. The image of the
"mulatto" used in this ad represents what people (or at least the makers of
the image) want to believe and communicate about multiracials.

■ "I Am Tiger Woods": Multiracials as Symbols of the "New Economy"

Levi Strauss was not the only company to capitalize on the symbolism of
multiracials for marketing. Since the mid-1990s, companies like IKEA,
Tylenol, Nike, Verizon, and General Electric have featured multiracials in
their ads. Although multiracials were sometimes used to convey authenticity or rebellion, they were also used as symbols of the "new." The "unexpected" that marketers in the age of hip consumerism were after is embodied in the juxtaposition of racialized physical features in one body. This
"look" has been particularly sought after in an era of technological change
and globalization. According to casting agent Jerry Saviola, "The multiracial look screams 'current, youthful, and urban.' And it also evokes a certain authenticity. . . . Eight strawberry blondes in a cybercafe wouldn't be
realistic" (Whelan 2001). I think it is safe to assume that if this advertiser
saw several redheads in a café sipping lattes while surfing the Internet he
would find it perfectly *realistic*. What he means, rather, is that commercials
with all-white casts are conventional, but so too are those with integrated
casts. We have seen such images too often for them to signal something
new. Images of multiracial people, however, have been relatively rare in
media until now and thus awaken the viewer to a change because of their
difference. Says another casting agent, Paula Sindlinger, "The mix of Asian
facial features and kinky hair . . . conjures up an immediate sense of both

globalization and technology. The blended look says 'we're all in this together' and that the 'world's getting smaller'" (Whelan 2001).

It is perhaps not surprising that in the 1990s, when the rapid development of Internet commerce was hailed as the beginning of a "new economy" in which the old rules no longer applied, multiracials as a "new people" were chosen symbols. Perhaps the best known example of the marriage of multiracials and markets is the relationship between Nike and Tiger Woods. After he became the youngest person to win the Masters in 1997, commentators prophesied that Tiger would democratize the elitist and racially exclusionary game of golf. People of color, they reported, would now become interested in golf. Children from all walks of life would be able to compete on the green unfettered by old rules about money and pedigree (Dorman 1996).

Soon thereafter, Woods signed an endorsement deal with Nike worth an estimated $30 million. Nike enlisted Woods at a time when it was suffering serious attacks to its public reputation. During the 1990s, Nike had shipped most of its manufacturing jobs overseas to factories in which its employees labored in sweatshop conditions.[10] Nike's public relations offensive sought to rebuild its public image from that of ruthless profit maximizer to that of a "democratized, soulful corporation"—a strategy pursued by many firms at the time (Frank 2000: 252). One of the earliest Nike ads using Tiger's image featured children—boys and girls—of a wide variety of ethnicities on a misty golf course, clubs in hand, looking earnestly into the camera while each uttered in succession, "I am Tiger Woods." Every child, the ad implied, could be Tiger because Tiger was a little bit of everybody. By this time, Tiger's mixed ethnicity was quite well reported. Shortly after the Masters, he had explained to Oprah and her millions of viewers that as a child he had created a name for himself ("cablinasian") that incorporated all of his ethnoracial ancestry. In the Nike ads, Tiger's racial mixedness is positioned as a democratizing, unifying force.

Contrast this portrayal to the use of another famous athlete's image in advertising. Michael Jordan has received perhaps more endorsement deals than any other athlete. Jordan's black silhouette soaring to the hole is immediately associated with Nike.[11] In many of those ads, however, Jordan's athletic accomplishments are portrayed as almost superhuman. Although everyone may have wanted to "be like Mike," such a possibility was merely a fantasy.[12] "I *am* Tiger Woods," however, says we already are like Tiger, notwithstanding his extraordinary athletic accomplishments. Although they may be as out of reach as those of Jordan, his racial mixedness makes him accessible to all.

Woods is popular as an endorser because of his mixedness, not in spite of it—a point his father Earl Woods recognized early on. Commenting on Tiger's popularity with companies looking for endorsers, Earl Woods told a

Newsweek reporter, "For marketing purposes, Tiger's mixed heritage goes off the charts" (Leland and Beals 1997). However, the market appeal of mixed-race bodies extends beyond Woods himself. According to one of my contacts who manages talent featured in ad campaigns, he now receives many requests for so-called ethnically ambiguous actors. This practice is either widespread enough, sexy enough, or both to have warranted an article in a recent Sunday *New York Times* (La Ferla 2003). Why the appeal? Says one executive of an advertising and trend research company, "Both in the mainstream and at the high end of the marketplace, what is perceived as good, desirable, and successful is often a face whose heritage is hard to pin down" (La Ferla 2003: 1).

■ Consumer Culture and Racial Justice

The marriage of the market and multiraciality raises several questions about the relationship between consumption and racial justice. For example, what does it say about contemporary modes of racial domination that images invoking interracial mixing are increasingly sought after, when just a few years ago they were rare and when used, as in the Benetton ad, were employed as much for their ability to shock as to "fight racism"? Is multiracials' quest for representation in the marketplace significantly different from that of other ethnoracial groups? What does the focus on representation obscure about other aspects of racial inequality?

Racialized groups have long understood the connections between consumption and racial justice. Organizers of the sit-ins of the civil rights movement, for example, recognized that access to white consumer establishments was essential to ensure blacks' access to a full range of goods and services. They understood as well that the conditions of such access (segregated versus integrated) were symbolic of the level of dignity and respect afforded African Americans in the society at large. Moreover, civil rights organizers understood that owners respond when their profits or livelihoods are threatened. Their actions politicized consumption in order to achieve social justice.

Racialized groups have also understood the importance of representation in media in their quest for full and equal citizenship. Advertising's scope and reach is so extensive that it has the power to shape public perceptions of social groupings: which ones exist, their relevance, and their influence. As such, civil rights organizations like the National Association for the Advancement of Colored People (NAACP) and National Council of La Raza monitor the degree and kind of representations of African Americans and Latinos in advertisements.

Moreover, in public discourse of late, politicians explicitly equate consumption with democratic participation and good citizenship. Increasingly, they encourage citizens to view themselves in a market relationship to government. We are encouraged to shop around for social services and to "vote with our pocketbooks" to signal our political preferences and beliefs. In times of economic downturn, politicians and economic analysts encourage Americans to consume more as a means of doing our part for the country by way of stimulating the economy (see Cohen 2003; Klinenberg 2002).

Like other racialized groups in the United States, multiracials couch their demands for full recognition as citizens with calls for companies to recognize them as a market. Mary Murchison-Edwards of the Interracial Club of Buffalo, for example, encourages people to buy products with multiracial themes, whether or not they reflect one's family background. She says, "We need to show there's a market for these products by supporting the companies that make them" (Van Kerckhove 2005).

One could assume that Murchison-Edwards believes recognition as a market is a proxy for greater social recognition as a group. Given advertising media's reach, that is likely. The question, then, becomes whether social recognition is equivalent to social justice. It strikes me as an ironic twist of the politics of consumption that racialized groups not only welcome but also seek out the opportunity to be pitched to—to be *sold,* as it were. The danger in the marketing of multiracialism (or any other ethnoracial identity) is not that multiracials will receive social recognition.[13] Rather, it is when "recognition" (be it in the form of representation in advertisements or in the census) is substituted for a politics of civic and economic equality. Boycotts and representation in advertisements are not the same thing. The former uses consumption as a leverage point to secure something else—access to institutions, fair wages, or respect, for example. The latter treats consumption as a political end in itself and is oriented toward the right to consume more—to be marketed to—and is delinked from broader social concerns.

In the ways that multiraciality is being marketed, there is cause for both optimism and concern. A commercial for a pain reliever (Children's Tylenol, 2002) in which a white father stays home from work to care for his ailing Asian son is a welcome representation of interracial intimacy. The decision to use a white mother and her daughter of African descent in an ad for pain reliever (Motrin IB, 2001) when interracialism is not the focus of the message is a subtle recognition of changing social norms concerning race. Yet, although there are more representations of interracial intimacy in popular culture than in the past, such ads are rare. Many companies are reluctant to use such images, concerned that they are inconsistent with their brand's image or that they will offend their customer base.[14]

Currently advertisers use interracial imagery in a limited set of lifestyle contexts and to invoke a rather narrow set of feelings. Too often, advertisements featuring images of multiraciality repeat rather than challenge racial stereotypes. The images of multiracials now put forth by advertisers echo older images of the mulatto but include only those elements that are putatively positive in the age of hip consumerism. She is a bridge between racial groups, one who goes against social convention, and one who signals the future. Like the image of the Hispanic consumer generated by advertisers, the image of the multiracial is "not altogether an original development. Instead, it is better regarded as an archetype, constituted by motifs that, while adaptable, persist across generations" (Davila 2001: 61).[15]

Such "archetypes" obscure more about social reality than they illuminate. Although some analysts would like to claim that the marketing of multiraciality reflects a trend toward a "post-racial America" (Walker 2003), this assessment is premature. Note that nearly every article about multiracial public figures, be it Tiger Woods, Vin Diesel, or Mariah Carey, says something about the significance of their racial mixedness. That which receives so much attention can hardly have been transcended. Rather, I think it more accurate to say that the interest in mixed-race bodies and particularly in multiracial celebrities is an example of what Thomas Holt has identified as "a shift in the terrain of racism." "Could it be," he asks, "that the issue now is less the utter ignorance of other cultures, as in times past, but too great a surface (sound-bite) familiarity; less stereotypes of the other than the voracious consumption of its metonymic parts?" (2000: 108).[16]

The implications of the marketing of multiraciality for racial justice are economic as well. Some analysts suggest that the "ethnically ambiguous" trend signals the impending decline of niche marketing. The multiracial data, says one marketer, "takes the pressure off agencies to play it ethnically" (Whelan 2001). If many consumers connect with and respond to a multiracial actor, the logic goes, why craft several different campaigns targeted toward discrete ethnic communities? (Walker 2003).[17] In trying to develop consumers' identification with a message, some advertisers see the racial ambiguity of multiracial bodies as an asset because, it is presumed, viewers from many ethnoracial groups will search for and usually find something in an ambiguous appearance with which they can identify.[18] In other words, multiracials may help companies capture market share while simultaneously lowering their costs.

Attention to issues of multiculturalism and cultural hybridity is also influencing advertising firm creation. Firms specializing in ethnic markets have tended to specialize in one ethnic group (i.e., Asian American *or* African American consumers). These firms have tended to have a subcontractual relationship with what are known in the industry as "general market" (i.e., white) firms. Recently, however, ethnic niche firms have joined forces to combine their expertise in order to compete for a wider range of business. One such firm—GlobalHue—formed in 1999. Chief Executive Officer Don Coleman merged his African American urban market agency (DCA) with that of Montemayor Asociados, a Hispanic firm based in San Antonio, and Innovasia, an Asian American firm in Los Angeles. In 2003 it was ranked the top ethnic advertising agency in *Black Enterprise*'s annual survey (based on annual billings) (Hughes 2003). At the same time, other firms position themselves to reach consumers who cross traditional ethnic boundaries. The True Agency, formed in 2000, has published its own book detailing its marketing philosophy and strategy, called "Transculturalism." Despite the growth in multicultural marketing, however, the reality of racial segregation in the United States means that those companies who primarily advertise through direct mail or local media will continue to craft messages specific to one ethnoracial group (Wellner 2002).

Marketers explain their interest in multiracials as simply another form of ethnic target marketing, and that it is. But it is also part and parcel of a process of group making. Marketers have become aware of a multiracial market in large part because this population is now statistically visible. Ever in search of new markets, they will proceed by conducting research on this population so as to understand better how to appeal to its desires. Whether they actually uncover anything unique about this demographic's tastes, values, practices, or beliefs, marketers will continue to use images of multiracials in their advertising because they know this population is growing.[19]

In the world of advertising, increasingly marketers describe their research efforts as "ethnography," which implies that they have identified a social group whose habits and lifeways they seek to uncover. What this portrayal leaves out is the extent to which the cultures that marketers claim to merely represent are in part their own creations. The issue is not that marketers fabricate their messages independent of social context. Quite the contrary: they draw on existing culturally resonant narratives of the meaning of racial mixedness for the purpose of selling. In so doing, they shape social perceptions that multiracials exist as such. Through the marketplace, multiracials are being constituted as subjects. Given the abundance of marketing—its scope and reach—we cannot afford to ignore its impact on the racialization of groups.

■ Notes

1. I use the term "multiracial" to refer to a broad range of people, including those who identify or are identified by others as being of "racially mixed" ancestry, as well as to intermarried couples.

2. Market segmentation was first theorized in the late 1950s. It arose as a solution to marketers' concerns that in the aftermath of Americans' postwar purchasing frenzy, markets for various consumer goods were becoming saturated and profits could no longer be ensured. By identifying differences in the tastes and habits of consumers, marketers could appeal to those differences and stimulate demand. See Cohen (2003) for a history of market segmentation.

3. In her analysis of marketing to children, Susan Linn describes how marketers use the rationale of need to justify the creation and marketing of television programs to infants. The creators of *Teletubbies,* for example, argued that their show would reach an "underserved" market. The term "underserved," Linn points out, is "usually associated with people needing and not getting adequate health care and social services" (2004: 56). Infants' putative "need" to have programming directed at them is said to come out of their specific developmental stage of life. That almost

all infants go through these developmental stages constitutes them as a class and therefore a market.

4. A friend who saw a similar "spotlight" in *Lucky* first made me aware of Curls. *Lucky* is a magazine dedicated to shopping.

5. All hair is made up of the same substance. What distinguishes hair textures among people (not just women) is the shape of the hair follicle.

6. In American literature, themes of interracialism have been explored for over two centuries. A recent spate of popular films like *Far from Heaven* (2002), *Die Another Day* (2002), and *Save the Last Dance* (2001) have featured interracial couples (Jones 2002). In contrast, before the late 1990s, multiracials as such had been almost totally absent from advertising.

7. The list of these characterizations is extensive. In the 1920s, Marcus Garvey was particularly hostile to what he called the "traitorous mulatto leadership" of Negroes, and eugenicist Madison Grant wrote in *The Passing of the Great Race* (1921) that mixing between blacks and inferior immigrant groups produced an inferior, lower type. More recently, Japanese American leaders, responding to high rates of outmarriage in the 1990s, expressed concern that their community would "die out," and Molefi Asante, chair of African American studies at Temple University, stated that multiracial classification "could be very, very useful, because there is a need to define who is in and who is not. . . . In fact, I think we should go further than that—identify those people who are in interracial marriages" (Wright 1994).

8. Esprit and Cherokee are two other clothing companies that began featuring interracial casts, but unlike Benetton, their ads focused on interracial friendship rather than interracial intimacy.

9. For photos of Colored Francie and a collector's assessment of her value today, see http:/kattisdolls.crosswinds.net/faces/cousins.htm.

10. Holt states that the child workers in Indonesia who make Nike shoes earn roughly two dollars for an eleven-hour workday (2000: 110).

11. Nike paid Jordan $20 million *annually*—"more than the total annual wages earned by Indonesian workers who made the shoe" (Holt 2000: 110).

12. Gatorade's campaign with Jordan popularized a jingle with the refrain, "If I could be like Mike."

13. There are many competing analyses of the consequences of multiracial recognition for racial politics. Most center on the effects of state enumeration. Critics of such enumeration include Spencer 1997.

14. My evidence for this claim is anecdotal at present. During a rather serendipitous trip to a bookstore in Manhattan, a casting agent approached my niece and me because she wanted to use us in an ad for a linen company. When I asked her to describe the casting call (and told her of my academic interest in the subject), she rather sheepishly confessed that she was told to go out and find "white-looking black women" with their kids. If she finds a person she wants to photograph and it turns out they are part of an interracial family, she said, she has to refuse them. Such images, she surmised, do not fit the family image the company is after. In this ironic example, the company sought an image of racial mixedness ("white-looking black women") as a representation of African American families. Racial mixedness is desired as long as the social context of that mixedness (racially different parents, the family) is invisible. Apparently, company executives thought "black-looking black women" unsuitable representatives of African American families. An image of racial mixedness is employed to cultivate the sense that the company is sensitive to diversity without offending anyone. According to my contacts in an ad firm for a major beer company, company executives insisted on changes to one ad featuring a black man and white woman in an intimate setting. These marketers believe the

company executives did so because they were not personally comfortable with the intimacy displayed between the characters.

15. Arlene Davila (2001) contends that the image of the Hispanic consumer invoked by US advertising firms draws from dominant ideas constructed by Latin-American intellectuals about the distinctive nature of Latin American culture—one constructed in contrast to the United States. In this formulation Latin American is to family, religion, and tradition as the United States is to technological innovation, materialism, and a lack of culture.

16. The best (and certainly the funniest) distillation of the public's desire to consume mixed-race bodies is, in my opinion, comedian Dave Chapelle's "Racial Draft" sketch (Chapelle's Show, Comedy Central, 2004). In it, various famous mixed-race people are "drafted" by representatives of racial groups in a forum modeled on professional sports' drafts. "The Jews" take Lenny Kravitz, whereas Tiger is drafted by "the blacks," much to the Asian delegation's annoyance. They draft the black rap group Wu Tang Clan.

17. Ethnic marketing companies are unhappy about this development because of its potential to take business away from them.

18. According to a Barbie spokesman, Kayla, Madison, and Chelsea (Barbie's new friends) are designed to look ambiguous so as to appeal to little girls of a broad range of ethnicities (Walker 2003).

19. Says one marketing analyst, "By the time the next Census comes around, multiracials may not look like such strange creatures anymore and marketers may by then have found the appropriate visual language to address them directly" (author not listed, Marketing Trendz newsletter, June 6, 2003).

Part 3

Socialization in Multiracial Families

13

It All Starts at Home: Racial Socialization in Multiracial Families

Kerry Ann Rockquemore, Tracey Laszloffy, and Julia Noveske

The most consistent and controversial finding in the growing body of research on the multiracial population has been that wide variation exists in racial identification (Gillem 2001; Korgen 1998–1999; Rockquemore and Brunsma 2002a; Storrs 1999). Although much of the literature has focused on documenting the identities that mixed-race individuals develop (Kilson 2001; Renn 2004; Rockquemore and Brunsma 2002a; Wallace 2001), exploring the factors that influence that development (Rockquemore 2002; Root 1997; Wijeyesinghe 1992, 2003), and theoretically modeling multiracial identity development (Gibbs 1989; Jacobs 1992; Kerwin and Ponterotto 1995; Kich 1992; LaFromboise, Coleman, and Gerton 1993; Poston 1990; Rockquemore 1999; Root 1990), the fundamental pattern is clear: in the post–civil rights era United States, multiracial people choose between several different racial identities.

We have argued elsewhere that researchers studying racial identity development need to shift their gaze from the *racial label* that individuals use to the *process* by which they have come to adopt that label as a racial self-understanding (Rockquemore and Laszloffy 2005). In other words, it is not that any one label is, in and of itself, more psychologically healthy, correct, or appropriate than another label. Instead, any racial identification can be approached by healthy (or unhealthy) pathways; by refocusing on the process of identity development, researchers can best determine the factors that shape how mixed-race people understand the world and their place in it.

In this chapter, we first outline a systemic model for understanding racial identity development among multiracial children and adolescents. We then focus exclusively on the family component of that model in order to describe the racial socialization processes at work in interracial families and how those processes may be different than racial socialization in monoracial families (see Rockquemore and Laszloffy 2005). We focus on family processes because it is so critical to racial development for multiracial children and because it allows a deeper consideration of how structural patterns shape even the most intimate of individual activities: parenting.

■ A Systems Approach to Racial Socialization

Sociological models of racial identity formation assume that individuals' racial identities are entirely structurally imposed and there is no "choice" in the matter (Espiritu 1992; Lee 1993; Omi and Winant 1994; Waters 1990). Similarly, psychologically informed models frame racial identity as a developmental process toward a singular endpoint (Cross, Parham, and Helms 1991). Although both types of models have been analytically useful, they are contradicted by recent research on the multiracial population that has repeatedly demonstrated that some element of "choice" exists in racial identification (Kilson 2001; Renn 2004; Rockquemore and Brunsma 2002a; Wallace 2001). For example, among mixed-race people who have one black and one white parent, some identify as biracial (Bowles 1993; Gibbs and Hines 1992; Kerwin et al. 1993); some as black (Rockquemore 1999; Storrs 1999); others as white (Rockquemore and Arend 2004; Root 1998; Twine 1997); some shift between black, white, and biracial identities, depending on the racial composition of the group they are interacting within (Rockquemore 1999; Root 1990, 1996a; Stephan 1992), whereas others refuse any racial designation (Daniel 1996b; Rockquemore 1999; Zack 1993). In addition to the variation that exists, racial identification has been shown to shift according to where and when the individual is asked (Harris and Sim 2002; Renn 2004).

Given that multiracial people vary in their racial self-understanding, we approach racial identity development in interracial families from a theoretical framework that recognizes the structural and psychological factors that affect children today. Specifically, we approach racial identification using a systemic perspective that recognizes that children are embedded in a complex web of structural, institutional, and interpersonal relationships and shaped by historically and culturally rooted rules about racial boundaries, group alignments, and power. In terms of racial identification, multiracial children develop a sense of self-understanding that is subject to both the broad societal parameters of racial group identification, and the more subjective and negotiated microreality of interpersonal relationships.

Structural Factors

Mixed-race children in the United States are born into a social world in which norms of racial categorization arise from a foundation of white supremacy. For example, in the United States our understanding of who is black is determined by the one-drop rule of racial categorization that emerged during slavery

(Davis 1991). Although the multiracial movement has begun to question the one-drop rule (Spencer 1999) and multiracialism has become more common in the media and public discourse (see Chapter 12, this volume), mixed-race children with black ancestry continue to be considered black. Because racial categorization is determined by structural forces, parents' individual understanding of a child's identity may be in opposition to how the child is categorized in the broader world. Families do not decide the racial identity of their children independently but instead operate in a social context where longstanding racist rules determine racial group membership.

Institutional Factors

In addition to structural factors, families live in communities, their children attend schools, and they engage in local economies. Institutions have their own racialized attitudes, practices, and policies that reinforce and reproduce the prevailing societal definitions of race. Importantly, these institutions also serve as external socializing agents above and beyond the direct control of families and provide additional arenas in which children's racial identification can be validated or contested.

Relational Factors

Within and beyond families, children interact with others and, in the process, learn their social location by figuring out how they fit into the social world relative to others. In childhood, family members are the primary agents of socialization. As children age, they increasingly encounter others beyond the family. These extrafamilial relationships are often the testing ground for ideas, attitudes, and identifications that have been learned at home. At various times in their individual development (particularly in adolescence), the assessment of peers can supersede those of family members.

Individual Factors

Finally, individual children have unique physical characteristics that are largely unchangeable. These phenotypic traits are important because skin color, facial features, body types, and hair texture are associated with racial group categorization and constrain the choices that individuals have for racial identification.

We suggest this systemic model of racial identity development in order to provide a map of the multiple levels of factors that influence how mixed-race children learn to understand who they are and where they fit in our racialized social world. In this chapter, we focus exclusively on the parent-child link. We do so because parents are the primary agents of socialization in children's lives and because racial socialization in interracial families directly illustrates how the most intimate of microprocesses (racial socialization) are shaped by larger macropatterns in race relations.

■ Rethinking Racial Socialization

Parents are critical to children's development generally and to their racial identity development specifically because families are the primary learning environment for children. Ideally, families not only teach children about how to become responsible, caring human beings, but they also provide comfort, support, and protection for children as they face life in a racially stratified society. The task of raising children of color in a society that devalues them is a difficult task under the best of circumstances (Hardy and Laszloffy 1993). Because of the importance of race in shaping children's lives, minority families have a responsibility to consciously engage in racial socialization that will prepare them to effectively negotiate the complexities of a racialized world.

For decades, psychologists, sociologists, and social workers have studied the phenomenon of racial socialization within families of color to better understand how children learn about their roles, statuses, and location in the social structure. Research on racial socialization in African American families has focused on the ways in which black parents teach their children about racism, including preparing children for minority status, fostering positive beliefs about their cultural history and heritage that counter societal devaluation, and ensuring success in mainstream society (Hughes 2003). This literature suggests that most black parents engage in some process of racial socialization of their children (Bowman and Howard 1985) although women hold more responsibility for socializing than men (Thornton et al. 1990).

Racial socialization has typically been conceptualized as a way to understand how minority families transmit what it means to be a member of a particular racial group. However, we conceptualize racial socialization in a much broader way based on our belief that *all* parents teach their children specific racial attitudes, beliefs, and behaviors. In other words, it is not only minority parents who racially socialize their children but white parents as well. All parents, directly or indirectly, send their children messages about race and how to understand themselves racially. Those messages may be different in black and white families, but all children learn about racial difference.

In comparison to the explicit racial socialization strategies used by black families, the process in white families is both subtler and different in content. White children learn that they are white and to associate race with people of color. The extent of their racial awareness is limited to the rare occasions when they may find themselves in a situation where they are the racial minority (Frankenburg 1993). White privilege affords the opportunity to live one's life without having to think about how race shapes daily life and believing that race plays no role in opportunity structures (McIntosh 1998). Thus, white parents do indeed racially socialize their children. This process occurs indirectly, unintentionally, and subtly, but white children do, in fact, learn how to "be white," how to think about matters of race, how to locate themselves racially within the world around them, and how to view others on the basis of race (Lewis 2003).

Interracial families face unique challenges because of the historical legacy of white supremacy, the long-standing social barriers against interracial marriage, and the cultural norm of racial homogeneity in marriage patterns.[1] For interracial families, racial socialization is complicated for important several reasons. First, parents bring different racial identities, experiences, and ideologies to their relationship that may result in different ideas about how to racially socialize their children. In addition, the politics of race in our society are such that their mixed-race children exist in a marginal and undefined space. There is no clear community of mixed-race people or a comprehensive understanding of the mixed-race experience that can be used to guide racial socialization of mixed-race children in a positive, cohesive manner. Unlike white or black children, most multiracial children do not have a parent with whom they can directly identify as a multiracial person. Unless a parent is also mixed-race, the majority of mixed-race children learn about race from one or more adults who cannot completely understand their racial reality. This means that most mixed-race children rarely have the luxury of being raised by a parent whose own racial identity and socialization process are relevant to their experience.

Research on interracial families has largely focused on why people intermarry (Chow 2000; Heaton and Jacobson 2000; Matthijs 1993; Model and Fisher 2002; Qian 1997; Tucker and Mitchell-Kernan 1990; Yancey 2003c), societal attitudes toward interracial relationships (Fang, Sidanius, and Pratto 1998; Fiebert, Karamol, and Kasdan 2000; Korolewicz and Korolewicz 1985; Mills 1995), how interracial couples deal with external racism (Dalmage 2000; Hibbler and Shinew 2002; Hill and Thomas 2000; Root 2001; Zebrowski 1999), and how couples reconcile cultural differences within their relationship (Crohn 1995; Foeman and Nance 1999; Gaines 1997; Killian 2001; Luke and Luke 1998). However, no systematic investigation has been done of how interracial families racially socialize their children or how racial socialization affects children's racial identity development. This is a curious omission, given that individuals enter interracial relationships with different racial identities, group memberships, racial experiences, and worldviews. How they reconcile these differences and communicate them to their children should be a critically important area of research.

■ Factors That Influence How Individual Parents Approach Racial Socialization

The way that parents approach the racial socialization of their children depends not only on the broader societal definitions of race but on the socialization they received while growing up. For the sake of clarity, we discuss here the difference between racial socialization in black and white families. Most black parents try to instill in their children a sense of cultural pride, teach them about their group history and cultural practices, prepare them for racial bias, and help them learn how to function in a world stratified by race. As part of this process, black children learn that they live in a racially divided and unequal society where they are a member of a racially devalued group. This reality requires the development of skills for negotiating life in a racially oppressive environment. Whether overtly or covertly, consciously or unconsciously, most black parents prepare their children to cope with the challenges they may face. As a result, black parents of mixed-race children possess an explicit understanding of the realities of racism and racial inequalities and have a clear model for racially socializing their own children.

In contrast, most white children grow up to become adults who have never thought about what it means to "be white" and the benefits they derive as a result of their racial privilege.[2] Consequently, the vast majority of white children are implicitly socialized to associate "race" with "people of color" and therefore they do not learn to think of themselves as members of a race, nor do they learn to recognize the many ways in which their racial identity influences their lives. This can create a challenge for white parents of mixed-race children because these parents lack a clear model for actively addressing issues of race in parenting.[3]

Understanding white parents' racial socialization is particularly important because the majority of black/white interracial couples consist of a white female and a black male. Moreover, mothers provide most racial socialization of children in families. When we consider these two facts, it becomes clear that most black/white mixed-race children are raised in families in which the majority of their direct care and racial socialization come from white mothers.

Interracial couples, by definition, consist of individuals who have different racial identities, life experiences, and racial socialization. Each factor shapes a parent's ideological framework and directs how they articulate the social world to their children. Parents are constantly communicating both subtle and overt messages to their children about how the world works and their place in it. Whether or not they are conscious of it, parents prepare children to face the society as *they see it*. We use the concept *racial ideology* to describe the "racially based frameworks used by actors to explain and justify the racial status quo" (Bonilla-Silva 2003: 9). There are many different frameworks that individuals can use to understand contemporary race relations, but the dominant framework that has emerged in the post–civil rights era United States is "color blindness" (Bonilla-Silva 2003). Those with a color-blind ideology have a set of beliefs that deny the salience of race in the United States, ignore the existence of racial inequalities, and criticize those who speak about race. Underlying the belief in color blindness is the sense that the racial status quo is acceptable and that inequalities occur because of individual failings (as opposed to structural factors). In contrast to color blindness, individuals can view the racial status quo through various liberatory frameworks that challenge the current state of race relations, acknowledge the persistent reality of racial inequalities, and articulate the salience of race in shaping individual opportunities. Neither framework is specific to any particular racial group. Instead, we may find both blacks and whites who use color blindness as a framework to understand contemporary race relations.

Interracial couples challenge the racial status quo by their sheer existence. That often leads people to expect them to hold critical perspectives on race relations, given their experiences of racism, hostility, and disapproval from family members. However, researchers have often found the opposite. Erica Childs (2005) has documented how interracial couples frequently utilize color blindness as an ideological framework to understand their experiences, attributing racism to isolated incidents of individual prejudice and minimizing the effects of racism. Interracial couples who share a color-blind ideology claim that their friends, family, and others support their relationship. But later, they contradict their own narrative of family support by recalling various incidents and comments made by family members that indicate disapproval of their relationship (see Chapter 15, this volume). Childs also asserts that color blindness is not solely exhibited by white partners in interracial relationships. On the contrary, she also found black partners who described their own racial identity by saying, "I am a human," "I am part of the human race," or "I'm not a color."

Ultimately, racial ideology is the gas fueling the engine of racial socialization in interracial families. It directs the way that parents understand the social world and propels the explanations they give to their children. Although race is not a perfect predictor of racial ideology, we do know that interracial families are much more likely to have different ideologies present in the relationship than monoracial families. We turn now to a discussion of how differing ideologies translate into racial socialization practices.

▧ How Racial Ideology Affects Racial Socialization

Parents send various messages to their children about race that can become sites of tension for interracial families. We consider three types of racial socialization: (1) preparation for bias, (2) cultural socialization, and (3) racial group membership. Although each of these types of racial socialization has been discussed in the literature on African American families, we believe they manifest differently in interracial families. Specifically, we examine how each type of racial socialization occurs in interracial families, how they vary according to parents' racial ideology, and how that difference may affect their child's identity development.

Preparation for Bias

Most minority families prepare children for the potential discriminatory treatment they may encounter in the world because they are a person of color. This has been found to vary between groups such that African Americans are the most likely to prepare their children for the bias that they may experience as a black person in the United States (Hughes 2003). Even within black families, racial socialization messages vary by sociodemographic factors (Thornton et al. 1990). Thus, we can expect variation in interracial families in the degree to which they teach children that racism exists and how to identify and respond to discriminatory behavior.

Racial ideology is a critical factor in determining whether parents in interracial families prepare their children for bias. Those possessing a color-blind ideology tend to minimize the existence of discrimination and perceive racism in terms of individual acts of aggression. As a result, parents who have a color-blind ideology believe that discussing racism is only necessary *if* such an incident occurs. Preemptive work would only lead children to expect discriminatory treatment and may also create situations where children believe that racial discrimination is occurring when it is not. Given these views, we should not be surprised to find parents holding a color-blind ideology resistant to the idea of preparing children for bias.

In contrast, parents with ideologies that challenge the racial status quo believe that preparing children for the discrimination that they will *inevitably* encounter is a necessary component of raising children of color. In other words, parents holding a liberation ideology consider discrimination as an inherent part of the black experience. Thus, it would not make sense to raise children who are unable to identify and respond to racism. Preparation for bias may take on a number of different forms, ranging from explaining the difference between individual and institutional racism, to teaching skills to identify discriminatory behavior in both its subtle and overt forms, to encouraging strategies for dealing with bias, and/or to deciding when to confront racism and when to walk away.

Whether parents include preparation for bias in their racial socialization affects children's ability to respond to discriminatory behavior when it occurs. Adolescents often discuss the degree to which their parents prepared them (or failed to prepare them) for racism as critical to their ability to process such experiences. Derek Salmond is a fifteen-year-old boy whose story is featured in Pearl Gaskins's 1999 book, *What Are You? Voices of Mixed-Race Young People.* His narrative provides an illustrative example of racial socialization that includes a preparation for bias:

> Most people assume that I'm black. I always find that they're kind of surprised when they first meet my parents, or see them together, because they're black and white. And for the most part, no one's really had anything against it. I can only think of one problem that I've had. There was

a girl on my water polo team. We had started going out and doing stuff together with groups of friends. She told her father about me and he just wasn't going to have it. He didn't want his daughter to hang out with someone of another ethnicity. I was stunned at first, but I always knew it was going to happen eventually. It's something that both of my parents had prepared me for. They always made me aware that there is racism out there and that I was definitely going to stand out because I'm of a different ethnicity. In many cases, it was just my dad telling me about encounters he had had. And when I started seeing girls, he reminded me that I was different and that girls may decide not to like me because of that, or that their parents may have problems with that. And that just made it easier for me to cope. When it came about, it wasn't as striking a blow for me as it may have been for others who wouldn't have been prepared for it. (Gaskins 1999: 119–120)

For Salmond, preparation for bias was important in helping him understand why he was experiencing discrimination. It provided him with a broader social context so that he could conceptualize the behavior of his girlfriend's father as racism and not internalize the behavior as individual rejection. In this circumstance, racial socialization worked to soften the blow of discriminatory treatment and provided Salmond with the socio-psychological tools he needed to process it.

Importantly, Salmond notes that *both* his parents had prepared him for bias, even though he gives the specific example of how his father (who is black) taught him by sharing his own experiences. Although his parents felt that preparation for bias was important, we can just as easily imagine Salmond having parents whose color blindness led them to communicate nothing about discrimination. Such silence would have left him on his own to understand the racist incident.

Cultural Socialization

Minority parents often make attempts to foster positive beliefs about their group's cultural history and heritage that counter societal devaluation. These could include overt behaviors, such as reading about black history, celebrating group-specific holidays, and/or attending cultural events. But parents also send covert messages about cultural socialization by the lifestyle choices that they make, which include the racial composition of their neighborhood, friends, and voluntary associations.

Parents with different ideological orientations can send very different messages to their children. Those with a color-blind ideology, who wish to minimize racial and cultural difference, are likely to communicate to their children both overtly and covertly that they are members of the "human race." Or they may remain silent about the child's nonwhite ancestry, which is often equivalent to socializing the child as white. That is most likely to occur when the child is being raised solely by the white parent and that parent has a color-blind ideology, because she or he is both unlikely to make proactive efforts to teach children about their nonwhite cultural heritage or to see such practices as necessary. Charmaine Wijeyesinghe (2003) argues that some white parents fail to culturally socialize children and discourage them from developing a nonwhite identity out of a fear of being rejected in the process of the children's racial identity development.

Parents with challenging ideologies racially socialize their children in ways that are similar to minority parents. They proactively teach their child about what it means to be a black person in the United States because they believe that race is fundamentally important in shaping their child's reality. They also do not want to put their child at risk by failing to teach him or her about black culture as a primary cultural framework (Wallace 2001). In other words, they want their child to be able to fit in with, relate to, and feel comfortable around other black children.

One of the most important manifestations of cultural socialization for interracial families is also the subtlest. When multiracial young adults talk about their childhood cultural socialization, they frequently discuss the environment that their parents choose to live in and the racial composition of their social networks as sending powerful messages about blackness and whiteness. Kerry Ann Rockquemore and David Brunsma (2002b) found that one of the most salient predictors of what racial identity multiracial individuals choose is the racial composition of their social network. When children see people like them in their environment, it communicates the message that their parents value black people and black culture. Beverly Tatum argues that when a child with one black and one white parent grows up without ties to a black community, "it will be very difficult for the child to value his or her heritage. There will be no buffer against the negative messages about blackness in the wider society, posing a threat to the child's developing self-esteem" (1997: 177). She cautions that "white parents, especially, may tend to undervalue the importance of being able to see oneself reflected in one's environment." Marion Kilson (2001) supports Tatum's link between environment and identity by arguing that biracial children who are isolated from communities of color during childhood and adolescence can end up perceiving themselves to be culturally "white" and avoiding an identity of color and that light-skinned biracials will identify themselves racially as white.

Jared Medina Bigelow is a college student whose autobiographical narrative appears in Maria Root and Matt Kelley's *Multiracial Child Resource Book* (2003). Bigelow has one black and one white parent, and he explains how his parents culturally socialized him as white. He describes how their messages about whiteness both shaped his childhood identity and became a point of rebellion in adolescence:

> My life has always been supersaturated with the values and expectations of White America. From my youth, both my parents and the media subconsciously molded me to conform to the habits of my white peers. My peers accepted me to an extent, but somehow I was never "white enough"

to be one of them. I was "pretty cool for a Black kid," and I was always the one that stood out in a crowd, with my nappy head, caramel-colored skin and thick lips. My mother, who is White, always tried to make me see that it didn't matter whether or not I was Black or White because I was "special," I was both. Not a single one of my White friends could ever know what it was like to be me and I couldn't never fully know what it was like to be White. So my "specialness" rested on me being in a state of racial limbo that was impossible to describe to any member of either of my constituent races, an interesting place to be. Despite my mother's best efforts to comfort me, something still didn't feel right about my identity, and the other side of the spectrum would prove to be no less cold.

From my initial "White phase" I progressed to be "Black as can be" at age 15 or so. "White" became a four-letter word for me, and I'd have nothing to do with it for another three years. My household never fostered such feelings, so it follows that once I recognized my "Blackness" as an irreconcilable difference separating me from "them," I focused on it and nurtured it, making it my defining characteristic. (p. 160)

Bigelow's story ends with his development of a biracial identity after he went to college and was able to interact with other mixed-race people. His story is important, however, because it illustrates the way in which well-intentioned parents, operating from a stance of a color-blindness, can unintentionally create an unhealthy environment for racial identity development.

Racial Identification

Possibly the one area of greatest difference in racial socialization between interracial and monoracial families is how they socialize their children in terms of their racial identity. In same-race families, the focus of racial identity development is to try to encourage children to have a positive perspective on their blackness in spite of the pervasive societal devaluation of blackness. In short, there is an assumption that the child is black, and the parents work to build a positive black identity. However, in black/white interracial families, the child can identify as black, white, biracial, or as no race. This sets up a situation in which parents need to be in alignment with each other over the racial identification of the child and to send the child consistent messages about his or her racial group membership.

Here again, racial ideology creates a critical difference in how parents understand their child's racial identity. Among parents with a color-blind ideology, their denial of racism and racial inequalities leads them to encourage their children to identify as mixed-race with an emphasis upon whiteness. They may also orient their children to identify as white. In some instances, they may even orient their children to disavow race altogether by pretending it does not exist and, by default, reproduce their own white socialization. The common stories parents use to justify this position are that the children have "the best of both worlds," that they are teaching them to "not see race," and that "saying they are one or the other is like denying one of their parents."

Parents who have challenging ideologies are more likely to raise their children to identify as mixed-race with an emphasis on their blackness or to identify as black. This is in response to a recognition that the child will be viewed by others as black and that his or her opportunities will be affected by that designation. Adult children of interracial marriages often discuss how their parents' messages about racial identity influenced the way they came to understand themselves racially. Singer Lenny Kravitz described the relationship this way:

> Luckily, I was not one of those children [with insecurities about my racial identity]. I knew lots of them who were mixed "am I black? am I white? what am I?" I used to see kids at school who were fair like me or even more fair. They wanted to be white; they didn't want to be black because it's too hard being black. And then the white kids are like, "you're black, so get away from us," and the black kids are like, "you're white." I never had that. My mother had taught me: "your father's white, I'm black. You are just as much one as the other, but you are black. In society, in life, you are black." She taught me that from day one . . . you don't have to deny the white side of you if you're mixed, accept the blessing of having the advantage of two cultures, but understand that you are black. In this world if you have a spot of black, you are black. So get over it. (Norment 1994: 29)

Kravitz recounts a nuanced set of messages communicated to him by his black mother, who held a challenging ideology. She clearly understood his social location in a racially stratified society and had clarity about how he would be perceived by others. As a result, she was able to simultaneously affirm his existence as a mixed-race person while communicating the reality that he would be defined by others according to the one-drop rule. As an adult reflecting back on his childhood, Kravitz perceived this racial socialization as a benefit he had over other multiracial children and a significant factor in his racial identity development.

■ Conclusion

The United States is currently undergoing a transformation in race relations that can be seen in the blurring of racial categories in cultural representations, on bureaucratic forms, in public discourse, and most importantly in the ways that individuals understand their racial group membership. It is an awkward historical moment, where race is acknowledged to be socially constructed yet continues to influence opportunities and everyday interactions. Several decades after the passage of civil rights legislation, structurally rooted racial inequalities continue to exist. Yet, despite these persistent inequalities, Americans increasingly believe that race is declining in significance and are adopting "color-blind" ideologies. The simultaneous denial of racial inequalities and widespread desire to move "beyond race" provides a unique set of circumstances for parents raising mixed-race children. Their challenge is twofold: first, to become conscious of their own racial ideology and the messages they are sending to their children, and second, they must critically evaluate if the messages they are communicating create a healthy or unhealthy context for their children's racial identity development.

Yet, it is not only a difficult moment for parents raising multiracial children. It is equally awkward for researchers studying race relations. The confusing nature of what race is and how it functions begs serious questions for those studying racial identity development, several of which are implicit in our discussion. Primary among the unanswered questions is the distinction between parents' *race* and their *racial ideology* as an indicator of racial socialization. We have argued here that instead of assuming that parents' race determines how they racially socialize their children, a better indicator would be to consider their racial ideology. The examples chosen to illustrate various components of the model were intended to further the possibility that in the study of racial socialization, racial ideology may be more important than race.

In this chapter we have provided a conceptual model of how racial socialization in interracial families may manifest and how it influences racial identity development in multiracial children. In doing so, we have made several conceptual assertions that we hope will encourage further empirical investigation. Our aim is to provide a provocative framework in order to reorient two parallel streams of research. First, we hope to stimulate researchers focusing on racial socialization processes in minority families to consider the heuristic richness of interracial families, as well as the implications of broader ideological shifts in the post–civil rights era United States on racial socialization patterns. Second, we want to prod researchers studying multiracial identity to move beyond the documentation of variation in racial identification toward questions of psychosocial processes. How do multiracial individuals actually develop their racial identities, how is that process influenced by broader macrostructural changes in race relations, and how do their ever-increasing choices play a role in challenging or reproducing racial inequalities?

■ Notes

1. When discussing interracial families, it is important to clarify that "family" does not equal "two married heterosexual parents with children." Interracial families come in every imaginable configuration: unmarried cohabiting couples raising biological children; grandparents raising biological grandchildren; extended family members raising nieces, nephews, and cousins along with their own biological children; same-race parents raising adoptive mixed-race children; and homosexual domestic partners raising biological and/or adoptive biracial children. When we use the terms "parents," readers should assume that we are referring to the individuals who provide primary care for children.

2. According to theorists on racial identity development, blissful ignorance is synonymous with the primary stage of white identity development, whereby individuals

lack any overt understanding of themselves as a white person (Helms 1990). For whites who are at the primary level of racial consciousness, when their attention is drawn to issues of race, more often than not the focus is centered on people of color, with little attention directed to their own whiteness.

3. Sometimes white parents are raised in families where active attention is devoted to addressing and examining race and where children are encouraged to assume an antiracist stance. In such families children learn to be ever mindful of the meaning of their whiteness and to critically challenge notions of white supremacy. Those who were raised in this way have an advantage when it comes to raising mixed-race children because they are conversant with issues of race and have a parenting model that explicitly acknowledges racial issues.

14

Racial Logics and (Trans)Racial Identities: A View from Britain

France Winddance Twine

> I became pregnant and, in the innocent exultant power of the first day of a first and wanted pregnancy, I realized that I—my body and self—was no longer exactly white.
>
> —Jane Lazarre (1996: 3)

Much theorizing about "whiteness" and "white identities" in North America has focused upon white supremacy and its historical and legal constructions (Blee 1991; Haney-Lopez 1996), whiteness as a form of property (Harris 1993; Lipsitz 1998), white identity formations (Brodkin 1998; Dyer 1997; Ignatiev 1995; Roediger 1999; Winant 1997), and feminist analyses of white racism and antiracism (Pratt 1984; Segrest 1994; Ware 1992). The past two decades have produced a growing body of literature in this subfield of critical race studies.

Interracial families are a crucial theoretical site for an analysis of how racial logics are transformed and translated and thus provide insights into microcultural racial processes and projects. The meanings of whiteness and its negotiation within families have received little attention from critical race theorists. There remains a dearth of empirical research by race theorists that examines how white members of interracial families respond to and negotiate intrafamilial racism and their own racialization.

In 1993 Ruth Frankenberg published her groundbreaking book, *White Women, Race Matters: The Social Construction of Whiteness,* in which she provides an analysis of "white women's lives as sites both for the reproduction for racism and challenges to it" (229). Frankenberg, a white British feminist, was interested in analyzing the "daily experience of racial structuring and the ways race privilege might be cross-cut by other axes of difference and inequality" (6). Frankenberg delineates three dimensions of whiteness.

She argues that "whiteness is a location of structural advantage, of race privilege" (18) and that it is a "standpoint, a place from which white people look at ourselves, at others, and at society" (18). If we consider whiteness as both a position of structural advantage and as a "liability" or a position of "disadvantage," then we can examine how white members of interracial families employ shifting analytical frames. Rather than seeing them as occupying a fixed standpoint, we can trace the movements in their racial logics as they acquire new conceptual frames.

How do the white birth parents of African-descent children conceptualize their positions on the socioracial spectrum? How do they translate and transmit racial logics to their children of multiracial heritage? I employ the term "racial logics" to refer to ideas about "race" and racial difference that they hold. These are ideas and notions that they have acquired growing up and are not questioned. It is part of what Pierre Bourdieu would call their "habitus." In my field research I uncovered a range of competing and contradictory racial logics held by white family members and their black relatives. For example, among some black members of interracial families, I discovered that whiteness was viewed as both a position of structural advantage and as a cultural disadvantage—particularly when it was associated with working-class cultural values.

■ A View from Black Britain

In 1991, 50 percent of UK-born black men had chosen a white partner (Modood et al. 1997). These statistics from the UK census suggest that interracial family formation is neither taboo nor a deviation from the norm for women and men of African Caribbean origin in the United Kingdom. In the two urban communities where I conducted my research (London and Leicester), black/white interracial families were highly visible and not uncommon sights in public spaces. Although the prevalence of interracial families, particularly those involving black men and white women, suggests that these unions are not particularly transgressive, there remains resistance to and opposition to interracial family formation. In a national context where interracial intimacy between black men and white women is relatively routine, nevertheless, one encounters discourses *against* interracial family formation. In my research with interracial families, I also uncovered competing and contradictory racial logics about the impact of these unions upon the family.

■ Research Methods

In this chapter I draw on "racial consciousness biographies" collected in structured annual interviews, informal conversations, and participant observation conducted between 1995 and 2003. I draw primarily on interviews with white parents of African-descent children whom I classified as "racism-cognizant." They identified racism as a serious concern and a problem for their children, who, they believed, could be subjected to racism. They also argued that their children needed special resources (emotional, political, cultural) to assist them in coping with the various forms of racism that they anticipated they might encounter. In the spring of 1995, during the first phase of this ethnographic study, I conducted a pilot study in which I interviewed twenty-five white birth mothers of African-descent children in London and Leicester. In 1997 I began the second phase of my research. I moved to an urban neighborhood located approximately one mile from the city center in Leicester for eight months.[1] During this period I interviewed and reinterviewed sixty-one white birth mothers, including the women in my pilot study. The transracial mothers who volunteered to participate in my study were between twenty-eight and seventy years old. Sixty-one percent of the mothers interviewed were between the ages of thirty and thirty-nine years old. Twenty-seven percent were between the ages of forty and forty-nine years old. Twelve percent were over the age of fifty. The women in this study gave birth to their first child between 1959 and 1999. Irish women represented 12 percent of the women interviewed, with half of this group having been born in Ireland. They provided me with referrals to other women and to their black male partners. At the time of my first interview, their children ranged in age from three months to thirty-seven years old.

During the third phase of my research, I expanded my sample to include black fathers and black sisters-in-law. I requested permission from a selected group of white mothers to contact their black husbands, former domestic partners, and sisters-in-law. After interviewing fifteen black men, I divided them into the following categories: (1) second-generation black men of Caribbean origin born in the UK; (2) first-generation Caribbean-born black men who migrated as children to the UK; and (3) North American black men of non-Caribbean origin who had been born in the United States and migrated to the UK as part of the US military.

What follows are three dialogues that I had with white mothers and their "black" children to provide a theoretical frame for my analysis of competing racial logics.

■ Dialogue One: Racial Adjustments— A Portrait of a Transracial Mother

Lisa and Owen are social workers. I was referred to them by Rachel, the daughter of an Irish woman, and a man from Barbados who self-identifies as "black" and was employed as a social worker at the children's home that Owen manages.

Born in December 1972, Lisa is blond with hazel eyes and a cherubic face. She met her husband, Owen, also a native of Leicester, at a children's residential home while completing her internship as a social work student. They were both born in England, although Lisa grew up in Cyprus because her father worked for the British military. She earned a university degree with a major in women's studies in 1994. I met her in 1998 before she became pregnant with their first child. Now the mother of two sons under four years of age, she struggles to balance her career and her responsibilities as a mother. Lisa initially faced strong opposition from her black sister-in-law, who remains opposed to interracial marriage but told me that she has come to accept and admire Lisa. In a private conversation with Lisa's sister-in-law, I was told: "When I discovered that they were going out, I didn't want to meet her. He had had a few white girlfriends, and this had *always* been a contentious issue between us. He let the relationship develop before he told me that he was going to marry her." Lisa and Owen got married in September 1997 in Barbados. All their family members and selected friends attended. Two and half years later, Lisa gave birth to their first child, Oshi. Lisa gave birth to her second son, Zuri, on December 1, 2002.

On a spring morning in 2003, I met Lisa in front of the Phoenix movie theater. Zuri is strapped to Lisa's chest, while Oshi is riding a red bicycle in circles. *Real Women Have Curves,* a US film about a Mexican American high school girl's coming of age, is advertised on the billboards. Lisa is having her new house remodeled and has moved her family into temporary accommodations. They are now living in a small, two-bedroom flat located on the second story of a recently constructed brick building located across the street from the Phoenix Arts Center. We enter a locked gate and take the elevator to the second floor. After Lisa gives me a brief tour of her home, we sit down on the living room couch to catch up on events since the birth of her second son. Oshi, now three years old, runs up and reaches for Lisa. She pulls him up on her lap. Lisa explains to me that she has decided not to return to her old job after she gave birth because of the demanding work hours. She has accepted an on-call position where she can work from home and provide visiting social work services in the evenings when her husband is home from work. Owen takes care of the children in the evenings when he returns from his day job. Lisa is married to a man who is devoted to his family and actively involved in parenting. This is evident to me as I observe how they coordinate their work schedules. Yet, it is Lisa, not her husband, who has made the decision to quit her full-time job and take a position that enables her to be home all day to take care of her two sons.

Several months after the birth of their second son, I spent two evenings with them in their home discussing how race influenced their life. When asked to describe her experiences as a mother, Lisa began to present her view of what I term "secondhand" racism, which refers to her not being seen as the birth mother. She also described forms of racism that were not recognized by her black husband as constituting acts of racism, so we will see how definitions of racism may diverge and have to be negotiated among couples in interracial families. Describing a conversation that she recently had with her mother-in-law, who is now in Guyana on vacation, Lisa points out the difference between how she and her mother-in-law racialize her son, whom she consistently refers to as "black" in her conversation with me.

> I was shocked, really. There was no hostility. It was matter of fact. The other day Oshi was asking me what color he was. We got to talking and in the end I was saying different people might say he was mixed parentage or different terms. Other people might say he was black. And he said to me "Well, I'm black like Papa." And I said, "Yes, that's right." So that's how he sees himself. Well, Owen's mum had said something to me about this conversation because he obviously said to her "I'm black. I'm like you." And her and Camille [Oshi's aunt] were saying to me "Well, that's okay. He can think that *now*. But you're going to need to—because he doesn't understand the complexities of it. But as he gets older you're going to have to explain to him that he's not [black]." And it never occurred to me. But they don't actually perceive him as black like them.

In the view of Lisa's black Guyanese mother-in-law and sister-in-law, her son is not simply black. As the white birth mother, her whiteness affects their calculation of his position on a socioracial spectrum. Yet Lisa views her birth son as "black" and as being vulnerable to the same forms of racism that darker skinned children of African descent will encounter. Lisa has consistently described her son as black in my presence, and she has taught her white English parents to refer to him as black, rather than "half-caste" or "mixed-race," or "dual heritage." I listen to Lisa as she describes in detail her efforts to understand and negotiate the complicated color classification scheme of her black family members. She is learning that her black Guyanese mother-in-law and her black sister-in-law employ a different calculus to conceptualize degrees of blackness.

Lisa's two sons spend most of their time with their white grandparents, and both she and her husband described them as "not having a close relationship" with his Guyanese grandmother. Lisa's husband, Owen, sees his son as a lighter version of himself—as black. Yet, Oshi's light skin and wavy hair and the fact that he has a white mother mark him as "not quite black" to his aunt and grandmother. The gender of her son also appears relevant in his strong identification with the black side of his family: both of his parents reported that Oshi strongly identifies with the black side of his family, although he spends most of his leisure time with his white grandparents. His maternal grandparents adore him and told me that they pick up the boys virtually every weekend so that Lisa and Owen have a break. The family photograph albums testified to this as I saw various photos of parties organized for him by his maternal grandmother.

Lisa has to grapple with the contradictory and complex meanings of "race" that position her son not quite inside and not quite outside "blackness" from the view of her black relatives but clearly inside the "black" box from the perspective of white people. She goes on to describe how she experiences not being perceived as the birth mother of her sons because of their color.

Early one evening in the spring, I sit on a couch in the living room directly across from Lisa and Owen. Both Lisa and Owen are exhausted after a long day of work and child care. Lisa's mother and father are in the other room, playing games with Oshi and Zuri. Owen appears surprised, almost shocked, when Lisa describes the public response to her. At one point they begin to disagree on what "race" and "racism" mean:

> *Lisa:*   I do feel it *more* than you. And when we talk about sort of
> the issue of Oshi being mixed-parentage, dual-heritage, black,
> mixed-race, still can't decide on terms—I find that as sort of
> quite difficult as well, that sort of, you know. . . . He said to me,
> "Madeline has blond hair. You've got blond hair. I've got black
> hair." And I said, "Yeah." "Papa's got black hair. I want blond
> hair." He probably just said it in passing—fleeting—but
> I said to you [looks at her husband]. . . . For me, that generated
> quite a lot of anxiety. I wonder . . . at school if they're sort of
> favoring the blond children. What's that all about? And you were
> . . . but for me it was an issue. . . . In terms of racism, you've
> obviously experienced it and I think it's perhaps more difficult
> for me [to parent] in a sense that I haven't—not directly. Via
> being with you and having Oshi I have [experienced racism].
> But not growing up, particularly. I wonder if he's not being
> picked up [at nursery as much] because he's black.
>
> *Owen:*   See, I don't understand it to be racism as I knew [racism]
> growing up. I think that's partly what it is 'cause I see it as being
> more like I knew racism when I was growing up. You get chased,
> literally, from one side of the school to the other, by some older
> [white] kids. And that's what I understand to be racism. . . . And
> that sort of perception of it with Oshi, I don't see it as being
> racism. . . . Sometimes I'd go home and my dad would send me
> back out [to fight]. And I always used to think, "That's a bit
> rough, really." I don't think I'd send Oshi back out. I think I'd
> sort of go out on his behalf. I think his support mechanisms are a
> bit different than what I had growing up.

In the above quote we see that Owen presents his account of growing up black, which challenges Lisa's definition of racism. He points to his encounters with racial violence and what some call "bullying" at school. Lisa's concerns about Oshi being neglected at the nursery and not being picked up or receiving the same amount of attention as white children are not perceived as racism by Owen. Owen does not define the lack of attention as racism but limits it to more vulgar forms of physical violence. In his account of how his black Guyanese father responded to his being racially abused at school, his analysis is that his son has sources of emotional support that he lacked. In contrast to some other black fathers whom I interviewed, Owen does not define Lisa's whiteness as a problem or as a disadvantage for his son, but rather emphasizes the support that his son has. Lisa then challenges Owen's interpretation and pushes him to consider the way that her whiteness generates anxiety for her because she is not "recognized" as the birth mother of her son.

> *Lisa:*   I think if you're with him on your own as well, I think in
>   conversation people automatically assume you're his dad. And
>   I think there's an amount of pressure there [for me] because
>   I often get asked . . . on a number of occasions I've been asked,
>   "Are you looking after him?" Is he mine? That kind of thing. In
>   the bank the other day, that young girl, with Zuri. And I kind of
>   think possibly was. Did I tell you [speaking to me directly]?
> *Owen:*   I think it must have been one of those taking-your-daughter-
>   to-work days or something [he laughs].
> *Lisa:*   I can't dismiss it like that, Owen, because you would be
>   very . . . if someone sort of said to you, "Is he your son?"
>   you would be very affronted by it. Because you are very clear
>   "my boys." I think that feeling of someone questioning that—
>   you would find quite difficult.

Then Lisa goes on to describe what occurred at the bank. This story echoes other stories told to me by white birth mothers.

> *Lisa:*   She said to me, "Oh, let me see your baby." She must
>   have been about 19 or 20. "Let me see your baby." I was
>   carrying him in this thing. "Oh, he's so cute. He's so cute.
>   What's his name?"
>   "Zuri."
>   "Oh, that's unusual. That's so unusual. Where's it from?"
>   I said, "Oh, it's an African name."
>   She says "Oh, right. That's a really nice name." She carried
>   on. She was sorting my money out. And then she said to me,
>   "You must have really wanted him."
>   And I said, "Yeah."
>   And then she said, "To go all the way to Africa and get him."
>   Francine, she was sincere, and I just sort of looked at her. And
>   then she clicked. And then she was really embarrassed. 'Cause I
>   don't think. . . . "Oh my God," she said. "Is he yours?"
>   And I said, "Yeah, he is."

In this exchange Lisa expresses her frustrations as the mother of two sons for whom she is the primary caretaker. She is the one who takes the children to and from school and spends most of the day with them, yet she is often not perceived to be their "natural" mother. She experiences this as an assault since she feels that she labors daily to socialize them as "black" children. Lisa's description of this misrecognition echoed that of other mothers who expressed feeling erased and excluded because they were not seen as members of a "natural" family unit. They learned to read their "invisibility" as the natural mothers as a form of racism. Yet their black family members were often unaware of these experiences or did not consider them in their calculations of racism. Now, the questions that this raises are, what do these women learn from these experiences, and should we consider them a form of "secondhand racism" or, in the conceptual frame of Ruth Frankenberg, a form of "rebound racism"?

I would argue that this experience illuminates some of the racial logics that white mothers such as Lisa must negotiate as they learn that their perceptions of racism may diverge from that of their partners. They experience their racialization, in part, through the inability or refusal of other white people to "see" their birth relationships to their children of African descent. If their children are brown-skinned or clearly coded as being of recognizable African or Caribbean heritage, then white mothers may be perceived as "unqualified" for maternity, particularly if they are coded as middle-class and respectable. This presents a particular problem for them because their experiences may or may not be perceived as a form of what black and white family members term "racial abuse."

■ Dialogue Two

In *Black, White or Mixed Race? Race and Racism in the Lives of Young People of Mixed Parentage,* Barbara Tizard and Ann Phoenix (1993) provide an analysis of the experiences of fifty-eight young people of multiracial parentage attending thirty-two schools in London. Tizard and Phoenix assigned "scores" to young people for their experiences of racism, based on their answers to a series of questions. In analyzing the racial scores, they concluded that although they did not find gender or class to be a significant variable, the scores

> were significantly related to the extent of family communication about racism, and the extent to which they believed their parents had advised and influenced their attitudes to racism. They were also significantly related to the centrality of their own colour in their lives, and the extent to which they held politicized views and saw black and white people as having different lives and different tastes. (Tizard and Phoenix 1993: 105)

When considering the effect of the parents' racial identity upon children of multiracial heritage, Tizard and Phoenix concluded that:

> In about half of the families there was very little communication of any kind about racism initiated by either parent or child, so that each was unaware of what the other had experienced, and how they responded. And less than half of the parents were reported to have used the strategy of teaching their children to be proud of their mixed-parentage and their black heritage. . . . We found no evidence that, according to their children, black and white parents gave different advice, used different strategies themselves, or communicated more or less about racism. (Tizard and Phoenix 1993: 130)

Building upon the work of Tizard and Phoenix and extending my research on racism and racial literacy in Brazil to another national context, I now turn to the *first* dimension of racial literacy that I uncovered among one-fourth of the white parents interviewed.

The provision of conceptual tools at home is the first practice that I detected when analyzing parents' descriptions of their efforts to prepare their children of African Caribbean heritage to respond to racism. White parents also described a number of discursive practices in which they trained their children to discuss and critically evaluate media and textual representations of black people. In an analysis of the intergenerational transfer of race-related resistance strategies among US blacks, Janie Victoria Ward analyzed black parents' descriptions of their efforts to train their children to resist racism. Ward identifies "homespace" as an important site for teaching black children to resist. She argues: "In the safety of homespace of care, nurturance, refuge, and truth, Black mothers have learned to skillfully weave lessons of critical consciousness into moments of intimacy between a parent and child" (1996: 85). White parents and a number of their adult children described daily practices that prepared them to resist racism in ways not unlike those reported by African American parents. White parents who were racism-cognizant reported that they trained their children to describe in detail social interactions that occurred outside home. The discussion and evaluation of their child's experiences with "race" was a social practice that was central to transmitting analytical skills and comprises one dimension of racial literacy.

A "Black" Daughter of an Irish Mother

Taisha, a twenty-one-year-old university student, is the daughter of Mary Hunte, an Irish woman who immigrated to England at the age of nineteen in the late 1950s and later established a family with a black man from Barbados. Mary divorced her husband when Taisha was a child and raised her as a single parent after more than twenty years of marriage. The youngest of six children, Taisha is pursuing a master's degree in social work. Recalling her mother's practices when she was a child, she argued that her mother routinely discussed race and racism with her and thus provided her with a vocabulary for thinking about the political meaning of her black, Irish, and

British heritage. In her analysis of why she strongly identified with the African Caribbean community and has shifted from self-identifying as "mixed-race" to a "black" woman, Taisha cites the alternative history lessons that her mother provided at home.

Periodically breaking down in tears while we sat in the kitchen talking, Taisha described to me the forms of racial abuse she experienced at school and how her mother helped her to cope. Taisha identified her Irish mother's efforts to promote her political and cultural identification with black Caribbean people. Taisha described practices that remain beneath the radar of registered antiracist acts in sociological analyses precisely because they are improvised, informal, and in response to the daily experiences of children. These practices are not always part of a formal strategy, but over a parental career they may cohere into a pattern of strategies designed to soften the blow of racism. What distinguished Taisha's mother, Mary, from parents who were not "racism-cognizant" was that Mary identified racism as a recurrent and serious problem that required continual attention. She did not interpret incidents at school as "isolated" but as part of a larger pattern.

In Taisha's analysis of how she learned to resist racism at school and maintained her self-esteem as a woman of Irish and African Caribbean parentage, she recalls: "When I used to come home from school and tell her what I'd been through, she used to talk to me about [racism]." Taisha describes her mother's efforts to help her cope with being racialized. Taisha identifies alternative history lessons and discursive space that her mother offered her at home as central to helping her learn to analyze the erasure of blacks from discussions of colonialism in the school curriculum, except for brief textual appearances as slaves.

> When you're doing history, all of it is on the first and second World Wars. They never tell you that black soldiers fought in the war, or that they were put to the front line to be killed first. They never tell you about colonialism. They tell you about the British Empire, but they never tell you . . . how they achieved it. And I was always lucky in the sense that I knew that history [from my mother]. I knew all of the things like slavery . . . and not just the negative but the positive things that black people had contributed to world history. There's nothing there for you to relate to [in the British curriculum].

Taisha considered the informal and supplementary education that her mother provided as crucial: "Basically I think black kids are made by the educational system to feel ashamed of who they are and their heritage because there's never anything positive. It's always negative."

This supplementary education described by Taisha is a central component of racial socialization because it facilitated Taisha's ability to analyze racism and British colonialism. It is Taisha's belief that her mother provided her with conceptual tools, particularly the vocabulary and concepts necessary to identify and analyze patterns in the educational curriculum, such as ignoring the contributions of Caribbeans to British culture. If we accept Taisha's analysis, we can argue that the conceptual training that she received from her mother constitutes a form of racial literacy that enabled her to identify symbolic and systematic racism in the readings and visual images that she encountered at school and to begin to counter this form of racism (Rampton et al. 1981).

In an analysis of the "old" and "new" racisms in Britain, Paul Gilroy argues that:

> The school provides a ready image for the nation in microcosm. It is an institution for cultural transmission and therefore a means of integration and assimilation. It hosts two important and related confrontations which have been of great interest to the popular press. The first arises where conflicting cultures have to contend for the attention of the child who may be caught between them, and the second takes shape where the multicultural zealotry of the local authorities who set overall educational policy has had to struggle against the ideologies and politics of heroic, individual teachers who have sought to resist this unwholesome tide of politically motivated zealotry. Mother-tongue teaching, anti-racist and multicultural curricula are all under attack. (Gilroy 1993: 59)[2]

Supplementary Schools and Social Resources

The "black voluntary" school movement emerged in Britain in the late 1970s and has been described as "part of a broader political and education ideal that has directly risen from an assessment by Afro-Caribbeans of their social position in Britain and of the part that the existing white dominated education plays in its perpetuation" (Chevannes and Reeves 1987: 147). In their analysis of how voluntary or supplementary schools differ from other educational projects, Chevannes and Reeves note:

> The schools have been set up for the benefit of children of Afro-Caribbean descent: they are indeed black schools in aim and composition. The fact that there may be no deliberate colour bar (a white or Asian child may be allowed to enroll or a white volunteer invited to help) has little bearing on the organizer's view that the schools have been set up to provide in a predominantly black environment for the needs of black children. Black children attend because they are deliberately recruited from families where the parents believe in the need for their children to undertake extra study with children from the same racial group and to obtain support from teachers who understand what it is to be black in white society. (Chevannes and Reeves 1987: 148)

The African Caribbean Education Working Group (ACE) was founded and is staffed almost entirely by African Caribbean women and operates the

Saturday School.[3] The primary goal of the school is to foster black children's self-esteem (and racial/cultural pride) rather than to pursue a specific curriculum. The supplementary school in Leicestershire, known as "Saturday School" because it is held for two hours on Saturday morning during the official school term, has been operating since 1981. Children between the ages of five and sixteen years of age are welcome to attend.[4] Until three years ago, the school was free of charge, but a nominal fee of ten pounds per family has since been charged to cover the costs of the workbooks. Because it receives no permanent funding, the Saturday School depends upon annual grants and is operated by a small volunteer organization.

Providing children with access to privileged cultural knowledge and social relationships with black adults and children is the second practice that I identified as a crucial dimension of racial literacy. Sending their preteen children to supplementary schools run by blacks or enrolling them in black-run after-school clubs are practices that socially integrate their children into black friendship networks. Doing so required more work for middle-class parents who lived in predominantly white residential communities outside the inner city. This strategy is concerned with a dimension of racial literacy that differs from the discursive practices discussed earlier because it provides social experiences and integrates children into black social networks. White parents, particularly those who belong to the middle and upper middle classes, often reside in residential communities in which their children do not routinely meet blacks in schools or as neighbors. In contrast to working-class parents and parents who resided in inner-city communities, they were more likely to argue that it is potentially harmful for their children to be socially isolated from black children and to be unable to form social relationships with blacks.

◼ Dialogue Three: A Mother and Her Daughter Negotiate Racialization

Although blacks are concentrated in the major urban centers and are not evenly distributed across geographic regions in the UK, they nevertheless live in closer proximity to nonblacks and are more "exposed" to white English people than their counterparts in the United States.[5] When compared to North American blacks, blacks in Britain do not experience the same degree of social isolation or spatial segregation from whites as their US counterparts (Massey and Denton 1993/1995; Smith 1989). This presents particular dilemmas for white parents who are concerned that their children are overexposed to whites. In a study of mixed-race children, Anne Wilson (1987) identified spatial isolation from blacks and other ethnic groups as a problem for the interracial families she interviewed in the late 1980s. Approximately one-fourth of the parents I interviewed identified racial and social isolation from blacks as a liability for their children.

In *The First R: How Children Learn Race and Racism,* Debra Van Ausdale and Joe R. Feagin provide a penetrating analysis of playgroups involving children between the ages of three and six years old. Van Ausdale and Feagin argue that:

> Early friendships are often precursors of relationships formed later in children's lives. How and with whom children form relationships at this stage can influence how and with whom they will choose to affiliate as they grow up. Early friendships inform children on what social groups are suitable for them and what groups they can expect to be included in over time. Some recent research suggests that these early relationships are the foundation for social understanding, intelligence, self-evaluations, social comparisons and social competence. (2001: 90)

Justine, the daughter of an Australian mother and a Dutch father, is a striking thirty-six-year-old blond. Born in Brisbane, Australia, she spent her early childhood years in West Africa, where her father taught. When her parents split up, she was taken to Ghana by her father, where she attended her first school and established her first close friendships. As one of a handful of white children attending the school where her father taught, virtually all her early friendships were with black African children. Justine is one of the white women whom black women described to me as "living in the black."[6] She reported that she has only dated black men in her life. As a youth and community worker, she is employed by the coordinator of the African Caribbean Center to work with youth aged nine to twenty-five. She describes her job responsibilities as "to develop their educational and social skills." As a single mother of a teenage daughter, Saasqua, whose beautiful cinnamon-colored skin conceals her Dutch and Australian ancestry, she expressed her concern that her daughter does not strongly identify as black.

Mothers such as Justine expressed their fear that their children's social isolation from black children could result in their being rejected by the black community, another potential source of injury to their children's well-being. When I asked Justine to explain her motivation for sending her daughter to the local African Caribbean supplementary school for black children, she replied,

> I sent her to [Saturday School] to educate her. I mean she gets her European culture here [at home] so I would send her to Saturday school, which provides classes which tell her the conditions around being black and black culture and being about Africa and the West Indies and all that. But if I ask her how she identifies, she doesn't see herself as black. . . . And I'm quite upset because I've always said to her, "Look, you're black." She goes, "Well, I'm not black because if I say I'm black I'm disrespecting you." And I thought, "You have a good point there." But what I said to her was, "Okay, put it this way. Society sees you as black. And it's best that you know that because at the end of the day if it came to one or the other it would be black people that would accept you." The white people don't

see you as "mixed with white." . . . At the end of the day it's the black people who will look after you. If push comes to shove, it's the black people.
I'm not going to tell you any different. I'd rather you be safe, than be in a
position where you're not comfortable.

In this exchange between Justine and her daughter, we see that her
daughter rejects her mother's definition of her as "black." The desire that
their children identify with the black community often masks the disagree-
ments and struggles that some white parents have if their children strongly
identify with their white parents as positive role models. In this case, Justine's daughter's identification with her white mother is interpreted by Justine
as a problem because she fears Saasqua will not be prepared for the racism
she will encounter and will be unable to defend herself.

As a white woman who works in both predominantly white areas and
racially mixed areas, Justine has concluded that white people do not distinguish her daughter of mixed parentage from a black person of no visible or
known European parentage. Justine argues that in the eyes of the white people with whom she is familiar, her biracial daughter will be perceived as
"just a nonwhite person in their face." In contrast to her mother's perception, Saasqua resists and rejects her mother's racial prescription and insists
that her biological and cultural ties to her mother's whiteness be recognized. This conflict is an example of the troubled terrain and competing
conceptual maps that that white mothers (and fathers) reported encountering when they attempted to cultivate cultural and political allegiances to the
black community among their children of multiracial heritage. Their children sometimes interpreted this placement of them on the spectrum of
blackness to be a denial of central aspects of their cultural identity and
social experiences.

Claire Alexander (1996) and Les Back (1996) have both conducted extensive field research in London, during which they examined how racial
identities (and racism) were negotiated among youth. These two British
scholars have produced several insightful community studies carefully examining issues of racial hierarchies, racism, and racial performance. Their
work guided me as I listened to discussions between Justine and her daughter as they negotiated her place on the spectrum of whiteness and blackness.[7] Saasqua invoked a racial logic and linguistic code that differed from
the one used by her mother.

■ Constricted Eyes and Racial Visions

Writing of her transformation in the late 1970s from a respectable, married wife
and mother of two children living with her family in a town in eastern North
Carolina, Minnie Bruce Pratt describes how she became aware of the limits of
her life as a white woman. She describes how she acquired a different racial

and political vision—one that enabled her to see and form antiracist alliances with black women, Jewish women, and other women of color:

> I learned a new way of looking at the world that is more accurate, complex, multilayered, multidimensional, more truthful. . . . I feel the *need* to look differently because I've learned that what is presented to me as an accurate view of the world is frequently a lie . . . so I gain truth when I expand my constricted eyes, an eye that has only let in what I have been taught to see. (1988: 34)

These "constricted eyes" that Pratt mentions provide a metaphor that illuminates the investment of a subset of the white parents I interviewed in training their children to understand and see how they might be racialized in public spaces. For those parents who feared that their children would be subjected to forms of racial exclusion, abuse, and harassment, engaging in various and improvised practices to assist them in responding to racism made sense. Although these "racial literacy" projects did not always cohere into a "public" project that was visible to those outside of the home, I learned that there were strategies that children acquired. I recognized these projects as a form of "political" labor that flies under the radar of sociological analyses of antiracist social movements. Yet the daughters and sons of white mothers and fathers constitute a potential source of leadership for the "black" British community. Whether they self-identify as dual heritage, black, mixed race, multiracial, African Caribbean, or simply black, children from multiracial families occupy a potentially pivotal and paradoxical role in the racial futures of social justice movements in the United Kingdom. Examining how they learn to see or not see racial hierarchies and respond to them can provide insights into the microcultural processes in families as they respond to larger state "racial projects" (Omi and Winant 1994).

My goal here has been to advance critical race studies by providing an empirical case that offers theoretical insights into how white members of black/white families often struggle to transfer racial literacy to their children. We can see that some white parents may disagree with their black partners on the meanings of race and racism. Pratt's notion of the "constricted eye" is instructive because, like black children, children of multiracial heritage may be subjected to forms of racial abuse in the public sphere, particularly in institutions such as schools, public transportation centers, and police stations. In order to arm themselves and assist them in defending themselves from assaults on their self-esteem, a subset of white parents, usually white mothers, train their children to see and respond to various forms of racism. They teach them how their lives are structured by racial hierarchies and the legacies of British colonialism. Members of families that are not "racially unified" must acquire these racial literacy strategies and racial visions while learning to negotiate their racialized positions in families in which siblings, parents, and children may occupy divergent and different racial positions in the public sphere.

■ Notes

1. Leicester, a city located 99 miles north of London by rail, belongs to the East Midlands of Britain. It is one of the largest cities in the region and serves as the transportation hub for the county. In 1991 Leicester had a population of 293,400, including a student population of around 30,000 associated with the city's two universities. Leicester has the distinction of being the local authority with the highest percentage of all ethnic minorities, including the largest Asian Indian population in the United Kingdom. Asian Indians constitute 22.3 percent of the population. Blacks, however, constitute only 2.4 percent of the population, and Pakistanis and Bangladeshis constitute 1.4 percent.

2. In *Racialized Barriers*, Stephen Small (1994) provides an analysis of how racialized ideologies circulate among teachers, coaches, trainers, and managers of sports institutions. He notes that "while the state is central to the dissemination of some racialised ideologies, other racialised ideologies are important and are embraced and disseminated by groups outside the formal political arena" (14).

3. In Leicester, several of the women who have chaired and administered ACE and who regularly teach at the Saturday School are qualified teachers who earned their degrees in England and are committed community activists. As in other supplementary schools, there is no formal "syllabus," and the focus of the lesson plans varies considerably, depending upon the interests and areas of specialization of the volunteer teacher who leads that week's session.

4. The population of the Saturday School fluctuates between twenty and forty. Six of the twenty students who attended all year were "mixed-race." The retention of the preteens and teenagers was cited as a major problem by Taisha.

5. See *American Apartheid* by Douglass Massey and Nancy Denton (1993/ 1995) for an analysis of residential segregation by race and *The Politics of "Race" and Residence* by Susan J. Smith (1989) for an analysis of the British case.

6. Roughly half of the women I interviewed had either only dated black men or had married their black boyfriend as a teenager, often after having only casually dated a white male. The remaining women had either married or dated white men prior to establishing a relationship with a black man. Five of the women I interviewed had children fathered by a white man and then married or established a domestic partnership with a black man and had subsequent children. These mothers were all socially integrated into the black community and reported having at least one close black female friend.

7. I had a number of private discussions with Justine. But she thought it was important that I hear her daughter's perspective, so I had an opportunity to discuss these issues with the two of them. To my surprise, Saasqua self-identified as a "breed," which she explained was short for "half-breed," a term borrowed from Hollywood Westerns. In the Westerns, it was a pejorative term referring to individuals who were of mixed Anglo-American and American Indian parentage. One can find an example of this character from the John Wayne film *The Searchers*.

15

Black and White:
Family Opposition
to Becoming Multiracial

Erica Chito Childs

In contemporary society, most families are racially homogeneous, or at least identify monoracially. Since it is in families that the meanings and attachments to racial categories are constructed and learned, it might be expected that the family, as a social institution, plays a central role in maintaining the racial status quo. Not surprisingly, the overwhelming majority of both whites and blacks marry someone of the same race, thereby maintaining the racial makeup of their families. Although recent polls report that the majority of white and black Americans support interracial marriage, qualitative research paints a different picture of individuals who claim acceptance of interracial relationships in general but oppose them for themselves and their families (see Bonilla-Silva 2003; Childs 2005). In many ways, the family is often the source of the greatest hostility toward relationships across racial lines. Families rarely say that race or racial difference is the problem; instead a myriad of reasons are given why the relationships will not happen (not a personal preference, not physically attracted to other races, do not know anyone of another race) and do not work (lack of commonalities, cultural differences, and the opposition of the larger society). These familial attitudes and responses brought forth by interracial relationships (or even the possibility of one) are inextricably tied to ideas of family, community, and identity, drawing from available discourses on race and race relations in our society.

One of the most common issues both white and black families raise to explain why they would not approve or are unsure of interracial relationships is "the problem of the children." By referencing a concern about "innocent" children who may be hurt, mistreated, or at least hindered by problems, families can avoid acknowledging that they object to the relationship itself, instead blaming it on the "problems" the relationship can cause. Yet, what exactly are these perceived problems of interracial relationships and the biracial children they produce, and what is the basis of this expressed concern of white and black families? Furthermore, what does the "problem of the children" argument tell us about the acceptability of multiracial families in particular and the larger project of racial justice in general? It is these questions that I explore in this chapter, addressing the ways that white families and black families use the issue of biracial children as a reason to oppose interracial relationships. In what follows, I briefly outline the research and then address the overall views of white and black families toward interracial relationships, before moving into an in-depth discussion of the underlying meanings of the "problem of the children" statements.

■ Method

For this chapter I draw from research I conducted for a comprehensive study of societal responses to black/white interracial relationships. The three different data sources are in-depth interviews with fifteen heterosexual black/white couples;[1] separate focus group interviews with racially homogenous neighborhood church communities of a predominantly white Catholic church and a predominantly black Baptist church;[2] and separate focus group interviews[3] with white and black student groups on three different college campuses, including an elite Ivy League university, a private university, and a state university.[4]

Although the larger project focuses on many different aspects of the opposition of whites and blacks to interracial relationships, for this chapter, I have focused on what I call "the problem of the children" discursive strategy that was used by the church and college communities and referenced by the interracial couples interviewed when discussing the responses of their families to their relationship. Given that my primary interest was to look at how biracial children are used as a reason to justify opposition to interracial marriage, I have focused on the parts of the interviews and focus groups in which this discursive strategy was used. While conducting the various research, I was struck by the similar, sometimes verbatim responses that these different groups and individuals gave when discussing their views or their families' views on interracial marriage, as if they were reading from a script. After compiling the different data sources, I reviewed and analyzed the use of this "problem of the children" response, looking for relevant data, logical relationships and contradictions, and emergent themes. Drawing from the symbolic interactionist perspective, I use a reflexive framework not only to explore the "problem of the children" statements but also to understand the underlying meanings of why they are employed to oppose interracial relationships in families and what the larger implications for race relations in society might be. Though these responses are not generalizable, there are common threads that run through the varied views of the white and black respondents and add to our understanding of the ways families negotiate race, especially when it comes to interracial relationships and biracial children. In what follows, I provide a brief discussion of the general opposition of white and black families to interracial marriage before addressing the particular use of biracial children as a basis for this opposition.

■ Findings

Keeping It in the Family

While interracial marriage rates increase, the number of black/white marriages remains low. According to the 2000 census data, interracial marriages account for 1.9 percent of all marriages, yet the overwhelming majority of these marriages are white/Asian couplings (1.2 percent); white/black couplings account for significantly less (0.06 percent). Given these low rates on interracial marriage between blacks and whites, it is not surprising that many families object to a family member marrying interracially or at least prefer that their family members marry someone of the same race. Since the meanings and attachments to racial categories are constructed and learned within the family, one's family is "the most critical site for the generation and reproduction of racial formations" (Hartigan 1997: 184). This includes who is and is not an acceptable marriage partner. In white and black families, certain discourses are used when discussing black/white relationships that reproduce the image of these unions as different, deviant, even dangerous. Interracial relationships and marriage often bring forth certain racialized attitudes and beliefs about family and identity that otherwise are not expressed. Recent qualitative studies of black/white couples have documented the existing opposition these couples face from their families, both black and white, such as the outright rejection of being disowned to more subtle responses of negative comments, questions, and jokes (Childs 2005; Dalmage 2000; McNamara, Tempenis, and Walton 1999; Moran 2001; Romano 2003; Root 2001; Rosenblatt, Karis, and Powell 1995).

White families express opposition to interracial relationships in largely nonracial or color-blind terms, arguing that they "don't have a problem with interracial relationships," followed by reasons why they (and their family members) would not, could not, and should not date or marry interracially. This corresponds to a number of recent studies on general racial attitudes that have found that whites essentially deny racism and racial inequality by using a color-blind discourse when discussing racial issues (Bonilla-Silva 2003; Carr 1997; Feagin and O'Brien 2003; Frankenberg 1993). During the focus group interviews I conducted on college campuses with white college students, most described the unlikelihood that they would date outside their race, citing the influence of their parents. Yet their parents' preference for same-race dating was described as "concern," not racism. For example, one college woman's statement is representative of those made by the others: "It's not that my mom and dad would have a problem with it. . . . they would just be concerned about how difficult it would be, they are not prejudiced. . . . they are completely open-minded [but their concern] comes out of how others would act." Even while acknowledging societal opposition, whites often avoid stating that they are opposed. Rather they argue that they are concerned because "others" are opposed, using color-blind explanations to argue that race was not a problem but that other nonracial reasons were the issue.

Whites also argue that these relationships are "untraditional," "uncomfortable," and "unsuccessful" due to perceived differences. Interracial marriage remains something they believe happens elsewhere and would prefer that it remain that way. For example, during a focus group interview with white community members, the following exchange occurred. A married white man in his fifties with grown children stated that interracial marriage "is not common because people want to marry somebody like themselves. . . . [my children] married [whites of the same ethnicity] not because I would have cared or told them not to but that's where they feel comfortable." One of the women in the group agreed with him, stating "it is not a race issue [but based] on culture and wanting to be with people with same values and beliefs." All of these concerns, although not stated racially, imply that white families have a vested interest in keeping their families white and their racial position intact.

While white families attempt to maintain white privilege when they discourage their family members from engaging in interracial relationships, a significant piece of black familial opposition involves the perceived racism of whites in the larger society (Collins 2000; Dalmage 2000; Rosenblatt, Karis, and Powell 1995). Black families described their difficulty accepting a family member getting involved with a white person because of lingering racism and a distrust in whites in general. For example, during the focus group interviews on college campuses, most black college students— like white students—described how their families raised them to avoid interracial relationships, as represented in this one woman's statement: "My family raised me to [be] very proud of who I am, a black woman, and they instilled in me the belief that I would never want to be with anyone but a strong black man." This statement also touches upon another reason black families express opposition to interracial relationships, which is the desire to maintain the strength and solidarity of black communities (Collins 2000; Dalmage 2000; Kennedy 2003). For example, in separate focus groups conducted with members of a black church community, the following exchange occurred: One of the men remarked, "only black men who are removed from [their] race . . . black men who date white are weak. They want a weak sub-servient woman." A woman in the group agreed, stating that it comes "out of discrimination they face growing up . . . just be proud of your race." In many ways, black families view interracial relationships as a loss—the loss or devaluation of blackness, the loss of individuals to white society, and the weakening of families and communities.

Having looked at the general views of white and black families toward interracial relationships and the implicit desire to maintain the racial iden-tity of the family, now we will look specifically at how children from inter-racial relationships are used as part of this discursive strategy to express opposition.

What About the Children?

Although whites and blacks offer different reasons to oppose interracial dating and marriage, "the problem of the children" is used by both whites and blacks in their discussion of interracial relationships. These white and black families claim they don't "have a problem with interracial relation-ships" but simply *worry about the children*. In the community research, both whites and blacks discussed the issue of children as a central concern and reason to question and/or oppose interracial unions, especially how the children will identify their race and if they will be accepted. Yet these indi-vidual or familial concerns were articulated by different families in such similar ways that the concern they expressed sounded like they were all reading from the same script. It is true that interracial marriage blurs the color lines, but biracial children pose an even greater "threat," since these children inherit both a black and a white identity. As Michael Omi and Howard Winant argue, "the determination of racial categories is thus an intensely political process. . . . the census's racial classification reflects pre-vailing conceptions of race, establishes boundaries by which one's racial 'identity' can be understood, determines the allocation of resources, and frames diverse political issues and conflicts" (1994: 3). Therefore these claims of concern over biracial children in the family need to be interro-gated within the context of the larger implications of racial identity and race relations.

When discussing the issue of interracial marriage, many whites argue that they do not have a problem with interracial relationships but that bira-cial children are a cause for concern. This common discursive strategy of stating "the problem of the children" or that "it's just not fair to the chil-dren" was offered repeatedly. Some whites told stories of interracial cou-ples they knew with biracial children who had problems. For example, among the white college students, one young woman described how her parents forbade her from dating interracially because of some neighborhood biracial children she babysat for. She described the family in the following way: "the dad was 'real dark' and the mom was white . . . and they had *social* issues . . . just major issues." In separate focus group interviews with white community members, a married mother of two also commented that the "problems the children face" are the reason that she would "say no" on the issue of interracial relationships. The other focus group respondents also echoed these sentiments, like this white woman who described her views in the following way: "it's not because there's anything wrong with blacks . . . but [I oppose] based on the issues that marriage bring such as the children." When I pushed them to discuss what these problems were, the respondents specified that these children may have internal "problems," such as confusion over their identity and lack of acceptance among whites and blacks. This white father's description of the "problem" is representative of the responses: "Children from interracial unions have problems . . . confusion over their identity with the questions 'are they white, half and half, will they be accepted?'" His statements, like the others, justify their concern for the children based on the internal problems the children are imagined to face, as well as their lack of acceptance in society.

This strategy of naming the children as the reason for opposition also emerged in the narratives of the interracial couples about their families' responses. During individual interviews with couples, the white partners described how their families had expressed "concern" for the children, regardless of whether they had children. White women who are involved interracially, like Kayla, a twenty-eight-year-old divorced bar manager, often experience opposition from their parents when they become pregnant, with Kayla's parents even going so far as to suggest abortion as the best solution rather than bring a biracial child into the world.

> My parents told me they didn't think it was a good idea because all the things I would have to go through raising an interracial baby in Maine . . . that other people would be too cruel and that I had to think of the child and that it is not fair to bring a child into this world, interracial, knowing what was going to happen. They told me if I had the baby I was selfish.

Even among the black/white couples who were married and were not even thinking about having children yet, the white families expressed concern about biracial children. For example, the family of Jennifer, a white, twenty-two-year-old college student, had difficulty dealing with her relationship with her black boyfriend Lance:

> Well, my father told me . . . they'd always raised us not to judge people on the color of their skin, and my dad always said he didn't care if someone was purple, yellow, black, whatever as long as they were nice . . . but he has a hard time dealing with my relationship [with Lance] . . . my mother raises concerns, like she will say, "I'm not being racist, I'm not saying there is anything wrong with interracial dating, but I want you to take into consideration the stress and impact it's going to have on you. It's not

going to be a normal relationship." She was just trying to clue me in to the problems it might cause in the future as far as children.

Similarly Sara, a white, twenty-one-year-old college senior who has been dating Andre, a black, twenty-one-year-old college senior, described how her parents reacted to their relationship:

> I knew presenting myself and my relationship with Andre was going to be
> . . . I knew it was going to be a challenge with my family but . . . it's more
> subtle than overt. . . . I didn't experience the overt, you know "you can't
> date him." I didn't get any of that. It's more subtle. It's more like, "well,
> you don't understand" . . . I'm close to my mom. . . . I wouldn't really say
> she's supportive but she's not antagonistic. . . . My mom's big thing is that
> she's trying to understand and I get frustrated. I'm like, what are you talk-
> ing about? What are you trying to understand, you know? . . . My
> mother's thing is that if I'm happy then she'll be happy for me but she . . .
> I think, can't understand how I might be happy in this way and I think
> that's what it is . . . and my mother's big issue is if I got married and had
> kids. . . . My parent's disapproval or whatever . . . the first question is,
> well, what if you marry him . . . and have kids.

White opposition to biracial children and interracial relationships comes out of a sense of group identity based on a belief in the existence of distinct and separate cultural communities and justified by various excuses such as biology or the absoluteness of racial differences (see Frankenberg 1993: 126). Individuals who based their opposition to interracial marriages on the children seemed to be drawing on the dominant image of the offspring of black/white unions as "tragic mulattoes," predisposed to emotional and psychological problems. This idea that children produced through racial mixing are flawed (see Davis 1991; Spickard 1989) has a long history. Furthermore, whites have always maintained that children from interracial unions are to be considered black rather than white, which comes from social and legal traditions that construct the white race as a biologically pure group. Even one drop of black blood is thought to taint the individual and constitute that individual as black. Yet many in the black community also argue that children from interracial unions should identify as black, since they will be treated as "black" by both whites and blacks.

Among black families, the children were also mentioned as a cause for concern, based on the identity problems the children may face and the lack of acceptance from society. Many of the black focus group respondents echoed the same sentiments as this black father: "To be real, the problem is the kids you bring into it, what's going to happen to them [imitating a child]: 'Am I black? Am I white?'" During the focus group interviews, the black respondents repeatedly discussed this concern for the children by describing biracial children as having "problems" and referring to them as confused, maladjusted, or "mixed up."[5] Among the black partners in interracial relationships, there was also discussion of the families' concern over having biracial children as based on the dominant notion of biracial children as mixed-up. For example, one young black woman named Aisha, who is married to a white man named Michael, stated: "My mom said, 'What do you think kids will be like? . . . It is wrong to bring kids into a situation like this; kids will be confused. I don't want polka dot grandkids.'"

The attitudes members of black communities hold toward children of interracial unions further reveal the opposition to interracial relationships. As black feminist theorist Patricia Hill Collins argues:

> Currently, however, the birth of biracial and mixed-race children to so many White mothers raises new questions for African-American women. Even in the face of rejection by Black men that leaves so many without partners, ironically, Black women remain called upon to accept and love the mixed-race children born to their brothers, friends, and relatives. By being the Black mothers that these children do not have, these women are expected to help raise biracial children who at the same time often represent tangible reminders of their rejection. (2000: 165)

Not surprisingly, interracial relationships and biracial children are sometimes viewed negatively because they are perceived as attempts to distance oneself (or one's family) from black communities and black identity. Like white families, black families focused on the ways that biracial children would not be accepted in a society where communities and social worlds remain racially segregated. For example, in the community focus group, this woman's comments represented the feelings of the group: "The children definitely bear the brunt because it is difficult. Difficult being black and white when some people don't want you as either." The responses of the black families connect their concern over biracial children to their more general concern over interracial relationships, which are both seen as problematic based on the lack of acceptance by whites in the larger society, as well as the meanings attached to interracial couples and biracial children in black communities.

The black filmmaker Spike Lee addresses these issues in his movie *Jungle Fever,* which portrays Flip, a married black man who has an affair with Angie, a white woman. In one scene, Flip tells Angie that their relationship has no future, remarking how he wouldn't want to have "mixed up Oreo children." This idea is further touched upon when Flip's wife tells him how his affair with a white woman hurt her even more because as a light-skinned biracial black woman she struggled with rejection from blacks. She describes how she questioned her own identity because of the names others in the black community called her, such as "octoroon," "quadroon," and "high yella." Spike Lee's characters and the narratives of the black respondents illustrate how claiming a biracial identity (or even being biracial) can be seen by black communities as being "less black" and an internalization of white racism.

From these responses, it is evident that the discourses and images about biracial children are based on the existence of racial communities, "imagined" but no less real communities of others with whom we identify (Bonilla-Silva 2003: 181). In the current racial social structure, whites and blacks virtually exist in separate worlds, and both whites and blacks have a vested interest in their racial identity and membership in a racial community. The narrative of the interracial couple Danielle and Keith further illustrates this point. Danielle, an unemployed white woman in her midtwenties, and her husband Keith, a black factory worker, discussed how their families felt about them having children:

> *Danielle:*   My parents . . . they have been okay . . . but they did talk about worrying about the kids . . . that was before we had [our daughter], and it was wanting to be sure I understood how "difficult" it would be to raise darker-skinned kids being white and maybe some of it was they were worried what our children would be like, look like, or even how they would be with black grandkids . . . you know, even how others would treat them . . .
>
> *Keith:*   [at a different point in the interview] My family didn't really have a problem with us together but their main concern was with how are you going to raise the children? . . . Mainly they asking, are you gonna raise them black? Because I don't think they could picture having some white grandbabies or just that they couldn't relate to.

Even though race is not explicitly stated, Keith and Danielle's experiences with their families (as well as those of the earlier respondents) illustrate the racialized nature of the concern: for Danielle's white parents, it was concern over having black grandkids; for Keith's parents, it was the fear of the children being raised white. The underlying concerns and fears of Keith and Danielle's families tie in the historical beliefs and practices surrounding biracial children. Biracial children blur the racial divisions, the racial boundaries, and, in essence, the racial communities. For example, Danielle's family is no longer exclusively white if Danielle has a biracial or "black" baby. Biracial individuals are a threat to the all-pervasive power of race and its classifying character, because their very existence undermines the assertion that race is a mutually exclusive grouping. Historically, children of black/white unions were accepted into the black community and participated as members of the black community (see Collins 2000; Davis 1991). It was whites who created the one-drop rule and "forced all shades of mulattoes into the black community where they were accepted, loved, married and cherished as soul brothers and sisters" (Davis 1991: 138–139).

Yet more recently, the trend for children from interracial unions to identify as biracial instead of black is viewed negatively by many in black communities, who see it as an internalization of white racism and an attempt to disassociate from blackness (like Keith's parents, who expressed concern that their grandchildren would be raised white, or at least not black). Therefore, though both whites and blacks discuss the issue of children as a reason to object to interracial relationships, the underlying arguments are different. Whereas whites seem to object to the creation of "black" children through interracial unions who may be inferior or "pollute" the white race, black opposition seems to stem from a concern with maintaining or protecting black communities.

■ Conclusion

Families occupy an interesting role within the reproduction of race through their opposition to black/white relationships and biracial children. Naming the "children" as a reason to question interracial relationships reveals the complicated and layered meanings attached to interracial relationships and the ways that opposition is coded within particular arguments such as the children. This opposition undoubtedly reveals one of the central sociopolitical responses to intermarriage: the threatened outcome of the mixing of the races, a blurring and confusing of racial groups in society. The 2000 Census was the first to allow individuals to acknowledge their multiracialism by choosing multiple races, and these choices involving how interracial families and children choose to identify will undoubtedly have important bearings on the future of intermarriage in both white and black communities. What this chapter highlights are the ways in which the opposition of families to their members becoming involved interracially and having biracial children is also tied to the issue of identity—the identity of the family, of the individuals involved, and the children. Based on the common responses throughout the research, I argue that certain discursive strategies are drawn upon to express opposition to interracial relationships by white and black respondents and shared among these varied groups. This speaks to the importance of group membership and one's identity as part of certain communities that require that individuals follow certain scripts or guidelines for behavior, a "culturally routine structure of interaction" (Eliasoph 1999: 497). In these discourses on interracial relationships, there is a sense of blacks and whites as two distinct groups: an "us versus them" ideology clearly exists.

The concerns and beliefs about interracial relationships and biracial children demonstrate the centrality of race to our constructions of families and identities and, more importantly, the socially constructed nature of race, if one's relationship or child can change one's "race" in this society still divided by racial boundaries. Families express concern over the identities of the biracial children who will be produced, and there is a tendency for the white families to worry that the children will be "too black" and for the black families to worry about the children being "raised white." White families often object to the idea of a biracial child, not because they know biracial children who have problems, but because of their ideas and beliefs about interracial relationships and blacks in general. For example, Kayla's parents discouraged her from having a biracial child even after she was already pregnant because they feared others' response and how it would make their family and their daughter look in their all-white Maine suburb. Black families also discussed the "problem of the children," yet their concern was often based on the idea that biracial children would not be accepted by whites because of racism against blacks, but that these children would also face a more difficult time among blacks too. Race remains a "tribal stigma" that "can be transmitted through lineages and equally contaminate all members of a family," which plays into the added concern expressed about the biracial children these unions can produce (Goffman 1963: 4).

This "problem of the children" argument can also be understood as a color-blind discourse, where rather than admit race is the problem, the "concern for the children" is used as a valid reason to oppose interracial couples, deflecting attention from the *other* reasons why these groups may object. This color-blind ideology makes it unacceptable for whites to state that they do not want to work with, live near, or be friends with an African American. There are even the common discursive excuses, such as "one of my best friends is black," or "I don't care if you are red, black, blue, or green," which are drawn upon by whites to "prove" that they are not racist. Yet in these color-blind ideologies of race, it is acceptable, common, and even desirable to state that biracial children are a "problem" without being seen as racist. When the children are used as a basis for opposition, it places the blame on the couple for having children, rather than the groups in society who reproduce a social environment where it is not possible, or at least not easy, to be both black and white. Furthermore, white families, in particular, do not criticize the racism and prejudice of a society that creates the environment where biracial children (and interracial couples) would not be accepted. Rather than reject white racism and actively work against it, they participate in the racist structure and ideologies and instead work against their families becoming multiracial. By referring to the problems the children would face in "society," the respondents also exclude themselves from this "society of others" who would make it difficult for the children: this talk reveals an unwillingness on the part of the groups to admit that they are *themselves* part of a world that treats children badly. Instead they use an "alienated discourse," revealing an inability or unwillingness to construe race relations as something that they participate in or can change. There was no discussion or acknowledgment that any "problems" that children might have would clearly be a result of how individuals and communities responded to interracial families and biracial children (Rockquemore and Laszloffy 2005). This concern and desire to spare their child (or grandchild) the difficulties of being biracial illustrates white privilege and reveals how white families, without mentioning race, acknowledge that they do not want their family member to experience the racial discrimination and lessened opportunities that blacks face. I argue that families' concern for the children is a strategy used to express their own concern about their family's image and identity, which is often heavily vested in race, and for whites, their underlying racialized and prejudiced beliefs about blacks.

These familial views on interracial relationships and biracial children must be considered for what they tell us about the pursuit of racial justice. By opposing interracial relationships and problematizing biracial children, families are reproducing racial boundaries, maintaining ideas of essential racial differences, and reinforcing institutionalized racism and racial inequality. Therefore, opposition to interracial relationships and marriage signifies more than a personal decision or familial issue. Even though whites, in particular, present their choices not to intermarry as nonracial and individual, this collective opposition against interracial marriage forms part of the larger structure of institutionalized racism. Though laws banning interracial marriage were struck down by the Supreme Court in 1967, whites (and blacks) still draw upon certain images and ideas about black/white unions to discourage the occurrence of these relationships. The basis for white and black opposition affects not only social interaction between blacks and whites but also the social, economic, and political realms. If an individual finds the idea of a relationship with a person of another race unnatural, undesirable, or unacceptable, can we really assume that that does not affect how they view members of that race in other areas, such as the workplace, neighborhood, or political office?

So where do we go from here, and what, if anything, can be done? Although the focus of this work is on families' responses to interracial intimacy and marriage, certainly the goal is not to promote more interracial marriage. Yet we do need to work toward ending and changing the systematic inequalities and racist hierarchical social structure that allow whites to argue that they do not want their white son or daughter to have a child with a black person because the child would not be accepted by either family. This discursive strategy of citing the children as the reason for concern needs to be critiqued and challenged primarily because it based in the larger racism and racial inequality that permeates American society. Through the racialized words that others speak to black/white couples about having children, it is clear that race still divides us. Rather than advocate color blindness, ignoring race or allowing others to ignore it, and hoping it will go away, there needs to be an effort "to change the framework of the conversations about race by naming relationships to power within the context of our racial and political history" (Guinier and Torres 2002: 15). The same ideologies that make whites prefer not to marry interracially or produce biracial children and make blacks view interracial marriage and biracial children as a self-internalization of racism form the basis of racial inequality, the belief in and experience that whites and blacks are distinct separate groups. Gerald Torres, a University of Texas law professor, tells of how when he was young he dreamed of a raceless society and that by "mixing the colors together we could eliminate the invidious distinctions drawn solely on the basis of appearance" (Guinier and Torres 2002: 7). He remembers thinking that "the children of mixed unions were clearly the hope for the future, and black people should be prohibited from marrying black people and white people should be prohibited from marrying white people." Yet as an adult he came to see that changes do not come from "physical attraction or regulation . . . [but] through political action" (Guinier and Torres 2002: 9). By recognizing and challenging this discourse against biracial children and interracial relationships, not only do we work to improve the acceptance of these children and relationships, but also we work to break down racial boundaries, which are institutionalized and run throughout the words and thoughts of individuals like those I interviewed.

■ Notes

1. This interview project was conducted from 1999 to 2001 and included couples who were referred to me through personal and professional contacts or were encountered randomly in public. The couples ranged in age from twenty to sixty-nine, and all were in committed relationships from two to twenty-five years, with nine of them married. The education level varied, with all of the respondents having finished high school or its equivalent, twenty-one respondents having attended some college and/or received a bachelor's degree, and four respondents having advanced degrees. The socioeconomic status of the couples ranged from working class to upper middle class, with careers such as college student, waitress, manager, factory worker, university professor, and postal worker, among others. All couples lived in the northeastern region of the United States, ranging from Maine to Pennsylvania, yet many of the couples had traveled extensively and lived in other parts of the country such as California, Florida, and the South. The interviews lasted for two to three hours, and I ended up with over forty hours of interview data.

2. St. Matthews is a predominantly white Catholic church in a New England suburb, described by the priest as a neighborhood parish that is predominantly Italian and Irish and middle to upper middle class. Trinity Baptist church is a predominantly black Baptist church in New York City, described by the reverend as a 300-member African American congregation with working-class to middle-class roots.

3. A focus group was used to interview the church members and student groups. At the churches, the focus groups were conducted at a weekly or monthly meeting of church members, and at the universities, the focus groups were conducted at the student organizations' weekly meetings. In all focus groups, the respondents were asked to discuss their views on race relations in general and their views and perceptions of interracial dating and marriage. The focus groups at the churches and universities consisted of both men and women, averaging eighteen to

twenty people for the church groups and fifteen to thirty people for the student groups. For these focus groups, emphasis was placed on their perceptions of group and societal views, though many participants also offered personal perspectives and experiences. I also visited the churches and universities on a minimum of three separate occasions before and after the focus groups.

4. Collegiate University is an Ivy League university in New England, and the student groups included a coeducational student group that addressed issues of European culture and a coeducational student group that celebrated the African/African American experience. St. Stephen's is a private Jesuit university in New York, and the student groups included two student organizations that celebrated different European heritages and a student group based on the celebration of black culture. Central State University is a public state university, and the student groups included the Greek council for the black fraternities and sororities and a combined group interview with a (white) sorority and fraternity. Although the sorority and fraternity that I am identifying as white do not identify themselves in racial terms, both groups had only white members.

5. Even academic studies on biracial children tend to focus on the problems they encounter, often identifying biracial individuals to study from psychiatric or counseling centers or focusing on their identity development (see Brown 1995; Gibbs 1987; Lyles et al. 1985).

Part 4

Dilemmas of Multiracial Identity

16

Negotiating Racial Identity in Social Interactions

R. L'Heureux Lewis and Kanika Bell

Social identity theory posits a dichotomy between personal and social identity that may not be applicable to people of color in the United States. The racialized social system in the United States dictates that the social identities of marginalized group members are likely reflected in their personal identities. Building on David Harris and Jeremiah Joseph Sim's (2002) conceptualization of identity as an entity that is internally defined, externally ascribed, and behaviorally expressed, we argue that racial identity is both a personal and social identity for people of color in contemporary American society. We define personal identity as the organization and hierarchical alignment of an individual's social identities. In short, personal identity lies at the intersection of social reality and personal making of meaning.

With few exceptions (e.g., Deaux and Martin 2003; Stets and Burke 2000), social scientists have avoided blending the frameworks of sociology and psychology to address the complex nature of identity, even though for both genres, identity is a central topic. Though the sociology and psychology literatures have extensively covered racial identity, neither sociological nor psychological perspectives on identity development give enough credence to the role of race in one's personal *and* social identity development. We have explored and fused sociological and psychological models of racial identity and produced a model that addresses the intersection of individual behavior and social contexts. From this model, researchers and practitioners may better examine the ways in which people of color in the United States use identity negotiation as a catalyst to pursue racial justice. In this chapter we briefly review the key literature on racial identity in both psychology and sociology, then introduce the intersectional model of identity (IMI), and conclude with a discussion of the model's implication for racial justice in the contemporary United States.

■ Social Identity Theory and Self-Categorization

Approaches to Personal and Social Identity

Early social identity theory suggested that social behavior oscillated between being determined by group membership and being determined by individual characteristics. Henri Tajfel (1979) proposed a qualitative distinction between group and individual behavior. Questions raised from this hypothesis about the relationship between interpersonal and intergroup behavior and the characteristics associated with each led to the development of self-categorization theory (Turner 1984, 1999).

According to self-categorization theory, social identity is the definition of the self in terms of categorical memberships, and personal identity is the definition of the self in terms of personal attributes. John Turner (1984) suggested that because different situational variables elicited the salience of different identities, social identity must, at least at times, be able to operate completely outside personal identity and that the goal of social identity is ultimately group behavior.

The common assumption following the introduction of the interpersonal-intergroup continuum hypothesis was that the personal self and the social self were at opposite ends of the identity continuum. Personal and social identities were conceptualized as representing different levels of self-categorization. However, this hypothesis did allow for situations in which personal and social categorical levels of self-definition can *both* be salient. In short, Tajfel (1979) and Turner (1984) left room in their theories for the possibility that personal identity is influenced by social context.

Rupert Brown (1996) followed this line of theorizing and suggested that the group provides a new opportunity to perceive the self as a group member and as someone with characteristics that reflect the reference group. Brown further indicated that people think of themselves in terms of personal characteristics as well as group memberships and thus describe themselves as American, Baptist, father, college student, and so on. These labels are determined both internally by the individual and externally by the social group. However, for marginalized groups like African Americans, it may be more difficult to construct an identity that does not involve race in an environment that assigns it to such obvious attributes as skin color and hair texture and gives it so much power. Though brown-skinned people in the United States may use other descriptors such as politician, college professor, Catholic, or parent to define themselves, society at large will often perceive them as *black* politicians, *black* college professors, *black* Catholics, or *black* parents, regardless of their expressed identity. These societal labels often become internalized by the individual actor, and thus the personal identity and the social identity merge.

Though racial identity is considered to be a social identity, it can be argued that American society provides a consistent context for race to be both personal *and* social for racial minorities. This can be argued on two fronts: (1) group membership and feelings of collective worth affect individuals located in a group, and (2) the constant exposure to messages that devalue one's group may "personalize" a social identity by increasing its salience. Persistent racial injustice in American society often causes African Americans and other members of marginalized groups to either "protect" or deny the social identity of race, just as they would their individual attributes. This response to identity threat enmeshes the social identity of race within the personal identity.

The intersectional model of identity (IMI) is an *integration model* of identity structure and suggests that personal attributes and categorical memberships overlap within the cognitive frameworks of the individual. Anne Reid and Kay Deaux (1996) define an integration model as one that concedes that the individual has as many cognitive structures as he or she has social identities, and each identity is associated with a set of personal attributes.

Our model recognizes the contribution of the operational distinction of personal and social identity provided by classic social identity and social categorization theory but suggests that the nature of racial identity is far more complex than dichotomy hypotheses purport. The IMI attempts to take into account contextual shifts *and* individual agency in the structuring of an individual's identity.

Psychological Perspectives of Racial Identity[1]

Gordon Allport's (1968) analysis of the origin and development of social psychology acknowledged the importance of cultural influences in such concepts as "group mind" and "national character." Race was also one such concept, and it played a prominent role in the early history of social psychology. James M. Jones (1990) summarized social psychology's treatment of race in the first half of the century as rooted in racism and biological determinism. For a short period of time, the difference between racial groups was analyzed in terms of cultural evolution and diversity. However, before this approach had a chance to become firmly established, it was eclipsed by a new emphasis that centered on individual reactions to racial injustice rather than the cultural bases of these attitudes (J. M. Jones 1990). Instead of placing the focus on the injustice that tainted American society, the focus was solely on controlling the assumedly negative individual reactions of the victims of racism.

This concentration on the attitudes of the individual is illustrated by the work of social scientists such as Gunnar Myrdal, R. Sterner, and A. M. Rose (1944), who suggested that personal experiences of racial injustice caused African Americans to hate themselves. This self-hatred thesis held that identification with one's own racial group was normative and that the preferences shown by African American children in the racial identity studies of the time (e.g., Goodman 1952; Horowitz 1939) illustrated the negative effects of societal racism. Because of studies such as those of Kenneth and Mamie Clark (1939a, 1939b), in which black children identified themselves as black but showed an assumed white orientation (e.g., black children identifying white dolls as "nice" or "good"), some theorists held that black people had learned to dislike blackness (see Baldwin, Brown, and Hopkins 1991). The underlying assumption was that slavery and segregation robbed the African American of a genuine cultural identity other than the cultural stereotypes of the dominant society. Thus emerged the need for models based on internal definitions of the self, rather than externally defined identity.

Joseph Baldwin, Raeford Brown, and Reginald Hopkins (1991) countered the "black self-hatred" research and argued that Western-centered psychology denied that a distinct, healthy African American identity existed beyond negative reactions to the personal experience of racial discrimination. These researchers cited others such as Spencer (1984), Banks (1984), and McAdoo (1985) as contributing to the widely held belief that persons of color are able to separate their personal identities from their racial identities. The ever-popular racial preference studies conducted with black children over the years have suggested that African Americans may be able to uphold a white reference group orientation while still maintaining an intact, positive personal identity. Baldwin, Brown, and Hopkins (1991) argued that this notion is antithetical to an Afro-centric worldview, which resists division between the self and the group.

"Black self-hatred" theories dominated the first half of the twentieth century, but what we now know as black racial identity theories began to emerge in the psychological literature during the 1960s, when fear of black uprising against white society was prevalent among social scientists. Most of the psychological literature during that period involved deficit modeling (Helms 1990; Thomas and Sillen 1972), which described all the perceived deficiencies but none of the strengths in "the black personality" (Helms 1990). In addition, negative intrapersonal and interpersonal dynamics were assumed to be unique characteristics of black people (Helms 1990). For example, Thomas and Sillen (1972) spoke about the "cultural deprivation" theory, which cited language, behavioral, and economic differences between white and nonwhite persons as evidence for the cultural inferiority of people of color. This focus on cultural deprivation treated poverty as solely a personal attribute rather than a social condition. Responses to racism, such as anger and suspiciousness, were considered representations of the pathogenic black psyche rather than part of a complex interrelated system of individual behavior, social context, and situational stressors.

Nigrescence models were developed in response to the models that focused on the negative aspects of blackness. Nigrescence is defined as the developmental process by which a person "becomes black," where black is defined in terms of one's manner of thinking about and evaluating oneself and one's reference groups, an evaluation not based solely on skin color. Nigrescence models attempted to separate those aspects of black identity development that respond to racial oppression from those aspects that occur as a normal part of the human self-actualization process and to at least acknowledge that this process exists among black people. One example of this latter goal is the agenda of the black consciousness/black power movement and the stressed importance of a personal racial identity for a black individual.

Nigrescence theorists believed that overidentifying with white culture (i.e., having *assimilated* identities) was a psychologically unhealthy solution to the challenges that result from having to survive in a racist environment (Penn, Gaines, and Phillips 1993). The black consciousness/black power movement was also contrary to the "Anglo-conformity" model (Gordon 1964) or the "melting pot" concept that had prevailed in American society until that time—in which different racial and ethnic groups became Americanized and their traditions are adopted but muted by the larger culture (Helms 1990).

After the introduction of the Nigrescence models, the African American racial identity literature rapidly expanded. Concern emerged with the models' ability to take into account cultural and historical experiences and also the models' use of developmental perspectives with a value-laden end state (Sellers et al. 1998). In other words, some theorists found it unrealistic that racial subjects begin at an unhealthy externally defined identity stage and systematically matriculate throughout mutually exclusive stages until they finally rest upon a healthy, internally defined sense of self.

Overall, there were three major models of identity development in the modern sociopsychological literature, which can be classified as developmental, acculturation, and what we call identity-as-choice models. Although those who research these models had assumed that all individuals acquire identity in the same fashion, we suggest that different groups or individuals achieve identity through different means, depending on how closely tied they are to their ascribed identities. It may be true that all human beings are hardwired to struggle for identity, as the developmental models suggest; that according to the acculturation models, we all adapt in some way or another to our environments in the development of our identities; and that, as the identity-as-choice theories advocate, humans use personal and social, achieved and ascribed, information to construct their own group identity.

Identity-as-choice models (e.g., Hogg and Turner 1987; Taylor 1992) highlight the importance of overall group identity, but according to Helms (1994), contemporary theory has not acknowledged the role of racial-group identity in the conceptualization of the self. By eliminating the importance of group identity from the analysis of the self-concept, all information regarding values, attitudes, worldview, ideology, religious preference, racial preference, salience of ethnicity, or the influence of nationalism is ignored

(Cross 1991). In the development of a holistic, comprehensive picture of a person, both personal and group identity information are needed. Recent empirical analyses suggest that some scholars still operate under the assumption that there is no significant relationship between the personal and the social identity (e.g., Gonzalez 2002; Onorato and Turner 2004).

■ Sociology in Racial Identity Theory

Sociology has long been concerned with issues of race and racial identification (McKee 1993). To examine contemporary sociological theories of racial identity, we outline the separate lineages of identity and race studies. The study of racial identity in sociology is largely a contemporary phenomenon. Sociological conceptions of racial identity advance the role of reference groups, social context, and situation of encounter on dynamic processes of racial identification.

The relationship between the individual (self) and the group historically has been a focus of sociology (Cerulo 1997). Mead and Morris (1934) advanced the conception of self as a socially constructed being. Mead and Morris's discussion of the "I" and "me" moved the conceptualization of the self from an autonomous entity to a socially constructed being. The continual process of identity negotiation is thus informed by the individual's relationship to group(s). Simmel (1908) advanced the role of the group in the construction of the self. He suggested that the perception of difference between persons gives rise to delineation between the individual and the group, which results in in-group and out-group orientations. These works provide early evidence for the role of social interaction in the construction of self and the importance of a reference group to identity construction.

Early discussions of race were not as rooted in social interaction and social construction. The sociological study of race and the African American condition began by viewing African Americans as a problem (McKee 1993) and, like early psychological theory, used deficit reasoning to explain behavioral and cultural patterns. These models of race and behavior centered on the ideas that race and racial identity are inherited and primordial (Isaacs 1975). Treating race, racial identity, and behavior as fixed concepts remained the prevailing norm until recently. For a notable exception, see W. E. B. Du Bois's (1903) "double-consciousness" thesis.

Despite the contributions of George Herbert Mead and Charles W. Morris (1934) and Georg Simmel (1908), for years identity theory neglected the contributions of social interaction and environment on identity presentation. Sheldon Stryker (1980; Stryker and Burke 2000) asserted the role of symbolic interaction in identity formation and negotiation. As social interactions occur, actors work to present their most desirable self while at the same time reacting to the definitions and beliefs of others. This process is particularly important in the consideration of racial identity, where definitions and beliefs about race influence the perception of racial or ethnic minorities (Bonilla-Silva 2001).

Though earlier research concentrated on ascribed racial identities, recent research has explored the effect of internal definitions of community on racial identity. Anthony P. Cohen's (1985, 1994) work on symbolic communities challenged prior conceptions of communities as solely defined by geography and tangible distinctions. Cohen argued that (1) symbolic communities hold something in common and (2) this commonality distinguishes them from other groups. Boundaries between in-group and out-group are then created to solidify the construction of the community. Barth (1969) stated that considerable research has framed ethnic identity as an ascribed membership with social constraints, whereas Cohen's conception of community illuminated the role of voluntary association in racial and ethnic identity.

As identity theory expanded to understand the ways in which social interaction creates community and meaning, identity theory also reconceptualized its understanding of ethnicity as variable and socially constructed. William Yancey and his colleagues (Yancey, Erickson, and Juliani 1976) challenged the prevailing knowledge of identity as based upon rooted and transplanted cultural heritage. Instead they suggested that ethnicities emerge under particular social conditions. Thus, ethnic identities are informed by the social locations of groups and the larger social contexts in which groups reside (Nagel 1996).

This theory of variable ethnicity is complemented by Michael Omi and Howard Winant's (1986) theory that races are created via racial projects that define the social, political, and economic significance of racial categories. Omi and Winant's (1986) discussion centers on the social construction of macrolevel racial categories, but they also note the microlevel influence of racial formation on racial categorization of individuals and groups. Racial projects such as the "one-drop rule," or hypodescent, have delineated larger racial categories such as black but also have influenced the ways in which individuals define their own group membership (Davis 1991; Rodríguez 2000).

Contemporary sociological research in race, ethnicity, and identity has drawn heavily on psychological conceptions of racial identity while remaining focused on group membership and its subsequent social consequences. Early research on ethnic identity assumed assimilation into American mainstream culture as normative (Gordon 1964). These theories of assimilation and acculturation were later refined to discuss the ways in which individuals may hold multiple ethnic identities and exercise them in a variety of ways dependent upon social context (LaFromboise, Coleman, and Gerton 1993; Waters 1990). This new line of research is often mentioned when discussing changes to the meaning and significance of race in the post–civil rights era (Bonilla-Silva 2001).

Psychological and sociological racial and ethnic identity research is now grappling with the shifting color line. As the United States diversifies, it is imperative to understand how racial identity labels apply or do not apply to different groups (Brunsma and Rockquemore 2001; Waters 1999). This question has challenged social science to better understand the social construction of race. Subsequent questions have emerged about the variable meanings of racial categories and whether these categories will retain social significance in the twenty-first century. The increasingly complex under-standings of racial identity and race relations are the foundation for our model of racial identity.

■ Intersectional Model of Identity

Sociopsychological understandings of racial identity must acknowledge the interplay between the individual and group in a more complex manner. Through the lenses of sociology and psychology one may begin to see the structure of the intertwined personal and social identities that compose the self-concept for people of color. The IMI suggests that, in the case of racial identity for people of color, group identity informs personal identity and vice versa. The reciprocal nature of this relationship is important when attempting to understand marginalized groups.

Four components emerged in the literature concerning the development, maintenance, and expression of personal, social, and personal-social iden-tity. Because of a lack of consensus concerning the terminology used in the identity literature (e.g., personal and social versus individual and collective, etc.), we labeled the four components as follows: individual characteristics, social context, reference group orientation, and situation of encounter.

Individual Characteristics

Although our premise is that the individual is generally an "individual in context," we acknowledge that individual characteristics do contribute to one's identity. These characteristics reflect a person's goals, needs, values, expectations, and past experiences and manifest through behavior, even when social identity is salient. Social identity salience can trigger an auto-matic response that can vary among individuals (Turner et al. 1994). For example, many African Americans reacted in some manner to the video-taped beating of and subsequent court proceedings for Rodney King. Although the social identity of race was very salient for most African Americans at that time, there was great variation in the behavioral response to the incident, ranging from subtle hostility to rioting.

This component reflects three elements: (1) the response to changes in attitudes (e.g., mental health consequences of shifts in salience), (2) the function of identification (e.g., adaptability to situational and social contexts), and (3) mode(s) of identity expression (e.g., wearing of African clothing, participation in the feminist movement). Due to the tendency for such phenomena to vary across individuals, the motivation for identity choice and expression, as well as the individual and collective consequences of these choices, is key to this section of the model.

The overlapping and hierarchical ranking of an individual's social group membership are also important to this portion of the model. For example, one person might consider the categories of woman and black as overlapping, whereas another's adherence to feminist ideology complicates the merge of blackness with woman. At some point, a person who views her different categorical memberships as conflicting will have to prioritize them. Thus, the feminist woman may place her feminist construal of womanhood above her sentiments of racial attachment. The renegotiation of categorical priority not only varies between individuals but within the individual, based upon immediate context. The feminist woman may rearrange her category hierarchy while at a meeting of predominantly white females or at a meeting of predominantly black males.

Social Context

Social context refers to the societal milieu and must be considered at the international, intranational, and local levels. These three levels of social context influence the identification process for African Americans in the United States.

The global racial project of slavery that occurred largely between Europeans and Africans forms the basis for the international category of black in the United States (Omi and Winant 1986). It placed those identified as black at the bottom of the US racial hierarchy, and this ranked position remains relatively stable despite immigration (Bonilla-Silva 2000; Waters 1999). The racial hierarchy of the United States provides a social context in which the significance of race is demonstrated through processes of stratification that occur in various forms of racial oppression.

The backdrop of black as a lesser-valued social category is both complemented and complicated when considering the role of ethnicity. The construction of ethnicities emerges from power differentials within the nation-state (Balibar and Wallerstein 1991). In the case of the United States, the question of "Who is black?" yields a myriad of definitions. Ethnic differences and the boundaries of blackness remain in flux due to the changing racial and ethnic composition of the United States (Brunsma and Rockquemore 2002).

In the case of African Americans, external definitions of blackness have historically taken legal and social precedence over internal definitions (Davis 1991; Omi and Winant 1986). The Susie Guillory Phipps case of 1983 illustrated how definitions of blackness based on social norms can take on legal meaning in the contemporary United States. Notwithstanding, it is possible for African Americans to challenge and redefine the definitions and boundaries of

blackness. Challenges to internal and external definitions of group boundaries can result in a shift or retention of a given group definition. Under this
schema it is also possible to have multiple definitions of blackness.

Variations in geographic region can affect the boundaries and meanings
of racial or ethnic categories without completely deconstructing their boundaries (Barth 1969). Carol Stack (1996) explores the urban-rural dichotomy,
in which rural blackness is constructed as involving slow-moving, kinship-
centered behavior and urban blackness as street-savvy behavior between
small social networks. Though many find this urban-rural dichotomy to be
inaccurate, the dichotomy is still central in discussions of African American
identity.

Finally, local social context in the form of race socialization is important
to understandings of blackness. Families or other primary groups provide
early and consistent socialization messages about the meanings of race and
ethnicity (Bowman and Howard 1985; Thornton 1997). A large amount of
variation in meaning and messages occurs at this level of social context.
Localized messages about race may be inconsistent because messages are
given by multiple individuals and can be mediated by a number of factors,
such as gender, income, and marital status (Thornton et al. 1990). These messages can be linked to racial identity development by providing a basis for reference group orientation and transmitting the meaning of race to individuals.

As delineated, the international level of social context is likely the
most stable, but the intranational level is variable, and the local level is
highly variable. The levels of social context often provide different information about the meaning of race and ethnicity, making variations in understandings of race and ethnicity common. The influence of internalized race-
relevant social contexts is evident in everyday behavior. The lens through
which one views the social world is colored by intranational variations in
definitions of blackness, which are housed within a larger national discourse of blackness. Just as the answer to "Who is black?" will vary among
the levels, so will individual answers to the questions "Who am I?" and
"Who are we?" As the social context of race shifts, so must our understanding of the relation of the individual to the in-group and the in-group to
other social groups.

Reference Group Orientation

The concept of reference groups was first introduced by Sherif and Sherif
(1964), who were concerned with the creation of valid measures that
demonstrate how people orient themselves toward their ascribed groups or
communities. The term "reference group orientation" has been adopted here
to replace "group identity" because the former binds psychological studies
to the sociological literature on reference group theory (Cross 1991).

The reference group provides structure for organizing the self. Just as
the individual categorizes himself or herself based on social comparison

with other individuals, the reference group is shaped by comparison with other groups. Studies have purported that members of marginalized groups use the principle of relative deprivation to define their group status. Smith, Spears, and Hamstra (1999) suggested a distinction between individual and group deprivation. However, perceived injustice toward one's in-group often results in individual behavior geared toward the benefit of the collective, such as participation in social protest (Dube and Guimond 1986). Thus, individual behavior and reference group orientation overlap.

Studies on reference group orientation and racial identity usually required participants to choose attitudes toward their socially ascribed group. Most of these studies implied information about participants' self-concept or personal mental health, based mainly upon whether or not participants positively identified with their ascribed ethnic group. What discussions of these studies have missed is the overarching fact that regardless of positive or negative in-group identification, all stages of racial identity involve some analysis of the larger social context, the manifestation of such identity in individual attributes or behavior, and some particular encounters that have contributed to in-group and out-group attitudes.

Though race is a central reference group for many people of color, the potential to have multiple reference groups must be acknowledged. Earlier models (e.g., Nigrescence models; Worell, Cross, and Vandiver 2001) of racial identity have even been extended to explore the ways in which individuals situate themselves relative to multiple groups simultaneously while negotiating identity. This phenomenon is especially important when considering the identity negotiations of marginalized groups such as multiracial individuals and women of color (Collins 2000; Rockquemore and Brunsma 2002a).

In the case of multiracial individuals who espouse protean identities, their reference group is informed by the surrounding social and situational contexts. Though an individual may express allegiance and ties to differing racial groups dependent upon context, it is important to note that racial reference group orientation does not exclude the possession of other non-racial reference group orientations. The concept of womanism for black women illustrates the ways in which multiple reference groups work in the creation of a worldview. The significance of both race and gender create a unique social position for black females in which multiple forms of oppression interlock (Collins 2000).

As we have discussed, individuals may elect multiple reference groups, but the groups to which they subscribe are regulated by social context. Free movement between groups is often not afforded to people of color; thus, rather than having the option of subscribing to a reference group, one is often ascribed to these individuals. Though one may attempt to opt out of a given reference group, it is still an intrinsic part of that person's self because race is a central organizing feature of US society (Bonilla-Silva 2001). For those who do subscribe to an ascribed reference group orientation, it is likely due to a perceived similarity with the group or community. The meanings and relevance of selected reference groups are determined by social context. These three components—individual characteristics, social context, and reference group orientation—predominated in early identity theories that viewed identity as fixed, but recent sociological insights have moved away from this invariable notion of identity and introduced the importance of situation of encounter.

Situation of Encounter

"Encounter" is a concept that was considered crucial to psychological identity models that theorized that identity developed through stages. It was believed to represent the experience of either a negative event (e.g., racial discrimination) or a positive event (e.g., having a black role model) that challenges the individual's previous beliefs about his or her in-group. "Situation of encounter" refers to the specific context in which identity's salience shifts. This concept is akin to Sonia Roccas and Marilyn Brewer's (2002) notion of situational factors. These authors define situational factors as events in the immediate context that influence the salience of particular in-group identities. In their model, which addresses the complexity of social identity, Roccas and Brewer (2002) stress the influential nature of these encounter situations and provide evidence for their importance in social identity models such the one presented here. For example, they argue that immediate events require increased attention, especially when the individual is surrounded by out-group members (e.g., a black student attending a predominately white university). The individual is required to place more effort into information processing in the face of an immediate situation.

We suggest that situations of encounter are ubiquitous and present in the lives of all people but admit that this is likely the most elusive, immeasurable component of the IMI. The authors of this chapter can clearly identify the situations of encounter they experienced transitioning from historically black, single-sex colleges to predominantly white, coeducational universities for graduate school. But we are hard-pressed to be able to identify specific events that singularly transformed our identities. The transience of situations of encounter likely explains why this concept has not yet been measured effectively. As Janet Helms (1990) stated, it is difficult to measure a phenomenon consistently if the phenomenon itself is not consistent. However, encounter situations are nonetheless influential and equal contributors to the construction of racial identity.

Robert M. Sellers et al. (1998) suggested that racial identity may be central to a person's self-concept, but the extent to which racial identity is relevant and performed is not the same across all encounters. Situation-specific, or symbolic interactionist examinations of racial identity provide a more dynamic model of social identity for individuals and their surrounding social world.

By moving racial identity from a flat model that suggests that race will retain the same influence at all junctures, we embed the psychological self-concept in sociological symbolic interaction. Erving Goffman (1959) stressed the coded nature of the presentation of self in everyday life. His discussion of image management centers on the idea that the audience moderates one's expressed identity. An example of such self-presentation is a middle-class African American in a work setting. The presentation of self is moderated by the race of those present and the situation in which he or she interacts (Feagin and Sikes 1994). Discussing topics in which race is a factor, such as affirmative action or discrimination, may be strongly influenced by situation of encounter. If it is one in which diverse opinions are valued, then personal ideas regarding race and discrimination are more likely to be shared. Contrastingly, if the situation of encounter is one in which an individual must acquiesce to a popular opinion that runs counter to his or her own belief, then the presentation of personal ideas and beliefs may be subdued or even changed.

Like the other components in the IMI, situation of encounter does not hold much meaning as a stand-alone concept. The way in which a situation of encounter is perceived depends largely on the individual's reference group orientation, his or her individual characteristics, and the larger social context. A black woman in a middle-class working environment may not perceive the fact that her supervisor counts the number of copies she makes as discriminatory if it were not for the context of racial injustice that pervades US work environments, or the fact that she is a vigilant person, or the fact that she highly identifies with African American as a reference group. The social context of racism may have contributed to her vigilance, or her natural vigilance may make her more attuned to racism. She may not have identified so strongly with the black race had it not been for repeated situations of encounters such as these or that her strong identification has motivated her to expose herself to immediate contexts in which situations of encounter may occur. As one can see, the causal direction of influence is not readily apparent between the IMI components. This direction of causation is also not necessary to understand because the IMI is not a developmental model of racial identity. Without casual inference, we are still able to see that each component of the IMI contributes and relies upon the other components.

■ Identity Work, Threat and Coping, and Racial Justice

Racial Justice
In this chapter, we draw from the first premise of Rawls's (1971) theory of justice[2] to understand the processes of identity work and its relation to

racial justice. Rawls argues that in a space where a "justice of fairness" is practiced, all individuals enjoy the maximum amount of liberty possible without impinging on the freedoms of others. He also argues that the good of the collective must supersede individual conceptions of happiness. For this theory of justice to hold for people of color, increased opportunities across racial and ethnic groups must be achieved. The limited opportunities that are produced by racial injustice affect both social and material conditions, as well as the psychological processes of those toward whom it is targeted. The process of achieving racial justice has been attempted by large-scale social movements such as the US civil rights movement, but macrolevel efforts toward racial justice are limited by the national political climate (Morris 1984). In addition, as race becomes a more variable social factor, the continual pursuit of racial justice on a macroscale becomes increasingly difficult. In contrast, microlevel processes of identity work may be developed as coping mechanisms in the face of continual situational threats. We argue that people of color wage these microlevel negotiations of identity in the pursuit of racial justice.

Threat and Coping

The IMI attempts to provide a framework for further research on the function of identity, the motivation to identify or not to identify with a particular group, and the behaviors that reflect that motivation. Thus, the intersectional model may best be considered a model of identity *negotiation*. K. Deaux and K. Ethier (1998: 301) define identity negotiation as "agentic identity work carried out in response to contextual demands . . . an ongoing process, best conceived as continual efforts directed at maintaining existing identities as well as adapting to changing circumstances." Movement through the components of the model is theorized, in concordance with several other theorists (e.g., Smith and Bond 1999), to be fostered by the presence of internal or external threat.

Several theories of identity that cite threat as a significant impetus for salience assume that threat refers to a negative event, for example, a stereotype threat that occurs with encountering a hostile environment (e.g., Dovidio et al. 2001; Ethier and Deaux 1990; Helms 1990). As the individual internalizes outside information and uses those standards as bases of self-comparison, the possibility of internally derived threat is increased.

The examination of racial identity for people of color in the sociological and psychological literature has inevitably involved addressing their reactions to racial oppression (J. M. Jones 1990). The existence of color as a distinguishing feature of reference group orientation renders it difficult for people of color to assimilate into the larger society by voluntarily releasing psychological ties to their culture of origin. The strategies adopted for dealing with oppressive experiences are, to a large extent, determined by social context. For example, during and after slavery, it was adaptive for blacks to restrict affective expression and rely upon covert resistance strategies (Davis et al. 1941). During the 1960s and 1970s, strong affective responses, especially anger, bolstered positive black identity and pride.

African Americans employ a myriad of different coping strategies to survive and adapt. It is essential for researchers to identify the modes of dealing with racial difficulties because they are a central component of identity for persons of color (J. M. Jones 1990). Along with racial oppression, the identity makeup for black people is hypothesized by Jones (1990) to also include the influence of the majority culture, the influence of traditional African American culture, and individual and family experiences and endowments. Because these factors overlap, it is likely that each factor varies in salience depending upon the situation of encounter.

G. Breakwell's (1996) notions about how disadvantaged racial groups negotiate the color line suggest coping strategies for dealing with identity threat. *Isolation,* or voluntary exclusion from interracial interactions, is described as an easier choice than confronting stigma and discrimination. *Negativism* involves conflicting with anyone presenting a threat to the identity structure or acting against external pressures to assert social independence. *Passing* refers to removing oneself from threat by purposely disguising one's origins to gain acceptance (e.g., passing for white). It may also involve participating in the degradation of one's own group. *Compliance* is often used when other techniques have failed or one has witnessed the failure of others. Compliance involves the threatened person purposely fulfilling stereotypes to increase the chance of being accepted into the dominant group. Examples of compliance as a coping strategy are ever-present in US media (Bogle 2001). Many contemporary popular television shows cast the "hip-hop black teenager" or the "don't take no mess black woman" as two-dimensional archetypes. These characters do not threaten the others or the American audience because they behave in a predictable fashion.

In W. E. B. Du Bois's work *The Souls of Black Folk* (1903), he outlined the dissonance experienced by people of African descent struggling to gain acceptance in the United States against the backdrop of racism and oppression. Unsuccessful attempts at assimilating into the majority culture can lead to what Ralph Ellison (1952) called the invisibility of black Americans. A. J. Franklin (1999; cited in Parham 1999) stated that racial identity development can serve as a buffer against the internalization of the invisibility process. The buffer can be strengthened through the maintenance of a collective sense of self and culture: a collective identity.

The identity threat literature fails to consider the "flip side of the coin" to coping with negative reactions to racial injustice—the positive pursuit of racial justice. Threat is merely a situation that may result in an adjustment of one's identity attitudes. Thus, the existence of identity threat and subsequent coping strategies do not always reflect negative reactions to racial injustice. They may also represent positive actions toward the pursuit of racial justice. The latter explanation has received little scientific attention. Many more studies have identified the negative consequences of threats to identities (e.g., low self-esteem, lower self-efficacy in academic arenas, etc.) than have examined the positive responses. For example, in the city of Cincinnati, local community members started a coalition to work with the police to address racial profiling after a number of incidences of constable-civilian violence involving African American males. Research on responses such as these hold the potential to counter black self-hatred theses and deficit models that historically plagued discourse on how African Americans view themselves and respond to racial injustice. More research in that area would illuminate new methods of identity expression, not merely because they were *victims of* racial *in*justice but because they were soldiers in the fight for racial justice. The conceptualizations of threat and subsequent coping strategies must be expanded to include the diversity of the racial identity negotiation process, and more attention must be paid to the complexity of the identity structure of people of color.

■ Conclusion

The IMI provides a more inclusive and comprehensive understanding of racial identity among people of color in the United States. It is integrative, employing the understanding that the singular frameworks from which racial identity has been analyzed have been insufficient because they have failed to address the complexity of this subject.

Rather than being tied to a particular framework located within the disciplines of either sociology or psychology, the IMI comprises concepts borrowed from both traditions. Sociological and psychological theory were purposely merged to stress the point that racial identity is both a personal and social identity for people of color because it lies at the intersection of the elements that are purported to comprise the two.

The four components of the model are integrative and are theorized to hold different meanings, depending on whether they stand alone or are merged. Thus, the interaction of the four components provides the possibility for bounded variation in racial identification where social and personal identity intersect. Ultimately, race is a part of the construction of self for people of color in the United States, but behavioral manifestations of this relationship vary across individuals. We assert that the separation of race as a social identity from personal identity for people of color is incorrect. Our assertion challenges arguments that "assimilated" or "raceless" identities represent individuals for whom race is not central. Instead, we argue race is still central for these individuals, but their reaction to the phenomenon of race is different than those with more internalized racial identities.

Finally, strategies for pursuit of racial justice are strongly influenced by the situation of encounter. As previously stated, when encountering new contexts and situations, the individual begins a process of identity renegotiation. Because this process is theorized to initiate in response to a perceived threat, this renegotiation process can have both personal and social consequences. For example, black/white biracial college students may find their identity at college constantly under surveillance. These students will likely be questioned on the groups, friends, and social activities with which they choose to associate. These students may not agree with the construction of race, but at the same time their responses to the "threat of race" may cause them to alter their individual identity construct or their reference group orientation. The renegotiated identities that emerge attempt to provide the student with a maximum amount of liberties in the face of threat.

Adaptive responses to the impact of race in the historical and contemporary United States are variable but still illuminate how race remains a significant social fact as people, particularly people of color, attempt to define themselves in a society that is obsessed with the color line. The interrelated nature of individual characteristics, reference group orientation, social context, and situation of encounter coalesce to explain not only the negative consequences of threat and racial injustice but also positive reactions that contribute to the pursuit of racial justice. With integrative frameworks like the IMI in mind, empirical researchers may get closer to understanding—and thus appropriately analyzing—racial identity and its relation to racial justice among people of color in the United States.

■ Notes

1. In preparing this chapter, one of the tensions that emerged was the distinction between race and ethnicity in race theory and social psychology. In the case of race theory, race is defined as a large social grouping such as black that contains multiple ethnic categories, whereas ethnicity is conceptualized as divisions that emerged within the nation-state. Social psychology's conception of racial identity was largely founded on the identity of African Americans, which in race theory would constitute an ethnicity. To date, social psychology in both sociology and psychology has developed ethnic specific models of identity but has neglected to redress issues of nomenclature involving ethnic identity (e.g. African American identity, Nigrescence, etc.) that are still discussed as "racial" identities. In this chapter we attempt to use common language to resolve this tension by making clear conceptual distinctions, but areas remain where prior theorists have conflated the categories of race and ethnicity.

2. There are a number of challenges to Rawls's theory that are valid but not germane to our use of Rawls's work. For a detailed review of challenges to Rawls's theory, please see Robert Wolff's *Understanding Rawls* (1977).

17

Black/White Friendships in a Color-Blind Society

Kathleen Korgen and Eileen O'Brien

Today, antiracist activists confront a major challenge: the ideology of color blindness. As the ideology of color blindness increasingly permeates popular culture in the United States, few Americans are able or willing to argue against the seemingly commonsense notion that we should push aside racial differences and focus on the "common humanity" of all Americans. Ignoring all the cultural and structural evidence to the contrary (see Brown et al. 2003), advocates of color blindness maintain that if we act like race does not matter, it will not matter. In the process of ignoring race and focusing on our similarities, we will be able to wipe away any lingering antipathy from the pre–civil rights era (Demott 1995). This view of race relations is seductive, especially for white Americans, and has the potential to blunt antiracism efforts throughout the United States (Bonilla-Silva 2003; Brown et al. 2003; Hitchcock 2002).

Color-blind advocates find much support for their view that those who believe racism exists are just stoking a dying fire. Outdated sociological measures of prejudice (e.g., questions on surveys that measure prejudice that everyone "knows" how to answer in order to show they are not racially prejudiced) indicate that relatively few Americans still harbor racial prejudice (Bonilla-Silva 2003; O'Brien and Korgen 2004). Optimistic polls even indicate that the majority of Americans have cross-racial friends (Bonilla-Silva 2003; Korgen 2002; *Boston Globe* Poll 2000). Overall, white Americans are weary of racial issues and would like to simply move on from that topic (Bonilla-Silva 2003; O'Brien and Korgen 2004). The color-blind ideology that race no longer matters and should no longer be viewed as a societal issue allows them to do just that.

In order to counter this trend, sociologists must find new ways of answering the question: "What's race got to do with it?" Equally important, sociologists must make the case that Americans need to discuss race in order to find effective tools for combating racism. In the color-blind era, even close cross-racial friends may skirt issues of race while leaving racial inequities untouched. Doing so prevents these friendships from acting as a means of acknowledging individual and institutional racism and promoting racial justice, the fair and equal treatment of all races.

In this chapter, we focus on the efficacy of the intergroup contact hypothesis, a tenet of race relations for decades that is used in many situations as a tool for promoting racial justice. This theory of intergroup relations, developed by Gordon Allport (1954) and updated by Thomas Pettigrew (1997), leads us to expect that the more close contacts people of different races have with each other, the more progress we will make in terms of race relations. Therefore, close friendships between whites and blacks should be an ideal means of encouraging whites in such friendships to take an active stand against racism. However, this line of thinking has failed to take into account the powerful influences of racial ideology and homophily (like attracting like) and the relationship between them.

According to Allport's (1954) intergroup contact hypothesis, interracial group contact may have a positive effect in reducing prejudice if the following four conditions exist: (1) cooperation between the groups; (2) a common goal; (3) equal status of groups during contact; and (4) the support of authority, custom, or law. In 1997, Thomas Pettigrew updated the intergroup contact hypothesis by adding a fifth ingredient, friendship potential. However, as important as the contact hypothesis is for efforts to reduce intergroup anxiety and prejudice, it is, as Pettigrew would readily admit, no panacea for troubled race relations (Hewstone 2003). It is limited to prejudice reduction and does not provide an effective means of creating an impetus for establishing racial justice through antiracist activism.

We also make the case that the possible reduction in prejudice due to intergroup contact described by Pettigrew and Allport does not tend to lead to a desire among whites to advocate for structural equity between whites and blacks. Mary Jackman and Marie Crane made this point in their now classic work, "Some of My Best Friends Are Black . . ." (1986). They found that having black friends and acquaintances was much more likely to affect whites' warmth toward blacks and belief in stereotypes about blacks than it was to influence their public policy views. In other words, most whites who interact on a friendly basis with blacks do not feel any personal animosity toward blacks, but neither will they vote for policies that promote equality between the racial groups. According to Jackman and Crane, whites, as a group, are very reluctant to relinquish the inequality from which they benefit—even if they do view blacks as potential friends.

In this chapter we further examine the usefulness of the intergroup contact hypothesis as a tool for antiracist efforts by looking at the influence of *close* friendships between blacks and whites on the antiracist activism of the white friends. We define "antiracists" as those who commit to fighting racism on a daily basis in their lives. We can point to concrete activities (more than just having interracial social associations) they participate in that focus on reducing racism in society (O'Brien and Korgen 2004). Although Jackman and Crane noticed that the number of black contacts was more important than the level of intimacy among the contacts in predicting racial attitude change among whites, they did not attempt to explain why close friendships would not have more influence over whites' racial attitudes than less intense relationships with blacks. Most likely, Jackman and Crane's reliance on survey data limited their opportunities to analyze this fully.

We are able to take a closer look at friendships between blacks and whites by using interview data. Going beyond Jackman and Crane's political explanations based on the social policy self-interests of whites, we provide evidence that close friendship between blacks and whites is not a particularly progressive racial change agent for many whites due to (1) the influence of a "color-blind" ideology; (2) the tendency of cross-racial friends, like most friends, to focus on similarities (a.k.a. "homophily"), rather than differences; and (3) the mutually supportive relationship between 1 and 2. We provide evidence that these forces lead most black/white friends to distance race from the friendship and avoid dealing or being inspired to deal with racial justice issues.

◾ Methodology

The data utilized in this chapter come from semistructured, intensive interviews of forty pairs of black/white close friends, undertaken by the first author between 2000 and 2002. Each friend was interviewed separately. A larger study, based on these interviews, resulted in *Crossing the Racial Divide: Close Friendships Between Black and White Americans* (2002). The number of interviewees was determined primarily by the point of saturation. This was the point at which responses from interviewees became sufficiently similar to make the researcher confident of a clear pattern among them (Glaser and Strauss 1967).

The races attributed to the interviewees are based on their own racial self-definitions. "Close" friends are friends who would feel comfortable calling one another during the middle of the night, in case of an emergency ("3:00 A.M. friends"). All the pairs consisted of platonic friends, and all but one consisted of persons of the same sex. Please see Table 17.1 for a detailed list of the race, age, and social class of the interviewees, as well as an indication of the length of the friendship, region of the country from which the friendship pairs came, and whether the interviewee was an antiracism activist.

Table 17.1 Characteristics of Cross-Race Friendship Dyads

	Name	Race	Age	Class	Length of Friendship	Region
1	Steven	Black	19	Middle	4 years	South
	Jeff	White	19	Lower-Middle	4 years	South
2	Tammy	Black	50	Middle	22 years	Northeast
	Pam[a]	White	58	Middle	22 years	Northeast
3	Rod	Black	45	Middle	31 years	Northeast
	Vinnie[a]	White	45	Middle	31 years	Northeast
4	Ty	Black	24	Middle	10 months	Northeast
	Pete	White	21	Middle	10 months	Northeast
5	Pam	Black	53	Upper-Middle	16 years	South
	Ellen	White	59	Middle	16 years	South
6	Latrice	Black	18	Middle	7 months	South
	Jane[a]	White	20	Upper-Middle	7 months	South
7	Ese	Black	21	Upper-Middle	3 years	South
	Peggy	White	21	Upper-Middle	3 years	South
8	Keith	Black	21	Lower-Middle	3 years	Northeast
	Phil	White	21	Middle	3 years	Northeast
9	Kofi	Black	35	Middle	13 years	Northeast
	Dave	White	35	Middle	13 years	Northeast
10	Kathy	Black	29	Middle	18 years	Midwest
	Elaine[a]	White	30	Middle	18 years	Midwest
11	Yvette	Black	39	Lower-Middle	16 years	Northeast
	Cheryl	White	39	Lower-Middle	16 years	Northeast
12	Doris	Black	49	Upper-Middle	1.5 years	Northeast
	Hillary	White	50	Upper-Middle	1.5 years	Northeast
13	Joe	Black	18	Upper-Middle	8 months	Northeast
	Devin	White	18	Middle	8 months	Northeast
14	James	Black	18	Middle	9 months	Northeast
	Vern	White	19	Middle	9 months	Northeast
15	Patrick	Black	23	Middle	10 years	Northeast
	Kyle	White	23	Middle	10 years	Northeast
16	Valerie	Black	35	Middle	8 months	Northeast
	Kristin	White	37	Middle	8 months	Northeast
17	Janet	Black	47	Middle	10 years	Midwest
	Caroline[a]	White	53	Upper-Middle	10 years	Midwest
18	Harriet	Black	51	Middle	About 5 years	Northeast
	Marie Elena[a]	White	53	Middle	About 5 years	Northeast
19	Lil	Black	59	Middle	25–30 years	Midwest
	Barbara[a]	White	84	Middle	25–30 years	Midwest
20	Liz	Black	34	Middle	2 years	South
	Patty	White	37	Middle	2 years	South
21	Kia	Black	18	Middle	3 years	South
	Cindy	White	20	Middle	3 years	South
22	Bob	Black	43	Middle	About 8 years	Northeast
	Evan[a]	White	41	Middle	About 8 years	Northeast
23	Sandra	Black	50	Middle	8 years	South
	Beth	White	50	Middle	8 years	South
24	Charles	Black	18	Middle	6 months	Northeast
	Carl	White	18	Middle	6 months	Northeast
25	Martin	Black	46	Mid-Upper-Middle	15 years	South
	Tim[a]	White	48	Upper-Middle	15 years	South
26	Chris	Black	18	Lower	9 months	Northeast
	Matt[a]	White	18	Middle	9 months	Northeast

(continues)

Table 17.1 continued

	Name	Race	Age	Class	Length of Friendship	Region
27	Vanessa	Black	18	Middle	8 months	Northeast
	Mary Anne	White	18	Middle	8 months	Northeast
28	Maria	Black	20	Middle	3 years	Northeast
	Tabitha	White	19	Middle	3 years	Northeast
29	Kobe	Black	28	Low-Lower-Middle	5 years	Northeast
	Paula	White	26	Middle	5 years	Northeast
30	Betty	Black	46	Middle	6 years	Midwest
	Patricia	White	65	Middle	6 years	Midwest
31	Ebony	Black	19	Lower	8 years	Northeast
	Alison	White	34	Lower-Middle	8 years	Northeast
32	Joelle	Black	10	Middle	3 years	Northeast
	Maura	White	10	Lower	3 years	Northeast
33	Patrice	Black	19	Lower	7 years	Midwest
	Mary	White	38	Middle	7 years	Midwest
34	Louise	Black	45	Middle	6 years	West
	Elizabeth	White	47	Upper-Middle	6 years	West
35	Joan	Black	28	Middle	23 years	Midwest
	Jan	White	28	Middle	23 years	Midwest
36	Violet	Black	85	Middle	About 55 years	Midwest
	Gert[a]	White	82	Middle	About 55 years	Midwest
37	Ed	Black	23	Working-Middle	2 years	Northeast
	Arthur	White	23	Lower-Middle	2 years	Northeast
38	Nicole	Black	21	Middle	3 years	Northeast
	Candace	White	21	Middle	3 years	Northeast
39	Paulette	Black	44	Middle	1.5 years	Midwest
	Cynthia	White	50	Middle	1.5 years	Midwest
40	Christina	Black	23	Lower-Middle	8 years	Northeast
	Paula	White	24	Middle	8 years	Northeast

Note: a. Antiracism activist.

Respondents were recruited through advertisements in university and local newspapers, the snowball method (one interviewee suggesting another), and word of mouth. Eleven pairs responded to ads placed in newspapers. Kathleen Korgen found six pairs through the snowball method, contacted two pairs after reading published articles on their interracial friendships, and located the remaining twenty-one pairs of interviewees through word of mouth. She offered each interviewee $10 as a token of appreciation.

Participants in the study came from California, Kansas, Massachusetts, Missouri, New Jersey, New York, Rhode Island, Texas, and Wisconsin. Korgen interviewed each friend separately for between one and two hours. Sixty-seven interviews took place in person, at a location convenient for the interviewee (usually at an office, dorm lounge, coffee shop, restaurant, or some other public place), and thirteen were carried out over the phone. Two of the interviewees were ten-year-old girls; the rest ranged in age from eighteen to eighty-five (see Korgen 2002).[1]

■ **Avoiding the Issue of Race
in Close Black/White Friendships**

In order to address issues of racial justice, one must first acknowledge racial injustice. Close friendships between blacks and whites would seem one obvious place to find recognition and discussion of racial inequities. However, our data indicate that most close black/white friends stay away from the topic of race during conversations with one another. Despite being confidants, the majority of the friends in our sample avoided sharing their views on race with their close cross-racial friend. Both the white and black members of the large majority of the pairs of friends (twenty-nine out of forty) unconsciously or consciously developed strategies to distance race from their cross-racial friendship; thus, only eleven out of the forty pairs of black/white friends had discussed racial issues at length.

This tendency to separate the friendship from race relations in the larger society may protect the friendships from race-based divisiveness, but it also prevents them from becoming tools to alleviate racial discrimination in society. The combined effects of "color blindness" and homophily acted to prevent these friendships from becoming progressive racial justice change agents.

■ **Color Blindness and the Avoidance of Racial Issues**

As Americans have moved more and more to "not noticing" race, crossing racial boundaries is no longer having the transforming impact it once did. People of color may or may not be the bearers of alternative ideologies, and even if they hold one, they may not choose to share such worldviews with whites with whom they come into contact. As the ideology of color blindness and its message to "not notice" race grows in influence (Bonilla-Silva 2003; Carr 1997; Frankenberg 1993; Hitchcock 2002; Williams 1998), the absence of racial discussions in even close cross-racial friendships becomes increasingly common (Korgen 2002). More than half of the forty pairs of friends avoid discussing the issue of race in their friendships.

Kyle and Patrick provide a good example of avoiding the issue of race. As Kyle, a white middle-class college student from a primarily white suburb in the Northeast, puts it, race is "never" something that "enters into [their] relationship." These friends illustrate the "taboo against talking about race" that color blindness has inserted into American society (Hitchcock 2002).

> It's not even like something that comes up in like conversation. Even now, it's like me and him, and just, and all my friends and stuff. We just, you know, Pat is Pat. We don't look at him as being black or whoever, you know. I never. I mean, obviously we know he is. But it just never, it never like enters into our relationship. (Kyle, white, twenty-three)

One of the few times that Kyle remembers discussing race occurred when he, Pat, and some white friends were pulled over by the police in a car.

> They'd [the police] pull him over and they, you know, they pulled me and my friends and he'd be in the car and they'd think we'd be up to you know. . . . [We'd] say it's ridiculous. [We'd] say and Pat would say, "the reason they're doing this and that, you know, [is] because I'm black." It's a typical, you know, stereotype that if you're black, you're some kind of criminal. You know, and I know he's encountered that, stuff like that. And it offends him, you know; it's ridiculous. It offends, you know, it offends me; it offends my friends. (Kyle, white, twenty-three)

So even though, when pressed, Kyle can recognize and recite an example of the race-based differences between himself and his close black friend, he does not feel comfortable talking about them. This type of discomfort with racial discussions is increasingly common as those Jeff Hitchcock calls "radically colorblind white people" become increasingly pronounced in their efforts "to police expressions of racial consciousness among white people in general" (2002: 67).[2] Kyle, having grown up in the post–civil rights color-blind era, has been surrounded by messages in the media to avoid noticing or discussing racial differences (Demott 1995; Korgen 2002). The fact that he feels discomfort when discussing racial issues and tends to "not look at [his close black friend] as being black" reflects the powerful influence of the now dominant color-blind ideology.

Paula, a white, twenty-four-year-old, middle-class graduate student raised in a predominantly white immigrant urban community, remembers that one of the rare times she and her close black friend Christina ever discussed racism occurred when Christina was concerned about potential encounters with racism while hunting for an apartment. Echoing Kyle, Paula explains that she and Christina rarely talk about race because "it's never really been an issue." She does not think that racial issues pertain to their "personal lives."

Christina, brought up by Caribbean immigrants in an urban, primarily black, and working-class neighborhood, agrees that it wouldn't be "natural" for her and Paula to discuss racial issues often, saying, "We can talk about it. And Paula and I can talk about the issue of race without a problem but it's not something that really comes up, we've got other things more, more pressing to talk about" (Christina, black, twenty-four). She says that race is not something that crosses her mind when looking at Paula. Moreover, rather than bringing her and Paula closer together, she thinks that discussions of racial issues would be artificial and needlessly "divisive." Neither is very "politically minded," with any desire to, in Paula's words, "rehash" the topic of "racial equality or inequality" with one another.

Christina is one of the five young black interviewees whose statements indicate that they espouse a color-blind view of the world. Although she won't go so far as to say that there is *no* racial discrimination in the United States, she is uncomfortable discussing it and prefers to think in highly individualistic terms. When asked whether she thinks blacks or whites are disadvantaged in American society due to race, she replied:

> It's not something that I, that I try to dwell on or. I mean, I have a very positive attitude or at least I try to maintain a positive attitude. And I feel like, you get out of this world what you put into it. And if you're a hard worker, keep your nose clean, don't speak, you're going to be OK. At least, certainly in this particular [metropolitan] corner of the world. . . . but, you know, the more maybe rural, the more backwards areas, if you want to call it that, then sure I know that prejudice exists. (Christina, black, twenty-four)

Christina, having grown up in a "color-blind" era with predominantly white friends, would like to think that racism no longer needs to be addressed. She even used the phrase "don't speak," along with being a "hard worker" and "keep[ing] your nose clean" when describing what one should do to make it in American society. Race is not something that she and Paula spend much time discussing, and neither Paula nor Christina would describe themselves as antiracist activists. Instead, their cross-racial friendship is, for the most part, color blind. They don't think about, talk about, or, for the most part, even notice the race-based differences between them. Radically color-blind whites would be pleased.

Sociologists who study color blindness note that black Americans, although much less likely to completely accept all the tenets of color blindness, may accept some aspects of it (Bonilla-Silva 2003). Just like white Americans, they are exposed to the ideology of color blindness every day of their lives. Christina is a good example of a black person who, although realizing racism still exists (at least in some "backward" parts of the United States), espouses the color-blind point of view that "you get out of this world what you put into it. And if you're a hard worker, keep your nose clean, don't speak, you're going to be OK"—no matter what your race.

■ Color Blindness and the Use of Humor as a Means of Avoiding Race

Some friends handle the fact that they are different races by constantly trading racial barbs and slurs. However, although they may cross the boundaries of political correctness (and, in the process, appall radically color-blind white people), these friends never seriously confront racial issues. Although they bring race up, they do so in a facile way, without seriously discussing the effects of racism on each other or the larger society. This tactic of handling racial differences only through jokes supports the color-blind agenda of ignoring racial inequality just as much as the strategy of ignoring race altogether.

Nine of the forty pairs of friends fall chiefly into this category of black/white friends. Instead of generally ignoring the topic, this group deals with the issue of race by hurling racial insults at one another. Six of these pairs of friends consist of young men now in college. Three pairs of women also bring up race primarily through joking, though they also discuss individual incidents of racism that they have either faced or noticed.

Joe and Devin represent this second way that close black/white friends avoid the issue of race. Joe, raised in a primarily white, upper-middle-class, New York suburb, aptly sums up the role race plays in these friendships by saying, "You know, when I look at friendships in general or specifically my friendship with Devin, it's amazing how much race plays a role, but doesn't play a role. How much we joke about it, but we never talk about it seriously" (Joe, black, eighteen). To them, racial stereotypes can be used as "in" jokes that bring them closer together yet allow them to skirt the possibly divisive issue of race.

> We make a weird fun of each other's ethnic backgrounds so much; it's incredible. . . . Like we found each other's stereotypes—I'm Irish and German—so we're, we're pretty bad with it. . . . Like I saw him at lunch, we were eating, and I saw him come back from one of the meal booths . . . and I was like "What you got there—some fried chicken and Kool-Aid?" [He, in turn, might say something like] "Why don't you build a new gas chamber?" (Devin, white, eighteen)

By crossing the lines of political correctness with each other, these friends create a bond between themselves. They joke with each other in a way they would neither do with others nor allow others to do with them. However, although this means of dealing with the issue of race in their friendship brings them closer together on one level, it allows them to avoid seriously addressing racial issues.

Vern and James, college students who both grew up in lower-middle-class New Jersey neighborhoods with increasing numbers of blacks, also use the topic of race as fodder for put-downs of one another. When asked whether race has ever come up or been an issue in their friendship, Vern's succinct response was, "No, not at all. Except for when we're, like, ripping on each other" (Vern, white, eighteen). When asked the same question, separately, James's response was almost identical to Vern's, "Just like joking. We always joke about people's races all the time" (James, black, eighteen). Like Joe and Devin and the majority of the young, male, interracial friends, Vern and James use racial jokes as a means of both bonding and acknowledging the "elephant in the living room" without having to address, in any depth, the fact that race affects them both in different ways. By joking about yet "never talk[ing] about it seriously," the friends never have to address the broader patterns of inequalities between blacks and whites of which they are a part. Although effective for maintaining their friendship, this strategy does nothing to inspire either friend toward antiracist work. Moreover, although it flouts color-blind advocates' attempts to ignore racial differences, it also supports the color-blind ideology by acting as a deterrent to any serious discussion about racial issues.

■ Homophily and Close Friendships

Social psychologists who study friendship formation note that close friendships are the result of homophily, with "like attracting like" (Wiggins, Wiggins, and Vander Zanden 1994). Almost all of the close black/white friends in this study maintain that they became friends through common interests and experiences. Importantly, even though most black and white Americans live, work, and socialize in separate spheres (Bonilla-Silva 2003; Massey and Denton 1993/1995, 1999; Steinhorn and Diggs-Brown 2000), the lives of these men and women somehow connected with one another. Through this connection, they were able to see commonalities that drew them to each other and eventually led to their developing a close friendship.

For instance, Jane describes the connection she has with her close black friend, Latrice, whom she met when they were both attending the same college, by saying, "Like today, the shirt she has on is black, I had one in pink. The same one . . . We read the same book . . . We just have a lot in common. Like, expectations in friendships [and] expectations in relationships. Things we like to do for fun" (Jane, white, twenty). Latrice, echoing Jane's description, describes them as "two of the same person."

Such descriptions of similarities between the friends were very common. For instance, Bob and Evan, after working together on a project in their corporation, realized that they had enough similarities to create the basis for a very strong friendship. As Bob described it,

> We found . . . that, once we got a chance to spend some time together, that there are certain things that we both enjoy. For instance, he likes to fish and I like to fish. He has a son and I have a son whom we hold very near and dear. . . . Our wives are both professionals. And we've had an opportunity to talk about certain things [that] come up with wives who are professionals . . . both like to travel . . . both like to run. (Bob, black, forty-three)

The two became so close their coworkers referred to them as "Mutt and Jeff." Two other interviewees, Elaine and Kathy, now in their twenties, bonded as the only thirteen-year-olds chosen for parts in one of their local midwestern university's theater productions. Spending rehearsals laughing and giggling together, they realized they had both theatrical and athletic interests in common. Their experience with the university theater spawned a friendship that has lasted almost two decades.

However, in order to protect their friendship from the potentially divisive forces of racial inequality, the majority of these friends tend to avoid racial issues and focus only on what makes them similar to one another. The ability of close black/white friends to focus on their commonalities and either downplay or ignore the race-based differences between them allows them to experience with each other the interpersonal attraction common among same-race close friends. It also highlights the fact that friendships, like all relationships, are maintained through persistent efforts.

For instance, two people may see similarities between themselves, be attracted to those commonalities, and become friends. During their friendship, in order to retain or increase that level of attraction, they must continually find ways to see each other as alike and avoid potential topics that might create distance between them. As Erving Goffman pointed out in *Interaction Ritual* (1967), each friend follows unspoken rules of social interaction. If one brings to light an uncomfortable difference between them or otherwise behaves inappropriately, "repair work" must be done.

Although what Goffman called "impression management" takes place in all interactions, it is particularly important when major disparities exist between friends. For instance, friends from different economic classes tend to avoid discussing their finances with one another for fear of creating tension. Many tenure-track professors tend to discuss their work life only with colleagues, believing that friends outside the profession are unaware of the extensive demands of the field. Often, young adults who marry and have children find they must make an effort to avoid constantly talking about their children and thereby alienate their single friends. The single friends and the parents may make jokes about the sudden differences in their lives, trying to keep or perhaps "repair" the bond with their friends through humor. Whatever strategy is employed, the goal of portraying themselves as similar remains constant.

■ The Mutually Supportive Influence of Color Blindness and Homophily

The ideology of color blindness and homophily are mutually supportive and work together to encourage the black/white friends to distance race from their relationship. Differences in racial privileges that are exposed in conversation between white and black friends can be brushed over quickly or turned into fodder for jokes in order to assure both friends that race will not disturb the equilibrium between them. This strategy of distancing race from the friendship enables the friends to avoid dealing with the fact that (like most blacks and whites in the United States) the black and white friends have very different perspectives on racial justice in the United States. Most of the members of the pairs even manage to avoid acknowledging how race affects the life chances of the black and the white friends differently. Thirty-three of the forty black friends believed that their white friend had an advantage over them due to race; only thirteen of the white friends said that they were racially privileged in comparison to their black friend.[3] However, these differences were never acknowledged or addressed within the context of the overwhelming majority (75 percent) of these friendships.

Despite their distinct ways of internally dealing with the race-based differences between them, both the black and the white friends tended to distance race from their cross-racial friendship. Most of the white friends did not notice the hardships their black friends faced due to racism in the United States. The black friends, however, tended to be very aware of their disadvantage but distanced their white friend from any responsibility for racism in American society. Both the black and white friends tended to stress the similarities between them and brush over the race-based differences. These efforts to emphasize their similarities and avoid issues of racial injustice both reflect and support the ideology of color blindness. Although their perspectives on racial issues differ, the majority of both the black and the white friends prop up the ideology of color blindness by downplaying the racial differences that exist between them.

The Influence of Color Blindness and Homophily on the White Friends

Matt, a white college student, provides a good example of a white friend who, although realizing that racism exists, had a hard time recognizing his advantage over his black friend. Matt acknowledged that whites, as a group, are "holding all the cards" in American society. He also described how he makes a point of talking to black people in an effort to bridge the racial divide. However, he did not see that his race gives him an advantage over his black friend. Matt's response to the question of whether race plays a factor in how people are treated in the United States today was typical of someone with this tunnel vision on issues of race. Asked whether he sees Chris as having any advantages over him as a result of race, he responded, "No. And if I have any over him, I guess it's just more of a class thing. But, you know, I like to think we're on an equal playing field." He continued, with some equivocation, "For the most part. . . . I should hope [we're on an equal playing field]. . . . I would think so. I mean I would [treat us equally] if I were the boss. But then again I'm not" (Matt, white, nineteen). However, when asked again whether he believes that he and Chris are both on a relatively even playing field, Matt responded with an affirmative "mmm-hmm." Matt recognizes the larger social issue of racism, but he does not link it to his friend Chris's individual life or recognize how it affects him and Chris differently.

Like Matt, the majority of the white interviewees easily recognized racism on a societal level but had a difficult time seeing that racism benefits them and hurts their friends. For instance, after saying that his friend Kofi does not have "any particular advantage or disadvantage over me because of his race," Dave stated that "generally speaking, on a societal level, black people may have it tougher" than whites. When asked why Kofi does not have it tougher, Dave perceived the illogic in his thinking.

> Why wouldn't Kofi have it tougher? Maybe he has but he's just overcome. Because why wouldn't he, right? It's just so funny, I mean, I just see Kofi and he's just—he's Kofi, he's not the black Kofi. I don't know, that's odd. Yah. I'm kind of tripping myself up and not following my own logic but . . . African Americans do have it more difficult and Kofi probably has in ways I don't realize. . . . He's probably had to work harder than I or anyone else probably realizes to get there. . . . Maybe it's just something I really haven't given a lot of thought to before, to be honest with you. I'm really thinking about that for the first time now as we're speaking about it. . . . It's just not something I've had to think about. (Dave, white, thirty-four)

Dave, who has been a very close and loyal friend to Kofi for more than fifteen years, somehow managed to avoid thinking about how racism affects his black friend. Although he could recognize that racism exists in American society, he had, up until the moment of the interview, never thought about how it affected him and Kofi differently. He echoed Paula Rothenberg in *Invisible Privilege* (2000), when she said that "it's just not something I've had to think about."

Matt and Dave's avoidance of the racial inequity between themselves and their close black friends indicates the powerful relationship between color blindness and homophily. Color-blind ideology discourages acknowledgment or discussion of racial issues. At the same time, friends ("like being attracted to like") naturally tend to stress similarities and downplay differences between them.

Peggy, a white college student, also had a hard time relating the racism that she perceives at the societal level to her and her friend Ese's life chances. During the interview, she first said that she thought she and Ese have an equal chance of "making it" in society, despite their different races. She then stated that more white people discriminate against blacks than vice versa. When questioned about the two statements, she, like Dave, quickly realized her inconsistency as she responded, "Hmmm. . . . I think that we have an equal chance but she has. . . . I think that she's more likely to be discriminated against than I would be. Yah." When prompted to explain how things are equal, Peggy laughed, realizing her contradiction, and said, "I guess they aren't. Yah. So yah. I guess that I have a higher chance of making it than she does." Peggy stated that she had never thought about the race-based inequality between Ese and her, saying:

I guess I try to not think about things like that. . . . Um. I guess to protect her. And that's weird that I wouldn't think about it to protect her. Wow! What thoughts are running through my head! [laughs] Yah. I guess, you know, 'cause I don't want to see her hurt. So, I guess I just try not to think it. And maybe . . . because I think she can do anything. And so I'm in her mindset, too. You know, we share so much, I guess I'm thinking, well, I know what her plans are and what she's going to do and I don't see anything getting in her way. So, I guess that probably has the most to do with it. [I would like not to think] that she would ever have anybody say anything or be discriminatory against her at all. (Peggy, white, twenty-one)

Just as Dave has pride in Kofi's ability to succeed, Peggy likes to believe that nothing will hinder Ese's attempts to fulfill her aspirations. Peggy does not *want* to think about how Ese may suffer from racism because the thought pains her. She does not *have* to think about it because she is white.

As they are for most white Americans, the advantages Peggy received from her white skin are what Rothenberg calls "invisible privileges" (2000). Ruth Frankenberg (1993) explains that "among the effects on white people both of race privilege and of the dominance of whiteness are their seeming normativity, their structured invisibility." Peggy's membership in the dominant race makes her privileges seemingly normal rather than noticeable to her. Moreover, like the majority of the other white friends, the combined influence of a color-blind ideology and homophily has made Peggy blind to both the effects of racial injustice on her black friend's life chances and the need for whites to take an active stand against racism.

The Influence of Color Blindness and Homophily on the Black Friends

Kofi, like the majority of the other black interviewees, is fully aware that his white friend has race-based advantages over him. He did not hesitate when he answered the question of whether he or his white friend, Dave, has advantages over the other as a result of race: "Well, I think he's advantaged over me due to race. Yah. But, you know, he didn't ask for it [laughs]. He was born, and it, like, just happened. And, yah, I mean, I think so. Because it's the way this society is here" (Kofi, black, thirty-five). However, like the other black friends, he separates his friend from any negative connotations in his response. Yes, Kofi says, Dave is privileged, but "he didn't ask for it . . . it just happened." When comparing Kofi's and Dave's responses, it is obvious that Kofi has given the issue of racism considerably more thought than Dave. He is quick to say that his white friend has an advantage over him because of race. However, he does not allow that perception to cool his warm feelings toward his friend. Instead, he excuses Dave from any responsibility for that privilege, saying "he didn't ask for it." And they never discuss it.

With different strategies, these two friends have worked together to ensure that race does not come between them. Dave had simply never thought about the issue enough to realize that he had any race-based advantage over Kofi. Kofi, however, recognizes that Dave has advantages over him as a white man but maintains that "it's just the way society is here" and never brings mention of it into their friendship. Like most of the other black interviewees, he keeps this knowledge "on a shelf" and out of his relationship with his white friend. In doing so, they are able to keep their focus on what they have in common with their close cross-racial friend.

Not all the black interviewees stated as explicitly as Kofi their separation of racism in society from their relationship with their white friend, but most made comments about their friendship, such as "it's not about race" and "it's just personal." In ways different yet parallel to the efforts of their white friends, the black friends have managed to place their friendship outside the negativity associated with racial issues in American society. None mentioned having any negative feelings brought on by their white friends having a race-based privilege that they cannot share.

Two black interviewees, although well aware of structural injustices, did not believe that their particular white friend had race-based advantages over them. Another five of the black interviewees embraced the color-blind notion that whites no longer have an advantage over blacks in American society. All except one of these seven were born after the culmination of the civil rights movement and during the color-blind era. The exception is Harriet, a fifty-one-year-old. Although she first answered "Yes, as a white woman, yah, [Marie Elena] probably has an advantage over me," she began to backtrack, saying that "race might play the other side . . . if someone feels that they would have to do what's politically correct." She went on to say

> I guess I'm kind of waffling because I really never thought about it. She might and she might not. . . . Let's put it this way, it's a possibility she might. But it's a possibility again, depending on the climate. I know she's good at what she does. Anything she gets, she deserves. (Harriet, black, fifty-one)

In just a few sentences, Harriet began to say that whites are privileged in our society and then took back that statement when she began to think of her own friend in light of it.

Although one might argue that the other black interviewees who do not strongly maintain that their white friend has an advantage over them as a result of race are in denial or simply too young to have experienced the full impact of racism in the United States, Harriet was an active participant in the civil rights movement, took courses in black studies, and grew up in a family well connected with leaders in African American history. National and international antiracist activists like Langston Hughes and Oliver Tambo were family friends. Today, Harriet is a lay leader in her church who advocates for racial justice. The fact that she had not thought about her friend's white privilege is a testimony to both the power of homophily in friendships and the power of color blindness as an ideology.

■ Color Blindness and Homophily and Antiracist Activism Among Close Black/White Friends

Although their close cross-racial friendship did not lead them to avoid racial issues, neither did it inspire most of the antiracist activists among the white friends to become antiracist activists. The eleven white interviewees who are antiracist activists managed to avoid the disarming influence of color blindness by embracing an antiracist ideology. None of the eleven had difficulty discerning the costs of racism for their black friend or, for the most part, discussing that fact with their close black friend. Ten of the eleven white antiracist activists had serious and open discussions about racial justice with their close black friend.

However, as in most friendships, homophily influenced the close cross-racial friendships in which the white antiracists were involved. All the anti-racist activists made the point that their friendships did not focus on racial issues. Although ten of the eleven said they had frank discussions about racial injustice with their close black friend, they emphasized that they tend to focus on other issues, primarily on what they have in common with one another. Although they would feel comfortable talking about racial issues with their friend, they do not make race a center of their friendship. Further evidence of the cross-racial friendships' lack of influence as a progressive racial change agent is the fact that only four of the eleven became antiracists primarily due to their experiences in a close cross-racial friend-ship. Most were motivated to fight racial injustice through being exposed to an antiracist ideology by their religion (religions of white antiracists respondents included Quaker, Catholic, and Episcopalian).

The era in which the friends grew up seems to influence their level of antiracism activity. Nine of the nineteen white friends over the age of thirty discussed efforts they have made to fight racial discrimination, whereas very few of the younger white interviewees said that they actively work to alle-viate racism in American society. Only two of the twenty-one interviewees under thirty described seeking out ways to improve race relations between whites and blacks. Most of the younger adults in the sample are in college environments and just beginning to form a sense of how individuals may affect society. The increasing popularity of the color-blind perspective on race no doubt has also heavily influenced younger white Americans and made it especially difficult for them to perceive their race-based privilege.

However, it is important to note that even the white interviewees who do not actively fight racism articulated some degree of change in their perspec-tive on race through their close interracial friendships. Like the respondents in Jackman and Crane's sample of whites with black friends and acquaintances, their contact with blacks through these close cross-racial friendships have made them less likely to see blacks as stereotypical figures and more likely to view them as potential friends. Through these friendships and the tendency for "like to attract like," these close black/white friends tend to focus on their similarities and ignore their differences. This supports the intergroup contact hypothesis at the same time that it reveals the necessity to move beyond strategies for prejudice reduction and toward impetuses for antiracist activism.

■ Conclusion

This chapter examines the efficacy of Allport (1954) and Pettigrew's (1997) intergroup contact hypothesis as a strategy for promoting antiracist activism. Using a sample of forty pairs of close black/white friends, this research reveals that, although all the white friends attained more positive outlooks toward blacks, few became antiracist activists through their close friendship with a black person. This supports Allport and Pettigrew's contention that, under the right circumstances, cross-racial contact can lead to prejudice and anxiety reduction. It also reveals the inadequacy of the intergroup contact hypothesis as a strategy to encourage white Americans to become antiracist activists. In the post–civil rights color-blind era, reduced prejudice no longer leads to the progressive racial change it once did. Now that legal segregation no longer exists, it is increasingly easy for Americans to accept the color-blind notion that racism no longer exists. Unfortunately, that leaves us with a society in which even whites who become friends with blacks no longer feel compelled to give up or to even notice their white privilege.

Both the natural desire for homophily in friendships and the prevailing ideology of color blindness encouraged the black/white friends to focus on their similarities and ignore the race-based differences between them. Doing so enabled them to avoid the discomfort of having to acknowledge their differences and allowed them to experience the interpersonal attraction common among the majority of same-race close friends. It also kept them in tune with the now mainstream ideology of color blindness in American society.

However, the strategy of "impression management" displayed by the large majority of the cross-racial friends in this sample indicates that such friendships are not particularly useful for creating and/or spreading antiracist activism. These findings also challenge the efficacy of the intergroup contact hypothesis for antiracism work. In order to go beyond reducing negative feelings and make strides toward racial justice, antiracist activists must do much more than bring different races together in the manner outlined by the intergroup contact hypothesis. In order for whites to become antiracist activists, they must first encounter and embrace an antiracist ideology.

Simply becoming friends, even *close* friends, with black Americans will not motivate most white Americans to combat or even recognize racism in American society. In fact, involvement in such friendships may even discourage whites from noticing the race-based differences between themselves and their black friend. Although cross-racial friendships may be fulfilling for many individuals, they do not effectively combat racism in the United States. Racial justice advocates should leave behind efforts to promote interracial friendships and focus their energy on establishing an antiracist ideology that can effectively counter the prevailing color-blind ideology.

■ Notes

1. Interviewees were asked to discuss the following topics: (1) basic demographic information; (2) background on when and how friendship began; (3) how strong the friendship is (is it really a "close" friendship?); (4) their views on members of their friend's race before the friendship; (5) their views on members of their friend's race now; (6) general views on race relations in United States before the friendship; (7) general views on race relations in United States now; (8) how they believe race affects their close cross-racial friendship (if at all); (9) how their close cross-racial friendship has influenced how they view racial issues and act about racial issues (if at all); (10) reactions of friends, family, acquaintances, and strangers to close cross-racial friendship; (11) whether race was discussed in household of origin; (12) whether issues of race were discussed between close cross-racial friends; (13) race of parents' friends; (14) whether they are or have been prejudiced or have practiced discrimination against members of another race (if so, what race(s) and why); (15) how they feel about their own race generally; (16) whether they feel connected to members of their own race; (17) what is the racial makeup of their other friends and how close are these friendships; (18) if they went to a party where they did not know anybody, would they go over to the white side or the black side? Why?; and, (19) whether they think they or their friend has any advantages or disadvantages due to race (compared to the other).

2. Korgen faces at least one such well-meaning audience member during almost all her conference presentations. She also finds the college students she teaches raising such color-blind-based queries on a regular basis.

3. Another said that, although he faced much racial discrimination, this actually made him a stronger and more capable person than his white friend.

18

Black and Latino: Dominican Americans Negotiate Racial Worlds

Benjamin Bailey

As a group whose members are both Hispanic *and* largely of African descent, Dominican Americans must negotiate distinctive issues of identity in the United States.[1] Up to 90 percent of Dominicans have sub-Saharan African ancestry (Haggerty 1991), which would make them African American by historical, US one-drop rules (Davis 1991; Harris 1964). African-descent Dominicans range in phenotype, in a smooth continuum, from individuals who match stereotypes of African phenotype to those who match stereotypes of European phenotype. Though the phenotypes of many second-generation Dominicans match those associated with black and white American identities in the United States, few second-generation Dominican Americans think of themselves in US black/white racial terms. Rather, they think of their race as "Dominican," "Spanish," or "Hispanic," and their Spanish-language use and Latino cultural practices make this ethnolinguistic identity situationally salient to outsiders (Bailey 2002; Moya Pons 1996; Torres-Saillant and Hernández 1998). Everyday enactment of a Dominican American identity thus involves negotiating multiple and conflicting ascriptions of identity and resisting US black/white racial categorization, a fundamental form of social organization in the United States (Bailey 2000; Feagin 1991; Omi and Winant 1994; Rodríguez 1994).

Social categorization systems such as race are rooted in social history, but their historical, contingent bases are commonly veiled, giving them the appearance of a natural order in the present. In the case of Dominican immigration to the United States, individual migrants and their children confront and negotiate differences between historical US and Dominican racialization practices in their everyday lives (see Mittelberg and Waters 1992). This process brings historical differences in racialization practices into sharp relief in the present. The negotiation of these contrasting systems by individual Dominican Americans illuminates racial formation processes in the United States that are otherwise highly naturalized and can highlight links between historical, macrosocial dimensions of race, and individuals' agency in negotiating such structures.

These Dominican American identity negotiations are representative, in some ways, of new framings of social difference in the United States that result from large-scale, ongoing immigration from Latin America, the Caribbean, and Asia. For post-1965 immigrants, many forms of social differentiation—those based on language or national origins—are much more salient in everyday life than the perceived presence or absence of African ancestry.[2] By the late 1990s, over 20 percent of the US population consisted of first- and second-generation immigrants (Rumbaut and Portes 2001a). As the post-1965 immigrant population grows in the United States, such immigrants and their children are reframing notions of race and what constitutes significant social difference, particularly in the geographical areas where they are present in large numbers, thus reshaping color-line negotiations and the meanings of race in the United States (Bailey 2001).[3]

Dominican American enactments of identity illuminate contradictions in the historical US black/white racialization system particularly clearly for two reasons: (1) Dominican Americans, as a group, seemingly straddle the categories of black, white, and Latino; and (2) Dominican Americans maintain understandings of race and social categorization that directly contradict popular US discourses on race.

In terms of phenotype, individual Dominicans variously match traditional US criteria for inclusion in the categories "black" or "white," but in terms of language and cultural heritage, they match criteria for assignment to the popularly and officially recognized category "Hispanic." The multiple and crosscutting ways in which Dominican Americans fit these categories undermine the assumptions of discreteness and fundamental difference upon which categories of race are constructed. Dominican American enactment of ethnolinguistic identity problematizes the constructed category African American particularly clearly because African-descent *race* in the United States has historically been treated as equivalent to African American *ethnicity* (Waters 1991). The Spanish language of Dominican Americans—in addition to cultural practices involving food, music, religion, residential patterns, and transnational relations—makes their Hispanic ethnicity highly salient, which directly undermines the popular US construction of black identity as ahistorical, monolithic, and primordial.

Dominican immigrants also bring with them ways of understanding their African and European ancestry that are directly at odds with the ways in which such ancestry has historically been understood and has historically shaped social organization in the United States. In the United States, a white majority have maintained a color line for centuries, and popular notions of race are dominated by dichotomous categories of "black" and "white," which are popularly seen as representing unbridgeable difference. In the Dominican Republic, in contrast, the majority of the population range across a continuum of phenotypes encompassing both African and European ancestry, and there is little sense of social identity associated with perceived relative degrees of African and European ancestry (Davis 1994).

In this chapter, I emphasize the subjective and performed dimensions of social categories such as race. Although race and ethnicity are popularly seen as natural categories that capture the essential nature of members of a group, social scientists since the 1960s have emphasized that ethnic and racial categories—and reality more generally (Berger and Luckmann 1967; Schutz 1967)—are socially constructed. Race, as such, is not a static thing but part of an ongoing process of social differentiation, with different configurations and meanings across time and space. Referents of the English word "race" have varied even within the past century in the United States: various immigrant groups in the early 1900s, such as Jews, Italians, and Slavs, were referred to as races (Waters 1990), for example, whereas now they are more commonly described as ethnic groups.

In a seminal article, Frederick Barth (1969) argued that ethnic groups are defined by the *boundaries* that groups construct between themselves, rather than the characteristics of group members. Social categories are thus about the processes through which individuals and groups create, maintain, or diminish social boundaries, rather than about the avowed content of those categories. This formulation foregrounds the subjective, social reality of individual actors, in that it is their judgments and activities, rather than static characteristics of individuals, that serve to constitute categories. Social identity becomes a function of two subjective processes: "self-ascription"—how one defines oneself—and "ascription by others"—how others define one (Barth 1969: 13).

On the surface, such a formulation appears to minimize the role of history and structure in the performance of identity, but social history and hierarchy are omnipresent as everyday, Gramscian "commonsense" understandings of the world, as embodied history or *habitus* (Bourdieu 1990). Individuals only ascribe identities to themselves that are imaginable in a particular social and historical context, and they are only ratified in identities (through other-ascription) that social history makes available to them. The social categories to which individuals ascribe themselves and to which they are ascribed by others are thus linked to historical social processes, and negotiations of identity take place within the parameters that history has imposed in a particular time and place.

■ Dominican (American) Understandings of Race

Second-generation Dominican understandings of themselves as Dominican or Spanish, rather than black or white, have roots in traditional Dominican understandings of race and identity. In the Dominican Republic, there is no binary division among Dominicans into social categories based on the perceived presence or absence of sub-Saharan African ancestry, and Dominicans do not have a notion of race that differentiates among Dominicans in the way the folk notion of black/white differentiates among Americans (Duany 1998; Fennema 1987; Hoetink 1967, 1985; Itzigsohn and Dore-Cabral 2000; Moya Pons 1996). There is no sense of ethnicity or group identity based on or symbolized by relative degrees of African or European ancestry. For Dominicans, Dominican nationality, Dominican ethnicity, and Dominican race are more or less the same thing (Davis 1994; Del Castillo 1987).

Dominicans on the island see their essential identity as relatively unrelated to individual phenotype. When I surveyed fifteen Dominicans in Santiago, Dominican Republic, asking, "Cuál es tu raza?" (What race/people are you?), they answered, "dominicano/a" (Dominican) without regard to individual phenotype, and most treated this expression of identity as a statement of the obvious.[4] This categorical identification as dominicano/a occurred despite the placement of the question in my survey immediately after a question referring explicitly to skin color: "Cuál es el color de tu piel?" (What color is your skin?), which elicited one answer of "blanco" (white), one of "moreno" (dark, black), and thirteen answers of some form of "indio" (Indian-colored).[5] Although Dominicans recognize and label differences in phenotype, different phenotypes are not the basis for ethnic, racial, or social groupings. Following a pattern with parallels in other Latin American countries (Rout 1976), individual phenotype is much less relevant for social identity than individual education, income, and regional origins and whether one comes from a rural or urban background.[6]

Regardless of phenotype, few Dominicans on the island think of themselves as being black (*negro*), a term that they typically reserve for non-Latino, African-descent peoples such as West Indians, US African Americans, and Haitians.[7] In the United States the "one-drop" rule has made individuals with perceived, recorded, or imagined African ancestry count as "black" (Domínguez 1986), but in the Dominican Republic, a very different one-drop rule is in effect: perceived or imagined European ancestry makes an individual *not* black.

These traditional Dominican ways of conceptualizing Dominican race and identity directly inform the understandings and identity enactments of second-generation Dominicans, who resist black/white racialization. For the Dominican Americans whom I interviewed and recorded in Providence,[8] Dominican "race" does not refer to distinctions based on or symbolized by[9] phenotype but to linguistic and national-origin distinctions, much closer to dominant US notions of "ethnicity." In both interview and more discursive contexts, members of the second generation used the same set of labels— Spanish, Dominican, Hispanic, or Latino—to identify their race *and* their culture or ethnicity. When asked specifically how they identified their race ("If someone asked you, 'What's your race?' what would you say?"), individuals described their race as "Spanish" or "Hispanic" and sometimes as "Dominican" or "Latino," but never as "black" or "white," regardless of phenotype.

For Dominican-born individuals such as Wilson (age seventeen, arrived at age seven), race is nothing more than where one was before coming to the United States:

> *BB:* What does "race" mean to you?
> *Wilson:* If they're asking, "What race are you?" I just say what I am. Dominican, Spanish. It means like where you're from.

For US-born individuals such as Martin (age seventeen), race is typically defined in terms of where one's parents or grandparents were before they came to the United States:

> *Martin:* Where you're originally from, like your parents and your grandparents and things like that, that's what I take for your race.

Some adult Dominican Americans are conscious of the disjunctures between their understandings of race and the historical US system. Rafael (age twenty-eight), for example, was a highly educated professional who described his race as "Latino" but recognized that it was a distinctive way of conceptualizing race in the larger society:

> *BB:* If someone asked you, "What's your race?" what would you say?
> *Rafael:* Latino.
> *BB:* What do you understand when you hear the term "race"?
> *Rafael:* . . . The first thing that comes to mind is black and white. Because . . . typically that's where . . . that's the way things were characterized in American history. Either black or white. And as you know, they've had . . . if you had any type of black blood, you were considered black. That's what I think about when I hear the word "race." Where that leaves me as a Latino is kind of outside of that category. I look at it more as, "Where did your ancestors come from?" . . . So when I think about race, I think about color. Because I think that's the traditional way. But when I think about race when someone asks my race, I think about, "Where do you come from?" I group it more, I think, almost with ethnicity, to some degree.

This concept of race highlights the historical and cultural specificity of US notions of race, both popular and academic. Such Dominican American understandings of race are at odds with dominant US understandings, which privilege phenotype (as a marker of imputed descent) and collapse ethnic, cultural, and historical distinctions among African-descent peoples.

■ An Ethnolinguistic Basis for Race

The Spanish language of the Dominican immigrant community is a key to claiming and enacting identities outside the black/white racial dichotomy. In terms of ascription by outsiders, it is a defining criterion for assignment to a widely recognized, preexisting social category in the United States. In terms of everyday immigrant life, it enables full participation in a thriving ethnolinguistic community with its own churches, restaurants, stores, Spanish-language media, and community organizations, a world that exists in many ways parallel to and separate from Anglophone society. This thriving community validates the customs, language, and beliefs of the first generation, reinforcing a common cultural memory and identity for the second generation. The presence of a vibrant and visible local Dominican community—within a vibrant and growing national Latino community—is key to the second generation's maintenance of Dominican frameworks for racial categorization in the face of dominant US phenotype-symbolized racialization practices.[10]

The significance of the Spanish language for countering phenotype-racial identity ascriptions and communicating an ethnolinguistic identity in everyday encounters is evident in both (1) Dominican Americans' explanations of how outsiders know that they are Dominican/Hispanic rather than "black" or "white"; and (2) the common proof procedure that Dominicans use to counter others' assumptions that they are black or white American: they show that they can speak Spanish.

Martin (US-born, age seventeen), for example, used Spanish strategically to differentiate himself from white Americans:

> *Martin:*   I don't really look Spanish. . . . People don't think that I'm Spanish until I tell them I speak Spanish, or whatever. If they just look at me, "Oh, it doesn't look like he's Spanish."
> *BB:*   Do Dominicans tease you and say, "Oh, you're white"?
> *Martin:*   No—sometimes that'll happen. Sometimes they don't know I'm Spanish, and they'll say something or whatever and I'll say something back in Spanish but not directly to them, but just so they can hear it, though.

A much larger percentage of Dominican Americans are regularly perceived to be African American. Even in Providence, where (African-descent)

Caribbean Hispanics outnumber non-Hispanic African-descent groups, many Dominican Americans are assumed to be African American until they are heard speaking Spanish:

> *BB:*   If somebody asks you, "What are you?" what do
> you say?
> *Janelle* (US-born, age seventeen):   I usually say Spanish,
> Dominican. I'll usually say Dominican first, 'cause most people
> . . . most people think I'm black though. A lot of people think
> I'm black. A lot of people! . . .
> *BB:*   Can you think of a specific time when someone thought you
> were black?
> *Janelle:*   I was in the gym, and usually in school
> I don't really talk in Spanish, and I was talking to some
> kid in English, and some girl, I guess she was listening,
> and I said a word in Spanish, and she goes, "Oh my god,
> you're Spanish." No, she goes, "You know Spanish." She
> thought I was just a black who knew Spanish. I was like,
> "I am Spanish." She's like, "Oh my god, I thought you was
> Cape Verdean or Black." I was like, "No." A lot of people
> think I'm black. I don't know, it's usually just little things
> like that, just people be like, "What are you, black?" I'm like,
> "No, I'm Spanish."

In Janelle's reported exchange with an African American classmate, "Spanish" is treated not just as a language but also as an ethnic/racial identity. Janelle and her interlocutor treat the social category "Spanish" as parallel in type to the folk-racial category "black" but mutually exclusive from it. In local terms, if one is Dominican or Spanish-speaking, one doesn't count as "black," regardless of phenotype. An individual only counts as black and Spanish in this local context if he or she has a Spanish parent *and* a non-Hispanic African-descent parent.

This local system of classification does not necessarily privilege identities based on phenotype—specifically, perceived degrees of European and African ancestry—over those based on other social criteria such as language or national origins. Janelle's African-descent, or "black," phenotype remains constant, but she no longer *counts* as black when she speaks Spanish and claims a Spanish identity. Race is thus treated not as a static attribute of individuals, but rather as a locally and linguistically achieved identity. This agency is particularly striking in resistance to black/white racial ascription, which is the type of social identity ascription over which individuals have historically had least control in the United States (Mittelberg and Waters 1992; Smedley 1993).

■ The Interactional Negotiation of Race

I videotaped one instance in which a Dominican American explicitly negotiates his racial identity in everyday, naturally occurring interaction with
peers. In this segment of interaction (transcribed below) during a high
school class, a student of Southeast Asian descent, Pam, tells an African-
descent Dominican American, Wilson, "I never thought you were Spanish"
after seeing him converse in Spanish. She had assumed he was African
American but then came to realize that he was Spanish when she heard him
speak Spanish. As a joke, Wilson and a Dominican confederate, JB, pretend
that Wilson *is* black or African American and not Spanish.[11] Although Wilson never identifies himself as black or African American (his self-ascription
as "Spanish" or "Dominican," above, was typical in my interactions with
him), he and JB know that Wilson is regularly perceived to be African American.[12] This enables them to try to fool Pam by getting her to believe that
Wilson is black, a social category attribution that is implausible from a
Dominican perspective. The humor of this put-on depends on tensions and
disparities between Dominican and US sociocultural frameworks for understanding race and social categories.

When Pam cites Wilson's speaking of Spanish as evidence that he is
Spanish rather than black, JB and Wilson initially deny that he can speak
Spanish and then devise scenarios that could explain his apparent Spanish
use. They falsely claim, for example, that Wilson's father is black and that
his mother is black *and* Spanish and was born in the United States. (Wilson was born of Dominican parents in the Dominican Republic and came to
live in Providence with his father as a seven-year-old.) Wilson and JB are
engaged in an adolescent put-on, but at the same time they are negotiating
ethnic and racial categories and the criteria for defining a person as "black"
or "Spanish." (In the following dialogue, bracketed text indicates words
spoken in overlap or a translation of the immediately preceding Spanish.
Parentheses indicate uncertainty about the accuracy of transcribed words or
material that could not be heard clearly enough to transcribe. Double parentheses indicate nonverbal, visual, or background information.)

> ((Wilson has finished explaining to JB, in Spanish, the function of the
>   wireless microphone that he is wearing.))
> *Pam:*   Yo, the first time I saw you, I never thought you were
>   Spanish.
> ((short pause))
> *Wilson:*   [Who ?]
> *JB:*   [(He's)] black.
> Pam: I never—
> *Wilson:*   'Cause I'm black.
> *JB:*   (   )

Wilson: 'Cause I'm black.

Pam: No.

JB: His father [is black], her mother is . . . his mother is,
   uh . . .

Wilson: [I'm black.]

Pam: (Can he) speak Spanish?

JB: No.

Wilson: 'Cause I was . . . [I was]

Pam: [Yeah!]

JB: So why (   )?

Wilson: No, no, seriously. I'm black, and I was raised in the
   Dominican Republic. ((short pause)) For real.

Pam: Your mother's black?

Wilson: My mom? No, my father.

Pam: Your father's black, your [mother's Spanish?]

Wilson: [My mom's Spanish.]

JB: His mom is black—and she's Spanish.

Wilson: Is mixed.

JB: His mom was born over here.

((Pause. Wilson smiles at Pam and throws a piece of paper at her.))

JB: Wilson, don't throw anything to her.

Wilson: Excúsame, se me olvidó, que es la jeva tuya [Sorry, I forgot
   that she is your girlfriend].

JB: Callate, todavía no [Be quiet, not yet]!

Pam: English!

JB: English, yeah!

Wilson: I said I'm sorry.

JB: He can't speak Spanish.

Pam: I saw you were talking to him (   ).

The Spanish language is being treated in this segment as the key to racial/ethnic identity, preceding phenotype. When JB and Wilson claim that Wilson is not Spanish but black, Pam mentions that he has just spoken Spanish. The implication is that if Wilson can *speak* Spanish, then he *is* Spanish, rather than black. Wilson and JB also treat the Spanish language as the key to determining social identity, both for ratification as Spanish and for disqualification from the category "black." JB initially denies that Wilson can speak Spanish, despite immediately available counterevidence. Admitting that Wilson can speak Spanish would invalidate JB and Wilson's line that Wilson is not Spanish but black.

The term "Spanish" is used by participants here to refer to Spanish identity four times and to Spanish language twice. It is not only Dominican Americans who use the term "Spanish" to describe both language and race/ethnicity. Pam, a teenager of Southeast Asian descent, is using it as a social category that she explicitly juxtaposes with African American race/ ethnicity: "Your father's Black, your mother's Spanish?" "Spanish" is a local social category based on linguistic and cultural criteria that is treated as equivalent in type to traditional US phenotype-based racial categories such as black and white.

Social classification based on linguistic and cultural heritage may capture the local social reality at this high school much better than black/white classification. The US categories of black and white developed out of a particular centuries-long social history in the United States. The historical relations between white Americans and African Americans are not of primary importance to the vast majority of students at this school, where over 80 percent of the students are immigrants or the children of immigrants. Their families have only been in the United States since the late 1960s or later, that is, the post–civil rights era (or in the case of some of the Puerto Rican students, since the 1950s).

Binary racial categorization based on phenotype is less immediately relevant in this setting than students' immigrant languages and cultures. Fewer than 10 percent of the students at Central High School are non-Hispanic white, and only 16 percent are non-Hispanic black, many of them immigrants. In this largely immigrant context, Wilson's immigrant ethnolinguistic identity is a more useful guide to significant attributes about him than his phenotype. At Central High School, such a Spanish identity might suggest that one speaks Spanish at home, eats Caribbean Latino food, socializes with other Spanish speakers, goes to Spanish nightclubs and Spanish-language Mass, has multiple, ongoing ties to Latin America, translates for parents, and so on. Such a bilingual/bicultural immigrant identity is likely familiar to Pam and may have strong parallels in her own life.

Although Wilson's phenotype remains constant, his racial identity is locally constituted and negotiated through language. Such negotiations denaturalize popular notions of race as a static and essential attribute of individuals. In this case, Wilson's achievement of a Spanish identity in an interethnic encounter highlights both the agency of an individual to resist the hegemonic racial structuring of society and the subjective nature of identity constitution, as his identity is achieved through congruent self-ascription and other-ascription.

■ Implications for Racial Justice of Such Microlevel Identity Negotiations

According to Michael Omi and Howard Winant (1994), race is a system of inequality (rooted in Western imperialism and, more immediately for most African Americans, in US slavery) that makes reference to skin color or phenotype. This system is not static but processual: racial categories are constituted, challenged, inhabited, and reproduced in racial formation (Omi and Winant 1994). Following poststructural theories that link individual agency to social structure (Giddens 1984) and power to discourse and symbolic representation (Bourdieu 1984; Bourdieu and Passeron 1990; Foucault 1982; Williams 1961), Omi and Winant argue that race is a matter of both social structure and cultural representation. Race exists in concrete social structures such as segregation and inequality in schooling and labor market participation, as well as in cultural representations, such as the (everyday) assignment of individuals to particular social categories and attribution of group social characteristics to members of those categories (1994: 56, 59–60). Our commonsense racial understandings (cultural representations) help us both to interpret existing racial structure and to rationalize ongoing structural inequality. Social structural dimensions of race both reflect racial understandings and provide ongoing material evidence to support or reconstitute such racial understandings.

According to Omi and Winant, in the post–civil rights era United States, cultural representations of racial difference have become increasingly important for maintaining the racial organization of society. This racial organization was long enforced through direct corporeal coercion—for example, control of African American bodies with chains and whips and later, executive branch enforcement of segregation and Jim Crow—but racial formation in the post–civil rights era is driven by more hegemonic, symbolic means.

It is in this context—in which hegemonic cultural representations and "commonsense" racial ascriptions maintain racial organization—that Dominican American negotiations of identity have implications for racial justice. Dominican American enactment of identities outside the black/white dichotomy does not have direct effects on material inequality in US racial structure, but such identity enactments *do* counter hegemonic racial understandings, particularly in sociogeographical contexts with high concentrations of immigrants who fall outside the black/white dichotomy.

Being able to control racial representations of oneself or one's group marks a securing of symbolic power in the face of a racial system that relies on symbolic means for the maintenance of inequality. Successfully contesting the phenomenological, symbolic boundaries of race can also be a key to subsequently confronting its more static and structural dimensions. Symbolic boundaries are, in important senses, prior to more static, social boundaries, in that it is only when symbolic boundaries are widely recognized and agreed up that they can translate into more fixed social boundaries and patterns of exclusion (Lamont and Molnar 2002). Dominican American enactments of race call into question the notions of race in the United States that are otherwise commonsense. When the subjective, phenomenological bases of race are undermined, the underlying inequality that is the basis of race is brought into sharper relief, and the clash between such inequality and US ideals of equality and democracy becomes starker and less tenable in public discourse.

■ A White/Nonwhite Color Line

Successful resistance to the black/white dichotomy does not, in and of itself, represent the achievement of racial equality for the children of Dominican immigrants. Most Dominican Americans who successfully claim and enact identities outside the dichotomy are still excluded from the racial category white, with its attendant privileges. In the following exchange from an interview during a break at school, Janelle (seventeen, US-born), Jose (seventeen, arrived at age eight), and I (thirty-four, US-born, Anglo-American) grapple with various ascriptions of identity for US-born Janelle. Although Jose and Janelle agree that she is "American" in one sense and "Dominican" in another, Janelle points out that when people ask her, "What are you?" they do not want her to answer that she is "American."

> *BB:* If someone asks, "What's your race?" what would you say?
> *Janelle:* I would say Hispanic.
> *BB:* If a person says, "I'm American," what group do you think they belong to?
> *Janelle:* "American" to me would be white, but I consider myself American even though I would say Spanish.
> *BB:* If a person has Dominican parents but was born here and grew up here, should they say they're American or should they say they're Dominican?
> *Janelle:* See, that's what I think is American. You born here, the fact that you was born here, no matter what your parents are.
> *BB:* So what should those kids say?
> *Janelle:* What should they say? I say Dominican, but . . .
> I know I'm not really Dominican, my parents are.
> (Four turns are omitted during which Jose and Janelle discuss whether Janelle is really Dominican.)
> *Jose:* You're American.
> *Janelle:* I know I'm American, but—
> *Jose:* You're American, but you got the blood of Dominican.
> *Janelle:* But when people say, "What are you?" they usually want like "Dominican." I'm saying that's what they want, or "Puerto Rican," not "I was born here."

This interaction highlights a number of competing ways in which Dominican Americans think of themselves and are seen by others. Notions of race, citizenship, and belonging overlap in the exclusion Janelle experiences from the unmarked category "American." For Janelle, citizenship is racialized: "American" implies a white identity, which Janelle does not claim or enact. Even though she was US-born, thus fulfilling a defining and sufficient criterion for citizenship, she situationally excludes herself—and is excluded by others—from the category of "American." The very fact that Janelle faces the question, "What are you?"—and that she understands people to be relatively uninterested in her US birth and citizenship—implies a marked racial status for which a certain type of account needs to be given.

For some Dominican Americans, this exclusion can lead to explicit political solidarity with black Americans. Ana (US-born, twenty-nine, college graduate), for example, saw her race as "Hispanic." She did not match stereotypes of African American phenotype, and she did not report ever being perceived as African American, but she knew that white Americans would not include her in the category white.

> *BB:* If someone asked you, "What is your race?" how would you answer?
> *Ana:* Depending on the options. If you have the options—
> *BB:* . . . let's say someone is just talking to you . . .
> *Ana:* What race are you? Hispanic. Now as far as the forms are concerned, when—and this is a discussion I had with someone, maybe a couple of years ago—you know when you have the list of races—white, black, Asian, Indian, other—when you only have those options, I would check off black.
> *BB:* You would?
> *Ana:* I would. I wouldn't check off white. My skin color is not white, so an American would not believe that I'm white anyways.

Like Janelle, above, Ana is US-born, but she sees herself as situationally excluded from the full privileges of citizenship and belonging, which are reserved for white Americans.

Although Dominican American claims of Spanish or Hispanic identities represent the symbolic power to speak for oneself and reject commonsense categories, they also reflect the hegemonic racial structuring of the United States at a more subtle level. Pan-national labels such as "Spanish," "Hispanic," or "Latino" are US constructions (Itzigsohn and Dore-Cabral 2000; Oboler 1995; Rumbaut and Portes 2001a) that reflect and reproduce exclusion from the racial category white and its attendant privileges. The claim and enactment of "Spanish" identities can thus reproduce white privilege by reconstituting a white/nonwhite color line.

■ Conclusion

Dominicans form only one part of the larger, post-1965 immigrant stream, but their identity negotiations suggest future directions of US racial formation processes. Like their Caribbean, Latin American, and Asian compatriots,

Dominicans come from a part of the world that was once colonized by Europeans; most Dominicans do not count as white in the dominant United States racial hierarchy; and they bring with them systems of social categorization distinct from the ones that have been historically dominant in the United States. As post-1965 immigrants and their children and grandchildren comprise an ever-larger percentage of the US population over the next decades, US constructions of race and identity will necessarily shift to accommodate groups whose identities and understandings of social categories are only partially a function of pre-1965 US social history.

The Dominican American racial understandings and practices that are documented in this chapter serve to illuminate racial formation processes in the United States that are otherwise veiled. Although academics have emphasized since the 1960s that race is a social construction, race can seem like a natural order of the world to many Americans, for whom it is a commonsensical organizing principle of society, visible in patterns of residence, marriage, association, and behavior. Similarly, although poststructuralist theorists have emphasized that relationships between individual social actors and social structure are reciprocal, it is often difficult to discern the agency of social actors because they commonly reproduce existing patterns of social relations.

The notions of race maintained by many Dominican Americans and their everyday enactment of Spanish racial identities, in contrast, highlight the processual, constructed nature of racial categories and individuals' agency in the (re)constitution of categories. In proposing and maintaining a different way of understanding European and African descent, Dominican Americans collectively undermine the commonsense nature of received US racial categories. On an individual level, by resisting black/white ascription, Dominican Americans highlight the agency of individual social actors to respond to sociohistorical circumstances and reshape the available macrosocial categories, at least at the local level.

Being able to represent oneself in one's own terms marks a securing of symbolic power in the face of a US racial system that has increasingly come to rely on symbolic means for the maintenance of inequality. Such negotiations thus represent an achievement of a degree of racial justice at the local level. Contesting the phenomenological, symbolic boundaries of race is also a necessary, preliminary step to confronting its more static and structural dimensions.

While Dominican American claims of Spanish or Hispanic identities represent the symbolic power to speak for oneself and reject commonsense US categories, they may also reproduce the hegemonic privileges of whiteness in the United States. When African-descent Dominicans successfully enact nonblack identities, it denaturalizes the category black, but it does not alter or call into question the privileges associated with whiteness. The very agency that such Dominican Americans exhibit in claiming a racial identity outside the traditional system may simply be the insidious, inadvertent collaboration of the oppressed with their oppressors that is characteristic of hegemonic systems. Dominican American negotiations of identity may thus represent part of a shift of US racial organization from a black/white color line to a white/nonwhite color line.

■ Notes

1. I use the term "Dominican American" specifically to refer to US-raised Dominicans whose parents immigrated from the Dominican Republic. I do not include in this category adult Dominican immigrants or third- and fourth-generation Dominicans whose grandparents or great-grandparents immigrated.

2. The watershed event defining this new wave of immigration was the enactment of changes in US immigration law in 1965. Highly restrictive immigration quotas that were based on nationality and favored northwestern European countries were abandoned in favor of increased quotas based on hemisphere, not country. The result of these changes in immigration law was a new wave of immigration beginning in the late 1960s that represented the largest influx of immigrants to the United States since the 1880–1920 period.

3. Over two-thirds of the US immigrant population are concentrated in California, Texas, Florida, and greater New York. While representing over 20 percent of the total US population, immigrants and their children represent a far greater proportion of the population of many metropolitan areas, both in these magnet states as well as in many other destination states.

4. Informants were mostly male, ranging in age from their early teens to early twenties. I approached them at a public basketball court in the upper/upper-middle class neighborhood of Villa Olga and on the street in the more working-class Pueblo Nuevo neighborhood.

5. The term "indio" in the Dominican Republic differs both in denotation and connotation from the term "indio" in the many Latin American countries where it refers to contemporary indigenous groups and is considered pejorative. In the Dominican Republic it does not refer to a contemporary ethnic/social group but to a range of skin colors/phenotypes that do not count as "blanco" (white). The majority of Dominicans describe their skin color as some form of indio, and it is unmarked both as a phenotype and a term.

6. Frank Moya Pons (1995) attributes the relative lack of racial hierarchy in the Dominican Republic in part to historical periods of extreme poverty. The class, or power, hierarchy of the country was so flattened during these times that there were no power differentials to be mapped onto skin color. Both fairer-skinned and darker-skinned Dominicans ate the same food, did the same work, lived together, and so on.

7. Dominican understandings of their color, race, and nationality have been constructed in contradistinction to Haiti, which shares the island of Hispaniola with the Dominican Republic, both historically and in contemporary times (Moya Pons 1995).

8. The data in this chapter come from fieldwork in Providence, Rhode Island, and the Dominican Republic between July 1996 and July 2000. Providence had over 15,000 Dominicans, according to the 2000 census, and they were the largest Latino group in the city. Data collection methods included ethnographic observation, audio-recorded interviews, and videotaping of naturally occurring interactions in school, home, and community contexts. In addition to interviewing over thirty high school

students, fifteen adult members of the second generation, and various administrators, teachers, and graduates, I repeatedly observed six primary subjects at school before videotaping them throughout a school day and in one family or community context.

9. While it is common in the United States to speak of race as "based on" skin color, it is more accurate to think of it as based on historical power differentials, with skin color merely symbolizing these differences.

10. For non-Latino immigrants of African descent, there is either no distinct ethnolinguistic community (e.g., among West Indians) or a much smaller, less vibrant one (e.g., among US Haitians).

11. I use the terms "Spanish," "black," and "African American" in their local, emic senses, following the usage of participants in this interaction. The terms "black" and "African American" refer only to non-Hispanic, African-descent individuals. "Spanish" refers to individuals of Latin American descent. Although "Spanish" individuals may be phenotypically indistinguishable from "blacks," they do not belong to the same social category in this local context.

12. Wilson mentioned other people's confusion about his identity to me a number of times in interview situations:

> A lot of people confuse me for an African-American most of the time. They ask me, "Are you black?" I'm like, "No, I'm Hispanic." and they'll be like, "Oh I thought you were black or something." Most of the time I'll be talking with them, chilling, or whatever. They'll be thinking that I'm just African American. Because sometimes the way I talk, my hair, my skin color, it's just that my hair is nappy. I use a lot of slang. You can confuse a lot of Dominicans as African Americans by their color. So that's why a lot of people just ask me, "I thought you were black, I thought you were this."

19

Finding a Home:
Housing the Color Line

Heather Dalmage

Communities, like clothes, are held together at the seams. Social seams are the places people come together: stores, schools, parks, and street corners (Jacobs 1961).[1] Good fabric, like a good neighborhood, needs the seams. When individuals look for quality, they examine the seams. Most black/white multiracial families are highly aware of these spaces—we have to be, given the unique position of our families in a racist and divided society. Because of the dual and unjust nature of the housing market, multiracial families search for affordable and stable mixed-race areas where some of the forms of daily discrimination in the schools, streets, and stores will be muted, especially for the sake of the children. Children's self-esteem, identity, and interaction with others who can affirm their experiences are bound to the place called home. In my research, multiracial adults have repeatedly spoken to the priority parents of multiracial children ought to put on finding housing in racially diverse areas. In communities with reputations for being stable and racially mixed, we find a disproportionate number of multiracial families. In the parks, playgrounds, schools, and stores—at the seams—these communities can appear to be almost utopian with regard to race. And yet, a closer look reveals the flaws and injustices.

The black/white color line is maintained through individual and institutional effort. Those who cross the line through marriage or parentage face overt discrimination from both sides in the form of hostile actions, comments, and stares. These family members also face various forms of discrimination in institutions set up to protect white privilege. Historically, the color line has been portrayed as normal and worthy of upholding, while those who cross the color line have been labeled pathological. Until recently, most research about multiracial people and families focused on identity problems.[2] Throughout history, laws and court rulings denied the legal existence of multiracial families and people (DaCosta 2004; Romano 2003; Wallerstein 2002). Of course, the motives behind pathologizing and banning the legal existence of multiracial families have been inextricably linked to the (re)creation of systems of race, class, and gender injustice. In her insightful analysis of the construction of race and family in the United States, Kimberly McClain DaCosta points out: "Marriage is, after all, far more than the sentimentalized consecration of love that modern actors imagine it to be. It is also a legal mechanism that regulates the transmission of property" (2004: 26). In his recent book, *Tell the Courts I Love My Wife: Race, Marriage, and Law, An American History,* Peter Wallerstein explains:

> The law of interracial marriage could—and often did—prevent the conveyance of wealth from white to nonwhite. Whiteness brought wealth—absorbed it, retained it, kept it out of the hands of people who, aside from their racial identity, had an entirely legitimate claim on property they nonetheless could not get. In effect, the law of interracial marriage imposed a tax by one group on another, an estate tax that tended to apply to nonwhite people, who paid the tax to whites. (2002: 162)[3]

In other words, the patrolling or policing of multiracial families on an institutional level has worked alongside other legal and extralegal actions to protect white privilege and power.

■ Borders

Throughout history, individuals invested in maintaining the color line have set up borders (Ferber 1998). Racial borders include the contested, patrolled, and often hostile spaces near the color line. Historical creations, borders have become institutionalized and internalized. They exist in how society is structured as well as in how individuals learn to think about and act on race. Borders created to protect resources such as goods and power are kept in place by laws, language, cultural norms, images, and individual action, as well as by interlocking with other borders, including the nation, religion, politics, sex, gender, race, and age. Each has a unique history laden with power struggles. People are raised to understand their world through borders (Dalmage 2000) and are taught from an early age to know where the borders exist. To young children, categories and their borders do not yet represent power and exclusion, they are just puzzles to be figured out. The construction of the puzzle takes place where the physical body (skin color, physical features, hair texture) interacts with family, friends, teachers, the media, the neighborhood, and for many, religion. How children understand the world and themselves racially arises from all these interactions. As they grow, they learn about the power associated with the categories and the consequences (Van Ausdale and Feagin 2001). By doing and seeing what is considered appropriate, they reinforce the strength of the categories and build borders. After learning to see categories, they internalize the borders and assume the socially created differences and valuations of those differences are inherent and natural. In turn, they patrol ourselves and others and, in the process, strengthen the color line (Dalmage 2000).

Border patrolling on an institutional level is grounded in a system of white supremacy. In such a system, social institutions intersect to ensure racial groups are situated in a separate and unequal relationship. For instance, the housing market remains inextricably connected to injustices in the educational system through the processes of redlining, steering, and school funding based on property taxes (Anyon 1997; Brantlinger 2003). The educational system is intimately linked to economic opportunities. The media, in general, continue to spin stories in ways that facilitate whites' comfort with injustice (Entman and Rojecki 2000; Sommerville 2000). Robert Stam and Ella Shohat have written: "The residual traces of everyday language, and the media, engender a fictitious sense of the innate superiority of European-driven cultures and people" (quoted in Rodríguez 1998: 50). Taken together, racial injustices are distorted into an ahistorical question of individual morality and ability, white supremacy is distorted into normalcy, and the color line is normalized and strengthened, while those who cross it are pathologized (Dalmage 2004a).

■ Housing Institution: An Agent of Injustice

> Residential segregation is a key contemporary institution for creating and maintaining inequality, not only for individuals and racial groups, but also for neighborhoods and entire municipalities.
> —Gary Orfield (quoted in Nyden et al. 1998a: 4)

In the 1960s whites were claiming that because many blacks chose to separate themselves from whites, whites should not be culpable for segregation in society. In 1963, Malcolm X responded to these claims by noting that racial separation and racial segregation are not the same. Separation is a choice, whereas segregation occurs in the context of inequality and imposition. In his statement, "It's only segregated when it's controlled by someone from the outside," Malcolm X was making the power relations clear: segregation was about the use of power to maintain an unjust system (quoted in Peller 1995: 128). Manning Marable (1998) has argued that integration is not necessarily the solution because all-black or all-Latino neighborhoods are not the root of the problem. Instead, we should be concerned about the unfair distribution of resources and the underlying racism that devalues people of color in a white supremacist society. I agree. White supremacy is the underlying problem. I would further add that for multiracial families, racial "separation" also causes difficulties. Thus, multiracial families desire to live in integrated neighborhoods, and yet, these areas present a number of problems and reflect the pervasiveness of whiteness. In other words, integration is not the solution when it occurs in a way that maintains and strengthens an unjust racial (and class) order.

■ A Search for Housing Justice

Until recently, my family lived in Uptown, a "diverse" north-side Chicago community.[4] The neighborhood housing includes public housing; low-income, overcrowded rentals; section 8 housing; halfway houses; single-room occupancies; high-end condos; and a few single-family detached homes. In the streets and stores—in the social seams—large numbers of African, Asian, Eastern European, and Latino immigrants, along with black and white Americans, are brought into proximity, if not interaction. In addition, the area just to the west has long been home to a lesbian community, while Uptown has quickly become a new home for gay men who are unable to afford the housing in the wealthier and whiter adjacent gay community. Judging by the number of "for sale" signs, parking shortages, and the increasing number of white faces in the streets and stores, it was obvious that our area was changing at a rapid rate. We did not experience the panic peddling and white-flight transition of the 1960s and 1970s, but rather the constant conversion from rental to condo (white in-flight) transition of the 1990s and 2000s. Panic peddling created neighborhoods that transitioned from white to black and brown in a matter of a few years.[5] The constant conversion has created neighborhoods that have transitioned from black and brown to white in a matter of a few years. The conversions are part of a larger process of gentrification in which, as Harold McDougall states, "low income residents are being displaced by middle and upper income individuals interested in acquiring inner-city housing on the private market" (1981–1982: 179).

The value of property in the United States has historically been determined by the socioeconomic class of the folks in the neighborhood (Jackson 1985). In the housing market, whiteness is constructed as inherently valuable. Whites are viewed as most deserving of good housing, loans, and other subsidies, whereas blacks are devalued and denied access to good housing and loans—even when their credit scores are equal to or better than their white counterparts'.[6] A study by the Association of Community Organizations for Reform Now found that "On average nationally, African Americans were 2.38 times as likely to be denied a conventional purchase money mortgage as Whites" (Sichelman 2003). The outcome has been the maintenance of a segregated and unequal housing market. In such a system, whites who want a continued increase in the value of their property work to "rid the neighborhood of 'undesirables'" that detract from the value—including (or primarily) poor people of color (Gugliemo 2003: 166). As a result, the seams in our neighborhood were fraught with hostility as gentrifiers, generally young childless white professionals, attempted to impose their will on "others" in the neighborhood. Current research in this area by Jeffrey Edwards highlights the way these white gentrifiers are using institutional means to enforce their will: attending Chicago Alternative Policing Strategy (CAPS) meetings in groups and demanding the direction of police enforcement in their areas,[7] calling city inspectors on low-rent apartment buildings in an attempt to coerce landlords into selling or converting the rental building, and the constant calling of 911, particularly when "suspicious" males of color are near their newly acquired property.[8] Of course, these overt methods are primarily used against the youth of color who do not quietly leave the gentrifying neighborhood on their own.[9] In his study, McDougall found that gentrifiers use the courts to argue against the construction of affordable housing and public housing. In short, they work to "keep low income people and minorities from remaining in their own neighborhoods" and thus perpetuate the historical housing processes that value and reward whiteness (1981–1982: 180).

Given the race-class hostilities in our diverse, albeit unstable, neighborhood, we decided this area might not be the best place for our children to grow up. We moved to Hyde Park, the stable, middle-class, "liberal," and self-consciously planned integrated community on the south side of Chicago.[10] Not all integrated neighborhoods are alike (Maly 2005; Nyden et al. 1998a, 1998b). Some are created by circumstance through processes of immigration, diverse housing stock, and other factors, whereas some communities, like Hyde Park, are created quite consciously through organizational and political involvement (Taub, Taylor, and Dunham 1984). In their study of fourteen "diverse" urban communities in nine cities, Nyden and his fellow researchers (1998a, 1998b) found that when organizations intervene to create diversity, the neighborhood will tend to have two middle-class groups (white and black) instead of a broader diversity (race, class, national origins, sexuality). These areas tend to be less diverse, albeit more stable than areas that develop as a matter of circumstance (Nyden et al. 1998a, 1998b; Saltman 1990). Thus stable, black/white integrated communities tend to be middle class and less affordable than other areas.[11]

In their study of four communities that had self-consciously worked to create and maintain integration, Nyden and his fellow researchers found that three of these communities "earned median incomes substantially higher than the city average in 1990 (more than 40 percent higher)" (1998b: 25). My own research shows that many multiracial families would prefer stable racially mixed areas but are unable to afford to live in these middle-class areas. While interviewing members of multiracial families for *Tripping on the Color Line,* I asked "How did you decide on the community you live in now?" Responses included: "I couldn't afford Hyde Park," and "It would be nice to be someplace that's more integrated, but I don't even know if there are any integrated communities that have houses we can afford at this time"

(Dalmage 2000: 97). Many multiracial families that cannot afford the cost of living in stable mixed-race areas may default into single-race areas or the less stable diverse areas. Economic class mediates opportunities for all children, but multiracial children face an additional burden when their parents cannot afford to live in stable, racially mixed communities: heightened forms of racism and/or border patrolling. In short, parents who can afford stable mixed-race areas are better able to protect their children from the hurtfulness of border patrolling.

Although my family could afford Hyde Park, after years of researching the lives of multiracial family members, I had some reservations about moving to a self-consciously integrated area. I kept in mind what I had been told by a woman who ran an organization for multiracial families: "Being in an interracial neighborhood is the number one thing that [multiracial children] need because people I've talked with who had problems growing up biracial have grown up in monoracial neighborhoods. White or black, it doesn't matter: monoracial" (Dalmage 2000: 101). I understood this and yet still had reservations about going to a stable mixed-race area. My reservation lay in two other pieces of information that had become clear through my research: First, the historical creation of stable racially mixed areas is laced with classism and racism. The self-conscious destruction of low-income housing and the creation of middle-class housing continues to be used as a way to mediate the racial composition of the neighborhoods. For instance, in the Hyde Park section of Chicago, low-income housing was razed and replaced with middle-class housing (Taub, Taylor, and Dunham 1984). In a white supremacist system, race and class intersect to ensure a greater percentage of whites will have access to middle-income housing. In racially mixed communities, whites generally control the more desirable property and hold the institutional power (Dalmage 2000; West 1996). When the balance seems threatened, or put another way, when it seems whites are feeling threatened and begin to flee, community organizations may engage in "positive marketing," racial steering, or increased policing and other means to give whites a sense of safety and comfort.[12] Thus, even though a mixed-race community offers multiracial families a more comfortable racial space than other areas, that space has been created and maintained through injustices.

My second and related concern is that white liberals are attracted to and dominate these areas. A white mother from Montclair, New Jersey, with two multiracial sons put it like this: "In this town people want to show how liberal they are, so we are really sought after. It allows them [white liberals] to have friends of color and their children to have friends of color without them being too dark. And then you have the white mother to relate to if you are uncomfortable with African Americans. In my case, you've got this white mother—I'm acceptable" (Dalmage 2000: 97). A woman living in a racially mixed suburb of Chicago put it this way: "We were the couple to know if people wanted to prove they were liberal. There was this one lady in particular, she knew us when she needed us. If she was with a group of people and didn't want them to know she knew us, she wouldn't look in our direction. Other times she would come running over pell-mell" (Dalmage 2000: 98).

I heard similar stories from multiracial family members in other racially mixed areas—including Hyde Park. Thus although multiracial families find the greatest possibility of comfort in these areas, they are also confronted with a particularly troubling aspect of white liberalism: those people who think about diversity as bean counting. In this view nothing has to change; it is just a matter of bringing people together and being able to claim friendships with as many people of color as possible. Diversity is something to be consumed, something that is exercised when convenient and discarded when privileges are threatened (Dalmage 2000). Interestingly, in Hyde Park, when problems arise that are potentially racially charged (e.g., resolving public school curricula issues, addressing gangs and drug dealing, removing basketball hoops from playgrounds), I have heard white people remark, "I wish we had more blacks fighting with us, then this fight wouldn't seem racist," or "If a black person were here it wouldn't look so bad." In other words, beyond mere "bean counting," these white people want blacks (it seems any black body will do) to stand with them and support their perspectives. They are not necessarily concerned with sharing the power or being allies with blacks (Kivel 2003).[13] Instead, black people are seen as a useful means to achieving a particular preplanned agenda.

And Hyde Park is not alone. In integrated communities created through conscious effort, Nyden and his fellow researchers found that "a middle-class White perspective tends to be dominant" (1998a: 11). In her case study analysis of the neighborhood stabilization movement, Juliet Saltman found that in three stable racially mixed areas, "Leadership was primarily white and middle-class" (1990: 536). Based on these findings and the result of his own in-depth research, Michael Maly has concluded that the "test of stable integration is not in the percentages of groups, but the community's process to join different groups in such a way that there is respect and a sharing of power" (2005). For multiracial families, living in racially mixed areas means that some of the effects of border patrolling may be muted in the daily interactions, but behind the seams, a system of whiteness prevails.

■ Legacies

As I sit on my front porch in Hyde Park and look up and down the street, I notice that several of the homes have been "in the family" for decades. I think about the legal maintenance of whiteness and the systemic devaluation of blackness. Although restrictive covenants were declared illegal by the 1948 Fair Housing Act, racism in the housing market continues, and even as middle-class blacks are making some headway, covert forms of discrimination and inheritance laws ensure that housing remains the privilege of whites (both directly by passing along property and indirectly through money for down payments). Of the thirteen homes on my block, nine are owned by whites, three by interracial families (including my own, two couples consist of white women and black men, and one is a white man and Asian Indian woman), and one by a Japanese family. One of the neighboring families signed a restrictive covenant when they bought their home in 1945.

Restrictive covenants were broadly used by Realtors to assure whites and others that the value of their property would be protected. Thomas Guglielmo argues that as whites attempted to keep blacks out of the neighborhood, "the restrictive covenant—a mutual agreement among property owners not to sell or rent to particular people over a given period of time" was "by far the most effective weapon" (2003: 166). He further specifies that

> While the target of these covenants varied to some degree from one location to another, in Chicago, African Americans unquestionably bore the brunt of restriction. In their survey of 215 covenants on Chicago's South Side in 1944, sociologists Herman Lone and Charles Johnson found that all but 1.4 percent of these agreements targeted African Americans *exclusively.* While estimates vary greatly, by World War II, covenants covered no less than 40 percent of Chicago's residential neighborhoods. (2003: 166)

The agreements were between homeowners, yet they were endorsed and promoted by the Federal Housing Administration (FHA): "The FHA's Underwriting Manual recommended covenants for the 'prohibition of the occupancy of properties except by the race for which they are intended'" (Guglielmo 2003: 167). As an aside and an interesting twist on racial history in the United States, my neighbors who signed the restrictive covenant had come to Chicago following their experience of being forced into internment camps and losing all their property on the West Coast. The constant in each case is the construction of whiteness against groups of color. However, it becomes clear that whiteness constructs itself against an ever-shifting historical, political, and economic backdrop, often acting in a contradictory manner, yet always maintaining the strength to punish those viewed as the greatest threat to white privilege at a given moment.

Fifty-six years after this couple signed a restrictive covenant, my husband and I went to look at our current home—the house next door to this couple. In the years in between, the housing market changed dramatically in Hyde Park. Buildings that had been all-white have slowly become integrated. Yet, the legacy of racism remains pervasive. When we looked at the house, the seller's Realtor stated that "a firm offer was coming in on the house" and that she was "expecting a contract that afternoon." She curtly answered our questions and rushed us out of the house, stating that she had another appointment (despite the fact that we were on time for our appointment with her). Disappointed, we continued our house search. After these types of events began to happen with a bit of consistency, we wondered if Hyde Park Realtors had ideas about what kind of people should buy on particular streets (as we had been warned).

We could have and maybe should have sought a legal remedy based on the Fair Housing Act of 1988, which states that "it shall be unlawful—(a) to refuse to sell or rent after the making of a bonafide offer, or to refuse to negotiate for the sale or rental of, or otherwise make unavailable or deny a dwelling to any person because of race, color, religion, sex, familial status or national origin." We may have been able to make a case, but like a lot of racism that plays out in the post–civil rights color-blind era, the racism is covert and more difficult to address. Zina Greene and her colleagues argue: "Housing discrimination remains rampant in the housing market despite the passage and amendment of the Fair Housing Act. Housing discrimination is sometimes difficult to detect because of the subtle techniques used by real estate agents, managers, financial people, insurance providers, and others in the market place" (1996: 1).

Two months later, the house was still on the market. We were still looking and decided to revisit the same house. This time the Realtor—the same Realtor—was kinder and gave us more time. This time I had returned with my Realtor (a white man). My husband (a black man) had to work and could not join us. The difference in treatment was remarkable. We visited one more time, this time with my husband, and then made an offer. The disrespect and unprofessionalism that followed our offer was abhorrent. As I look around Hyde Park, I can identify predominantly black streets and white streets, black buildings and white buildings. This housing pattern is the outcome, no doubt, of racist real estate dealings at the intersection of educational, economic, and racial inequality; the outcome of a society in which inheritance of property, wealth, and status are racialized and ensure a color line that protects injustice and white privilege.

■ Raising Our Children Beyond Borders and Struggling for Social Justice

Once our housing issue was settled, our next adventure was locating an acceptable preschool for our then two-year-old. I was told by a few whites about the high-quality schooling at two particular places. I decided to visit and, not surprisingly, found predominantly white children and white teaching staffs. After observing in one preschool and thinking about the problems my daughter would encounter, I asked a director: "Is this pretty standard as far as diversity in the school?" She beamed, "Oh, yes! We are a very diverse school." And then, unwittingly illustrating the tragic and global nature of whiteness (and the problems with the term "diversity"), she added: "We have children from many different countries here." I wanted to point out: *many different white/European countries*. I let it go and continued my search.

I visited another preschool recommended by a black friend, the same preschool a white person told me "is not what it used to be." This preschool was racially mixed and had a wonderful environment; I breathed and relaxed. I had found a place where learning and humanity could join forces. Here, in racially mixed Hyde Park, despite the geographical proximity of blacks and whites, many whites remain in racial isolation where socializing and education happen in predominantly white spaces, generally in white-controlled spaces. The threads that weave the legacy of slavery and white supremacy into our current communities become apparent. In these seams, power is created and maintained, even as white liberals may struggle in word and action against racism.

And yet, I have never been more racially comfortable in an area. From Milwaukee, to Chicago's north side, to Brooklyn and Queens, Hyde Park is by far one of the most wonderful places for multiracial families. Every day I interact with many other multiracial family members. My family does not often face questions about our relationship to one another; in this place we are not a rarity. Now in the neighborhood public school, my daughter has a classroom and school that is racially mixed; two of her teachers and several classmates come from multiracial families (the school also has twenty-one different native languages represented). The streets, stores, and parks are racially mixed and relaxed. Overt displays of white power erupt from time to time, such as when the basketball courts were removed from a local school (read: no young black men congregating), and when the chess tables were removed from a local retail square (read: not too many black men congregating). Yet, in many ways, the seams are wonderfully threaded in black and white. Some explicit discussions of race and racism occur across racial lines. Many whites, for instance, were quite vocal about (and against) the underlying racism that led to the removal of the chess tables, and a group of white youths organized a rally against the decision. Analyzing racially mixed areas and the experiences of multiracial families helps to highlight that although the color line may be clear and stark (as seen in the housing market), it is likewise elusive and constantly changing (as seen in human interaction).

If a quality garment is made in a sweatshop with exploited labor, then the quality was gained through injustice. How comfortable can we be with that? We need to look closely at the social and historical context of the seams. Those who believe that we just need to get people together and the world will change need to look deeper into the dynamics of racism. In racially mixed communities, whiteness is not subverted. In fact, these communities may actually strengthen white supremacy by hiding racism and racial injustice behind the seams. As members of multiracial families concerned with liberation and justice, we need to understand the historical and contemporary context of the places we call home, even as we attempt to do what is best for our children. In other words, we need to understand what is happening behind the seams so that we are best prepared to raise our children to both live beyond borders and struggle for social justice.

■ Notes

1. In her oft cited book *The Death and Life of Great American Cities,* Jane Jacobs writes about the need to create diverse seams (places where a variety of people will intermingle and thus connect various sections of a city) rather than "border vacuums" (sites that demarcate one area from another and thus become dividers of neighborhoods and people). Interestingly, her discussion of border vacuums mirrors closely much of the discussion of the experiences of multiracial family members in a society structured around racial borders and speaks to the concrete or material realities that multiracial families negotiate: "People who live behind project borders and who feel estranged and deeply unsafe about the city across those borders are not going to be much help in eliminating district border vacuums, or even in permitting replanning aimed at rejoining them with the fabric of a city district" (1961: 402). Multiracial family members, of course, live on racial borders and thus often look for housing near racially defined social seams. Unfortunately, what may appear to be a seam can in short time become a racial border vacuum, as in the cases of gentrification and panic peddling.

2. Two books in particular shifted the discussion from the study *of* multiracial people to the discussion of perspectives and analyses *by* multiracial people. These two books are *Racially Mixed People in America* by Maria P. P. Root (1992a) and *Black, White, Other: Biracial Americans Talk About Race* by Lise Funderburg (1994). In addition, by the early 1990s, multiracial family organizations began to grow in strength and numbers. A shift occurred: instead of being talked about and named by others, multiracial family members were now doing the talking and naming and claiming their own experiences.

3. The interconnection between property relations, citizenship, inheritance, and the construction of whiteness have been explored in great detail. See for instance, Harris (1995), as well as Sommerville (2000).

4. For in-depth analyses of the Uptown section of Chicago, see Maly and Leachman (1998) as well as Maly (2005).

5. Taub, Taylor, and Dunham (1984) found that, referring to an Austin neighborhood, "between the years of 1966 to 1973 blocks changed over from white to black at the rate of 37% per year" (p. 46). My own research indicates that multiracial families often moved into neighborhoods that appeared to me racially mixed, only to find out that the neighborhood was undergoing transition—often that transition would take place in a matter of just a few years (see Dalmage 2000: 75–78).

6. According to a 2002 Urban Institute study prepared for the Department of Housing and Urban Development, *All Other Things Being Equal: A Paired Testing Study of Mortgage Lending Institutions: Final Report,* by Margery Austin Turner et al., the discrimination is both covert and multilayered. For instance, in Chicago whites received "follow-up" from the lending institute at a higher rate than blacks. Likewise, whites received "coaching" from lenders, whereas blacks did not. Moreover, whites were consistently quoted higher loan amounts. In its report the Urban Institute also addresses those who contend that credit history rather than race explains the differential treatment. The Urban Institute report counters this contention by noting that "existing research evidence concludes that minority homebuyers in the United States

do face discrimination from mortgage lending institutions. Although significant gaps remain in what we know, a substantial body of objective and credible evidence strongly indicates that discrimination persists" (2002: 8; see also Browne 1995).

7. Chicago Alternative Policing Strategy was created to address problems in policing. CAPS meetings, held monthly in most districts, bring together residents, local beat officers, commanders, and other interested parties to discuss the priorities of policing in that particular district. The beat officers will prioritize their policing strategies to reflect the information received in the meetings and the demands of the residents. For a more in-depth discussion and analysis of CAPS, see the US Department of Justice July 2002 report, "Taking Stock: Community Policing in Chicago," prepared by Wesley G. Skogan, Lynn Steiner, Jill DuBois, J. Erik Gudell, and Aimee Fagan at the Institute for Policy Research, Northwestern University.

8. In Chicago, police presence in a neighborhood is based in part on the number of 911 calls dispatchers receive from particular areas. In CAPS meetings, local residents are encouraged to call 911 often and to form calling trees, so that as many residents call as possible. The greater the number of calls, the more likely police presence in a neighborhood will be increased. In some cases, the number of 911 calls is used as one determinant as to whether the Chicago Police Department will assign special tactical unit officers to a neighborhood (especially if the calls are about suspected gangbangers/drug dealers). Thus, in gentrifying neighborhoods, the policing system works with the housing market to encourage the constant policing of black and brown males.

9. These findings are part of a larger research project Jeffrey Edwards is conducting in Uptown and Edgewater. His larger project examines the politics and actions of gay men in the process of neighborhood gentrification.

10. For a brief history of Hyde Park, see Taub, Taylor, and Dunham (1984: 89–118). For a contemporary analysis of the seams in Hyde Park, see Duneier (1992).

11. In *Paths of Neighborhood Change*, Taub, Taylor, and Dunham quote a local Hyde Park comedian who once quipped that in Hyde Park, we will find "black and white together . . . shoulder to shoulder against the poor" (1984: 99).

12. Based on personal interviews with organizational members of a Fair Housing Action group in a racially integrated city. See also the vast literature on "racial tipping points."

13. In "Being a Strong White Ally," Paul Kivel (2003: 401) writes: "Being an ally to people of color . . . includes listening to people of color so that we can support the actions they take, the risks they bear in defending their lives and challenging white hegemony. It includes watching the struggle of white people to maintain dominance and the struggle of people of color to gain equal opportunity, justice, safety and respect." My experiences and my research show that many whites (although not all) in racially mixed communities ultimately reproduce white hegemony, even as they assert themselves as being engaged in a struggle against it.

20

Confronting Racism in the Therapist's Office

Kwame Owusu-Bempah

> The American "mixed blood" . . . is not the dejected, spiritless out-cast, neither is he the inhibited conformist. He is more likely to be restless and race conscious . . . radical, ambitious and creative. The lower status to which he is assigned naturally creates disconnected and rebellious feelings. From an earlier spontaneous identification with the white man, he has, under the rebuffs of a categorical race prejudice, turned about and identified with the Negro race.
>
> —Evertt Stonequist (1937: 24–25)

Stonequist made this observation in the early decades of the last century. Two of the fundamental questions that we must ask ourselves in the twenty-first century are why social and political efforts to classify the offspring of African and white unions as a distinct racial group continue and also why the issue still engenders emotionally charged debate among all and sundry. Why, as social scientists and/or helping professional practitioners, do we experience misgivings in our relations with these individuals? In Western societies, the answers to these questions lie in the history of black and white relations, particularly in the manner in which black and white sexual liaisons have been historically perceived and their offspring treated by a racist society.

This history must begin with North American antimiscegenation laws. US antimiscegenation laws not only outlawed interracial sex and marriage but also defined racial identity and reinforced and enforced racial hierarchy. For people of African descent, the laws explicitly identified them as a diminished, inferior race doomed to slavery (Guthrie 1976; Moran 2001). These laws further classified as a "mulatto" the child or grandchild of a "Negro," decreed that mulattoes must be made black, defined the bondage of "blacks," and made it universal (Moran 2001). This led to the universal adoption and application of the "one-drop rule." To aid identification and classification of mulattoes by officials, this rule defined as black anyone with traceable African ancestry. Thus, a further classification of these individuals based on (superficial) anatomical features soon followed, resulting in the following categories of the offspring of black and white unions:

- Sambo: a person of seven-eighths (87.5 percent) "black blood" and one-eighth (12.5 percent) "white blood";
- Mango: a person who was three-quarters (75 percent) black and one-quarter (25 percent) white;
- Meamelouc: a person who was one-sixteenth (6.25 percent) black and 93.75 percent white; and
- Sang-mele: a person who was one sixty-fourth (1.56 percent) black and sixty-three sixty-fourths (98.44 percent) white (see Herskovits 1934; Moran 2001).

The aim of this classification was not just to deny but, more crucially, to obliterate their white side. By sociopolitically scraping out their white heritage, the racial classification scheme converted them into black; it turned them into individuals who might have been generated by a single biological parent, who might have been cloned. The object was to formally disenfranchise them; it precluded them from claiming their birthright and from gaining official recognition of their white ancestry, thereby denying them inheritance and privileges based on their white origins. This process applied also to their mothers. Under a 1661 Maryland antimiscegenation law, for example, "freeborne English women" who married "Negro slaves" and their children were made slaves to their husbands' masters during their husbands' lifetimes (Moran 2001). Furthermore, it identified and classified the children as "mulattoes." Elsewhere in the Western world and at other times they were variously referred to as "métis" (French for a mongrel dog), "mixed-breed," "half-breed," "half-caste," and so forth. In Britain, such terms as "tinted," "half-caste," and "mixed-breed" are still current among "politically incorrect" groups and individuals.

Obviously, this perverse system of classification blatantly lacked biological or scientific precision. Attempts to remedy this problem led to an equally preposterous revision of categories or degrees of "African ancestry," as opposed to "European ancestry": mulatto (a person of one-half African blood), quadroon (a person of one-quarter African blood), and octoroon (a person of one-eighth African blood and seven-eighths white European blood). The likely confusion that these classifications and reclassifications might have engendered in these individuals, especially those who were classified as one-sixteenth black and one-sixty-fourth black, as "only" 93.75 percent and 98.44 percent white, respectively, prompted scholars in the late 1920s and throughout the 1930s, notably Robert Park (1928, 1931) and Stonequist

(1937), to coin the term "marginal man" to symbolize their experiences, thereby changing the terminology among the community of social scientists. Both Park and Stonequist defined the marginal man as a person who did not fall "neatly" into black or white groupings in the United States at the time. That is, although marginal persons naturally belonged to both black and white communities, often neither was prepared to accept them. They were therefore said to be living in limbo; they were characterized as culturally, socially, emotionally, and psychologically confused.

■ The Mulatto Hypothesis: The Societal Legacy

Following the publication of the United Nations Educational, Scientific, and Cultural Organization's (UNESCO's) (1967) Statement on Race, reaffirming its previous statement in 1964, the prevailing public view today is that "race" is a sociopolitical invention (Banton 1987; Howitt and Owusu-Bempah 1994; Montagu 1974; Owusu-Bempah and Howitt 2000). Yet, the recognition that "race" as applied to homo sapiens is a fallacy has not resulted in the abandonment of racial categories and subcategories or the differential treatment of individuals and groups based upon these categories. Current efforts not to abandon the "mulatto" category (i.e., people of 50 percent African ancestry and 50 percent European ancestry), for example, but rather to replace it with a "biracial" category, is further evidence of the obsession with (if not vested interest in) race. The public acceptance that "race" is a pernicious myth has not led to the abandonment of social and economic boundaries separating not only major racial/ethnic groups but also shades of "black." In short, can we expect a change in terminology—labeling the offspring of black and white unions as "biracial," as opposed to "mulatto," "marginal man," or "mango"—to result in changes to the status quo? Will it encourage dominant white society to change its false belief in and practice of hypodescent? The following predictions by observers of the "one-drop" rule indicate the likelihood of that happening: "no amount of white ancestry, except one hundred percent, will permit entrance to the white race" (Myrdal, Sterner, and Rose 1944: 113); and, "it seems unlikely that the one-drop rule will be modified in the foreseeable future, for such a move would generally be opposed by both whites and blacks" (Davis 1991, in Rockquemore and Brunsma 2002a: 113). Stonequist (1937) had earlier made this observation when he pointed out the unwillingness of white society to distinguish between the so-called "mixed blood" (mulattoes) and "full blood" (Negroes).

F. James Davis's (1991) observation has implications for the "black community" also. In other words, how do we reconcile our abhorrence for the one-drop rule (hypodescent) with our desire and demand for a two-drop rule (biracialism)? As a corollary, what difference would statutory endorsement of a "two-drop" rule, a biracial category, make? One is inclined to agree with such contemporary commentators as Rockquemore and Brunsma (2002a) that by demanding an independent governmental designation for mixed-race people, we are quintessentially arguing for the abolition of the one-drop rule. A caveat, though, is the very likelihood of replacing it with a "two-drop" or "three-drop" rule. In view of the discussion so far, if that actually happened, would individuals who fall into these various categories be accepted by both or indeed either of the dominant groups, the black and white communities? Even within the black community, contemporary commentators have noted the internalization of the one-drop rule (e.g., Owusu-Bempah 2003, 2005; Owusu-Bempah and Howitt 1999a). Readers familiar with the literature relating to US antimiscegenation laws will not be surprised that both the pro and con camps for the call for a biracial category comprise black, white, and mixed-race individuals. Neither will they be surprised that the leading proponents of the pro camp are predominantly white mothers of biracial children. Unlike their historical counterparts, such as Nell Butler (Irish Nell) (see Moran 2001) who accepted their harsh lot under US anti-miscegenation laws, they are challenging the contemporary system to ensure equality for their children and themselves.

■ Professional Thinking and Practice

> The Negro would give anything to change his colour; so too the white man hates to admit that he has been touched by the black.
> —Carl Jung (1930: 196)

While the political wrangling concerning a formal racial/ethnic classification of the offspring of black/white unions rages on, we need to seriously consider also the ways in which society as a whole and, for our purposes, professional practitioners perceive and relate to them. Throughout history, the offspring of black/white unions have typically been disparaged not only on ideological grounds but also on (pseudo) scientific ones (Guthrie 1976; Williams 1980). In Western society, indeed, beyond sub-Saharan Africa, "race" or caste is still seen as an unbridgeable divide, such that people of African descent are not accepted in the same way as other "racial" or ethnic groups are. In a racially divided world, sex and marriage between a black person and a white person or a person of another group presumed to be superior to Africans are automatically considered pathological, the target of irrational fears and bigotry. Consequently, the resultant offspring have historically been vilified and treated less favorably than others in similar circumstances.

Psychology, as a discipline and institution, is a microcosm of the social structure. Thus, understanding the influence of race on psychological theories and practice should aid in understanding its dynamics in the wider society. Since its inception, psychology has been heavily influenced by race theories, beliefs, and assumptions. These, in turn, have generally biased and distorted clinicians' perceptions, assessments, and treatment of people of African ancestry and their needs (Williams 1980). In this section I discuss some of the ways in which race continues to influence psychological practice today. I use therapists' and other helping professionals' misassumptions about the self-concept of children and youths of mixed-race parentage and their putative "negative self-identity" as an illustration of my profession's insensitivity to the adverse structural (socio-politico-economic) circumstances facing them; we tend to use race in various ways as the chief explanatory factor in these children's problems and needs (Owusu-Bempah 1994).

Psychology, of all the social science disciplines and practices, has played a key role in pathologizing the offspring of black/white unions and Africans generally (Holdstock 2000; Howitt and Owusu-Bempah 1994; Owusu-Bempah and Howitt 1994, 2000). Edward Strickland summarizes psychology's historical role: "The history of psychology reveals tragic episodes of the misuse of psychological concepts and methods. Some of these misassumptions continue to influence the psychology practice today" (2000: 3310).

These misassumptions include those about the psychological functioning of mixed-race individuals. In Britain, for example, the entrenched belief in the mulatto hypothesis, the idea that "mixed-blood" individuals are flawed, that psychologically they are plagued by feelings of identity confusion and low self-worth, has spawned specialist units and psychological consultants, black and white, specializing in "identity work" with black children. This type of work recognizes racism as the cause of the children's difficulties but seeks the remedy in the victims themselves, the children. Indeed, it is a misnomer to call it "psychotherapy." An appropriate tag would be "race therapy" or "race work," since it is predominantly race-based, focusing on "black identity," "racial identity," "black culture," and so forth. Intervention programs mainly involve providing the children with information about their "black cultural background," including information about black historical figures, and/or counseling them to take pride in their "blackness" (see Owusu-Bempah 2002; Owusu-Bempah and Howitt 1999a). The claim is that such information will neutralize the damaging psychological effects of the racism they experience in their daily lives and thereby enhance their self-esteem. This type of therapy, identity work, is so preoccupied with race or "blackness" that it tends to lose sight of other salient factors in the children's lives. Banks illustrates this unfortunate oversight very clearly in the case of Nathan:

> The . . . client families that have been referred to me have usually been single parent white women with one or several children of mixed ethnicity . . . there is often some anger about the absence of the Black father. . . . This resentment may lead to a considerable amount of psychological aggression (and sometimes physical abuse) directed toward the child. . . .

As one mother repeatedly said in a session in the presence of her eight year old boy: "Every time I look at him he reminds me of that black bastard and what he did to me. If Nathan ever grows up to be like him I'll kill him." (1992: 33–34)

This case suggests a profound problem requiring intervention aimed at dealing with the mother's anger toward Nathan's father. However, Banks's recommended "therapeutic" intervention (cognitive ebonization) deals with Nathan's putative identity problem. Lamentably, although expectedly, such questionable psychological ideas and methods have been embraced, often wholesale, by other disciplines and professions, notably counseling, social work, and teaching (Owusu-Bempah 1994, 2005; Owusu-Bempah and Howitt 1999b).

The following includes comments made by social work students about a fictitious child of mixed-race parentage: "Stephen's best friends are white [and] so may be confused about his identity; . . . awareness of being different, i.e., colour, feeling of shame about his origin. Stephen has problems reconciling with his own identity, he may be trying to be white" (Owusu-Bempah 1994: 132). The students (102 total) participated in a study that investigated the prevalence and extent of the influence of the mulatto hypothesis on children and family social work. They responded individually to three randomly distributed vignettes that were identical, with the sole exception of the racial/ethnic backgrounds of the principal characters: a white boy, a boy of mixed-race parentage, and a black boy. The respondents' task was to identify the possible causes of the children's behavioral problems and to assess their developmental needs. They were also required to suggest possible intervention programs to promote the children's social, emotional, and psychological well-being.

The students' responses were analyzed according to the frequency with which particular causes of the children's behavior and particular intervention programs to address their needs were mentioned. Causal factors mentioned ranged from identity confusion to family circumstances, including parenting. Analysis of the results revealed racial differences in the respondents' attributions and recommendations. Eighty-five percent of those who responded to the vignette involving the child of mixed-race parentage attributed his difficulties to identity crisis, but 59 percent and only 25 percent of those who responded to the vignettes involving the black child and the white child, respectively, mentioned identity crisis as a causal factor in the children's difficulties. The respondents' recommended intervention programs were equally telling: identity work was the commonest recommended intervention for the child of mixed-race parentage (55 percent). To an extent, that was also true for the black child (35 percent), whereas identity work was hardly recommended for the white child (9 percent). In addition, the provision of information about cultural heritage went virtually unmentioned in the case of the white boy (3 percent) but was recommended for the boy of mixed-race parentage (39 percent) and the black boy (19 percent). These attributions and recommendations ignored the core cause of the children's difficulties, especially in the case of the child of "mixed-race" parentage. In other words, the social work trainees' assessments and recommendations were not based upon objective facts; instead, they were heavily influenced by centuries-old racial myths and consequently recommended psychologically potentially noxious intervention programs, particularly for the child of mixed-race parentage.

In the context of the present discussion, one may wonder if the participants would have responded differently to Stephen, had he been described as "biracial," as opposed to mixed-race. Research suggests that the answer must be in the negative. It suggests that apart from being "free persons" (as opposed to slaves), apart from being referred to or classified as "biracial," "mixed-race," or "dual heritage" (as opposed to "samboes," "mulattoes," "half-caste," and so forth), very little has changed in the ways in which modern racist society perceives and treats the offspring of black and white intimate unions, especially those who come into contact with statutory agencies, including the police and the courts, and professionals. Evidence suggests that very little has changed; they still face hostility and disdain in important sectors of society: education, health and social care, housing, and employment. Today, the offspring of black and white unions are still pathologized by both black and white professionals—social workers, teachers, and therapists. Practitioners hang on to the myth that personality and other psychological problems plague these individuals, young and old, as a consequence of their presumed inability to integrate both sides of their biological and cultural heritage (Owusu-Bempah 2005; Owusu-Bempah and Howitt 1999a).

In recent years, Ravinder Barn (1993, 1999; Barn, Sinclair, and Ferdinand 1997) has carried out a series of investigations and reviews of studies of children entering UK local authority care. These studies and reviews indicate that children of mixed-race parentage continue to be disadvantaged in the system, are disproportionately overrepresented, and are more likely to be admitted into local authority care than other children. In one of their reviews, Barn, Ruth Sinclair, and Dionne Ferdinand concluded that "while African Caribbean and Asian families are considered suitable for children of African Caribbean and Asian backgrounds [respectively], children of mixed parentage presented a dilemma for social workers" (1997: 281). Other research in both Britain and the United States over the years has consistently reported similar findings (e.g., Barth 1997; Batta, McCulloch, and Smith 1975; Batta and Mawby 1981; Courtney et al. 1996; Foren and Batta 1970; Katz 1996).

Given the foregoing discussion, it is not so difficult to see why these children represent a challenge to child care professionals. Historically, the "one-drop" rule decreed that they be seen and treated as black. Today, duplicitous political correctness mandates that they be seen as something else (Owusu-Bempah 2003), yet there is no consensus regarding their ethnic category or how they ought to be treated. Thus, in situations of uncertainty or ambiguity, practitioners resort to myths, stereotypes, assumptions, and prejudices concerning these children. In clinical work, as in social work, education, and health care, the marginal man notion provides prêt-à-porter stereotypes and assumptions (Owusu-Bempah 1994). This notion holds that mixed-blood individuals are inferior to others and portrays them as culturally, socially, and psychologically wretched. Evidence regarding the influence of these assumptions on contemporary child care practice in the UK abounds (Connolly 1998).

■ Should They Not Have a Say?

In Britain, much of the therapeutic work claiming to deal with these youngsters' putative psychological disturbance has essentially involved explicitly or implicitly denying their white heritage (e.g., Banks 1992, 1993; Maximé 1991a, 1993). Kwame Owusu-Bempah (1994) has unequivocally described this type of clinical work as victim blaming; it is racist and damaging. Still, practitioners seem oblivious to evidence suggesting the undesirability of this practice and its exacting psychological and emotional anguish on these youngsters (Katz 1996; Owusu-Bempah and Howitt 1999a; Tizard and Phoenix 1993).

The influence of race theories, beliefs, and assumptions on child care practices with children of mixed-race parentage refuses to abate (Kirton 1999; Owusu-Bempah 1994). In the UK, as in the United States, the current vogue is, once again, for child care professionals and others to reconfigure these children's ethnicity and self-concept. For example, the title of a 1999 article by Beverley Goldstein, "Black, with a White Parent: A Positive and Achievable Identity," outwardly championing the interest and welfare of children of mixed-race parentage, reveals the continuing marginalization of these children. As the title indicates, it focuses on "black children with a white parent" in Britain. The paper describes the psychopolitical process of their identity development and advocates that a viable means by which they can normalize is to identify themselves not as biracial but as "black with a white parent." It claims that doing so will enable them to reject the forces that pathologize them. From what the author claims to be a "postmodernist black perspective," it concludes: "the 'racial' self-concepts that are available to this group, identifying their underlying agendas and their consequences . . . the availability of the self-concept 'black with a white parent,' offered in the framework of change, multiplicity and individuality, is beneficial" (Goldstein 1999: 285). Whatever this assertion may mean, it raises several revealing questions. For example: to whom is the imposed self-definition, "black with a white parent," beneficial, the children or proponents of the one-drop rule? Alternatively, why can they not identify themselves as "white with a black parent," and why will this self-concept not be equally beneficial? In short, this definition may be regarded as yet another euphemism for "sambo," "mulatto," and so on, a surreptitious attempt to continue to deny these children self-definition, something most of us take for granted.

Typically, clinicians and other practitioners do not view the efforts of individuals of black/white heritage to claim dual membership in black and white groups as an acceptable option for them; often, they regard such efforts as symptomatic of personality disturbance requiring psychological intervention (e.g., Banks 1992; Maximé 1991a, 1991b; Milner 1975, 1983), despite the fact that mixed-race individuals have a legitimate claim to both groups. They disregard the fact that exerting pressure upon patients to be "either/or" obliges them to make a choice between black, white, or "other" worlds (Hall 1992). In other words, instead of helping them to develop their own sense of "monoracialism," "biracialism," or "multiracialism," as the case may be (Connolly 1998; Owusu-Bempah 2005; Rockquemore and Brunsma 2002a, 2002b), clinicians strive to impose upon their patients the culture or membership of the group to which the clinicians belong. Placing them in this position is not just unnecessary but, more importantly, damaging, as much research has indicated (e.g., Brown 1993; Owusu-Bempah 1997, 2002, 2005; Tizard and Phoenix 1993).

In our unrelenting efforts to configure and reconfigure their racial/ethnic group and concomitantly their social identity and self-concept, clinicians need to pause and ponder these and other important questions: What is our political, social, or psychological agenda? In whose interest are these efforts, our own or theirs? What damage may we be inflicting upon their psychological functioning, as well as their life-chances, as a result of our denying them self-definition? Concerning children and young persons, research warns of the potential harm to them when child care professionals collude with society to pressure them to accept the racial/ethnic identity we impose over their self-concept and that when this happens, feelings of confusion, isolation, and loss of orientation frequently result (e.g., Brown 1993; Bowles 1993; Connolly 1998; Hall 1992; Owusu-Bempah 1997, 2002; Tizard and Phoenix 1993). Dorcas Bowles (1993), for example, believes that the current debate regarding the racial/ethnic category of the offspring of black and white unions has, up until now, been about the political dimension of biracialism. Namely, this stance has not taken sufficient note of the psychological dimension of biracialism.

■ Racial Equality Without Social Justice?

Paradoxically, race is simultaneously a biological myth and a social reality that has not only traditionally defined the allocation of power and resources but also sanctioned interracial relations, particularly interracial sexual relations. However, do we, as twenty-first-century intellectuals and professional practitioners, want to keep alive this pernicious canard? Do we want to continue to police the taboo on black and white sexual intimacy on behalf of a racist society? In short, do we want to continue to lecture, practice, and thus perpetuate the one-drop rule in our work with children and adults of mixed-race parentage? If not, can we realistically rid our thinking and practice of its influence simply by replacing it with a "two-drop" rule (i.e., labeling them "biracial") without attending to the structural impediments they face that make such nonsensical rules "necessary"? Forty years ago, UNESCO charged us with this important duty: "In order to undermine racism it is not sufficient that biologists should expose its fallacies. It is necessary that psychologists and sociologists should demonstrate its causes. The social structure is always an important factor" (1967: Statement 10). Thirty years previously, Stonequist (1937) noted that the social position of mixed-blood persons is inextricably intertwined with the larger issue of racism; the complex web of individual, institutional, and cultural racism perpetuates distinct status differentials for those who are not white in a white society, without giving them full membership in any group. The duty upon us now, therefore, is not just to disapprove of or refrain from acts of racism. We must accept it as our duty to counteract racial injustice not only in our practice but, equally importantly, in society at large. This requires our unflinching, resolute commitment to racial justice.

Many see this duty as merely reducing racial antipathy and discrimination against black people (e.g., Mays 2000). Others (e.g., Dreier 1998) regard economic justice as the essential precondition for racial justice. The question is whether it is possible to reduce discrimination—unfair treatment of others—or achieve economic justice and hence racial justice in a climate of social injustice. UNESCO's response is that "Social and economic causes of race prejudice are particularly observed in . . . societies wherein are found conditions of great disparity of power and property, in areas . . . where individuals are deprived of equal access to employment, housing, political participation, education, and the administration of justice" (1967: Statement 11a). It is fair to acknowledge that, in Western societies, black people are not the only group who experience disadvantage in these essential sectors of society. Other groups, which include white individuals, also experience social inequalities on the grounds of class, gender, age, and so forth. Of course, within each of these groups, being black or of African ancestry becomes a compounding factor; we must not lose sight of this fact.

In every sector of a given Western society, the very air we breathe is saturated with racial injustice. Research aside, everyday observation alone renders it trite to talk about the gross disparities between people of African ancestry and others, disparities in physical and mental health, mortality, education, housing, and employment (e.g., Brown 1984; Caputo 2004; Lott and Bullock 2001; Modood et al. 1997; Owusu-Bempah and Howitt 2000; Schulz et al. 2000; Sheppard 2002). In commenting on the disparity in mental health between black people and other groups, Jill Sheppard (2002) has emphasized that African Caribbeans experience considerably greater disadvantage in economic, material, and opportunity terms when compared with the white population; that they are systematically disadvantaged in terms of life opportunities in areas such as education, housing, and employment; and that they are, of course, subject to racial harassment and discrimination. In brief, their life chances are far less than other groups in British society. Twenty years ago, Brown (1984) reported very similar findings from a UK national survey. Sheppard summarizes these disadvantages:

> Social injustice is not just about material wealth, and its absence, and differential distribution of resources within society. It is not simply a matter of fairness or unfairness. It should be no surprise that disadvantage and despair can go hand in hand. It is perhaps this relationship to which differential rates of mental health problems point, when we compare different groups in society. (2002: 794)

■ Conclusion: Undoing What Has Been Done

Racism is undeniably harmful to all who experience it in their daily lives, but it is not their ethnicity or self-worth that is damaged by it. Rather, their life chances are restricted by racism, especially institutional/professional racism. Institutional racism thwarts their dreams, efforts, and aspirations and very likely makes them embittered and angry. Structural inequality is their encounter daily, and the problem for us and society as a whole is removing structural barriers against fulfilling their dreams and achieving their aspirations; we do not need to provide them with *soma* (psychotherapy) or relabel them. Measures such as therapy are palliative. We must dismantle the structural barriers to equality so that everyone's life chances are greatly improved. Our target, therefore, must be the racist system rather than the psychology of the individual or their race or ethnicity.

How may psychologists and other social scientists repair the damage our disciplines and practices have, over the centuries, caused people of African ancestry? Simply, social justice must be our guiding principle in our daily activities, in our teaching, research, practice, and social relations. In this endeavor, Strickland (2000) counsels courage: the future of our disciplines and practices requires us to be prepared to articulate, teach, and develop a body of science informed by social justice, and we must not be afraid to teach, engage in practice, and develop public policy and research about racism, sexism, classism, homophobia, and other divisive perspectives that enable people to treat those who are different from themselves unfairly. Echoing Hall (1997), Strickland warns that psychology's progress as a discipline and practice depends on our ability to include everyone in the future—to be fair to all, not just to some. He argues further that no one should have their future, their health, or their well-being compromised for reasons of race/ethnicity, class, gender, national origin, physical and psychological abilities, religion, or sexual orientation or as a result of unfair distribution of resources. He implores us to work diligently to ensure the brightest future for all.

The following recommendations derive from the preceding discussion:

1. With regard to teaching, we need to revise our curricula and acknowledge the limitations of our theories. The world is a complex web of cultures, groups, and individuals; we need to take into account this diversity of humankind. We need to impress upon our students the right of people to be different both individually and collectively. We need to overcome our arrogance that what applies to us should apply to all and sundry. It is imperative that we revise our curricula to take these simple facts into account.

2. Regarding professional training, it should seek to reflect the reality of the social, economic, and political worlds in which clients live; that is, they live in different social, cultural, and economic contexts from our own. In short, training should equip trainees to be socially, politically, and culturally competent practitioners in a socially, politically, and culturally diverse community (including the global community). Professional training should seek to equip trainees to effectively address the needs of the victims of social injustice. It is important to recognize that race, color, or ethnicity is just a compounding factor of social injustice. This point needs to be properly understood. To be competent practitioners, trainees need to understand the circumstances of their clients and know and understand their clients' worldviews.

3. We also need to improve research by developing theories that derive from perspectives other than the Euro-American, male, middle-class perspective. If we approach different groups and impose our theories or way(s) of life on them, then we are not recognizing or accepting their worldviews. Apart from everything else, such an approach precludes us from understanding others, and often ourselves.

4. To achieve the ultimate goal of justice for all, it is also incumbent on students and trainees to demand that, instead of being recruited and trained to be guardians of the status quo, to prop up the establishment (e.g., by providing psychotherapy to its victims), they be educated and equipped with skills to become agents of social change so that they can better the structurally adverse circumstances in which disadvantaged groups live.

In conclusion, to undo the historical damage that psychology and allied disciplines and practices have done to people with "traceable" African blood, social justice should be our guiding principle in our daily activities, in our teaching, research, practice, and social relations. At the heart of social justice, of course, is the notion of equal treatment for all. Advocating racial justice in a prevailing ethos of social injustice is a pipedream.

21

Culture and Identity in Mixed-Race Women's Lives

Debbie Storrs

The recent US Census decision to allow individuals to mark more than one racial box in their self-identification process, due in large part to pressures from the mixed-race movement (Spencer 1997), is hailed by some as a significant shift in the racial terrain in the United States. Multiracial, or border, identification is seen as a rejection of the hegemonic construction of race that posits mutually exclusive racial categories. However, the resulting development of the novel racial category and identity "multiracial" is not the only oppositional practice to racial fictions. Multiracial individuals can also develop a protean identity, a fluid and shifting identity in which individuals construct and claim two or more monoracial identities as well as a multiracial identity (Rockquemore and Brunsma 2002a). Still another potentially oppositional strategy is the process of broadening membership in existing categories through challenging and reconstructing the meanings of those categories. Shifting racial borders is potentially oppositional as it induces fissures in the static borders and essentialist foundations upon which the prevailing racial terrain rests. For example, Julia Sudbury (2001) argues that black British women in community organizations construct a "multiracial blackness" that encompasses Asians and Caribbeans as an effective political strategy to unify women against gendered racism. Similarly, Nell Bernstein (1995) describes white teens in the United States who embrace the identities and practices of Mexican Americans and other nonwhite racial identities. In this chapter, I explore a similar phenomenon: the shifting of racial boundaries by mixed-race women, some of whom can pass as white, to include themselves under the rubric of nonwhite racial categories and communities. Rejecting the option of identifying with the category "multiracial," the women favored a nonwhite identity and challenged community and institutionalized notions of racial belonging through linguistic and other cultural markers. The ideological root of their cultural identity work is essentialism that, unfortunately, does more to reproduce our racial terrain than fracture it.

■ Methodology

The data used in this chapter are part of a larger data set that examines the racial and gendered identity constructions of mixed-race women. This study employed a selective, nonrandom, nonclinical sample of thirty women with mixed racial ancestry from the northwestern region of the United States. Women ranged in age from eighteen to fifty. The sample included nine women with Asian and Caucasian ancestry, six women with Native American and Caucasian ancestry, nine women with black and Caucasian ancestry, three women with Mexican and Caucasian ancestry, two women with Asian and black ancestry, and one woman with Mexican and Native American ancestry. The majority of women (twenty-seven out of thirty) with white and nonwhite racial ancestry identified with their nonwhite ancestry. Interviews were conducted in subjects' homes or in my office. All interviews were taped and later transcribed, coded, and analyzed using a comparative method.

The sample used in this study is relatively small and has the unique characteristic of being from a predominantly white racial region of the United States. The purpose of this research is not to generalize the specific findings of this group of women to all mixed-race individuals in the United States but instead to reveal the way racial subjectivities are achieved discursively, to highlight the agency of individuals in the cultural process of racialization, and to comment on the ability of such discursive strategies to challenge racial ideologies.

■ The Racial Terrain

The racial terrain encompasses the meanings, identities, categories, and ideologies surrounding race. The racial terrain as it currently exists is based on essentialist, static, and mutually exclusive categories of belonging that shape corresponding identities. In addition, these categories are embedded in a social system that unevenly distributes resources along those racial lines. Thus, it is an unjust racial terrain.

One way to examine how individuals engage, collude, and participate in such a terrain is to analyze what Wetherell and Potter (1992) refer to as their "interpretative repertoire"—the linguistic ways in which women construct racial boundaries and meanings. The use of language is fundamental in the placement of oneself within racial categories and in the very meaning of categories themselves, yet there are different linguistic repertoires one can employ. For example, scholars have attended to the repertoire of the physical, the use of phenotypical characteristics, in biracial individuals' identity constructions. Brunsma and Rockquemore's (2001) research revealed that the way one talks about how others perceive one's physical appearance is a significant factor in one's identity choice (Brunsma and Rockquemore 2001). Alternatively, Verkuyten, De Jong, and Masson (1995) explored the linguistic deployment of stories people use to position themselves within racial categories. Such research reveals how racial identities are "an acquired and used feature of human identity, available for employment by either participant in an encounter and subject to presentation, inhibition, manipulation, and exploitation" (Lyman and Douglas 1973: 351). Of course, multiracial individuals' identity work does not occur within a vacuum. Instead, their constructions are constrained, limited, and shaped by the structural and ideological societal underpinnings concerning race (Jenkins 1994). In this chapter I explore the repertoire of culture, specifically the material and symbolic markers of culture that women employed in their narratives of self, revealing the ideological foundations of such identity work. Women used the cultural heritage associated with their nonwhite ancestry to locate themselves within recognizable racial boundaries and to provide meaning to their subjectivities. The most common cultural signifiers are rooted in "material culture," which includes food, objects, and symbolic holiday observances. Mixed-race women with black ancestry employed a more specific cultural notion by emphasizing common historical experiences of racism, what I refer to as "problems culture," a finding that suggests that physical and cultural repertoires are linked.

After outlining the construction of culture, I reveal the ways in which cultural racial discourse rests upon essentialism. The relationship between essentialism and culture is evident through issues of ownership and authenticity. Racial ancestry, or biology, is the premise upon which mixed-race women legitimately access nonwhite cultures, even though cultural knowledge must be learned. I discuss the various ways women access, learn, and come to "own" cultural practices and knowledge, given their predominantly white racial environments and biographies. I conclude by considering whether mixed-race women's use and meaning of culture is superficial or superfluous. In comparison, I explore similarities and differences between white ethnics and mixed-race women to support my conclusions about the ways in which women use their cultural repertoire to effectively challenge the hegemonic racial terrain.

■ The Meaning of Culture

Culture, like race, is socially constructed, shifting and changing over time. The concept of culture generally refers to the "symbolic-expressive aspect of human behavior," including language, practices, beliefs, ideologies, and so on (Wuthnow, Hunter, and Kurzwell 1987: 3). Developments in anthropology and cultural studies conceive of culture in a dynamic sense, socially constructed and contested. Rather than a static entity passed on generationally, culture is "the semantic space, the field of signs and practices, in which human beings construct and represent themselves and others, and hence their societies and histories" (Comaroff and Comaroff 1992: 27).

What exactly is the relationship, then, between culture and race? Applying a social constructionist framework to racial identity, race is conceptualized as a culturally and historically specific process that shapes group boundaries and provides meanings for those groups. Nagel provides a useful metaphor of the shopping cart to visually distinguish between group boundaries and their meanings:

> We can think of ethnic boundary construction as determining the shape of the shopping cart (size, number of wheels, composition, etc.); ethnic culture, then, is composed of the things we put into the cart—art, music, dress, religion, norms, beliefs, symbols, myths, customs . . . culture is not a shopping cart that comes to us already loaded with a set of historical cultural goods. Rather we construct culture by picking and choosing items from the shelves of the past and the present. (1994: 162)

As race constructs boundaries by references to "different types of human bodies," culture provides the content and meaning of these boundaries (Omi and Winant 1994: 55). In this chapter I reveal how women's talk sustains race and how the interpretive repertoire of culture rests on essentialist notions of race.

■ Material Culture

The substance and meaning of women's racial identities were framed in terms of cultural knowledge and specificity. Women's assessment of their own and others' cultural knowledge served as a mechanism for determining group membership and boundaries as well as the meaning of such membership.

Food

According to Steinberg (1989), food is one of the last bastions of ethnicity. Although white ethnics have shed most other attachments to their ethnic heritage, "ethnic foods" continue to be a part of their life. The commercialization and availability of ethnic foods allow individuals of all ethnic backgrounds to partake in their consumption. Although ethnic foods continue to be consumed, they have become a commodity one can purchase, by choice, rather than something integral to a larger everyday cultural milieu.

The consumption of ethnic foods was a central theme in the mixed-race women's narratives I collected. The key foods in these narratives were tied to women's nonwhite ancestry. Food both provided women with meaning for their racial identities and secured membership within racial boundaries through its proper consumption. For example, Geri identified rice as the "ethnic food" of the Japanese, although rice must be consumed in a particular way:

> I was always really interested in being Asian and always kind of thought I was more Asian than anything else. We always ate rice. One time I had a friend over and she said, "Oh, do you have cinnamon and sugar for your rice?" And I'd never eaten cinnamon and sugar on my rice, and she wanted milk on it! And I was shocked because I always pour soy sauce on it and stuff. . . . The other night a friend of mine that I gave a rice maker to, she said, "Hey, I made rice in your rice cooker and I put cinnamon and sugar on it," and I was just like "Ugh! I can't believe you did that!" because that's something that's so totally foreign to me. I never did that.

Geri's comment that she was always interested in being Asian more than anything else reveals her attempt to provide continuity to her racial subjectivity, but it also highlights the voluntary and selective nature of her racial identity. Geri's discussion of rice and the appropriate way to eat it were central in her cultural construction of being Japanese. Geri's narrative demonstrates that, in order to locate oneself within a particular racial boundary, one must learn the appropriate practices and symbols. Adding cinnamon, sugar, and milk to one's rice clearly placed one outside the boundaries of Japanese cultural practice. The appropriate Japanese way to eat rice was plain or with soy sauce. Because Geri preferred her rice this way, she positioned herself as authentically Japanese. Although Japanese food was important to her identity as Japanese, it was not a part of her everyday life. Geri explained this inconsistency in her narrative by the inaccessibility of Japanese food:

> *Interviewer:* Do you eat Japanese food every day?
> *Geri:* Some days, not every day. But my mom does. But not me.
> I think I've just grown up in a fast-food generation where I just throw something in the microwave. But if there were more easy ways to make Japanese food I would probably do it. . . . When I lived in town I would go out and get sushi and things like that every night. But I don't anymore because I live in the valley and it's not accessible.

Geri attributed the difference between her and her mother's consumption of Japanese foods to generational differences, but her mother's consistency in eating Japanese food helped legitimate Geri's identity claims. Although that may be an important factor, another possible explanation is that her own consumption is similar to the common practice of all people to consume various ethnic foods because of their commodification and availability. Her mother's daily consumption may be less a function of her not being part of the "fast-food generation" and more due to her embeddedness within Japanese cultural practices.

Food as a cultural signifier was used less by mixed-race women with black ancestry. Sherry's ambiguity over what constituted "black foods" was common among women with black ancestry:

> I had never eaten gumbo or okra or whatever except when I went to my grandmother's house. We ate a lot of fried chicken, I guess that's considered a black food. But my mother, who is white, eats a lot of fried chicken too. So I didn't really know what kinds of food were considered black foods. So I went down to visit my grandparents and they had all that stuff, ribs and a bunch of good stuff. I just tried greens. I tried it at my mother-in-law's house, who introduced me to greens, and they talk about grits a lot.

Sherry hesitantly identified gumbo, okra, chicken, greens, and grits as "black foods" but questioned whether fried chicken constituted "black food" since her white mother also consumed it. Sherry's irregular consumption of these food items and the improper way she ate them (with butter as opposed to honey) was not as critical to her own subjectivity as eating rice the appropriate way was for Geri. No doubt this lesser importance of food as a cultural signifier stems from the importance of real or perceived physical signifiers of difference that were most salient for women with black ancestry, as well as the legacy of the hypodescent policy.

Objects

Cultural symbols of race include artifacts and objects that signify one's race to oneself and others. For example, Patty discussed the ways in which she publicly identified herself as Japanese:

> *Patty:* When I went to Los Angeles I found the first book ever . . . about biraciality. And the first story was wonderful in that this young woman basically said as long as she could make a paper crane that made her Japanese. That was her hold on her Japanese; I think she's a quarter Japanese. And I . . . do some of those things to let people know I'm Japanese.
>
> *Interviewer:* Like what?
>
> *Patty:* Like, for example, last year at my job I made cranes for everyone and let everyone know I'll be . . . celebrating New Year's.

Patty's discussion of cultural practice reveals how elements of essentialist and cultural repertoires work hand in hand. References to the woman's quantifiable amount of Japanese ancestry (a quarter) were paired with her need to publicly assert her authenticity through the use of cultural features.

Another example of how cultural and essentialist discourse are tied to one another was revealed in Patty's discussion of the different stages of her identity. Patty recalled as a young child attempting to be different from her mother, who, for her, signified her difficulties in school and lack of acceptance by others. She remembered "trying to be as white as I could be, more like my dad." This conscious attempt to disassociate herself from her mother focused on both the cultural and physical:

> I hated Japanese food, didn't want to talk to her, hated when she sang songs to me and stuff. . . . And I remember one time . . . walking in and she was cleaning the sink and scrubbing it out and I thought that was a really good idea. So I took a bath and this was when I was in the fifth grade and I scrubbed myself with a brillo pad that she used to have, trying to make myself a bit lighter. And I remember at a very young age putting stuff on me and in the summers wearing long shirts because I didn't want to get darker at all.

Trying to be white meant that Patty had to successfully eliminate all markers of racial difference, both physical and cultural. This attempt to embrace her whiteness lasted until the eighth grade, at which time she "decided to be more Japanese." Again, her repositioning focused primarily on the cultural: "I started wearing kimonos and stuff . . . and I started eating Japanese food . . . and I remember setting the table and telling Mom I wanted to learn Japanese. So I used to set the table and she would name the plate and I would say the plate in Japanese. And we'd sing stupid Japanese songs and stuff." Patty's decision "to be more Japanese" was shaped in large part because she discovered that she could not be white, largely due to external categorizations based on physical cues. Thus, although she focused on the cultural when embracing her Japanese ancestry, it was integrally linked to the external positioning of her as nonwhite based on physical markers.

Patty's stories of identity reflect the shifting developments, initiated by both external and internal forces, and the attempts of most women to construct a continuous and consistent subjectivity. Women did so in different ways. Although Patty highlighted her struggles with identity, her narrative revealed continuity through her final discovery that she could never be and never was white. Decisions to be more this or that indicate the degree of choice that many mixed-race women had in terms of identity. These choices, however, were tempered by external categorizations.

A key theme in women's interviews was the lack of context for cultural symbols in their childhood. For example, Roxie's mother was Chinese American and her father was African American. During her youth, she spent very little time with her mother's extended family, who lived several states away. In the following quote, Roxie revealed the periphery of cultural objects in her childhood:

> We don't really acknowledge a lot of the Asian culture at all. We do the food. My mom has tons of Asian things around her home that we grew up with looking at and seeing them. . . . And then there's a game, I can't even think of the name right now, oh, maybe is it Mai Tai? No, that's a drink.

There's a game, it's just like dominos, but it's a Chinese game version of it. It's got little pictures of bonsai trees and stuff like that on it. So we played with that when we were younger and that sort of thing. We do Chinese food all the time. And greens and chitlins and all that too, a little bit. My dad doesn't really care for it, but if we go to Texas where our grandparents are then it's all there.

Roxie's inability to correctly name the Chinese game of mah-jongg is indicative of the lack of cultural context for such objects. In addition, her discussion of "Chinese food" and "black food" revealed how cultural signifiers were less important in shaping her racial subjectivity than were physical signifiers of difference. Roxie identified as African American because that was how others viewed her and because of the barriers she faced due to this racialization, but the meaning of African American racial boundaries does not rest simply on external categorizations or physical cues. The role of cultural objects in the construction and meaning of "blackness" is revealed in Roxie's following statement: "But our African American culture, it's just been a natural part of our life. . . . I mean even my mom listens to Marvin Gaye and stuff like that, whereas when she was a teenager she listened to the Bee Gees and to Elvis and stuff like that. And when she got with my dad she kind of adopted this whole culture as well." Although Roxie hinted at essentialist ideas when she explained how "natural" the African American culture had been in her life, it was also something that could be adopted and learned, as evidenced by her mother's incorporation of African American music and cultural practices. Her discussion of "natural" was more a function of the way she had been racialized, her lack of involvement with Asian Americans, and her association with African Americans.

Robyn, whose mother was Native American and whose father was white, identified as Indian. When I asked her why, she initially responded by using physical criteria: "Because I show more Indian features than I do white." Although that remark seemed to suggest that cultural markers were unimportant in her construction of racial boundaries, in reality, culture played an important role in her personal understanding of who she was. Robyn's statement, "I'm Native American but inside I'm more white," was recognition of how she was externally categorized and perceived. In addition, such a statement reveals a different internal measure of who she is. Her internal understanding of what constituted "Indianness" was based on cultural knowledge and practice. It was most evident when she compared herself to her Native American husband, whom she perceived as both externally (physically) Indian and internally (culturally) Indian. Robyn argued that "I look more Indian, but inside I feel more white, probably just because of the way I grew up." Robyn grew up in an urban setting and spent little time with her Indian relatives. She spent three years at an Indian boarding school, where she met her common-law husband, whom she referred to as a "reservation Indian." Robyn moved to her husband's reservation after the birth of their child. After separating from her husband, Robyn relocated to a large urban city. She explained that her husband would not follow her to the city because: "He's too set in his traditional Indian ways. He's always been on a reservation. And he does Indian dances, he sings in an Indian drumming group, he listens to those crazy tapes with flute music, birds, and stuff like that. He's even been in sun dances. And I mean he really believes in his Indian beliefs. If he came here to live with me, he couldn't sweat." Robyn's characterization of her husband as a "traditional reservation Indian" was based on cultural criteria. The importance of cultural criteria over physical ones was evident when she discussed her four-year-old daughter who lived with her father on a reservation:

> My little girl is way lighter than I am, she's really light. But I want her to know about who she is. She's Indian and she's kind of already doing that on her own with her dad. Because she'd rather listen to his crazy Indian music and I really don't have all that much. I mean I could go to a pow-wow . . . but it's not something I could just sit and watch forever like they do. But she knows she's Indian because she always wants to be Pocahontas. . . . My niece made her an Indian outfit so she's dancing.

Robyn's statement that she didn't "have all that much" was in reference to her cultural knowledge and interest, which was again opposed to her husband's knowledge and practice of Native American culture. References to her daughter's skin color recognized external categorization processes that depended on physical markers of difference. For Robyn, however, her daughter was Indian because of her interest in and knowledge of cultural practices. Robyn felt less Indian than her husband because of her lack of cultural knowledge yet still identified as Indian because relative to whites, she was more culturally knowledgeable and experienced in "Indian ways."

Material culture was necessary for some mixed-race women to feel nonwhite in light of their physical ability to pass as white and served as external cues for others of their racial and cultural identities. Likewise, cultural objects and materials provided women with the meaning of their racial subjectivities, although the depth and meaning for such objects and practices varied by women's biographies and cultural milieu.

Holidays

Women described family customs they deemed as culturally specific and, in doing so, helped construct a continuous and stable cultural history and subjectivity. Yet even as the mixed-race women I interviewed discussed how their families recognized and celebrated particular holidays, the significance and meaning of cultural symbols seemed ambiguous or lost in their interpretation. Women attempted to reinforce their subjectivities through holiday rituals, but for many women this practice was inconsistent, unclear, and ambiguous. For example, Patty whose mother was Japanese American and whose father was white, described how she celebrated New Year's:

> A celebration that I do a lot and I've done all the time is I celebrate New Year's, kind of like Japanese-style, in that the first seven days we aren't supposed to cook and stuff like that. And you're supposed to reflect who you're gonna be around for the first seven days, that reflects the rest of your year. So I've always taken . . . the first week of January off. And I've done different things like I go to this New Year's celebration where they have food and wish each other a New Year's. The Japanese community puts that on.

The way Patty celebrated the Japanese New Year, "kind of like Japanese-style," reflects her attempt to blend her understanding of cultural practices from information provided to her by her Japanese-born mother with celebrations sponsored by "pure" members of the "Japanese community."

A common theme that emerged in women's narratives was the sporadic nature and lack of cultural context in recognizing and celebrating "ethnic holidays." Jamie, whose mother identified as African American, white, and Jewish and whose father was Italian American, discussed how her family celebrated a range of "ethnic holidays": "We're also Jewish—my grandmother on my mother's side is Jewish—so one year we did Passover, which was really fun. We did Hanukkah and stuff like that too. And then my dad's family is Italian but we didn't have any special holidays for that but we always have the big Italian feast and stuff like that." "Ethnic holidays" like Hanukkah and Passover were inconsistently practiced in Jamie's family. When celebrated, they were "fun" rather than consistent and culturally meaningful holidays and events, in contrast to their regular celebration of Christmas.

"Ethnic holidays" were inconsistently practiced and took on ambiguous meanings for the mixed-race women I interviewed. Women participated in cultural holidays as adults at their discretion and intermittently, without a larger cultural context to enhance their meaning. It appeared women implemented what they viewed as cultural holiday practices and rituals at their own whim and without clear understanding of the various reasons for engaging in such practices. For many women, this inconsistency was also true of their childhood experiences with their nonwhite parent's cultural practices. Even without a larger cultural milieu, women fondly remembered their family's unique celebrations and continued to practice them as adults because it gave them a sense of being special, unique, and "ethnic."

■ Problems Culture

Gans (1979) coined the term "problems culture" to refer to the symbolic nature of ethnic culture for American Jews. Symbolically, the meaning of

Judaism is reduced to a focus on problems such as anti-Semitism. Knowledge of a group's history of oppression was a common cultural signifier for some mixed-race women. Mixed-race women with African American ancestry were particularly prone to utilizing this discursive strategy.

Kate, a mixed-race woman with white and black ancestry, was adopted as a young child and raised by white parents in a predominantly white community. As a child isolated from blacks, she often wished she was white. Her first contact with other blacks occurred when she attended college. Her initial reaction to blacks she met in this racially diverse college environment was to distinguish herself from them. When approached by other blacks to join a black student union, she responded: "I'm not like you, get away. I did not even want to be connected with them." After befriending blacks and realizing the complex diversity among blacks in terms of skin color, personalities, and backgrounds, she became more interested in identifying as black, but doing so after a lifetime of rejecting blackness in the absence of a black cultural context presented identity problems for Kate. Kate viewed herself as culturally ignorant of blacks and was embarrassed that her knowledge of black history did not begin until the age of nineteen in a black sociology class:

I had never been taught anything in my family or in history. I was nineteen years old before I knew Martin Luther King existed. And when I looked at black Americans dying to fight for me and when I looked at some of the horrific times they lived through and they still bore children. . . . they fought to change it and fought for rights and now I can vote, I can drive down the street, I can read books, and I can educate myself. When I looked at what they had actually done . . . it gave me a pride. I stood up and looked at myself in the mirror, and I thought, how dare you to try to deny my blackness, how dare you try to look in the mirror and say I'm white? How dare you slap all those people for your race?

Identifying with the historical legacy of black protest and struggles, Kate began to embrace her blackness and hungrily consumed black history to educate herself on her new group identity. Blackness for her began to constitute itself culturally through black struggle and resistance:

I thought the history was so cool because I thought this is a part of me. Even though I may not be a direct descendant of Malcolm X, my name isn't Kate X, but it was like this is a part of me. This is a part of where I fit in. This is a part of how I felt I was treated growing up. And even though segregation wasn't allowed, I was still segregated in the fact that I wasn't included in the same, I wasn't treated the same.

For Kate, black culture involved discrimination, struggle, and resistance. In her own life, raised by a white family in a white community, she too experienced ostracism—both from being racialized as nonwhite and from being adopted. Linking her own personal pain and struggles of acceptance with the history of black struggle was her way of aligning herself culturally with other blacks.

Similarly, Mary, who was raised by her white mother and black father, had little exposure to other blacks until high school. Mary came of age during the civil rights movement, which she described as monumental in shaping her racial subjectivity:

> In high school I became more aware of what was happening in the world around me. . . . What was happening in the south, dogs going after people, spraying them with fire hoses. I remember vividly watching with tears and . . . I remember the scene and I thought . . . those are people like me and look what's happening to their lives. . . . it's outright prejudice and racism.

Mary identified with the African Americans she saw being discriminated against on television, even though she personally had little experience with racism or discrimination. Stories of racial discrimination were shared by her African American father. Mary aligned herself culturally with blacks' struggle for civil rights and, as a teenager, joined a student nonviolent committee and picketed a local hotel over unfair hiring practices.

Others have found that when black/white biracial individuals experience negative treatment from whites, that is a push factor in adopting a monoracial black identity (Brunsma and Rockquemore 2001). Beyond personal experiences of discrimination, the mixed-race women in this study used their knowledge of group oppression to linguistically situate themselves within racial borders. Although other mixed-race women also represented themselves as members within oppressed racial groups by relaying personal examples of racism, they did this less so than mixed-race black women and used it as one of many cultural markers of difference.

Women's play, use, and selection of cultural markers appear, on the surface, to challenge the hegemonic racial terrain in that they may look white but act and identify, through their cultural markers, as nonwhite. Women's cultural use has the potential to break the illusion of continuity between racial categories and behaviors associated with them, yet the potential of this strategy to challenge the racial terrain is muted by its rootedness in essentialism.

■ Relationship Between Essentialism and Culture: Ownership and Authenticity

Women's use of cultural signifiers to locate themselves within recognizable boundaries does not effectively challenge the racial terrain because it is founded upon essentialist beliefs. One way in which women's discussion of the cultural reveals essentialism was through references to who has legitimate access to cultural practices and behaviors.

Their racial ancestry or biology was the premise upon which women could legitimately access cultural signifiers. This point was made most explicitly by Julia, who recently learned of her Puerto Rican ancestry, when she distinguished between biological and cultural roots:

> I think there are genetic roots and cultural roots. And it would be nice if we didn't have to make that distinction, but the world does that for us. My roots are genetic. Culturally I was raised as an Anglo. . . . I'm trying to learn the cultural part of my heritage in a way that does not seem threatening to people who are not only genetically but also culturally identified with the group. To let them know I'm not trying to take your culture away from you, I'm trying to find a way to honor your culture and honor my genetic roots. And I feel like I have a right to do that.

Julia made a distinction between individuals who were culturally and biologically pure, those who had nonwhite biological ancestry regardless of degree, and those who had no biological or cultural roots. For Julia, those who could document some biological ancestry were justified in pursuing information about that culture. Julia's right to investigate and practice Puerto Rican culture was due to her racial ancestry.

The dependence on essentialism in the interpretive repertoire of culture was most evident in women's discussion of legitimate practitioners of cultural customs. Many mixed-race women referred to "wannabes" and "New Agers," whom they contrasted to themselves, authentic and rightful owners of cultural practices and customs. The right to practice nonwhite customs resided in women's nonwhite ancestry, regardless of their physical ability to pass. The essentialist basis of women's racial selves suggests the limitation of this discursive strategy as it corresponds with historical and contemporary assumptions about racial categories. For too long, racial categories have been presumed to be real and innate, with clear racial boundaries, though the historical records indicate that such hegemonic ideas have no scientific basis and have been propagated in an attempt to maintain racial hierarchies and subordination. Those in pursuit of racial justice have publicly criticized essentialist logic, hoping to reveal the politicized nature and purpose of racial boundary making. For women to utilize the same essentialism that historically led to the racial subordination of peoples of color suggests their racial identity work fails to meet the test of racial justice. I return to this issue of racial justice in the conclusion.

Although mixed-race women positioned themselves as legitimate practitioners on essentialist grounds, those who could pass as white faced dilemmas when others more racially "pure" often perceived them as "wannabes." One way mixed-race women resolved this dilemma was to appeal to those more racially "pure" to acknowledge their right to practice. Kelley, who only recently discovered her Mexican American heritage and who often passed as white, used this mechanism to contrast herself to "wannabes." Kelley participated in a La Raza community meeting, where she was the "lightest" person there. She expressed her fear of being rejected by "pure" others at this meeting because of her ability to pass, to a Mexican American woman who was active in the Mexican American community. Kelley was relieved by her colleague, who told her not to worry about her physical appearance because only those with an "untrained" eye would assume she was white. References to "untrained" eyes referred to those who were not authentic or legitimate decisionmakers of communities. Clearly, the converse, "trained eyes," were those like herself, full-fledged members of the Mexican American community. The reassurance and acceptance of a "racially and culturally pure" member reaffirmed Kelley's desire to identify as Mexican American and to say: "This is who I am, and I do belong here!" Kelley found her colleague's response reassuring, but I note that the judgment of both "trained" and "untrained" eyes depends on the same signifiers in making membership judgments—physical cues.

Like Kelley, Tammy's identity was validated by those she identified as firmly within Native American borders, Native American elders: "I think one of the ways I've tried to increase my identity is to learn more of the old ways. And to spend time with elders so I can learn and then it validates me." Tammy's identity as Native American was secured by learning the "old ways," references to "traditional" cultural practices. Those who were authorities of the traditional were the elderly, and thus, through learning from Native American elders, her identity as Native American was more securely fashioned and authentic.

In women's discourse, culture took on a static form based on tradition. Authentic cultural forms were those that resided in the past rather than the present or future. This emphasis on a "pure" and "traditional" culture of the past has several consequences, one of which is to freeze culture into a static body of practices and behaviors. The construction of culture as pure and real also results in the construction of the fake and inauthentic, creating limiting and narrow versions of racial subjectivity and practice. The construction of an ancient and traditional culture in talk about authenticity and ownership reveals the relationship between essentialism and cultural signifiers.

■ Learning Culture

Even though one's access to cultural practice is often based on essentialist grounds, cultural knowledge must be learned. The way in which the mixed-race women I interviewed talked about learning their heritage, history, and ethnic practices revealed both an intermittent practicing and a lack of context for interpretation and understanding of such practices. The majority of women I interviewed grew up in predominantly white neighborhoods and had little contact with their nonwhite extended families. For example, Roxie, whose father was African American and whose mother was Chinese American, seldom saw her Chinese relatives. As a result of external categorization, Roxie identified as African American, although her Chinese ancestry was a source of pride for her:

> And I don't remember what it was that made us know we were Chinese as well. . . . I do know there were conversations and to make us understand our situation and the fact that we have two different cultures. . . . My mom has always, in the absence of the Asian culture as far as religion or the language, she's always made it available for us. She'd ask us, "Do you want to learn the language?" When we were younger we never did, we were never around it. . . . I do know that she always made it very clear to us that she was proud of her heritage and proud of being Chinese. And that we did have the other side to us. We didn't really acknowledge one over the other, it just became more of a society type thing that, you know, we look black.

The availability of her Chinese American culture came by way of her request rather than from being immersed within a larger cultural milieu. Roxie was proud of her Chinese heritage, but it was not part of her daily life. This, in conjunction with how others racialized her and her friendships with other blacks, resulted in her primary identification as African American.

Some women described how their parents' attempts to assimilate and "just be American" limited their access to cultural practices and meanings, whereas others were able to access information from their nonwhite parents about their family history and cultural heritage. For example, Kelley was recently introduced to the Mexican culture when she reestablished ties with her biological father. Kelley's parents were divorced when she was quite young. She was raised by her white mother and white adoptive father and had little contact with her biological father as a child. As an adult in her midthirties, Kelley started to examine her mixed racial ancestry and identified as Mexican American. Kelley used her father to glean information about her heritage and Mexican culture:

> My father would just take me to Mexican events. It was never really talked about. It's more or less he's taking me through the culture. . . . And he's taken me to Mexico a couple of times. I mean he's really shown me Mexico. Not the tourist parts, he's taken me to the factories, where Levi is getting dollar-a-day employees. And we talk to people on the streets. And he's taken me to the ghettos. . . . And those are the kinds of things that I learn.

Although Kelley's father never explicitly talked about Mexican culture, he took her into what Kelley perceived to be "real" rather than "tourist" culture. "Real" and "tourist" were synonymous with "authentic" and "fake." Kelley's father's firm and unambiguous identity as Mexican American by virtue of his full ancestry and cultural competency positioned him as a cultural authority for Kelley. However, because Kelley and her father lived in different states, she saw him irregularly. Thus, as an adult, like her childhood, there was little consistency or context in which to situate and practice her newly acquired knowledge.

Because of the lack of information provided by mixed-race women's families of origin, many of the multiracial women I interviewed had or were taking ethnic studies courses in their desire to know more about their nonwhite racial history and ancestors. Formal sources, rather than familial ones, were their primary source of knowledge about their heritage. Cultural knowledge and history become abstract pieces of knowledge rather than embedded links of experience and knowledge tied together within a cultural environment, which had the effect of reinforcing static conceptions of culture. Carrie's idea of culture provides an example. She grew up in a small town that was predominantly Native American. Through an Indian education program, her brothers learned "traditional" carving skills at the cultural center. Carrie was denied this opportunity because of her responsibilities of cleaning and cooking for family members while her parents worked. As a result, Carrie considered herself ignorant of her Native American history and culture and talked about them in an abstract way. She believed that it was only recently that she began to learn more about her culture and identity after moving to a predominantly white racial environment where her children began to participate in an Indian education program:

> After we moved to here to go to school and my kids became involved in the Indian Education is when I actually learned more information about myself. I learned about me being a Native American. As part of their project they had to learn about their own native culture so I learned more from that than I learned from my own childhood. I learned what my ancestors dressed like, what their regalia is.

Carrie's understanding of culture was static, traditional, and limited. She argued that her children's "nativeness" started when they went to the Indian education program. This was the case even though Carrie lived in a highly culturally relevant milieu. Carrie was one of the few women I interviewed whose racial environment was characterized by regular and consistent interaction with nonwhite relatives, where her primary associations and friendships were with other Native Americans, and who resided in and attended predominantly Native American neighborhoods and schools. Even so, Carrie felt ignorant of her Native American culture until she left her small community and moved to a predominantly white community, where she became involved with an American Indian educational program. The curriculum in this program focused on "traditional" Native American history and culture, reinforcing static and rigid conceptions of culture and identity.

Her understanding of her heritage and identity was in terms of what her ancestors did, how they lived, and what they dressed like in the past, rather than on both historical and contemporary cultural practices and experiences.

■ The Meaning and Practice of Culture: Superficial or Syncretic?

A major focus in the study of ethnicity has been on its sustainability in the modern era. Research on successive generations of European immigrants has detailed the assimilation of groups and the waning meaning and practice of ethnicity, suggesting that ethnicity is no longer viable (Alba 1990; Farley 1991; Steinberg 1989; Waters 1990). For example, Waters's (1990) research on third- and fourth-generation white Americans reveals how ethnicity is flexible and voluntary. For most white ethnics, ethnic identities are primarily leisure-oriented activities. The meaning and practice of culture in white ethnics' lives are fairly superficial, which is revealed by the picking and choosing of certain elements of traditional cultures and the occasional and sporadic practice of cultural customs. White ethnics do not live structurally ethnic lives because they are seldom employed in ethnic enclaves, do not live in ethnic neighborhoods, and rarely speak a language other than English (Steinberg 1989).

The latitude and voluntary character of white ethnic identities are often contrasted in the literature with the experiences of nonwhite groups, who experience involuntary political, economic, and social consequences of being racialized as nonwhite. Many nonwhite racialized groups live structurally segregated lives, evidenced by the concentration of certain groups in particular occupations and low rates of interracial marriages. In addition, Asian and Hispanic groups still maintain high levels of native language skills sustained by waves of new immigrants.

Comparing the meaning and practice of culture between white ethnics and nonwhite racialized minorities often takes the form of authentic and inauthentic. Ethnicity for white ethnics is often characterized as symbolic, shallow, and intermittent, whereas racial identity for nonwhite group members is often characterized as real, consistent, and meaningful. Although clearly there are differences in the degree of choice and constraint in ethnic and racial identities, this comparison misses the mark. In fact, characterizing racial identity as real and meaningful and ethnic identity as symbolic and shallow supports an essentialist view of race and a static view of culture. Such contrasts lead to assumptions that because white ethnic identities are voluntary and symbolic, they are trivial and unimportant in their lives. Waters (1990) argues that revealing the intermittent nature of ethnicity for white ethnics does not necessarily mean that these are unimportant psychologically to ethnic group members. Individuals can and do have meaningful attachments to ethnic collectivities, even when their lives are not structured physically, politically, or socially by ethnic ties.

In the case of the mixed-race women I interviewed, cultural signifiers were central in their placement of themselves and others within racial boundaries. Cultural markers work in tandem with biological essentialism to further strengthen women's identities. Like Nagel's shopping cart, biological essentialism provides the racial boundaries, and cultural signifiers often provide the material with which to fill the cart. Cultural symbols become important particularly when the shopping cart of racial ancestry is not quite as solid due to conceptions of "biological impurity."

The practices women engaged in to construct a sense of self were intermittent and unintegrated into a larger cultural matrix of meaning. However, though cultural practices were intermittent and seemingly absent of deep symbolic meanings, that did not diminish their importance in the construction of women's racial subjectivities. The degree to which women's discourse about cultural identity was integral and salient in their daily lives was a factor of their personal biographies and racial environments. One important factor in shaping the strength and meaning of cultural practices was the race of one's mother. When mothers were members of nonwhite racialized groups, women often experienced more consistency in cultural practices, although that was tempered by some families' desires to assimilate. Because of the gendered nature of work in the family—the fact that women were relegated the responsibility for feeding the family and nurturing the children—their cultural heritage was often explicitly or implicitly a part of mixed-race women's childhood. A second factor that shaped the meaning and practice of cultural practices in women's adult lives was the contemporary racial context for the various women. Like Waters's white ethnics, racially mixed women who grew up in a predominantly white neighborhood, who learned of their nonwhite racial heritage as adults, or whose mothers were white, not only had more options in their racial identification but had a seemingly less integral and meaningful sense of culture.

Women's narratives revealed that racial identity was very important in many women's lives, even though they had varying degrees of latitude in racial identity choices and even though their everyday life was not structured along explicit and conscious racial or cultural lines. Almost all the women I talked with discussed their desires to belong and feelings of being different. Racial identities and cultural practices were mechanisms through which women could begin to feel a sense of belongingness to larger racial collectivities, even if they were not embedded within a larger cultural matrix.

The fact that women's narratives for the most part did not reveal a deep attachment to cultural practices does not mean their identities were superfluous. Waters (1990) explains the importance of and appeal to ethnicity as one way in which people feel important, special, and connected while at the same time maintaining their individuality. For the same reasons white ethnics embrace a largely symbolic ethnic identity, mixed-race women's racial identities matter psychologically even though they are, to various degrees, symbolic. Through such identifications, women's desires for belonging, structure, and sense of place are satisfied, even if in a tenuous way.

The lack of a secure place of belonging is due to rigid notions of what constitutes boundaries. Communities provide borders, a sense of place and being, at the same time they require conformity and rigidity. Part of this conformity for mixed-race women is the required identification of a "pure" racial essence rather than a mixed-race identity. Women's conceptions of cultural practices often took the form of traditional, unchanging, and static nostalgic references to authentic culture—that too is a result of the rigidity of communities. Women used and accepted such limiting and narrow versions of cultural expression because those "who deviate from familiar forms of racial identity and cultural expressions" are often viewed as inauthentic (Dyson 1994: 222). Because women had mixed racial ancestry and because some of them could pass as white, they perceived their membership within nonwhite racial boundaries as unstable, making it risky for them to explicitly challenge static and familiar forms of cultural expression. In other words, women did not expand the meaning of "blackness" or "Asianness" but instead tried to employ familiar cultural expressions despite their lack of cultural knowledge, training, and exposure.

Although some may interpret mixed-race women's cultural expression as inauthentic or evidence of passing, such a characterization assumes culture is a coherent, consistent sum of practices and behaviors. Once we take a more fluid conception of culture as historically situated and encompassing a variety of signifiers, we can begin to view their syncretism as creative choices as they incorporate pieces of mainstream "American" culture with the cultural practices and traditions of their nonwhite ancestors. Women selectively chose some cultural practices over others within a body of familiar cultural expressions and signifiers to actively represent themselves as members of racial and cultural groups and to provide meaning to these identities.

Women were restricted by larger discursive constructions of culture as traditional and authentic but often discarded that which seemed oppressive. The freedom and degree of choice mixed-race women had in doing so is illustrated by Anita's reflections on the differences between three generations of women in her family. Anita identified primarily as Mexican but also recognized her Native American and Lebanese ancestry. As an adult in her midthirties, Anita spoke of actively working to bring these three ancestries together into a coherent whole. She revealed the freedom she had in selecting cultural practices and symbols through the metaphor of tortillas:

> Tortillas have become a symbol of empowerment for me and yet [were] a symbol of oppression for my mom, as she had no choice but to make them, but I do. . . . And so my grandmother never questioned making

them, they were the livelihood of the family. My mother often questioned, but had no choice but to make them. And now I have choices about the traditions I can follow and the ones that feel oppressive to me. And I just look a lot at how things have been handed down, and if I want to continue using these or if they're not gonna work for me.

The conscious choices Anita and other mixed-race women made in constructing and practicing culture reveals the work of identity. The freedom women had in picking and choosing cultural elements stemmed from their mixed racial ancestry, predominantly white racial environments, and the waning cultural context. Anita revealed how isolation from a cultural context provided her the freedom in making choices that her forebears did not have. Thus culture is not a static entity passed on that women simply employ but instead is discursively produced and mediated.

The women in this study articulate a racial identity in ways that surprise many members of their communities as they opt to construct an identity as nonwhite. In some ways, this construction seems to challenge the racial order in the United States as they disregard whiteness in favor of nonwhiteness. Women's esteem of nonwhiteness inverts the traditionally conceptualized racial pecking order. In addition, women discard that which is culturally oppressive. Despite these seemingly challenging practices, women's racial identity work and the identity constructions of others, including that of multiracial activists, are not as oppositional or counterhegemonic as they appear, for several reasons. First, although it may be psychologically rewarding for women to discard that which is culturally oppressive, the selection process and practice have the tendency to reinforce essentialist cultural practices and mutually exclusive racial categories. Thus, even as women secure their identities through actively participating in the continuing and unfolding construction of racial boundaries and meanings, they do little to shift the terrain of race. Second, even as women reject whiteness, the essentialist foundations of their identity work do little to contest the racial terrain. The expansion of racial borders in and of themselves is not oppositional if this broadening is completed through the use of essentialist logic. In women's rhetoric, essentialism is the root of their "right" to practice and "own" culture.

An important distinction may assist in our evaluation of whether racial projects effectively challenge the larger landscape of race in the United States. On the one hand, the construction by individuals of racial subjectivity and meaning can be psychologically rewarding. The mixed-race women in this study found their identity work to be an empowering means to participate in a community and create their own identity. Women felt a sense of belonging and of uniqueness because of the construction of themselves as members of recognized nonwhite racial groups. On the other hand, their linguistic repertoire does little to challenge the racial order on a structural basis because it remains founded on hegemonic essentialist cultural understandings. The real test of whether discourse effectively can move the United States closer to racial justice is whether it addresses both individual psychological need and the structural need to reorder US thinking about race itself. Such a discourse remains to be seen.

References

Adams, R. 1937. *Interracial Marriage in Hawaii: A Study of the Mutually Conditioned Processes of Acculturation and Amalgamation.* New York: Macmillan.
———. 1969. "The Unorthodox Race Doctrine of Hawaii." Pp. 81–90 in *Comparative Perspectives on Race Relations,* edited by M. Tumin. Boston: Little, Brown.
African Regional Preparatory Conference for the World Conference Against Racism, Racial Discrimination, Xenophobia and Related Intolerance. 2001/2003. "Declaration and Recommendations for a Programme of Action, Dakar, January 22–24." Pp. 344–353 in *Should America Pay? Slavery and the Raging Debate on Reparations,* edited by Raymond A. Winbush. New York: Amistad.
Aiyetoro, A. 2003. "The National Coalition of Blacks for Reparations in America N'COBRA: Its Creation and Contribution to the Reparations Movement." Pp. 209–225 in *Should America Pay? Slavery and the Raging Debate on Reparations,* edited by Raymond A. Winbush. New York: Amistad.
Alba, R. 1990. *Ethnic Identity: The Transformation of White Identity.* New Haven, CT: Yale University Press.
———. 1999. "Immigration and the American Realities of Assimilation and Multiculturalism." *Sociological Forum* 14(1):3–25.
Alba, R., and V. Nee. 1997. "Rethinking Assimilation Theory for a New Era of Immigration." *International Migration Review* 31(4):826–874.
———. 2003. *Remaking the American Mainstream: Assimilation and Contemporary Immigration.* Boston, MA: Harvard University Press.
Alexander, C. 1996. *The Art of Being Black: The Creation of Black British Youth Identities.* Oxford: Oxford University Press.
Allen, H. G. 1982. *The Betrayal of Liliuokalani, Last Queen of Hawaii.* Honolulu: Mutual Publishing.
Allen, R. 1990. *Black Awakening in Capitalist America: An Analytic History.* Trenton, NJ: Africa World Press.
Allport, G. W. 1954. *The Nature of Prejudice.* New York: Doubleday.
———. 1968. *The Person in Psychology: Selected Essays.* Boston: Beacon Press.
Altheide, D. 2000. "Identity and the Definition of the Situation in a Mass-Mediated Context." *Symbolic Interaction* 23(1):1–27.
Anderson, A. 2001. "The Complexity of Ethnic Identities: A Postmodern Reevaluation." *Identity* 1(3):209–223.
Anderson, T. 1992. "Comparative Experience Factors Among Black, Asian, and Hispanic Americans." *Journal of Black Studies* 23(1):27–38.
Anner, J., ed. 1996. *Beyond Identity Politics: Emerging Social Justice Movements in Communities of Color.* Boston, MA: South End Press.

Anyon, J. 1997. *Ghetto Schooling: A Political Economy of Urban Educational Reform.* New York: Teachers College Press.

Anzaldúa, G. 1999. *Borderlands: The New Mestiza,* 2nd ed. San Francisco, CA: Aunt Lute Books.

Arnett, E. C., and T. Pugh. 1997. "Mixed-Race Unions Up." *Denver Post,* December 6, p. A2.

Asante, M. K. 2003. "The African American Warrant for Reparations: The Crime of European Enslavement and Its Consequences." Pp. 3–13 in *Should America Pay? Slavery and the Raging Debate on Reparations,* edited by Raymond A. Winbush. New York: Amistad.

Azibo, D. 1989. "African-Centered Thesis on Mental Health and a Nosology of Black/African Personality Disorder." *Journal of Black Psychology* 15(2):173–214.

Back, L. 1996. *New Ethnicities and Urban Culture: Racism and Multiculture in Young Lives.* London: University College London Press.

Bailey, B. 2000. "Language and Negotiation of Ethnic/Racial Identity Among Dominican Americans." *Language in Society* 29(4):555–582.

———. 2001. "Dominican-American Ethnic/Racial Identities and United States Social Categories." *International Migration Review* 35(3):677–708.

———. 2002. *Language, Race, and Negotiation of Identity: A Study of Dominican Americans.* New York: LFB Scholarly Pub.

Baldwin, J. A. 1979. "Education and Oppression in the American Context." *Journal of Inner City Studies* 1:62–83.

———. 1990. "African (Black) Psychology: Issues and Synthesis." Pp. 125–135 in *Black Psychology,* edited by R. L. Jones. Berkeley: Cobb and Henry.

Baldwin, J. A., R. Brown, and R. Hopkins. 1991. "The Black Self-Hatred Paradigm Revisited: An Africentric Analysis." Pp. 141–165 in *Black Psychology,* 3rd ed., edited by Reginald L. Jones. Berkeley: Cobb and Henry Publishers.

Balibar, E., and I. Wallerstein. 1991. *Race, Nation, and Class: Ambiguous Identities.* London: Verso.

Ball, E. 1998. *Slaves in the Family.* New York: Farrar, Straus, and Giroux.

Ballhatchet, K. 1980. *Race, Sex, and Class Under the Raj.* London: Camelot.

Banks, J. A. 1984. "Black Youths in Predominantly White Suburbs: An Exploratory Study of Their Attitudes and Self-Concepts." *Journal of Negro Education* 53(1): 3–17.

Banks, N. 1992. "Some Considerations of 'Racial' Identification and Self-Esteem When Working with Mixed Ethnicity Children and Their Mothers as Social Services Clients." *Social Services Research* 3:32–41.

———. 1993. "Identity Work with Black Children." *Educational and Child Psychology* 10:43–46.

Banner-Haley, C. T. 1994. *The Fruits of Integration: Black Middle-Class Ideology and Culture, 1969–1990.* Jackson: University of Mississippi Press.

Banton, M. 1955. *The Coloured Quarter: Negro Immigrants in an English City.* London: Jonathan Cape.

———. 1987. *Racial Theories.* Cambridge: Cambridge University Press.

Barn, R. 1993. *Black Children in the Public Care System.* London: Batsford.

———. 1999. "White Mothers, Mixed-Parentage Children and Child Welfare." *British Journal of Social Work* 29:269–284.

Barn, R., R. Sinclair, and D. Ferdinand. 1997. *Acting on Principle: An Examination of Race and Ethnicity in Social Services Provision for Children and Families.* London: British Association for Adoption and Fostering.

Barth, F. 1969. *Ethnic Groups and Boundaries: The Social Organization of Cultural Differences.* Boston: Little, Brown.

Barth, R. P. 1997. "Effects of Age and Race on the Odds of Adoption Versus Remaining in Long-Term Out-of-Home Care." *Child Welfare* 27:285–308.

Bates, K. 1993. "Color Complexity." *Emerge* (June):38–39.

————. 1994. "The Trouble with the Rainbow: Will Blackness Have a Place in a Truly Multiracial America?" *Utne Reader* (November–December):91–92.

Batta, I., and R. Mawby. 1981. "Children in Local Authority Care: A Monitoring of Racial Differences in Bradford." *Policy and Politics* 9(2):137–149.

Batta, I., J. McCulloch, and N. Smith. 1975. "A Study of Juvenile Delinquency Amongst Asians and Half-Asians." *British Journal of Criminology* 15:32–42.

Baudrillard, J. 2000. "The Ideological Genesis of Needs." Pp. 57–80 in *The Consumer Society Reader,* edited by J. B. Schor and D. B. Holt. New York: New Press.

Bean, F. D., and G. Stevens. 2003. *America's Newcomers and the Dynamics of Diversity.* New York: Russell Sage Foundation.

Beechert, E. D. 1985. *Working in Hawai'i: A Labor History.* Honolulu: University of Hawai'i Press.

Bennett, L., Jr. 1962. *Before the Mayflower: A History of the Negro in America, 1619–1962.* Chicago: Johnson.

Benson, S. 1981. *Ambiguous Ethnicity: Interracial Families in London.* Cambridge: Cambridge University Press.

Berger, P. L., and T. Luckmann. 1967. *The Social Construction of Reality: A Treatise in the Sociology of Knowledge.* New York: Doubleday.

Berlin, I. 1998. *Many Thousands Gone: The First Two Centuries of Slavery in North America.* Cambridge: Harvard University Press.

Bernard, J. 1966. "Note on Educational Homogamy in Negro-White and White-Negro Marriages." *Journal of Marriage and the Family* 28:24–27.

Bernstein, N. 1995. "Goin' Gangsta, Choosin' Cholita." *Utne Reader* (March–April): 87–90.

Berry, B. 1963. *Almost White.* New York: Macmillan.

————. 1965. *Race and Ethnic Relations,* 3rd ed. New York: Houghton Mifflin.

Biegel, H. G. 1966. "Problems and Motives in Interracial Relationships." *Journal of Sex Research* 2:185–205.

Bilbo, T. G. 1947. *Take Your Choice: Separation or Mongrelization.* Poplarville, MS: Dream House Publishing.

Blalock, H. M., Jr. 1967. *Toward a Theory of Minority-Group Relations.* New York: Capricorn Books.

Blank, R. 2001. "An Overview of Trends in Social and Economic Well Being, by Race." Pp. 21–39 in *America Becoming: Racial Trends and Their Consequences,* edited by Neil Smelser. Washington, DC: National Academy Press.

Blassingame, J. W. 1972. *The Slave Community: Plantation Life in the Antebellum South.* New York: Oxford University Press.

Blau, P., T. Blum, and J. Schwartz. 1982. "Heterogeneity and Intermarriage." *American Sociological Review* 47(1):45–62.

Blauner, B. 1972. *Racial Oppression in America.* New York: Harper and Row.

Blaustein, A. P., and C. C. Ferguson, Jr. 1957. *Desegregation and the Law.* New Brunswick, NJ: Rutgers University Press.

Blee, K. 1991. *Women of the Klan: Racism and Gender in the 1920s.* Berkeley: University of California Press.

Blum, L. M. 2000. *At the Breast: Ideologies of Breastfeeding and Motherhood in the Contemporary United States.* Boston: Beacon Press.

Blumer, H. 2003. "Race Prejudice as a Sense of Group Position." Pp. 99–105 in *Rethinking the Color Line: Readings in Race and Ethnicity,* 2nd ed., edited by Charles A. Gallagher. New York: McGraw-Hill.

Bobo, L. 2000. "Race and Beliefs About Affirmative Action." Pp. 137–164 in *Racialized Politics: The Debate About Racism in America,* edited by D. O. Sears, J. Sidanius, and L. Bobo. Chicago: University of Chicago Press.

———. 2001. "Racial Attitudes and Relations at the Close of the Twentieth Century." Pp. 264–301 in *America Becoming: Racial Trends and Their Consequences,* edited by Neil Smelser. Washington, DC: National Academy Press.

Bobo, L., and D. Johnson. 2000. "Racial Attitudes in a Prismatic Metropolis: Mapping Identity, Stereotypes, Competition, and Views on Affirmative Action." Pp. 83–166 in *Prismatic Metropolis,* edited by L. Bobo, M. Oliver, J. Johnson, and A. Valenzuela. New York: Russell Sage Foundation.

Bobo, L., J. R. Kluegel, and R. A. Smith. 1997. "Laissez-Faire Racism: The Crystallization of a 'Kindler, Gentler' Anti-Black Ideology." Pp. 15–42 in *Racial Attitudes in the 1990s: Continuity and Change,* edited by Steven A. Tuch and Jack K. Martin. Westport, CT: Praeger: 15–42.

Bobo, L., and R. Smith. 1998. "From Jim Crow Racism to Laissez Faire Racism: The Transformation of Racial Attitudes." In *Beyond Pluralism: The Conception of Groups and Group Identities in America,* edited by Wendy Katkin, Ned Landsman, and Andrea Tyree. Chicago: University of Illinois Press.

Bobo, L., C. Zubrinksy, J. Johnson, Jr., and M. Oliver. 1995. "Work Orientation, Job Discrimination, and Ethnicity." *Research in the Sociology of Work* 5:45–85.

Bogle, D. 2001. *Toms, Coons, Mulattoes, Mammies, and Bucks: An Interpretive History of Blacks in American Films,* 4th ed. New York: Continuum.

Bonacich, E. 1995. "Inequality in America: The Failure of the American System for People of Color." Pp. 138–143 in *Sources: Notable Selections in Race and Ethnicity,* edited by A. Aguirre, Jr., and D. V. Baker. Guilford, CT: Duskin Publishing.

Bonilla-Silva, E. 1997. "Rethinking Racism: Toward a Structural Interpretation." *American Sociological Review* 62(3):465–480.

———. 2000. "'This Is a White Country': The Racial Ideology of the Western Nations of the World-System." *Sociological Inquiry* 70(3):188–214.

———. 2001. *White Supremacy and Racism in the Post–Civil Rights Era.* Boulder, CO: Lynne Rienner.

———. 2002. "We Are All Americans! The Latin Americanization of Racial Stratification in the USA." *Race and Society* 5(1):3–17.

———. 2003. *Racism Without Racists: Color-Blind Racism and the Persistence of Racial Inequality in the United States.* New York: Rowman and Littlefield.

———. 2004a. "Where Is the Love? A Rejoinder by Bonilla-Silva on the Latin Americanization Thesis." *Race and Society* 5(1):105–116.

———. 2004b. "From Biracial to Tri-Racial: The Emergence of a New Racial Stratification System in the United States." Pp. 224–239 in *Skin Deep: How Race and Complexion Matter in the "Color-Blind" Era,* edited by C. Herring, V. M. Keith, and H. D. Horton. Urbana: University of Illinois Press.

Bonilla-Silva, E., and G. Baiocchi. 2001. "Anything but Racism: How Sociologists Limit the Significance of Racism." *Race and Society* 4:117–131.

Bonilla-Silva, E., and A. Doane, eds. 2003. *White Out: The Continuing Significance of Racism.* New York: Routledge.

Bonilla-Silva, E., and K. S. Glover. 2004. "We Are All Americans! The Latin Americanization of Race Relations in the USA." In *The Changing Terrain of Race and Ethnicity: Theory, Methods and Public Policy,* edited by Maria Krysan and Amanda E. Lewis. New York: Russell Sage Foundation.

Bonilla-Silva, E., and A. E. Lewis. 1999. "The New Racism: Toward an Analysis of the U.S. Racial Structure, 1960s–1990s." In *Race, Nation, and Citizenship,* edited by P. Wong. Boulder, CO: Westview Press.

Bonilla-Silva, E., and R. Saenz. 2000. "'If Two People Are in Love . . .' : Color Blind Dreams, (White) Color-Coded Reality Among White College Students in the USA." Unpublished paper.

Boston Globe Poll. 2000. "Views on Race in America." *Boston Globe* Online. Retrieved May 17, 2000, http://www.Boston.com/Globe/Nation/Packages/ Rethinking_Integration/.

Boston, T. D. 1988. *Race, Class and Conservatism.* Boston: Unwin Hyman.

Bourdieu, P. 1984. *Distinction: A Social Critique of the Judgment of Taste.* Cambridge: Harvard University Press.

———. 1986. "The Forms of Capital." Pp. 241–258 in *Handbook of Theory and Research for the Sociology of Education,* edited by J. Richardson. New York: Greenwood.

———. 1990. *The Logic of Practice.* Stanford: Stanford University Press.

Bourdieu, P., and J. C. Passeron. 1990. *Reproduction in Education, Society, and Culture.* London and Newbury Park, CA: Sage, in association with Theory Culture and Society, Department of Administrative and Social Studies, Teesside Polytechnic.

Bowles, D. D. 1993. "Bi-Racial Identity: Children Born to African-American and White Couples." *Clinical Social Work Journal* 21:417–428.

Bowman, P., and C. Howard. 1985. "Race-Related Socialization, Motivation, and Academic Achievement: A Study of Black Youths in Three-Generation Families." *Journal of the American Academy of Child Psychiatry* 24:134–141.

Bracey, J. R., M. Y. Bamaca, and A. J. Umana-Taylor. 2004. "Examining Ethnic Identity and Self-Esteem Among Biracial and Monoracial Adolescents." *Journal of Youth and Adolescence* 33(2):123–132.

Brantlinger, E. 2003. *Dividing Classes: How the Middle Class Negotiates and Rationalizes School Advantage.* New York: RoutledgeFalmer.

Brayboy, T. L. 1966. "Interracial Sexuality as an Expression of Neurotic Conflict." *Journal of Sex Research* 2:179–184.

Breakwell, Glynis Marie. 1996. "Identity Processes and Social Changes." Pp. 13–27 in *Changing European Identities: Social Psychological Analyses of Social Change,* edited by Glynis Marie Breakwell and Evanthia Lyons. Woburn, MA: Butterworth-Heinemann, International Series in Social Psychology.

Brodkin, K. 1998. *How Jews Became White Folks: What That Says About Race in America.* New Brunswick, NJ: Rutgers University Press.

Brooks, R. L. 1990. *Rethinking the American Race Problem.* Berkeley: University of California Press.

Brown, C. 1984. *Black and White Britain: The Third PSI Survey.* London: Heinemann.

Brown, Hedy. 1996. "Themes in Experimental Research on Groups from the 1930s to the 1990s." Pp. 9–62 in *Identities, Groups, and Social Issues,* edited by Margaret Wetherell. Thousand Oaks, CA: Sage.

Brown, J. N. 1998. "Black Liverpool, Black America, and the Gendering of Diasporic Space." *Cultural Anthropology* 13(3):291–326.

Brown, M. K., M. Carnoy, E. Currie, T. Duster, D. B. Oppenheimer, M. M. Shultz, and D. Wellman. 2003. *White-Washing Race: The Myth of a Color-Blind Society.* Berkeley: University of California Press.

Brown, N. G., and R. E. Douglass. 1996. "Making the Invisible Visible: The Growth of Community Network Organizations." Pp. 323–340 in *The Multiracial Experience: Racial Borders as the New Frontier,* edited by M. P. P. Root. Thousand Oaks, CA: Sage.

———. 2003. "Evolution of Multiracial Organizations: Where We Have Been and Where We Are Going." Pp. 11–124 in *New Faces in a Changing America:*

Multiracial Identity in the Twenty-First Century, edited by L. I. Winters and H. L. Debose. Thousand Oaks, CA: Sage.

Brown, P. M. 1993. "Biracial Identity and Social Marginality." *Child and Adolescent Social Work* 7:319–337.

Brown, Rupert. 1996. *Prejudice: Its Social Psychology.* Cambridge, MA: Blackwell.

Brown, U. 1995. "Black/White Interracial Young Adult: Quest for a Racial Identity." *American Journal of Orthopsychiatry* 65(1):125–130.

Brown, Y. A., and A. Montague. 1992. *The Colour of Love: Mixed-Race Relationships.* London: Virago.

Browne, L. E. 1995. "Mortgage Lending in Boston—a Response to the Critics." *New England Economic Review* (September–October):53–78.

Brunsma, D. L., and K. A. Rockquemore. 2001. "The New Color Complex: Appearances and Biracial Identity." *Identity: An International Journal of Theory and Research* 1(3):225–246.

———. 2002. "What Does 'Black' Mean? Exploring the Epistemological Stranglehold of Racial Classification." *Critical Sociology* 28(1–2):101–121.

Burma, J. G. 1946. "The Measurement of Passing." *American Journal of Sociology* 52:18–22.

Butcher, K. F. 1994. "Black Immigrants in the United States: A Comparison with Native Blacks and Other Immigrants." *Industrial and Labor Relations Review* 47:265–284.

Butler, J. 1990. *Gender Trouble: Feminism and the Subversion of Identity.* New York: Routledge.

Byrd, C. 1994. "Wedowee: Opportunity Missed!" *Interracial Voice,* September, http://www.webcom.com/intvoice/editor94.html.

———. 1995. "About Race: The Census' One-Drop Rule." *Interracial Voice,* September–October, http://www.webcom.com/intvoice/editor2.html.

———. 1996. "Kwesi Mfume: Perpetuating White 'Racial Purity.'" *Interracial Voice,* March–April, http://www.webcom.com/intvoice/editor4.html.

———. 1997a. "Government Officially Nixes Multiracial Category." Interracial Voice, October 30, http://www.webcom.com/intvoice/this_in3.html.

———. 1997b. "Leftist Socialism or Multiracial Libertarianism: Our Community's Two Choices?" *Interracial Voice,* November–December, http://www.interracial voice.com/editorial13.html.

———. 1997c. "OMB's Preliminary Recommendations and an IV Commentary." *Interracial Voice,* July 12, http://www.interracialvoice.com/omb_iv.html.

———. 1997d. "The Political Color Continuum." *Interracial Voice,* July–August, http://www.interracialvoice.com/editor12.html.

———. 1997e. "The Speaker's Apparent Endorsement of a Multiracial Classification." *Interracial Voice,* June 20, http://www.webcom.com/intvoice/this_in3.html.

———. 1997f. "Untitled Speech." Presented at the First Annual Multiracial Solidarity March, August 9, Washington, DC.

———. 1998. "Census 2000 Protest: Check American Indian." *Interracial Voice,* January 7, http://www.interracialvoice.com/protest.htmlkjm5.

———. 1999. "An Interview with Ward Connerly." *Interracial Voice,* April 24. http://www.webcom.com/intvoice/interv6.html.

———. 2000a. "The Political Realignment: A Jihad Against 'Race'-Consciousness." *Interracial Voice,* September–October, http://www.interracialvoice.com/jihad.html.

———. 2000b. "The Third Wave: Meditations on a New-Era Synthesis." *Interracial Voice,* http://www.interracialvoice.com/editor26.html.

———. 2003. "Racial Privacy Initiative and Religion's Failure." *Interracial Voice,* September–October, http://www.interracialvoice.com/editor35.html.

Caldwell, C. H., L. P. Kohn-Wood, K. H. Schmeelk-Cone, T. M. Chavous, and M. A. Zimmerman. 2004. "Racial Discrimination and Racial Identity as Risk or Protective Factors for Violent Behaviors in African American Young Adults." *American Journal of Community Psychology* 33(1–2):91–105.

Cannon, P. 1956. *A Gentle Knight: My Husband, Walter White.* New York: Rinehart.

Caputo, R. K. 2004. "Women Who Die Young: The Cumulative Disadvantage of Race." *Affilia* 19:10–23.

Carr, L. 1997. *"Color-Blind" Racism.* Thousand Oaks, CA: Sage.

Carr, S. C., and M. Maclachlan. 1993. "Asserting Psychology in Malawi." *Psychologist* 6:408–413.

Carter, D. T. 1996. *From George Wallace to Newt Gingrich: Race in the Conservative Counterrevolution, 1963–1994.* Baton Rouge: Louisiana State University.

Casper, L., and J. Fields. 2001. "America's Families and Living Arrangements." *Current Population Reports,* June 2001.

Castles, S., and M. Miller. 1993. *The Age of Migration: International Population Movements in the Modern World.* Hong Kong: Macmillan.

Catterall, H. T., ed. 1926–1937. *Judicial Cases Concerning American Slavery and the Negro.* Vols. 1–5. Washington, DC: Carnegie Institute.

Censo Nacional de Población y Vivienda. 2002. *Bolivia: Caraterísticas de la Población.* Serie Resultados 4. La Paz: Ministerio de Hacienda.

Centre for Contemporary Cultural Studies. 1982. *The Empire Strikes Back: Race and Racism in 70s Britain.* London: Routledge.

Cerulo, K. A. 1997. "Identity Construction: New Issues, New Directions." *Annual Review of Sociology* 23:385.

Chan, S. 1991. *Asian Americans: An Interpretive History.* Boston: Twayne.

Chang, J. 1996. "Local Knowledge: Notes on Race Relations, Panethnicity and History in Hawai'i." *Amerasia Journal* 22(2):1–29.

Chase, S. 1995. "Taking Narrative Seriously: Consequences for Method and Theory in Interview Studies." Pp. 1–26 in *Interpreting Experience: The Narrative Study of Lives,* vol. 3., edited by R. Josselson and A. Lieblich. Thousand Oaks, CA: Sage.

Chemerinsky, E. 2003. "Why California's Racial Privacy Initiative Is Unconstitutional." CNN, August 22, http://www.cnn.com/2003/law/08/22/findlaw.analysis.chemerinsky.race/).

Chevannes, M., and F. Reeves. 1987. "The Black Voluntary School Movement: Definition, Context, and Prospects." Pp. 147–148 in *Racial Inequality in Education,* edited by B. Troyna. London: Tavistock.

Childs, E. 2005. *Navigating Interracial Borders: Black-White Couples and Their Social Worlds.* Piscataway, NJ: Rutgers University Press.

Chow, S. 2000. "The Significance of Race in the Private Sphere: Asian Americans and Spousal Preference." *Sociological Inquiry* 70:1–29.

Choy, P. 2000. "Anatomy of a Dancer: Place, Lineage, and Liberation." In "Whose Vision? Asian Settler Colonialism in Hawai'i," special edition of *Amerasia Journal* 26(2):234–252.

Church's Chicken Press Release. "Converging on the Crunch," July 29, 2004.

Clark, K. B., and M. K. Clark. 1939a. "The Development of Consciousness of Self and the Emergence of Racial Identification in Negro Preschool Children." *Journal of Social Psychology* 10:591–599.

———. 1939b. "Segregation as a Factor in the Racial Identification of Negro Pre-School Children." *Journal of Experimental Education* 8:161–163.

Clemetson, L. 2000. "Color My World: The Promise and Perils of Life in the New Multiracial Mainstream." *Newsweek,* May 8, pp. 70–74.

Cohen, A. P. 1985. *The Symbolic Construction of Community.* London: Tavistock.

————. 1994. *Self Consciousness : An Alternative Anthropology of Identity.* London: Routledge.

Cohen, L. 2003. *A Consumer's Republic: The Politics of Mass Consumption in Postwar America.* New York: Alfred A. Knopf.

Cohen, R. 1997. *Global Diasporas: An Introduction.* Seattle: University of Washington Press.

Collins, P. H. 2000. *Black Feminist Thought: Knowledge, Consciousness, and the Politics of Empowerment.* New York: Routledge.

Collins, S. F. 1951. "The Social Position of 'White' and 'Half-Caste' Women in the Coloured Groupings in Britain." *American Sociological Review* 16:796–802.

Comaroff, J., and J. Comaroff. 1992. *Ethnography and the Historical Imagination.* Boulder, CO: Westview.

Conley, D. 2000 *Honky.* Berkeley: University of California Press.

Connerly, W. 2000. "A Homecoming with Too Much Color." *Interracial Voice,* May–June, http://www.interracialvoice.com/connerly.html.

————. 2001a. "Let's Rid Ourselves of Those Silly Race Boxes." *Abolitionist Examiner,* August–September, http://www.multiracial.com/abolitionist/word/connerly .html.

————. 2001b. "The Racial Privacy Initiative." *Interracial Voice,* November–December, http://www.interracialvoice.com/connerly5.html.

————. 2001c. "Towards a Twenty-First Century Vision of Race: Why We Should Get Rid of the Boxes Altogether." *Interracial Voice,* May–June, http://www .interracialvoice.com/connerly3.html.

————. 2002. *Creating Equal: My Fight Against Race Preferences.* San Francisco: Encounter Books.

Connolly, P. 1998. *Racism, Gender Identities and Young Children: Social Relations in a Multi-Ethnic, Inner-City Primary School.* London: Routledge.

Conyers, J., Jr., and J. N. Watson. 2003. "Reparations: An Idea Whose Time Has Come." Pp. 14–21 in *Should America Pay? Slavery and the Raging Debate on Reparations,* edited by Raymond A. Winbush. New York: Amistad.

Cornell, S., and D. Hartmann. 1997. *Ethnicity and Race: Making Identities in a Changing World.* Thousand Oaks, CA: Pine Forge Press.

Courtney, M., R. P. Barth, J. D. Berrick, D. D. Brooks, D. Needel, and L. Park. 1996. "Race and Child Welfare Services: Past Research and Future Directions." *Child Welfare* 75:99–137.

Crass, C. N.d.. "Still We Rise: Conversations with Organizers on Building a Global Justice Movement and Ending War." Unpublished manuscript, http://colours .mahost.org/articles/crass11.html.

Crawford, J., W. Nobles, and J. D. Leary. 2003. "Reparations and Health Care for African Americans: Repairing the Damage from the Legacy of Slavery." Pp. 251–282 in *Should America Pay? Slavery and the Raging Debate on Reparations,* edited by Raymond A. Winbush. New York: Amistad.

Crohn, J. 1995. *Mixed Matches: How to Create Successful Interracial, Interethnic, and Interfaith Relationships.* New York: Balantine Books.

Cross, W. E., Jr. 1991. *Shades of Black.* Philadelphia: Temple University Press.

Cross, W., T. Parham, and J. Helms. 1991. "The Stages of Black Identity Development: Nigrescence Models." Pp. 319–228 in *Black Psychology,* 3rd ed., edited by R. L. Jones. Berkeley: Cobb and Henry.

C-SPAN. 2000. "Racial Classifications on Census Forms." Program ID: 156340-1, News Conference, Washington, DC, March 31.

DaCosta, K. M. 2004. "All in the Family: The Familial Roots of Racial Division." Pp. 19–42 in *The Politics of Multiracialism: Challenging Racial Thinking,* edited by Heather Dalmage. Albany, NY: SUNY Press.

Dalmage, H. 2000. *Tripping on the Color Line: Black-White Multiracial Families in a Racially Divided World*. New Brunswick, NJ: Rutgers University Press.

———. 2004a. "Protecting Racial Comfort: Protecting White Privilege." Pp. 203–218 in *The Politics of Multiracialism: Challenging Racial Thinking,* edited by Heather Dalmage. Albany, NY: SUNY Press.

———, ed. 2004b. *The Politics of Multiracialism: Challenging Racial Thinking.* Albany, NY: SUNY Press.

Daniel, G. R. 1992. "Beyond Black and White: The New Multiracial Consciousness." Pp. 333–341 in *Racially Mixed People in America,* edited by M. P. P. Root. Newbury Park, CA: Sage.

———. 1996a. "Racism: Past and Present." Znet October. Retrieved October 31, 2004, http://www.zmag.org/gettingstarted.htm.

———. 1996b. "Black and White Identity in the New Millennium: Unsevering the Ties That Bind." Pp. 121–139 in *The Multiracial Experience: Racial Borders as the New Frontier,* edited by M. P. P. Root. Thousand Oaks, CA: Sage.

———. 1997. Testimony before the House Subcommittee on Government Management, Information, and Technology of the Committee on Government Reform and Oversight, May 22, 1997, Federal Measures of Race and Ethnicity and the Implications for the 2000 Census: Hearing. 105th Cong., 1st sess.

———. 1998. "Black No More or More Than Black: Multiracial Identity Politics and the Decenial Census." Presented at Colorlines in the Twenty-first Century: Multiracialism in a Racially Divided World. September 26, Roosevelt University, Chicago, IL.

———. 2000a. "Black No More or More Than Black." Presented at the annual meeting of the American Sociological Association, August 14, Washington, DC.

———. 2000b. *More Than Black: Multiracial Identity and the New Racial Order.* Philadelphia: Temple University Press.

Davidson, J. R. 1992. "Theories About Black-White Interracial Marriage: A Clinical Perspective." *Journal of Multicultural Counseling and Development* (October):150–157.

Davila, A. 2001. *Latinos, Inc.: The Marketing and the Making of a People.* Berkeley: University of California Press.

Davis, A., B. B. Gardner, M. R. Gardner, and W. L. Warner. 1941. *Deep South: A Social Anthropological Study of Caste and Class.* Chicago: University of Chicago Press.

Davis, A. Y. 1981. *Women, Race, and Class.* New York: Vintage Books.

Davis, F. J. 1991. *Who Is Black? One Nation's Definition.* University Park: Pennsylvania State University Press.

———. 1995. "The Hawaiian Alternative to the One-Drop Rule." Pp. 115–131 in *American Mixed Race: The Culture of Microdiversity,* edited by Naomi Zack. Lanham, MD: Rowman and Littlefield.

Davis, K. 1941. "Intermarriage in Caste Societies." *American Anthropologist* 43(3): 376–395.

Davis, M. E. 1994. "Music and Black Ethnicity in the Dominican Republic." Pp. 119–155 in *Music and Black Ethnicity: The Caribbean and South America,* edited by G. Behague. New Brunswick, NJ: Transaction.

Daws, G. 1968. *Shoal of Time: A History of the Hawaiian Islands.* New York: Macmillan.

Dawson, M. C. 1994. *Behind the Mule: Race and Class in African American Politics.* Princeton, NJ: Princeton University Press.

———. 2000. "Slowly Coming to Grips with the Effects of the American Racial Order on American Policy Preferences." Pp. 344–358 in *Racialized Politics,* edited by D. Sears, J. Sidanius, and L. Bobo. Chicago: University of Chicago Press.

Day, D. 1979. *The Adoption of Black Children: Counteracting Institutional Discrimination.* Lexington, MA: Lexington Books.

Deaux, K. 1992. "Personalizing Identity and Socializing the Self." Pp. 9–33 in *Social Psychology of Identity and the Self-Concept,* edited by G. Breakwell. London: Academic Press.

Deaux, K., and K. Ethier. 1998. "Negotiating Social Identity." Pp. 301–323 in *Prejudice: The Target's Perspective,* edited by J. Swim and C. Stangor. San Diego: Academic Press.

Deaux, K., and D. Martin. 2003. "Interpersonal Networks and Social Categories: Specifying Levels of Context in Identity Processes." *Social Psychology Quarterly* 66:101–117.

DeGenova, M. K., and F. P. Rice. 2005. *Intimate Relationships, Marriages, and Families.* New York: McGraw-Hill.

De La Fuente, A. 1998. "Race, National Discourse, and Politics in Cuba: An Overview." *Latin American Perspectives* 25(3):43–69.

De La Garza, R. O., L. Desipio, C. Garcia, J. Garcia, and A. Falcon, eds. 1993. *Latino Voices: Mexican, Puerto Rican, and Cuban Perspectives on American Politics.* Boulder: Westview Press.

Del Castillo, J. A. M. M. 1987. "Migration, National Identity and Cultural Policy in the Dominican Republic." *Journal of Ethnic Studies* 15(3):49–69.

Demott, B. 1995. "Put on a Happy Face: Masking the Differences Between Blacks and Whites." *Harper's,* September, pp. 31–38.

Dickson, L. 1993. "The Future of Marriage and Family in Black America." *Journal of Black Studies* 23:472–491.

DiMaggio, P. 1994. "Culture and Economy." Pp. 27–57 in *The Handbook of Economic Sociology,* edited by N. Smelser and R. Swedberg. Princeton, NJ, and New York: Princeton University Press and the Russell Sage Foundation.

DiTomaso, N., R. Parks-Yancy, and C. Post. 2003. "White Views of Civil Rights: Color Blindness and Equal Opportunity." In *White Out: The Continuing Significance of Racism,* edited by A. W. Doane and E. Bonilla-Silva. New York: Routledge.

Dodd, V. 2000. "Black Women Win Payout for Soldier's Racial Abuse." *Guardian,* September 16, p. 18.

Domínguez, V. R. 1986. *White by Definition: Social Classification in Creole Louisiana.* New Brunswick, NJ: Rutgers University Press.

Dorman, L. 1996. "On Golf: 'We'll Be Right Back, After This Hip and Distorted Commercial Break.'" *New York Times,* September 1, retrieved October 26, 2004, from LexisNexis Academic database.

Dougherty, M. 1992. *To Steal a Kingdom.* Waimanalo, HI: Island Style Press.

Douglas, M., and B. Isherwood. 1996. *The World of Goods: Towards an Anthropology of Consumption.* New York: Routledge.

Douglas, N. 1996. "Semantic Inequality." Speech presented at the Multiracial Solidarity March, August 9, Washington, DC.

———. 1997a. "I Solemnly Swear." *Interracial Voice,* May 22, http://www.interracialvoice.com/natdoug3.html.

———. 1997b. "Leaving the Scene of a Crime." *Interracial Voice,* July 12, http://www.interracialvoice.com/natdoug4.html.

———. 1997c. Testimony before the House Subcommittee on Government Management, Information, and Technology of the Committee on Government Reform and Oversight, May 22, 1997, Federal Measures of Race and Ethnicity and the Implications for the 2000 Census: Hearing. 105th Cong., 1st sess.

————. 1998a. "The Kinky Hair Machine." Project Race Website, January 5. http://www.projectrace.com/zcommentary/archive/commentary-002.php.

————. 1998b. "What We're Up Against." *Interracial Voice,* March–April, http://www.interracialvoice.com/nathan.html.

Douglass, F. [1857] 1985. "The Significance of Emancipation in the West Indies." Speech, Canandaigua, New York, August 3, 1857. P. 204 in the *Frederick Douglass Papers. Series One: Speeches, Debates, and Interviews.* Vol. 3, 1855–1863, edited by J. W. Blassingame. New Haven, CT: Yale University Press.

Douglass, R. 1997a. Testimony before the House Subcommittee on Government Management, Information, and Technology of the Committee on Government Reform and Oversight, May 22, 1997, Federal Measures of Race and Ethnicity and the Implications for the 2000 Census: Hearing. 105th Cong., 1st sess.

————. 1997b. Personal correspondence with G. Reginald Daniel, June 21.

Dovidio, John F., Samuel L. Gaertner, Yolanda Flores Niemann, and Kevin Snider. 2001. "Racial, Ethnic, and Cultural Differences in Responding to Distinctiveness and Discrimination on Campus: Stigma and Common Group Identity." *Journal of Social Issues* 57(1):167–188.

Drake, S. C. 1954. "Value Systems, Social Structures, and Race Relations in the British Isles," University of Chicago. Unpublished doctoral dissertation. Department of Anthropology.

Drake, S. C., and H. R. Cayton. 1945. *Black Metropolis: A Study of Negro Life in a Northern City.* Chicago: University of Chicago Press.

Dreier, P. 1998. "There's No Racial Justice Without Economic Justice: Shortcomings of Clinton's Race Initiative Report." *Social Policy* 29:41–50.

Duany, J. 1998. "Reconstructing Racial Identity: Ethnicity, Color, and Class Among Dominicans in the United States and Puerto Rico." *Latin American Perspective* 25(3):147–172.

Dube, L., and S. Guinmond. 1986. "Relative Deprivation and Social Protest: The Personal-Group Issue." In *Relative Deprivation and Social Comparison: The Ontario Symposium,* edited by J. M. Olson, C. P. Herman, and M. P. Zanna. Hillsdale, NJ: Lawrence Erlbaum.

Du Bois, W. E. B. 1903. *The Souls of Black Folk: Essays and Sketches,* 3rd ed. Chicago: A. C. McClurg.

DuCille, A. 1996. "Toy Theory: Black Barbie and the Deep Play of Difference." Pp. 259–280 in *The Consumer Society Reader,* edited by J. B. Schor and D. B. Holt. New York: New Press.

Dudley, M. K., and K. K. Agard. 1993. *A Call for Hawaiian Sovereignty.* Honolulu: Nä Käne O Ka Malu Press.

Duke, D. 1999. *My Awakening.* Mandeville, LA: Free Speech Press.

Duneier, M. 1992. *Slim's Table: Race, Respectability, and Masculinity.* Chicago: University of Chicago Press.

Durkheim, E. 1960. *The Division of Labor in Society.* Translated by G. Simpson. New York: Free Press.

Dyer, R. 1997. *White: Essays on Race and Culture.* New York: Routledge.

Dyson, M. E. 1994. "Essentialism and the Complexities of Racial Identity." P. 218 in *Multiculturalism: A Critical Reader,* edited by D. T. Goldberg. Cambridge, MA: Blackwell.

East-West Center. 1999. "EWC Mission and Overview." East-West Center. Retrieved May 20, 2004, http://www.eastwestcenter.org/about-ov.asp.

Eastland, T. 1997. *Ending Affirmative Action: The Case for Colorblind Justice.* New York: Basic Books.

Eckard, E. W. 1947. "How Many Negroes Pass?" *American Journal of Sociology* 52:498–503.

Eliasoph, N. 1999. "'Everyday Racism' in a Culture of Political Avoidance: Civil Society, Speech, and Taboo." *Social Problems* 46(4):479–502.

Ellison, R. 1952. *Invisible Man.* New York: Random House.

Emerson, M., R. T. Kimbro, and G. Yancey. 2002. "Contact Theory Extended: The Effects of Prior Racial Contact on Current Social Ties." *Social Science Quarterly* 83(3):745–761.

Emerson, M., and C. Smith. 2000. *Divided by Faith: Evangelical Religion and the Problem of Race in America.* Oxford: Oxford University Press.

Emerson, M., G. Yancey, and K. Chai. 2001. "Does Race Matter in Residential Segregation? Exploring the Preferences of White Americans." *American Sociological Review* 66(6):922–935.

Entman, R., and A. Rojecki. 2000. *The Black Image in the White Mind: Media and Race in America.* Chicago: University of Chicago Press.

Epstein, J., and K. Straub, eds. 1991. *Body Guards: The Cultural Politics of Gender Ambiguity.* New York: Routledge.

Espiritu, Y. L. 1992. *Asian American Panethnicity: Bridging Institutions and Identities.* Philadelphia: Temple University Press.

Espiritu, Y. L., and D. L. Wolf. 2001. "The Paradox of Assimilation: Children of Filipino Immigrants in San Diego." Pp. 157–186 in *Ethnicities: Children of Immigrants in America,* edited by R. G. Rumbaut and A. Portes. Berkeley: University of California Press.

Essed, P. 1991. *Understanding Everyday Racism: Towards an Interdisciplinary Theory.* Thousand Oaks, CA: Sage.

Ethier, K. A., and K. Deaux. 1990. "Hispanics in Ivy: Assessing Identity and Perceived Threat." *Sex Roles* 22:427–440.

Fagan, E., et al. 2002. "Farmer-Paellman vs. Fleetboston, Aetnainc., Csx." Pp. 354–366 in *Should America Pay? Slavery and the Raging Debate on Reparations,* edited by Raymond A. Winbush. New York: Amistad.

Falkerstein-Jordan, K. 1995. "Clinton Needs to Hear from You." *Spectrum: The Newsletter of MASC,* June, p. 4. Los Angeles: Multiracial Americans of Southern California.

Fang, C. Y., J. Sidanius, and F. Pratto. 1998. "Romance Across the Social Status Continuum: Interracial Marriage and the Ideological Asymmetry Effect." *Journal of Cross-Cultural Psychology* 29:290–305.

Farley, J. E. 2000. *Majority-Minority Relations,* 4th ed. Upper Saddle River, NJ: Prentice-Hall.

Farley, R. 1991. "The New Census Question About Ancestry: What Did It Tell Us?" *Demography* 28:411–429.

Farley, R., and W. Allen. 1987. *The Color Line and the Quality of Life in America.* New York: Russell Sage Foundation.

Farmer-Paellmann, D. 2003. "Excerpt from Black Exodus: The Ex-Slave Pension Movement Reader." Pp. 22–31 in *Should America Pay? Slavery and the Raging Debate on Reparations,* edited by Raymond A. Winbush. New York: Amistad.

Fausto-Sterling, A. 1993. "The Five Sexes: Why Male and Female Are Not Enough." *Sciences* 33:20–25.

Feagin, J. 1991. "The Continuing Significance of Race: Antiblack Discrimination in Public Places." *American Sociological Review* 56:101–116.

———. 2000. *Racist America.* New York: Routledge.

Feagin, J., and C. Feagin. 1996. *Racial and Ethnic Relations,* 5th ed. Upper Saddle River, NJ: Prentice-Hall.

Feagin, J., and E. O'Brien. 2003. *White Men on Race: Power, Privilege, and the Shaping of Cultural Consciousness.* Boston: Beacon Press.

Feagin, J., and M. P. Sikes. 1994. *Living with Racism: The Black Middle-Class Experience.* Boston: Beacon Press.

Feagin, J., and H. Vera. 1995. *White Racism: The Basics.* New York: Routledge.

Fennema, M. 1987. *La Construcción de Raza y Nación en la República Dominicana.* Santo Domingo, Dominican Republic: Editorio Universitario.

Ferber, A. L. 1998. *White Man Falling: Race, Gender, and White Supremacy.* Lanham, MD: Rowman and Littlefield.

———, ed. 2004. *Home-Grown Hate: Gender and Organized Racism.* New York: Routledge.

Fernandez, C. A. 1992. "La Raza and the Melting Pot." Pp. 126–143 in *Racially Mixed People in America,* edited by M. P. P. Root. Newbury Park, CA: Sage.

———. 1995. "Testimony of the Association of Multiethnic Americans Before the Subcommittee on Census, Statistics, and Postal Personnel of the U.S. House of Representatives." Pp. 191–210 in *American Mixed Race: The Culture of Microdiversity,* edited by Naomi Zack. Lanham, MD: Rowman and Littlefield.

———. 1997. Testimony before the House Subcommittee on Government Management, Information, and Technology of the Committee on Government Reform and Oversight, May 22, 1997, Federal Measures of Race and Ethnicity and the Implications for the 2000 Census: Hearing. 105th Cong., 1st sess.

Fernandez-Kelly, P., and S. Curran. 2001. "Nicaraguans: Voices Lost, Voices Found." Pp. 127–156 in *Ethnicities: Children of Immigrants in America,* edited by R. G. Rumbaut and A. Portes. Berkeley: University of California Press.

Fiebert, M. S., H. Karamol, and M. Kasdan. 2000. "Interracial Dating: Attitudes and Experience Among American College Students in California." *Psychological Reports* 87:1059–1064.

Fields, B. J. 1990. "Slavery, Race and Ideology in the United States of America." *New Left Review* 181:95–118.

Fleming, Jim, ed. 1984. *Marx Beyond Marx: Lessons on the Grundrisse.* South Hadley, MA: Bergin and Garvey.

Flores-Gonzales, N. 1999. "The Racialization of Latinos: The Meaning of Latino Identity for the Second Generation." *Latino Studies Journal* 10(3):3–31.

Foeman, A. K., and T. Nance. 1999. "From Miscegenation to Multiculturalism: Perceptions and Stages of Interracial Relationship Development." *Journal of Black Studies* 29:540–557.

Forbes, J. D. 1993. *Africans and Native Americans: The Language of Race and the Evolution of Red-Black Peoples.* Chicago: University of Illinois Press.

Foren, R., and I. Batta. 1970. "'Colour' as a Variable in the Use Made of a Local Authority Child Care Department." *Social Work* 27(3):10–15.

Forman, T., R. Martinez, and E. Bonilla-Silva. N.d. "Latinos' Perceptions of Blacks and Asians: Testing the Immigrant Hypothesis." Unpublished manuscript.

Foster, E. 1998. "Jefferson Fathered Slave's Last Child." *Nature,* November 5, pp. 27–28.

Foster, J. 1999. "An Invitation to Dialogue: Clarifying the Position of Feminist Gender Theory in Relation to Sexual Difference Theory." *Gender and Society* 13:431–456.

———. 2004. "Strategic Ambiguity Meets Strategic Essentialism: Multiracial, Intersex, and Disability Rights Activism and the Paradoxes of Identity Politics." *Research in Political Sociology* 13.

Foucault, M. 1982. *The Archaeology of Knowledge* and *The Discourse on Language.* New York: Pantheon Books.

Frank, T. 1997. *The Conquest of Cool: Business Culture, Counterculture, and the Rise of Hip Consumerism.* Chicago: University of Chicago Press.

————. 2000. *One Market Under God: Extreme Capitalism, Market Populism, and the End of Economic Democracy.* New York: Doubleday.

Frankenberg, R. 1993. *White Women, Race Matters: The Social Construction of Whiteness.* Minneapolis: University of Minnesota Press.

————. 1997. *Dis-Placing Whiteness: Essays in Social and Cultural Criticism.* Durham, NC: Duke University Press.

————. 2001. "Mirage of an Unmarked Whiteness." In *The Making and Unmaking of Whiteness,* edited by B. B. Rasmussen, E. Klineberg, I. Nexica, and M. Wray. Durham, NC: Duke University Press.

Franklin, Anderson J. 1999. "Invisibility Syndrome and Racial Identity Development in Psychotherapy and Counseling African American Men." *Counseling Psychologist* 27(6):761–793.

Fraser, N. 1997. *Justice Interruptus: Critical Reflections on the "Postsocialist" Condition.* New York: Routledge.

Frenzen, J., P. M. Hirsch, and P. C. Zerrillo. 1994. "Consumption, Preferences, and Changing Lifestyles." Pp. 403–425 in *The Handbook of Economic Sociology,* edited by N. Smelser and R. Swedberg. Princeton, NJ, and New York: Princeton University Press and the Russell Sage Foundation.

Frey, W. H., and R. Farley. 1996. "Latino, Asian, and Black Segregation in U.S. Metropolitan Areas: Are Multi-Ethnic Metros Different?" *Demography* 33(1): 35–50.

Fuchs, Lawrence H. 1961. *Hawaii Pono: A Social History.* New York: Harcourt Brace.

Fujikane, C. 2000. "Asian Settler Colonialism in Hawai'i." In "Whose Vision? Asian Settler Colonialism in Hawai'i," special edition of *Amerasia Journal* 26(2):xv–xxii.

Funderburg, L. 1994. *Black, White, Other: Biracial Americans Talk About Race.* New York: Morrow.

Fuss, D. 1989. *Essentially Speaking: Feminism, Nature, and Difference.* New York: Routledge.

Gadberry, J. H., and R. A. Dodder. 1993. "Educational Homogamy in Interracial Marriages: An Update." *Journal of Social Behavior and Personality* 8:155–163.

Gaines, S. O. 1997. "Communalism and the Reciprocity of Affection and Respect Among Interethnic Married Couples." *Journal of Black Studies* 27:352–364.

Gallagher, C. A. 1995. "White Construction in the University." *Socialist Review* 24(1–2):165–187.

————. 1997. "White Racial Formation: Into the Twenty-first Century." Pp. 6–11 in *Critical White Studies: Looking Behind the Mirror,* edited by R. Delgado. Philadelphia, PA: Temple University Press.

————. 2003a. "Playing the White Ethnic Card: Using Ethnic Identity to Deny Contemporary Racism." In *White Out: The Continuing Significance of Racism,* edited by A. W. Doane and E. Bonilla-Silva. New York: Routledge.

————. 2003b. "Color-Blind Privilege: The Social and Political Functions of Erasing the Color-Line in Post-Race America." *Race, Gender, and Class* 10(4):22–37.

————. 2003c. "Miscounting Race: Explaining Whites' Misperceptions of Racial Group Size." *Sociological Perspectives* 46(3):381–396.

————. 2004a. "Transforming Racial Identity Through Affirmative Action." Pp. 153–170 in *Race and Ethnicity: Across Time, Space and Discipline,* edited by R. D. Coates. Boston: Brill.

————. 2004b. "Racial Redistricting: Expanding the Boundaries of Whiteness." Pp. 59–76 in *The Politics of Multiracialism: Challenging Racial Thinking,* edited by H. Dalmage. Albany, NY: SUNY Press.

Gallup Organization. 1997. "Black/White Relations in the U.S." June 10, pp. 1–5.
———. 2001. "Black and White Relations in the United States: Update, Special Reports." July.
Gamson, J. 1996. "Must Identity Movements Self-Destruct? A Queer Dilemma." Pp. 395–420 in *Queer Theory/Sociology*, edited by S. Seidman. London: Blackwell.
Gans, H. 1979. "Symbolic Ethnicity: The Future of Ethnic Groups and Cultures in America." *Ethnic and Racial Studies* 2:1–18.
———. 1999. "The Possibility of a New Racial Hierarchy in the Twenty-First Century United States." In *The Cultural Territories of Race: Black and White Boundaries*, edited by M. Lamont. Chicago: University of Chicago.
———. 2004. "The American Kaleidoscope." In *Reinventing the Melting Pot: The New Immigrants and What It Means to Be American*, edited by Tamar Jacoby. New York: Basic Books.
Garcia, J. A. 1995. "A Multicultural America: Living in a Sea of Diversity." Pp. 29–38 in *Multiculturalism From the Margins: Non-Dominant Voices on Differences and Diversity*, edited by D. A. Harris. Westport, CT: Bergin and Garvey.
Gaskins, P. F. 1999. *What Are You? Voices of Mixed-Race Young People*. New York: Henry Holt.
Geertz, C. 1963. "The Integrative Revolution: Primordial Sentiments and Civil Politics in the United States." Pp. 105–157 in *Old Societies and New States: The Quest for Modernity in Asia and Africa*, edited by C. Geertz. New York: Free Press.
Gelman, D., K. Springen, K. Brailsford, and M. Miller. 1988. "Black and White in America." *Newsweek*, March 7, pp. 18–23.
Gibbs, J. T. 1987. "Identity and Marginality: Issues in the Treatment of Biracial Adolescents." *American Journal of Orthopsychiatry* 57(2):265–278.
———. 1989. "Biracial Adolescents." Pp. 332–350 in *Children of Color: Psychological Interventions with Culturally Diverse Youth*, edited by J. T. Gibbs and L. N. Huang. New York: Jossey-Bass.
Gibbs, J. T., and A. M. Hines. 1992. "Negotiating Ethnic Identity: Issues for Black-White Biracial Adolescents." Pp. 223–238 in *Racially Mixed People in America*, edited by M. P. P. Root. Newbury Park, CA: Sage.
Gibson, C., and K. Jung. 2002. "Historical Census Statistics on Population Totals by Race, 1790 to 1990, and by Hispanic Origin, 1970 to 1990, for the United States, Regions, Divisions, and States." Working Paper No. 56, U.S. Census Bureau Population Division, Washington, DC.
Giddens, A. 1984. *The Constitution of Society: Outline of the Theory of Structuration*. Berkeley: University of California Press.
Gilbertson, G. A., J. P. Fitzpatrick, and L. Yang. 1996. "Hispanic Outmarriage in New York City—New Evidence from 1991." *International Immigration Review* 30.
Gillem, A. R. 2001. "Black Identity in Biracial Black/White People." *Cultural Diversity and Ethnic Minority Psychology* 7:182–196.
Gilroy, P. 1993. *Small Acts: Thoughts on the Politics of Black Culture*. New York: Serpent's Books.
Gingrich, N. 1997. "Letter from Newt Gingrich, Speaker of the U.S. House of Representatives, to Franklin D. Raines, Director of the OMB. From the Speaker." Project Race Website, July 1, http://www.projectrace.com/hotnews/archive/hotnews-070197.php.
Gingrich, N., and W. Connerly. 1997. "Face the Failure of Racial Preferences." *New York Times*, June 15, section 4, p. 5.
Gist, N. P., and R. Dean. 1973. *Marginality and Identity*. Leiden: Brill.

Gladwell, M. 2000a. *The Tipping Point: How Little Things Can Make a Big Difference.* New York: Little, Brown.

———. 2000b. "Lost in the Middle." In *Half and Half: Writers on Growing Up Biracial and Bicultural,* edited by Claudine C. O'Hearn. New York: Pantheon.

Glaser, B. G., and A. Strauss. 1967. *The Discovery of Grounded Theory.* Chicago: Aldine.

Glazer, N., and D. P. Moynihan. 1963. *Beyond the Melting Pot: The Negroes, Puerto Ricans, Jews, Italians, and Irish of New York City.* Cambridge, MA: MIT Press.

Glick, C. E. 1980. *Sojourners and Settlers: Chinese Migrants in Hawaii.* Honolulu: Hawaii Chinese History Center and University Press of Hawaii.

Goffman, E. 1959. *The Presentation of Self in Everyday Life.* Garden City, NY: Doubleday.

———. 1963. *Stigma: Notes on the Management of Spoiled Identity.* Englewood Cliffs, NJ: Prentice-Hall.

———. 1967. *Interaction Ritual.* New York: Doubleday.

Goldberg, D. T. 1993. *Racist Culture: Philosophy and the Politics of Meaning.* Oxford: Blackwell.

Goldstein, B. P. 1999. "Black, with a White Parent: A Positive and Achievable Identity." *British Journal of Social Work* 29:285–301.

Gonzalez, J. A. 2002. "Personal and Social Identity in Organizations: A Study of Organizational Commitment." Ph.D. diss.

González, J. L. 1993. *Puerto Rico: The Four-Storeyed Country.* Princeton, NJ: Markus Wiener.

Goodman, M. E. 1952. *Race Awareness in Young Children.* Oxford: Addison-Wesley.

Gordon, A. 1996. *Ghostly Matters: Haunting and the Sociological Imagination.* Minneapolis: University of Minnesota Press.

Gordon, M. M. 1964. *Assimilation in American Life.* New York: Oxford University Press.

Gould, S. J. 1981. *The Mismeasure of Man.* New York: Norton.

Graham, S. R. 1995. "Grassroots Advocacy." Pp. 185–189 in *American Mixed Race: The Culture of Microdiversity,* edited by N. Zack. Lanham, MD: Rowman and Littlefield.

———. 1996. "The Real World." Pp. 37–48 in *The Multiracial Experience: Racial Borders as the New Frontier,* edited by M. P. P. Root. Thousand Oaks, CA: Sage.

———. 1997a. Testimony before the House Subcommittee on Government Management, Information, and Technology of the Committee on Government Reform and Oversight, May 22, 1997, Federal Measures of Race and Ethnicity and the Implications for the 2000 Census: Hearing. 105th Cong., 1st sess.

———. 1997b. "Advocates to Continue to Fight for Multiracial Classification." Project Race Website, July 25, http://www.projectrace.com/hotnews/archive/hotnews-072597.php.

———. 1997c. "From the Executive Director." Project Race Website, October 29, http://www.projectrace.com/hotnews/archive/hotnews-102997.php.

———. 1997d. "Newt Confirms." Project Race Website, July 15, http://www.projectrace.com/hotnews/archive/hotnews-061597.php.

———. 1997e. "Newt Said It." Project Race Website, January 7, http://www.projectrace.com/hotnews/archive/hotnews-010797.php.

———. 1997f. "The Speaker Says." Project Race Website, July 19, http://www.projectrace.com/hotnews/archive/hotnews-061997.php.

———. 1997g. Personal Communication to Multiracial Community Leaders and Activists.

———. 2003. "May the RPI (Racial Privacy Initiative) RIP (Rest in Peace)." Project Race Website, October 17, http://www.projectrace.com/hotnews/archive/hotnews-101703.php.

Graham, S., and J. Landrith. 1999. "Blood Pressure." Project Race Website, April 21, http://www.projectrace.com/hotnews/archive/hotnews-02un99.php.

Gramsci, A. 1971. *Selections from the Prison Notebooks of Antonio Gramsci.* New York: International Publishers.

Grant, G., and D. M. Ogawa. 1993. "Living Proof: Is Hawaii the Answer?" *Annals of the American Academy of Political and Social Science* 530:137–154.

Grant, Madison. [1921] 1970. *The Passing of the Great Race; or, The Racial Basis of European History,* 4th ed. New York: C. Scribner's Sons.

Grantham, T. C., and D. Y. Ford. 2003. "Beyond Self-Concept and Self-Esteem: Racial Identity and Gifted African American Students." *High School Journal* special issue: Addressing the Needs of Multicultural Populations in Educational Settings: Implications for Teachers and Counselors 87(1):18–29.

Green, K. K. 2002. "Colonialism's Daughters: Eighteenth- and Nineteenth-Century Westerners' Perceptions of Hawaiian Women." Pp. 221–252 in *Pacific Diaspora: Island Peoples in the United States and Across the Pacific,* edited by P. Spickard, J. L. Rondilla, and D. H. Wright. Honolulu: University of Hawai'i Press.

Greene, Z. G., C. R. Torres, and E. B. Skolnick. 1996. *Fair Lending in Montgomery County: A Home Mortgage Lending Study.* Montgomery County, Maryland Human Relations Commission, Rockville.

Grieco, E. M., and R. C. Cassidy. 2001. *Overview of Race and Hispanic Origin 2000.* Washington, DC: US Government Printing Office.

Grier, W. H., and P. M. Cobbs. 1968. *Black Rage.* New York: Basic Books.

Grosby, S. 1994. "The Verdict of History: The Inexpungable Tie of Primordiality." *Ethnic and Racial Studies* 17(1):164–171.

Grosz, G. 1989. "From Sea to Shining Sea: A Current Listing of Interracial Organizations and Support Groups Across the Nation." *Interrace* 1:24–28.

Guglielmo, T. A. 2003. *White on Arrival: Italians, Race, Color, and Power in Chicago, 1890–1945.* New York: Oxford University Press.

Guinier, L., and G. Torres. 2002. *The Miner's Canary: Enlisting Race, Resisting Power, Transforming Democracy.* Cambridge, MA: Harvard University Press.

Gulick, S. L. 1937. *Mixing the Races in Hawaii: The Coming Neo-Hawaiian Race.* Honolulu: Hawaiian Board Book Rooms.

Guthrie, R. 1976. *Even the Rat Was White: A Historical View of Psychology.* New York: Harper and Row.

Gwaltney, J. L. 1980. *Drylongso: A Self-Portrait of Black America.* New York: Vintage.

Haggerty, R. A. 1991. *Dominican Republic and Haiti: Country Studies.* Washington, DC: Library of Congress, Division of Federal Research.

Haizlip, S. T. 1994. *The Sweeter the Juice: A Family Portrait in Black and White.* New York: Simon and Schuster.

Haley, A. 1976. *Roots: The Saga of an American Family.* Garden City, NY: Doubleday.

Haley, A., and D. Stevens. 1993. *Queen.* New York: Avon.

Hall, C. 1992. "Please Choose One: Ethnic Identity Choices for Biracial Individuals." Pp. 250–264 in *Racially Mixed People in America,* edited by M. P. P. Root. London: Sage.

———. 1997. "Cultural Malpractice: The Growing Obsolescence of Psychology with the Changing U.S. Population." *American Psychologist* 52:642–651.

———. 2000. "Introduction: Thinking the Postcolonial, Thinking the Empire." Pp. 1–33 in *Cultures of Empire: A Reader: Colonisers in Britain and the Empire in the Nineteenth and Twentieth Centuries,* edited by C. Hall. Manchester, England: Manchester University Press.

Hall, P., ed. 1997. *Race, Ethnicity, and Multiculturalism: Policy and Practice.* Missouri Symposium on Research and Educational Policy. New York: Garland.

Halter, M. 2000. *Shopping for Identity.* New York: Schocken Books.

Hanchard, M. 1994. *Orpheus and Power: The Movimiento Negro of Rio de Janeiro and São Paulo, Brazil, 1945–1988.* Princeton, NJ: Princeton University Press.

Haney-Lopez, I. 1996. *White by Law: The Legal Construction of Race.* New York: New York University Press.

Hapa Issues Forum. 2003. "Vote No on Prop. 54: HIF Joins Coalition to Defeat Racial Privacy Initiative, Better Known as the Racial Ignorance Initiative (Prop. 54)." Hapa Issues Forum, http://www.hapaissuesforum.org/community/pr_rpi.html.

Hardy, K., and T. Laszloffy. 1993. "Deconstructing Race in Family Therapy." *Journal of Feminist Family Therapy* 5:5–33.

Harper's. [2000] 2003. "Does America Owe a Debt to the Descendants of Its Slaves?" Pp. 79–108 in *Should America Pay? Slavery and the Raging Debate on Reparations,* edited by Raymond A. Winbush. New York: Amistad.

Harris, C. 1993. "Whiteness as Property." *Harvard Law Review* 196 (June 1993): 1709–1791.

———. 1995. *Whiteness of Property: Critical Race Theory: The Key Writings That Formed the Movement.* New York: New Press.

Harris, D. 2002. "Does It Matter How We Measure? Racial Classification and the Characteristics of Multiracial Youth." Pp. 62–101 in *The New Race Question: How the Census Counts Multiracial Individuals,* edited by J. Perlmann and M. Water. New York and Annandale-on-Hudson, NY: Russell Sage Foundation and the Levy Economics Institute of Bard College.

Harris, D., and J. Sim. 2002. "Who Is Multiracial? Assessing the Complexity of Lived Race." *American Sociological Review* 67:614–627.

Harris, M. 1964. *Patterns of Race in the Americas.* New York: Walker.

Hartigan, J. 1997. "Locating White Detroit." Pp. 180–213 in *Displacing Whiteness: Essays in Social and Cultural Criticism,* edited by R. Frankenberg. Durham, NC: Duke University Press.

Hartsock, N. 1999. *The Feminist Standpoint Revisited and Other Essays.* Boulder, CO: Westview.

Hazama, D. O., and J. O. Komeiji. 1986. *Okage Sama De: The Japanese in Hawai'i, 1885–1985.* Honolulu: Bess Press.

Heaton, T. B., and C. K. Jacobson. 2000. "Intergroup Marriage: An Examination of Opportunity Structures. *Sociological Inquiry* 70:30–41.

Helg, A. 1990. "Race in Argentina and Cuba, 1880–1930: Theory, Policies, and Popular Reaction." Pp. 37–70 in *The Idea of Race in Latin America, 1870–1940,* edited by R. Graham. Austin: University of Texas Press.

Helms, J. 1990. *Black and White Racial Identity: Theory, Research and Practice.* New York: Greenwood Press.

———. 1994. "The Conceptualization of Racial Identity and Other 'Racial' Constructs." Pp. 285–311 in *Human Diversity,* edited by E. J. Trickett, R. J. Watts, and D. Birman. New York: Jossey Bass.

Herring, C. 2002. "Bleaching Out the Color Line? The Skin Color Continuum and the Tripartite Model of Race." *Race and Society* 5(1):17–30.

Herring, C., and C. Amissah. 1997. "Advance and Retreat: Racially Based Attitudes and Public Policy." Pp. 121–143 in Racial Attitudes in the 1990s: Continuity and Change, edited by J. K. Martin. Westport CT: Praeger.

Herring, C., V. M. Keith, and H. D. Horton, eds. 2004. *Skin/Deep: How Race and Complexion Matter in the "Color Blind" Era.* Urbana and Chicago: Institute for Research on Race and Public Policy and University of Illinois Press.

Herskovits, M. J. 1934. "A Critical Discussion of the 'Mulatto Hypothesis.'" *Journal of Negro Education* 3(3):389–402.

Herzog, T. 1997. "Hybrids and Mischlinge: Translating Anglo-American Cultural Theory Into German." *German Quarterly* 70:1–17.

Hewstone, M. 2003. "Intergroup Contact: Panacea for Prejudice?" *Psychologist* 16(7):352–355.

Hibbler, D. K., and K. J. Shinew. 2002. "Interracial Couples' Experience of Leisure: A Social Network Approach." *Journal of Leisure Research* 34:135–156.

Hill, M., and V. Thomas. 2000. "Strategies for Racial Identity Development: Narratives of Black and White Women in Interracial Partner Relationships." *Family Relations* 49:193–200.

Hitchcock, J. 2002. *Lifting the White Veil.* Roselle, NJ: Crandall, Dostie and Douglass Books.

Hochschild, J. 2003. "From Nominal to Ordinal: Reconceiving Racial and Ethnic Inequalities in the United States." Presented at the Harvard Color Lines Conference, September 2003, Cambridge, MA.

Hoetink, H. 1967. *Caribbean Race Relations: A Study of Two Variants.* London: Oxford University Press.

———. 1985. *"Race" and Color in the Caribbean.* Washington, DC: Woodrow Wilson International Center for Scholars.

Hogg, M. A., and J. C. Turner. 1987. "Intergroup Behavior, Self-Stereotyping and the Salience of Social Categories." *British Journal of Social Psychology* 26: 325–340.

Holdstock, T. L. 2000. *Re-Examining Psychology: Critical Perspectives and African Insights.* London: Routledge.

Holmes, S. 1997. "New Categories on Race and Ethnicity Adopted by Administration." *New York Times,* October 30, p. A1.

Holt, T. C. 2000. *The Problem of Race in the Twenty-First Century.* Cambridge, MA: Harvard University Press.

hooks, bell. 2000. *Feminist Theory: From Margin to Center.* Boston, MA: South End Press.

Horne, L., and R. Schickel. 1965. *Lena.* Garden City, NY: Doubleday.

Horowitz, R. E. 1939. "Racial Aspects of Self-Identification in Nursery School Children." *Journal of Psychology* 7:91–99.

Horton, H. D. 1999. "Critical Demography: The Paradigm of the Future?" *Sociological Forum* 14(3):363–367.

———. 2002. "Rethinking American Diversity: Conceptual and Theoretical Challenges for Racial and Ethnic Demography." Pp. 261–278 in *American Diversity: A Demographic Challenge for the Twenty-First Century,* edited by N. Denton and S. Tolnay. Albany, NY: SUNY Press.

Horton, H. D., and L. Sykes. 2003. "Critical Demography and the Measurement of Racism: A Reconsideration of Wealth, Status and Power." *Race and Society* 4:207–217.

———. 2004. "Toward a Critical Demography of Neo-Mulattoes: Structural Change and Diversity Within the Black Population." Pp. 159–173 in *Skin Deep: How Race and Complexion Matter in the "Color-Blind" Era,* edited by C. Herring, V. Keith, and H. D. Horton. Chicago: University of Illinois Press.

House Subcommittee on Government Management, Information, and Technology, Committee on Government Reform and Oversight. Hearings on Federal Measures of Race and Ethnicity and the Implications for the 2000 Census. Federal Measures of Race and Ethnicity and the Implications for the 2000 Census,

Serial No. 105-57, Statement of Congressman John Conyers, July 25, 1997, p. 535.

Houston, B. 1996. "Multiculturalism and a Politics of Persistence." http://www.ed .uiuc.edu/PES-Yearbook/96_docs/houston.html.

Howard, A. 1980. "Hawaiians." Pp. 449–452 in *Harvard Encyclopedia of American Ethnic Groups,* edited by S. Themnstrorn. Cambridge, MA: Harvard University Press.

Howard, D. 2001. *Coloring the Nation: Race and Ethnicity in the Dominican Republic.* Boulder, CO: Lynne Rienner.

Howitt, D., and J. Owusu-Bempah. 1994. *The Racism of Psychology: Time for Change.* Hemel Hempstead: Harvester Wheatsheaf.

Huckleberry, T. M. 2002. "Moving Beyond Race: Examining the Multidimensional Self-Concept of African-American College Students." Ph.D. diss., University of Texas at Austin.

Hu-Dehart, E. 2001. "Twenty-First-Century America: Black and White and Beyond." Pp. 79–97 in *Race in Twenty-First-Century America,* edited by C. Stokes, T. Meléndez, and G. Rhodes-Reed. East Lansing: Michigan State University Press.

Hughes, A. 2003. "United Colors of Global Hue." *Black Enterprise,* June, pp. 186–194.

Hughes, D. 2003. "Correlates of African American and Latino Parents' Messages to Children About Ethnicity and Race: A Comparative Study of Racial Socialization." *American Journal of Community Psychology* 31:15–33.

Humphreys, J. M. 2002. "The Multicultural Economy 2002: Minority Buying Power in the New Century." *Georgia Business and Economic Conditions* 62(2): 1–27.

Hunter, M. 2002. "Rethinking Epistemology, Methodology, and Racism: or, Is White Sociology Really Dead?" *Race and Society* 5(2):119–138.

Huntington, S. P. 2004a. *Who Are We: The Cultural Core of American National Identity.* New York: Simon and Schuster.

———. 2004b. "The Hispanic Challenge." *Foreign Policy,* March–April.

Hurk, W., and K. Kim. 1989. "The 'Success' Image of Asian Americans: Its Validity, and Its Practical and Theoretical Implications." *Ethnic and Racial Studies* 12: 512–538.

Ifekwunigwe, J. 1998. *Scattered Belongings: Cultural Paradoxes of "Race," Nation, and Gender.* London: Routledge.

Ignatiev, N. 1995. *How the Irish Became White.* New York: Routledge.

Isaacs, H. R. 1975. "Basic Group Identity: The Idols of the Tribe." In *Ethnicity: Theory and Experience,* edited by Nathan Glazer and Daniel P. Moynihan. Cambridge, MA: Harvard University Press.

Itzigsohn, J., and C. Dore-Cabral. 2000. "Competing Identities? Race, Ethnicity and Panethnicity Among Dominicans in the United States." *Sociological Forum* 15(2):225–247.

Jackman, M. R., and M. Crane. 1986. "Some of My Best Friends Are Black . . . : Interracial Friendship and Whites' Racial Attitudes." *Public Opinion Quarterly* 50(4):459–486.

Jackman, M. R., and M. J. Mahu. 1984. "Education and Intergroup Attitudes: Moral Enlightenment, Superficial Democratic Commitment, or Ideological Refinement." *American Sociological Review* 49:751–769.

Jackson, K. T. 1985. *Crabgrass Frontiers: The Suburbanization of the United States.* New York: Oxford University Press.

Jacobs, J. 1961. *The Death and Life of Great American Cities.* New York: Vintage.

Jacobs, J. H. 1992. "Identity Development in Biracial Children." Pp. 190–206 in *Racially Mixed People in America,* edited by M. P. P. Root. Newbury Park, CA: Sage.

Jacobsen, M. F. 1999. *Whiteness of a Different Color: European Immigrants and the Alchemy of Race.* Cambridge, MA: Harvard University Press.

Jane Doe v. Louisiana. 1983. 479 S.2d 369–72 D. La.

Jenerette, V. 1996. "The New Face of America—Moving Beyond Race." Presented at the Multiracial Solidarity March I, August 9, Washington, DC.

Jenkins, R. 1994. "Rethinking Ethnicity: Identity, Categorization, and Power." *Ethnic and Racial Studies* 17:197–223.

Johnson, A. 1997. *The Forest and the Trees: Sociology as Life, Practice, and Promise.* Philadelphia: Temple University Press.

———. 2001. *Privilege, Power, and Difference.* New York: McGraw-Hill.

Johnson, J., S. Rush, and J. Feagin. 2000. "Doing Antiracism and Making a Nonracist Society." *Contemporary Sociology* 29(1):95–110.

Johnston, J. H. 1970. *Race Relations in Virginia and Miscegenation in the South, 1776–1860.* Amherst: University of Massachusetts Press.

Jones, A. C. 1990. "Psychological Functions in African Americans: A Conceptual Guide for Use in Psychotherapy." Pp. 577–590 in *Black Psychology,* edited by R. L. Jones. Berkeley: Cobb and Henry.

Jones, H. 1990. *How I Became Hettie Jones.* New York: E. P. Dutton.

Jones, J. M. 1990. "The Concept of Race in Social Psychology." Pp. 441–468 in *Black Psychology,* edited by R. L. Jones. Berkeley: Cobb and Henry.

Jones, V. E. 2002. "Mixing and Matching: Interracial Romances, Once Hollywood Taboo, Are Creating Sparks on the Big Screen." *Boston Globe,* November 12, retrieved October 26, 2004, from LexisNexis Academic database.

Jorge, A. 1979. "The Black Puerto Rican Woman in Contemporary American Society." Pp. 134–141 in *The Puerto Rican Woman,* edited by Edna Acosta-Belén. New York: Praeger.

Josselson, R., and A. Lieblich. 1995. *Interpreting Experience: The Narrative Study of Lives.* Vol. 3. Thousand Oaks, CA: Sage.

Jung, C. G. 1930. "Your Negroid and Indian Behavior." *Forum* 83:193–199.

Kaeser, G., and P. Gillespie. 1997. *Of Many Colors: Portraits of Multiracial Families.* Amherst: University of Massachusetts Press.

Kaiser Family Foundation. 2001. *Race and Ethnicity in 2001: Attitudes, Perceptions and Experiences.* Washington, DC: Kaiser Family Foundation.

Kalmijin, M. 1993. "Trends in Black/ White Intermarriage." *Social Forces* 72(1): 119–146.

Kame'eleihiwa, L. 1992. *Native Land and Foreign Desires.* Honolulu: Bishop Museum Press.

Kanahele, G. H. S. 1986. *K? Kanaka: Stand Tall: A Search for Hawaiian Values.* Honolulu: University of Hawai'i Press.

Kane, C. 1998a. "Levi Strauss Is Trying to Regain Market Share for Its Jeans, Especially Among Young Consumers." *New York Times,* May 5, retrieved October 26, 2004, from LexisNexis Academic database.

———. 1998b. "TBWA/Chiat Day Brings 'Street Culture' to a Campaign for Levi Strauss Silver Tab Clothing." *New York Times,* August 14, retrieved October 26, 2004, from LexisNexis Academic database.

Kaplan, J., ed. 2000. *Encyclopedia of White Power: A Sourcebook on the Radical Right.* Walnut Creek, CA: Alta Mira.

Kasinitz, P., J. Battle, and I. Miyares. 2001. "Fade to Black? The Children of West Indian Immigrants in Southern Florida." Pp. 267–300 in *Ethnicities: Children of Immigrants in America.* Berkeley: University of California Press.

Katz, I. 1996. *The Construction of Racial Identity in Children of Mixed Parentage: Mixed Metaphors.* London: Jessica Kingsley.

Kauanui, J. K. 1998. "Off-Island Hawaiians 'Making' Ourselves 'at Home': A [Gendered] Contradiction in Terms?" *Women's Studies International Forum* 21(6): 681–693.

———. 2000. "Rehabilitating the Native: Hawaiian Blood Quantum and the Politics of Race, Citizenship, and Entitlement." Ph.D. diss., University of California at Santa Cruz.

———. 2002. "The Politics of Blood in Rice V. Cayetano." *Polar* 25(1):110–128.

Keith, V. M., and C. Herring. 1991. "Skin Tone and Stratification in the Black Community." *American Journal of Sociology* 97(3):760–778.

Kelly, S. 2004. "Underlying Components of Scores Assessing African Americans' Racial Perspectives." *Measurement and Evaluation in Counseling and Development* 37(1):28–40.

Kennedy, R. 2003. *Interracial Intimacies: Sex, Marriage, Identity, and Adoption.* New York: Vintage.

Kent, N. J. 1983. *Hawaii: Islands Under the Influence.* New York: Monthly Review Press.

Kerwin, C., and J. G. Ponterotto. 1995. "Biracial Identity Development: Theory and Research." Pp. 199–217 in *Handbook of Multicultural Counseling,* edited by J. G. Ponterotto, J. M. Casas, L. A. Suzuki, and C. Alexander. Thousand Oaks, CA: Sage.

Kerwin, C., J. G. Ponterotto, B. L. Jackson, and A. Harris. 1993. "Racial Identity in Biracial Children: A Qualitative Investigation." *Journal of Counseling Psychology* 40:221–231.

Kessler, S., and W. McKenna. 1978. *Gender: An Ethnomethodological Approach.* Chicago: University of Chicago Press.

Khanna, Nikki. 2004. "The Role of Reflected Appraisals in Racial Identity: The Case of Multiracial Asians." *Social Psychology Quarterly* 67(2):115–131.

Khimm, S. 2003. "Avalanche Against Prop 54." *Alternet,* October 17, http://www.alternet.org/story/16972/.

Kich, G. K. 1992. "The Developmental Process of Asserting a Biracial, Bicultural Identity." Pp. 304–317 in *Racially Mixed People in America,* edited by M. P. P. Root. Newbury Park, CA: Sage.

Killian, K. D. 2001. "Reconstituting Racial Histories and Identities: The Narratives of Interracial Couples." *Journal of Marital and Family Therapy* 27:27–42.

Kilson, M. 2001. *Claiming Place: Biracial Young Adults of the Post–Civil Rights Era.* Westport: Bergin and Garvey.

Kim, C. J. 2000–2001. "Playing the Racial Trump Card: Asian Americans in Contemporary Politics." *Amerasia Journal* 26(3):35–65.

Kimmel, M., and A. Ferber, eds. 2003. *Privilege: A Reader.* Boulder, CO: Westview.

Kimura, Y. 1988. *Issei: Japanese Immigrants in Hawai'i.* Honolulu: University of Hawai'i Press.

Kinder, D. R., and L. M. Sanders. 1996. *Divided by Color: Racial Politics and Democratic Ideals.* Chicago: University of Chicago Press.

Kirton, D. 1999. "Perspectives on 'Race' and Adoption: The Views of Student Social Workers." *British Journal of Social Work* 29:779–796.

Kitano, H. L., and G. R. Daniels. 1995. *Asian Americans: Emerging Minorities,* 2nd ed. New Jersey: Prentice-Hall.

Kivel, P. 2003. "Being a Strong White Ally." Pp. 401–412 in *Privilege: A Reader,* edited by M. S. Kimmel and A. L. Ferber. Boulder, CO: Westview.

Klinenberg, Eric. 2002. *Heatwave: A Social Autopsy of Disaster in Chicago.* Chicago: University of Chicago Press.

Kluegel, J. R., and E. R. Smith. 1986. *Beliefs About Inequality: Americans' View of What Is and What Ought to Be.* New York: Aldine De Gruyter.

Knight, A. 1990. "Racism, Revolution, and Indigenismo: Mexico, 1910–1940." Pp. 71–114 in *The Idea of Race in Latin America, 1870–1940,* edited by R. Graham. Austin: University of Texas Press.

Koopmans, R., and P. Statham. 1999. "Challenging the Liberal Nation-State? Postnationalism, Multiculturalism, and the Collective Claims Making of Migrants and Ethnic Minorities in Britain and Germany." *American Journal of Sociology* 105:652–696.

Korgen, K. O. 1998–1999. *From Black to Biracial: Transforming Racial Identity Among Americans.* Westport, CT: Praeger.

———. 2002. *Crossing the Racial Divide: Close Friendships Between Black and White Americans.* Westport, CT: Praeger.

Korolewicz, M., and A. Korolewicz. 1985. "Effects of Sex and Race on Interracial Dating Preferences." *Psychological Reports* 57:1291–1296.

Kosasa, E. 2000. "Ideological Images: U.S. Nationalism in Japanese Settler Photographs." In "Whose Vision? Asian Settler Colonialism in Hawai'i," special edition of *Amerasia Journal* 26(2):66–91.

Kotlowski, D. 2002. *Nixon's Civil Rights: Politics, Principle, and Policy.* Cambridge, MA: Harvard University Press.

Kovel, J. 1970. *White Racism: A Psychohistory.* New York: Columbia University Press.

Kuykendall, R. S., and A. G. Day. 1961. *Hawaii, a History: From Polynesian Kingdom to American State,* revised ed. Englewood Cliffs, NJ: Prentice-Hall.

Kuzenski, J. C., C. S. Bullock, and R. K. Gaddie. 1995. "Introduction." Pp. xi–xv in *David Duke and the Politics of Race in the South,* edited by J. C. Kuzenski, C. S. Bullock, and R. K. Gaddie. Nashville: Vanderbilt University Press.

Lacayo, R. 1989. "Between Two Worlds: The Black Middle Class Has Everything the White Middle Class Has, Except a Feeling That It Really Fits In." *Newsweek,* March 13, pp. 58–68.

Ladner, J. A. 1977. *Mixed Families: Adopting Across Racial Boundaries.* Garden City, NY: Anchor/Doubleday.

Laenui, P. 1994. *Report to the People of Hawaii Via the State Legislature of Hawaii: Another View on the Subject of Hawaiian Sovereignty and Self-Determination.* Waianae, HI: Diane Publishing Company.

La Ferla, R. 2003. "Generation E. A.: Ethnically Ambiguous." *New York Times,* December 28, retrieved October 26, 2004, from LexisNexis Academic database.

LaFromboise, T., H. L. K. Coleman, and J. Gerton. 1993. "Psychological Impact of Biculturalism: Evidence and Theory." *Psychological Bulletin* 114:395–412.

Laham, N. 1998. *The Reagan Presidency and the Politics of Race: In Pursuit of Colorblind Justice and Limited Government.* Westport, CT: Praeger.

Lamont, M., and V. Molnar. 2002. "The Study of Boundaries in the Social Sciences." *Annual Review of Sociology* 28:167–195.

Landrith, J. A., Jr. 2000. "Free Will (or the Right To Not Decide)." *Abolitionist Examiner,* October–November, http://www.multiracial.com/abolitionist/word/landrith.html.

———. 2001a. "Drama Overload." *Interracial Voice,* May–June, http://www.interracialvoice.com/landrith5.html.

————. 2001b. "Statement on the Racial Privacy Initiative." *Abolitionist Examiner,* October–November, http://www.multiracial.com/abolitionist/word/landrith3 .html.

Lazarre, J. 1996. *Beyond the Whiteness of Whiteness: Memoir of a White Mother of Black Sons.* Durham, NC: Duke University Press.

Lee, K. K. 1998. *Huddled Masses, Muddled Laws.* Westport, CT: Praeger.

Lee, S. M. 1993. "Racial Classifications in the U.S. Census: 1890–1990." *Ethnic and Racial Studies* 16:81–84.

————. 2001. "Using the New Race Categories in the 2000 Census." Washington, DC: The Annie E. Casey Foundation and Population Reference Bureau.

Leland J., and G. Beals. 1997. "In Living Colors." *Newsweek,* May 5, pp. 58–60.

Lew, J. 2000. "Guidance on Aggregation and Allocation of Data on Race for Use in Civil Rights Monitoring and Enforcement." OMB Bulletin No. 00-02. Washington, DC: Office of Management and Budget.

Lew, S. 2003. "Chicago No. 2 in Mortgage Racial Gap, Acorn Study Says." *Chicago Tribune,* October 26.

Lewis, A. 2003. *Race in the Schoolyard: Negotiating the Color Line in Classrooms and Communities.* New Brunswick, NJ: Rutgers University Press.

Lewis, J., and S. Jhally. 2004. "Television and the Politics of Racial Representation." Pp. 403–414 in *Rethinking the Color Line: Readings in Race and Ethnicity,* edited by C. A. Gallagher. New York: McGraw-Hill.

Lili'Uokalani. [1898] 1964. *Hawaii's Story by Hawaii's Queen.* Rutland, VT: Tuttle.

Lim, J. H. 2001. "Affirmative Action on Trial." *Asianweek,* http://www.asianweek .com/2001_04_06/news2-umichigan-trial.html.

Lind, A. 1946. *Hawaii's Japanese: An Experiment in Democracy.* Princeton, NJ: Princeton University Press.

Lind, M. 1997. "The End of the Rainbow: The Poverty of Racial Politics and the Future of Liberalism." *Mother Jones* 22: 39–44.

Linn, S. E. 2004. *Consuming Kids: The Hostile Takeover of Childhood.* New York: New Press.

Lipsitz, G. 1998. *The Possessive Investment in Whiteness: How White People Profit from Identity Politics.* Philadelphia: Temple University Press.

Locke, Michelle. 2005. "Controversial Regent Retires." Associated Press. *Daily Breeze,* January 16, p. A6.

Logan, J. R. 2001. *Many Shores: Asians in Census 2000.* Albany, NY: Lewis Mumford Center for Comparative Urban and Regional Research, University of Albany.

Lorber, J. 1999. "Crossing Borders and Erasing Boundaries: Paradoxes of Identity Politics." *Sociological Focus* 32:355–369.

Lott, B., and H. E. Bullock. 2001. "Who Are the Poor?" *Journal of Social Issues* 57:189–206.

Luke, C., and A. Luke. 1998. "Interracial Families: Difference Within Difference." *Ethnic and Racial Studies* 21:728–754.

Lusane, C. 1997. *Race in the Global Era: African Americans at the Millennium.* Boston: South End Press.

Lyles, M. R., A. Yancey, C. Grace, and J. H. Carter. 1985. "Racial Identity and Self-Esteem: Problems Peculiar to Biracial Children." *Journal of the American Academy of Child and Adolescent Psychiatry* 24:150–153.

Lyman, S. M., and W. A. Douglas. 1973. "Ethnicity: Strategies of Individual and Collective Impression Management." *Social Research* 40:345–365.

Lynch, F. R. 1989. *Invisible Victims: White Males and the Crisis of Affirmative Action.* New York: Greenwood Publishing.

Macpherson, D. A., and J. B. Stewart. 1992. "Racial Differences in Married Female Labor Force Participation Behavior: An Analysis Using Interracial Marriages." *Review of Black Political Economy* (Summer):59–68.

Maitre, M. 2004. "Connerly Sets New Tack on UC Forms." *Oakland Tribune,* March 11.

Major, B., M. Testa, and W. Bylsma. 1991. "Response to Upward and Downward Social Comparisons: The Impact of Esteem-Relevance and Perceived Control." Pp. 237–260 in *Social Comparison: Contemporary Theory and Research,* edited by J. Suls and T. A. Wills. Hillsdale, NJ: Lawrence Erlbaum.

Makalani, M. 2003. "Rejecting Blackness and Claiming Whiteness: Antiblack Whiteness in the Biracial Project." Pp. 81–94 in *White Out: The Continuing Significance of Racism,* edited by A. W. Doane and E. Bonilla-Silva. New York: Routledge.

Maly, M. T. 2005. *Beyond Segregation: Multiracial and Multiethnic Urban Neighborhoods in the United States.* Philadelphia: Temple University Press.

Maly, M. T., and M. Leachman. 1998. "Rogers Park, Edgewater, Uptown, and Chicago Lawn, Chicago." *Cityscape: A Journal of Policy Development and Research* 4(2):131–160.

Marable, M. 1998. "Beyond Color-Blindness." *Nation,* December 28, p. 12.

Martha, N. 1992. "Korean and Black Symposium Raises Tough Issues and Questions." *Asianweek* 13(41):12.

Martin, E., T. J. Demaio, and P. C. Campanelli. 1990. "Context Effects for Census Measures of Race and Hispanic Origin." *Public Opinion Quarterly* 54(4):551–566.

Martinez, E. 1993. "Beyond Black/White: The Racism of Our Times." *Social Justice* 20(1–2):22–34.

Massey, D., and N. Denton. 1987. "Trends in the Residential Segregation of Blacks, Hispanics and Asians: 1970–1980." *American Sociological Review* 52:802–825.

———. 1988. "Residential Segregation of Blacks, Hispanics, and Asians by Socioeconomic Status and Generation." *Social Science Quarterly* 69:797–817.

———. 1993/1995. *American Apartheid: Segregation and the Making of the Underclass.* Cambridge, MA: Harvard University Press.

———. 1999. "The Construction of the Ghetto." Pp. 178–201 in *Majority and Minority: The Dynamics of Race and Ethnicity in American Life,* edited by N. R. Yetman. Boston: Allyn and Bacon.

Mathabane, M., and G. Mathabane. 1992. *Love in Black and White: The Triumph of Love Over Prejudice and Taboo.* New York: HarperCollins.

Matsuda, M. J. 1996. *"Where Is Your Body?" and Other Essays on Race, Gender and the Law.* Boston: Beacon Press.

Matthijs, K. 1993. "Trends in Black/White Intermarriage." *Social Forces* 72:119–146.

Maximé, J. E. 1991a. "Some Psychological Models of Black Self-Concept." Pp. 100–116 in *Social Work with Black Children and Their Families,* edited by in S. Ahmed, J. Cheetham, and J. Small. London: B. T. Batsford.

———. 1991b. *Black Like Me Workbook One: Black Identity.* Beckenham: Emani Publications.

———. 1993. "The Importance of Racial Identity for the Psychological Well-Being of Black Children." *Association of Child Psychology and Psychiatry Review and Newsletter* 15(4):173–179.

Mays, V. M. 2000. "A Social Justice Agenda." *American Psychologist* 55:326–327.

McAdoo, Harriette Pipes. 1985. "Racial Attitudes and Self-Concept of Young Black Children over Time." Pp. 213–242 in *Black Children: Social, Educational, and*

Parental Environments, edited by Harriette Pipes McAdoo and John Lewis McAdoo. Sage Focus Editions, vol. 72. Thousand Oaks, CA: Sage.

McBride, J. 1996. *The Color of Water: A Black Man's Tribute to His White Mother.* New York: Riverhead Books.

McDougall, H. 1981–1982. "Gentrification: The Class Conflict over Urban Spaces Moves into the Courts." *Fordham Urban Law Journal* 10(2):177–213.

McDowell, S. F. 1971. "Black-White Intermarriage in the United States." *International Journal of Sociology of the Family,* special Issue 1:49–58.

McGregor, D. P. 2002. "Recognizing Native Hawaiians: A Quest for Sovereignty." Pp. 331–354 in *Pacific Diaspora: Island Peoples in the United States and Across the Pacific,* edited by P. Spickard, J. Rondilla, and D. Wright. Honolulu: University of Hawai'i Press.

McIntosh, P. 1998. "White Privilege: Unpacking the Invisible Knapsack." Pp. 147–152 in *Re-Visioning Family Therapy: Race, Culture and Gender in Clinical Practice,* edited by M. McGoldrick. New York: Guildord Press.

McKee, J. B. 1993. *Sociology and the Race Problem: The Failure of a Perspective.* Urbana: University of Illinois Press.

McNamara, R. P., M. Tempenis, and B. Walton. 1999. *Crossing the Line: Interracial Couples in the South.* Westport, CT: Praeger.

Mead, G. H., and C. W. Morris. 1934. *Mind, Self, and Society from the Standpoint of a Social Behaviorist.* Chicago: University of Chicago Press.

Merton, R. K. 1941. "Intermarriage and Social Structure: Fact and Theory." *Psychiatry* 4:361–374.

Meyer, S. G. 2000. *As Long as They Don't Move Next Door: Segregation and Racial Contact in American Neighborhoods.* New York: Rowman and Littlefield.

Michener, J. A. 1959. *Hawaii.* New York: Random House.

Miles, R. 1993. *Racism After Race Relations.* New York: Routledge.

Mills, C. W. 1997. *The Racial Contract.* Ithaca, NY: Cornell University Press.

Mills, J. K. M. 1995. "A Note on Family Acceptance Involving Interracial Friendships and Romantic Relationships." *Journal of Psychology* 129:349–351.

Milner, D. 1975. *Children and Race.* Harmondsworth: Penguin.

———. 1983. *Children and Race: Ten Years On.* London: Ward Lock Educational.

Min, P. G. 1996. *Caught in the Middle: Korean Communities in New York and Los Angeles.* Berkeley: University of California Press.

Mindiola, T., M. Rodríguez, and Y. F. Niemann. 1996. *Intergroup Relations Between Hispanics and Blacks in Harris County.* Houston, TX: University of Houston, Center for Mexican American Studies.

Mittelberg, D., and M. C. Waters. 1992. "The Process of Ethnogenesis Among Haitian and Israeli Immigrants in the United States." *Ethnic and Racial Studies* 15(3):412–435.

Model, S. 1991. "Caribbean Immigrants: A Black Success Story?" *International Migration Review* 25:248–276.

Model, S., and G. Fisher. 2002. "Unions Between Black and Whites: England and the U.S. Compared." *Ethnic and Racial Studies* 25:728–754.

Modood, T., R. Berthoud, J. Lakey, J. Nazroo, P. Smith, S. Virdee, and S. Beishon. 1997. *Ethnic Minorities in Britain: Diversity and Disadvantage.* London: Policy Studies Institute.

Monahan, T. P. 1970. "Are Interracial Marriages Really Less Stable?" *Social Forces* 48:461–473.

———. 1971. "Interracial Marriage in the United States: Some Data on Upstate New York." *International Journal of Sociology of the Family* 1(1):94–105.

———. 1973. "Marriage Across Racial Lines in Indiana." *Journal of Marriage and the Family* (November):632–639.

————. 1976a. "The Occupational Class of Couples Entering into Interracial Marriages." *Journal of Comparative Family Studies* 7(2):175–189.

————. 1976b. "An Overview of Statistics on Interracial Marriage in the United States, with Data on Its Extent from 1963–1970." *Journal of Marriage and the Family* (May):223–231.

————. 1977a. "Interracial Marriage in a Southern Area: Maryland, Virginia, and the District of Columbia." *Journal of Comparative Family Studies* 8(2):217–239.

————. 1977b. "Interracial Parentage as Revealed by Birth Records in the United States, 1970." *Journal of Comparative Family Studies* 8(1):65–76.

Montagu, A. 1974. *Man's Most Dangerous Myth: The Fallacy of Race.* New York: Oxford University Press; 6th ed., Walnut Creek: Altamira Press, 1997.

Moore, E., Jr. 2004. "White Privilege, White Supremacy, and the Prison Industrial Complex." Presented at the Fifth Annual Conference on White Privilege, April 28–May 1, Central College, Pella, IA.

Moran, R. F. 2001. *Interracial Intimacy: The Regulation of Race and Romance.* Chicago: University of Chicago Press.

Morner, M. 1970. *Race and Class in Latin America.* New York: Columbia University Press.

Morris, A. D. 1984. *The Origins of the Civil Rights Movement: Black Communities Organizing for Change.* New York and London: Free Press and Collier Macmillan.

Morrison, T. 1992. *Playing in the Dark: Whiteness and the Literary Imagination.* New York: Random House.

Moskos, C. C., and J. S. Butler. 1996. *All That We Can Be: Black Leadership and Racial Integration the Army Way.* New York: Basic Books.

Moya Pons, F. 1995. *The Dominican Republic: A National History.* New Rochelle, NY: Hispaniola Books.

————. 1996. "Dominican National Identity: A Historical Perspective." *Punto 7 Review: A Journal of Marginal Discourse* 3(1):14–25.

MSNBC. 2003. "Racial Privacy Initiative Defeated." MSNBC, October 7, http://www.msnbc.com/news/976981.asp?cp1=1.

Myers, Jr., S. L. 1997. "Preface." Pp. vii–xiv in *Civil Rights and Race Relations in the Post Reagan-Bush Era,* edited by S. L. Myers. Westport, CT: Praeger.

Myrdal, G., R. Sterner, and A. M. Rose. 1944. *An American Dilemma.* New York: Harper and Row.

Nagel, J. 1994. "Constructing Ethnicity: Creating and Recreating Ethnic Identity and Culture." *Social Problems* 41:152–176.

————. 1996. *American Indian Ethnic Renewal: Red Power and the Resurgence of Identity and Culture.* New York: Oxford University Press.

Nakashima, C. L. 1992. "An Invisible Monster: The Creation and Denial of Mixed-Race People in America." Pp. 162–178 in *Racially Mixed People in America,* edited by M. P. P. Root. Newbury Park, CA: Sage.

Negri, A. 1984. *Marx Beyond Marx: Lessons on the Grundrisse.* South Hadley, MA: Bergin and Garvey.

Nelson, J. 1997. "ACRI Criticizes Federal Government's Rejection of a Multiracial Census Box." American Civil Rights Institute, ACRI News, July 9, http://www.acri.org/news/070997.html.

"New Multiracial Classification Spotlights Hawaii." 2001. *USA Today,* February 21.

Nicholls, D. 1981. "No Hawks or Pedlars: Levantines in the Caribbean." *Ethnic and Racial Studies* 4:415–431.

Niemann, Y., L. Jennings, R. Rozelle, J. Baxter, and E. Sullivan. 1994. "Use of Free Response and Cluster Analysis to Determine Stereotypes of Eight Groups." *Personality and Social Psychology Bulletin* 20(4):379–390.

Nobles, M. 2000. *Shades of Citizenship: Race and the Census in Modern Politics.* Stanford, CA: Stanford University Press.

Nordyke, E. C. 1988. "Blacks in Hawaii: A Demographic and Historical Perspective." *Hawaiian Journal of History* 22: 241–255.

Norment, L. 1994. "Lenny Kravitz: Brother with a Different Beat." *Ebony.*

Noyes, M. H. 2003. *And Then There Were None.* Honolulu: Bess Press.

Nyden, P., J. Lukehart, M. T. Maly, and W. Peterman. 1998a. "Neighborhood Racial and Ethnic Diversity in U.S. Cities." *Cityscape: A Journal of Policy Development and Research* 4(2):1–18.

———. 1998b. "Overview of the 14 Neighborhoods Studied." *Cityscape: A Journal of Policy Development and Research* 4(2):19–28.

Nzingha, Y. A. 2003. "Reparations + Education = The Pass to Freedom." Pp. 299–314 in *Should America Pay? Slavery and the Raging Debate on Reparations,* edited by Raymond A. Winbush. New York: Amistad.

Oboler, S. 1995. *Ethnic Labels, Latino Lives: Identity and the Politics of (Re)Presentation in the United States.* Minneapolis: University of Minnesota Press.

———. 2000. "It Must Be a Fake! Racial Ideologies, Identities, and the Question of Rights in Hispanics/Latinos." In *The United States: Ethnicity, Race, and Rights,* edited by J. Jorge, E. Garcia, and P. Degreiff. New York: Routledge.

O'Brien, E. 2000. "Are We Supposed to Be Colorblind or Not? Competing Frames Used by Whites Against Racism." *Race and Society* (3):41–59.

———. 2001. *Whites Confront Racism: Antiracists and Their Paths to Action.* Lanham, MD: Rowman and Littlefield.

O'Brien, E., and K. O. Korgen. 2004. "It's the Message, Not the Messenger: The Declining Significance of Black-White Contact." Presented at the annual meeting of the American Sociological Association, August, San Francisco, CA.

Ogawa, D. M. 1978. *Jan Ken Po: The World of Hawaii's Japanese Americans.* Honolulu: University Press of Hawaii.

Ojito, M. 2001. "Best of Friends, Worlds Apart." Pp. 23–40 in *How Race Is Lived in America.* New York Times. New York: Time Books.

Okamura, J. Y. 1980. "Kanaka Me Ke Aloha 'Aina: Local Culture and Society in Hawaii." *Amerasia Journal* 7(2):119–137.

———. 1994. "Why There Are No Asian Americans in Hawai'i: The Continuing Significance of Local Identity." *Social Process in Hawai'i* 35:161–178.

———. 1998. "The Illusion of Paradise: Privileging Multiculturalism in Hawai'i." Pp. 264–284 in *Making Majorities: Constituting the Nation in Japan, Korea, China, Malaysia, Fiji, Turkey, and the United States,* edited by D. C. Gladney. Stanford, CA: Stanford University Press.

Okihiro, G. 1994. *Margins and Mainstreams: Asians in American History and Culture.* Seattle: University of Washington Press.

Oliver, M. L., and T. M. Shapiro. 1997. *Black Wealth, White Wealth: A New Perspective on Racial Inequality.* New York: Routledge.

Olumide, J. 2002. *Raiding the Gene Pool: The Social Construction of Mixed Race.* London: Pluto Press.

Omi, M. 2001. "The Changing Meaning of Race." Pp. 243–263 in *America Becoming: Racial Trends and Their Consequences,* edited by Neil Smelser. Washington, DC: National Academy Press.

Omi, M., and H. Winant. 1986. *Racial Formation in the United States: From the 1960s to the 1980s.* New York: Routledge and Kegan Paul.

———. 1994. *Racial Formation in the United States: From the 1960s to the 1990s,* 2nd ed. New York: Routledge.

Onorato, R. S., and J. C. Turner. 2004. "Fluidity in the Self-Concept: The Shift from Personal to Social Identity." *European Journal of Social Psychology* 34(3):257–278.

Osorio, J. K. 2002a. "'What Kine Hawaiian Are You?' A Mo'Olelo About Nationhood, Race, History, and the Contemporary Sovereignty Movement in Hawai'i." *Contemporary Pacific* 13(2):359–379.

———. 2002b. *Dismembering Lāhui: A History of the Hawaiian Nation to 1887.* Honolulu: University of Hawai'i Press.

Ottley, R. 1943. *New World A-Coming.* Cleveland: World Publishing.

Outrigger Hotels. 2004. "Island Culture." Retrieved May 20, 2004, http://ohanahotels.com/travelguide_region.aspx?regiondetail=1anddestination=5.

Outterson, K. 2003. "Slave Taxes." Pp. 135–149 in *Should America Pay? Slavery and the Raging Debate on Reparations,* edited by Raymond A. Winbush. New York: Amistad.

Owusu-Bempah, K. 1994. "Race, Self-Identity and Social Work." *British Journal of Social Work* 24:123–136.

———. 1997. "Race." Pp. 50–56 in *The Blackwell Companion to Social Work,* edited by M. Davies. Oxford: Basil Blackwell.

———. 2002. "Culture, Ethnicity and Identity." Pp. 304–312 in *The Blackwell Companion to Social Work,* edited by M. Davies. Oxford: Basil Blackwell.

———. 2003. "Political Correctness: In the Interest of the Child?" *Educational and Child Psychology* 20:53–63.

———. 2005. "Mullato, Marginal Man, Half-Caste, Mixed-Race: The 'One-Drop' Rule in Professional Practice." In *Working with Children of Mixed Parentage,* edited by T. Okitikpi. Lyme Regis: Russell House.

Owusu-Bempah, K., and D. Howitt. 1994. "Racism and the Psychological Textbook." *Psychologist* 7:163–166.

———. 1999a. "Even Their Soul Is Defective." *Psychologist* 12(3):126–130.

———. 1999b. "Educational, Psychological, and the Construction of Black Childhood." *Educational and Child Psychology* 16:17–29.

———. 2000. *Psychology Beyond Western Perspectives.* Oxford: Blackwell.

Padilla, M. T. 2000. "Hispanics Stay Quiet on Affirmative Action." *Orlando Sentinel,* January 22.

Page, C. 1996. *Showing My Color.* New York: Harper and Collins.

Pak, G. 1992. *Watcher of Waipuna and Other Stories.* Honolulu: Bamboo Ridge Press.

Palumbo-Liu, D. 1999. *Asian/American: Historical Crossings of a Racial Frontier.* Stanford, CA: Stanford University Press.

Parham, Thomas A. 1999. "Invisibility Syndrome in African Descent People: Understanding Cultural Manifestations of the Struggle for Self-Affirmation." *Counseling Psychologist* 27(6):794–801.

Park, R. 1928. "Human Migration and the Marginal Man." *American Journal of Sociology* 33:881–893.

———. 1931. "The Mentality of Racial Hybrids." *American Journal of Sociology* 36:534–551.

Pauley, G. E. 2001. "Modern Presidency and Civil Rights: Rhetoric on Race from Roosevelt to Nixon." Presidential Rhetoric Series No. 3. College Station: Texas A&M University Press.

Pedraza, S. 1985. *Political and Economic Migrants in America: Cubans and Mexicans.* Austin: University of Texas Press.

Peller, G. 1995. "Race-Consciousness." Pp. 127–158 in *Critical Race Theory: The Key Writings That Formed the Movement,* edited by K. Crenshaw, N. Gotanda, G. Peller, and K. Thomas. New York: New Press.

Penn, M., S. Gaines, and L. Phillips. 1993. "On the Desirability of Own-Group Preference." *Journal of Black Psychology* 19:303–321.

Perlmann, J., and R. Waldinger. 1997. "Second Generation Decline? Children of Immigrants, Past and Present—a Reconsideration." *International Migration Review* 31(4):893–922.

Perlmann, J., and M. Waters, eds. 2002. *The New Race Question: How the Census Counts Multiracial Individuals.* New York: Russell Sage Foundation.

Pettigrew, T. F. 1997. "Generalized Intergroup Contact Effects on Prejudice." *Personality and Social Psychology Bulletin* 23:173–185.

Pewewardy, C. 2004. Personal Communication at Conference Session, "Should America Pay? Racism, Privilege, and Reparations." Fifth Annual Conference on White Privilege: White Privilege, White Supremacy, and the Prison Industrial Complex, Central College, Pella, Iowa. April 30.

Pierce, J. 2003. "'Racing for Innocence': Whiteness, Corporate Culture, and the Backlash Against Affirmative Action." In *White Out: The Continuing Significance of Racism,* edited by A. W. Doane and E. Bonilla-Silva. New York: Routledge.

Pierce, L. 2004. "'The Whites Have Created Modern Honolulu': Ethnicity, Racial Stratification, and the Discourse of Aloha." Pp. 124–154 in *Racial Thinking in the United States,* edited by P. Spickard and G. R. Daniel. Notre Dame: University of Notre Dame Press.

———. 2005. "Creating a Racial Paradise: Citizenship and Sociology in Hawai'i." In *Race and Nation: Ethnic Systems in the Modern World,* edited by P. Spickard. New York: Routledge.

Pinkney, A. 1984. *The Myth of Black Progress.* New York: Cambridge University Press.

Pinkus, F. L. 2003. *Reverse Discrimination: Dismantling the Myth.* Boulder, CO: Lynne Rienner.

Porterfield, E. 1982. "Black-American Intermarriage in the United States." *Marriage and Family Review* 5(1):17–34.

Portes, A., and R. Rumbaut. 1990. *Immigrant America: A Portrait.* Berkeley: University of California Press.

Portes, A., and M. Zhou. 1993. "The New Second Generation: Segmented Assimilation and Its Variants." *Annals of the American Academy of Political and Social Science* 530:74–97.

Porteus, S. D. 1945. *Calabashes and Kings: An Introduction to Hawaii.* Palo Alto, CA: Pacific Books.

Poston, C. W. 1990. "The Biracial Identity Development Model: A Needed Addition." *Journal of Counseling and Development* 69:152–155.

Prakash, G. 2000. "Subaltern Studies as Postcolonial Criticism." Pp. 120–136 in *Cultures of Empire: A Reader: Colonisers in Britain and the Empire in the Nineteenth and Twentieth Centuries,* edited by C. Hall. Manchester, England: Manchester University Press.

Prashad, V. 2000. *The Karma of Brown Folk.* Minneapolis: University of Minnesota Press.

Pratt, Minnie Bruce. 1984. "Identity, Skin, Blood, Heart." In Elly Bulkin, Minnie Bruce Pratt, and Barbara Smith, *Yours in Struggle: Three Feminist Perspectives on Anti-Semitism and Racism.* New York: Firebrand Books.

Pritchard, J. 2003. "Debate Highlights Health Care's Role as Prop. 54 Issue." *Santa Barbara News-Press,* September 30, p. A9.

Qian, Z. 1997. "Breaking the Racial Barriers: Variations in Interracial Marriage Between 1980–1990." *Demography* 34:263–276.

Rademaker, J. A. 1947. "Race Relations in Hawaii, 1946." *Social Process in Hawaii* 11.

Rampton, A., et al. 1981. *West Indian Children in Our Schools: Interim Report of the Committee of Inquiry into the Education of Children from Ethnic Minority Groups.* London: Her Majesty's Stationery Office.

Rawls, J. 1971. *A Theory of Justice.* Cambridge: Belknap Press of Harvard University Press.

Reddy, M. 1994. *Crossing the Color Line: Race, Parenting, and Culture.* New Brunswick, NJ: Rutgers University Press.

Reed, T. E. 1969. "Caucasian Genes in American Negroes." *Science* 165:762–768.

Reid, A., and K. Deaux. 1996. "Relationship Between Social and Personal Identities: Segregation or Integration?" *Journal of Personality and Social Psychology* 71: 1084–1091.

Renn, K. 2004. *Mixed Race Students in College: The Ecology of Race, Identity, and Community on Campus.* Albany: State University of New York Press.

Reuter, E. B. 1969 [1918]. *The Mulatto in the United States.* Boston: Badger.

Ridgeway, C. L. 1991. "The Social Construction of Status Value: Gender and Other Nominal Characteristics." *Social Forces* 70(2):367–386.

Ringer, B. B., and E. R. Lawless. 1989. *Race-Ethnicity and Society.* New York: Routledge.

Robinson, Randall. 2000. *The Debt: What America Owes to Blacks.* New York: Dutton.

Roccas, Sonia, and Marilynn Brewer. 2002. "Social Identity Complexity." *Personality and Social Psychology Review* 6(2):88–106.

Rockquemore, K. A. 1999. "Between Black and White: Exploring the Biracial Experience." *Race and Society* 1:197–212.

———. 2002. "Negotiating the Color Line: The Gendered Process of Racial Identity Construction Among Black/White Biracials." *Gender and Society* 16:485–503.

Rockquemore, K. A., and P. Arend. 2004. "Opting for White: Choice, Fluidity, and Black Identity Construction in Post–Civil Rights America." *Race and Society* 5(1):51–66.

Rockquemore, K. A., and D. L. Brunsma. 2002a. *Beyond Black: Biracial Identity in America.* Thousand Oaks, CA: Sage.

———. 2002b. "Socially Embedded Identities: Theories, Typologies, and Processes of Racial Identity Among Black/White Biracials." *Sociological Quarterly* 43(3):335–356.

Rockquemore, K. A., and T. Laszloffy. 2003. "Exploring Multiple Realities: Using Narrative Approaches in Therapy with Black/White Biracials." *Family Relations* 52:119–128.

———. 2005. *Raising Biracial Children.* Lanham, MD: Altamira.

Rodríguez, C. 1994. "Challenging Racial Hegemony: Puerto Ricans in the United States." Pp. 131–145 in *Race,* edited by S. G. A. R. Sanjek. New Brunswick, NJ: Rutgers University Press.

———. 2000. *Changing Race: Latinos, the Census, and the History of Ethnicity in the United States.* New York: New York University Press.

Rodríguez, N. M. 1998. "Emptying the Content of Whiteness: Toward an Understanding of the Relation Between Whiteness and Pedagogy." Pp. 31–62 in *White Reign: Deploying Whiteness in America,* edited by J. Kincheloe, S. R. Steinberg, N. Rodríguez, and R. Chennault. New York: St. Martin's Griffin.

Rodríguez, R. 2003. Brown: *The Last Discovery of America.* New York: Penguin.

Rodríguez, V. M. 1999. "Boricuas, African Americans, and Chicanos in the 'Far West': Notes on the Puerto Rican Pro-Independence Movement in California, 1960s–1980s." Pp. 79–110 in *Latino Social Movements: Historical and Theoretical Perspectives,* edited by R. D. Torres and G. Katsiaficas. New York: Routledge.

Roediger, D. R. 1999. *The Wages of Whiteness: Race and the Making of the American Working Class.* New York: Norton.

Romano, R. C. 2003. *Race Mixing: Black-White Marriage in Postwar America.* Cambridge, MA: Harvard University Press.

Root, M. P. P. 1990. "Resolving 'Other' Status: Identity Development of Biracial Individuals." *Women and Therapy* 9:185–205.

———, ed. 1992a. *Racially Mixed People in America.* Newbury Park, CA: Sage.

———. 1992b. "Within, Between and Beyond Race." Pp. 3–11 in *Racially Mixed People in America,* edited by M. P. P. Root. Newbury Park, CA: Sage.

———, ed. 1996a. *The Multicultural Experience: Racial Borders as the New Frontier.* Thousand Oaks, CA: Sage.

———. 1996b. "The Multiracial Experience: Racial Borders as Significant Frontier in Race Relations." Pp. xii–xxviii in *The Multiracial Experience: Racial Borders as the New Frontier,* edited by M. P. P. Root. Thousand Oaks, CA: Sage.

———. 1997. "Mixed Race Women." Pp. 157–174 in *Race/Sex: Their Sameness, Difference, and Interplay,* edited by N. Zack. New York: Routledge.

———. 1998. "Experiences and Processes Affecting Racial Identity Development: Preliminary Results from the Biracial Sibling Project." *Cultural Diversity and Mental Health* 4:237–247.

———. 2001. *Love's Revolution: Interracial Marriage.* Philadelphia: Temple University Press.

Root, M. P. P., and P. Arend. 2002. "Opting for White: Choice, Fluidity and Racial Identity Construction in Post–Civil Rights America." *Race and Society* 5:51–66.

Root, M. P. P., and M. Kelley, eds. 2003. *Multiracial Child Resource Book.* Seattle: MAVIN Foundation.

Rosa, J. P. 2000. "The Massie Case Narrative and the Cultural Production of Local Identity in Hawai'i." *Amerasia Journal* 26(2):93–115.

Rose, A. M. 1956. *The Negro in America.* Boston: Beacon Press.

Rosenblatt, P. C., T. A. Karis, and R. D. Powell. 1995. *Multiracial Couples: Black and White Voices.* Thousand Oaks, CA: Sage.

Rossomando, J. 2001. "California Initiative Seeks to End Racial Classifications." CBS News, December 31, http://www.cbsnews.com/politics/archive/200112/pol20011231a.html.

Rothenberg, P. 2000. *Invisible Privilege: A Memoir About Race, Class, and Gender.* Lawrence: University of Kansas Press.

Rout, L. B. 1976. *The African Experience in Spanish America, 1502 to the Present Day.* Cambridge and New York: Cambridge University Press.

Rumbaut, R. G., and A. Portes. 2001a. *Ethnicities: Children of Immigrants in America.* Berkeley and New York: University of California Press and Russell Sage Foundation.

———. 2001b. "Introduction—Ethnogenesis: Coming of Age in Immigrant America." Pp. 1–20 in *Ethnicities,* edited by R. Rumbaut and A. Portes. New York and Los Angeles: University of California Press and Russell Sage Foundation.

Russell, K., M. Wilson, and R. Hall. 1992. *The Color Complex: The Politics of Skin Color Among African Americans.* Orlando, FL: Harcourt Brace.

Saenz, R., and M. C. Morales. 2005. "Demography of Race and Ethnicity." In *The Handbook of Population,* edited by D. L. Poston, Jr., and M. Micklin. New York: Klewer Academic/Plenum Publishers.

Saito, L. T. 1998. *Race and Politics: Asian Americans, Latinos, and Whites in a Los Angeles Suburb.* Urbana: University of Illinois Press.

Sakoda, K., and J. Siegel. 2003. *Pidgin Grammar: An Introduction to the Creole Language of Hawai'i.* Honolulu: Bess Press.

Saltman, J. 1990. "Neighborhood Stabilization: A Fragile Movement." *Sociological Quarterly* 31(4):531–549.

Sample, H. A. 2000. "Connerly Joins Foes of 'Silly' Queries on Census Forms: He Weighs Ballot Drive to Limit Race Data, Capitol Alert." Sacramento Bee News. April 1, http://www.capitolalert.com/news/capalert02_20000401.html.

Sanders, J. 2003. "Prop. 54 Campaign Funding Questioned." *Santa Barbara News Press,* August 19, p. A5.

Sanjek, R. 1996. "Intermarriage and the Future of Races in the United States." Pp. 103–130 in *Race,* edited by S. Gregory and R. Sanjek. New Brunswick, NJ: Rutgers University Press.

San Juan, E., Jr. 2000. "The Limits of Ethnicity and the Horizon of Historical Materialism." In *Asian American Studies: Identity, Images, Issues Past and Present,* edited by E. M. Ghymn. New York: Peter Lang.

Sawicki, J. 1991. *Disciplining Foucault: Feminism, Power, and the Body.* New York: Routledge.

Schmitt, R. C. 1968. *Demographic Statistics of Hawai'i, 1778–1965.* Honolulu: University of Hawai'i Press.

———. 1977. *Historical Statistics of Hawai'i.* Honolulu: University Press of Hawai'i.

Schoenbaum, D., and E. Pond. 1996. *The German Question and Other German Questions.* New York: St. Martin's.

Schulz, A., B. Israel, D. Williams, E. Parker, A. Becker, and S. James. 2000. "Social Inequalities, Stressors and Self Reported Health Status Among African American and White Women in the Detroit Metropolitan Area." *Social Science and Medicine* 51:1639–1653.

Schuman, H., C. Steeh, L. Bobo, and M. Krysan. 1997. *Racial Attitudes in America: Trends and Interpretations.* Cambridge: Harvard University Press.

Schutz, A. 1967. *The Phenomenology of the Social World.* Evanston, IL: Northwestern University Press.

Sears, D. O., J. J. Hetts, J. Sidanius, and L. Bobo. 2000. "Race in American Politics." Pp. 1–43 in *Racialized Politics: The Debate About Racism in America,* edited by D. O. Sears, J. Sidanius, and L. Bobo. Chicago: University of Chicago Press.

Secours, M. 2003. "Riding the Reparations Bandwagon." Pp. 286–298 in *Should America Pay? Slavery and the Raging Debate on Reparations,* edited by Raymond A. Winbush. New York: Amistad.

Segrest, M. 1994. *Memoir of a Race Traitor.* Boston: Beacon Press.

Sellers, R. M., M. A. Smith, J. N. Shelton, S. A. J. Rowley, and T. M. Chavous. 1998. "Multidimensional Model of Racial Identity: A Reconceptualization of African American Racial Identity." *Personality and Social Psychology Review* 2(1):18–39.

Selznick, G., and S. Steinberg. 1969. *The Tenacity of Prejudice: Anti-Semitism in Contemporary America.* New York: Harper and Row.

Sen, R. 2003–2004. "Winning Race." *Colorlines* 6(4):7–8.

Senna, D. 1998. "The Mulatto Millennium." Pp. 12–27 in *Half and Half: Writers on Growing up Biracial and Bicultural,* edited by C. O'Hearn. New York: Pantheon.

Sheppard, M. 2002. "Mental Health and Social Justice: Gender, Race and Psychological Consequences of Unfairness." *British Journal of Social Work* 32:779–797.

Sherman, G. W. T. [1865] 2003. "In the Field, Savannah, Georgia, Special Field Orders, No. 15." Pp. 331–333 in *Should America Pay? Slavery and the Raging Debate on Reparations,* edited by Raymond A. Winbush. New York: Amistad.

Sherif, M., and C. W. Sherif. 1964. *Reference Groups.* New York: Harper and Row.

Shils, E. 1957. "Primordial, Personal, Sacred, and Civil Ties: Some Particular Observations on the Relationships of Sociological Research and Theory." *British Journal of Sociology* 8:130–145.

Sichelman, Lew. 2003. "Minorities More Likely to Be Rejected." *Reality Times,* October 22, http://realtytimes.com/rtcpages/20031022_minorities.htm.

Simmel, Georg. 1908, 1955. *Conflict and the Web of Group Affiliations.* New York: Free Press.

Simmel, G., and K. H. Wolff. 1950. *The Sociology of Georg Simmel.* Glencoe, IL: Free Press.

Skogan, W. G., et al. 2002. "Taking Stock: Community Policing in Chicago." Institute for Policy Research, Northwestern University, Evanston, IL.

Small, S. 1994. *Racialized Barriers: The Black Experience in the United States and England in the 1980s.* New York: Routledge.

Smedley, A. 1993/1999. *Race in North America: Origin and Evolution of a Worldview.* 1st and 2nd eds. Boulder, CO: Westview.

Smith, H. J., R. Spears, and I. J. Hamstra. 1999. "Social Identity and the Context of Relative Deprivation." Pp. 205–229 in *Social Identity: Context, Commitment, Content,* edited by N. Ellemers, R. Spears, and B. Doosje. Oxford: Basil Blackwell.

Smith, P. B., and M. H. Bond. 1999. *Social Psychology Across Cultures.* Boston: Allyn and Bacon.

Smith, R. C. 1995. *Racism in the Post–Civil Rights Era: Now You See It, Now You Don't.* Albany: State University of New York Press.

Smith, S. 1989. *The Politics of "Race" and Residence: Citizenship, Segregation, and White Supremacy in Britain.* Cambridge, UK: Polity Press.

Smith, V., ed. 1998. *Not Just Race, Not Just Gender: Black Feminist Readings.* New York: Routledge.

Solaun, M., and S. Kronus. 1973. *Discrimination Without Violence.* New York: John Wiley.

Solomos, J. 1989. *Race and Racism in Britain,* 2nd revised ed. New York: St. Martin's.

Sommerville, S. B. 2000. *Queering the Color Line: Race and the Invention of Homosexuality in American Culture.* Durham, NC: Duke University Press.

Sousa, D. D. 1996. "The One-Drop-of-Blood-Rule." *Forbes Today,* December 2, pp. 48.

Sowell, T. 1985. *Civil Rights: Rhetoric or Reality.* New York: William Morrow.

Spears, A. K. 1999. *Race and Ideology: Language, Symbolism, and Popular Culture.* Detroit: Wayne State University Press.

Spencer, J. M. 1997. *The New Colored People: The Mixed-Race Movement in America.* New York: New York University Press.

Spencer, M. B. 1984. "Black Children's Race Awareness, Racial Attitudes, and Self-Concept: A Reinterpretation." *Journal of Child Psychology and Psychiatry* 25(3):433–441.

Spencer, M. E. 1994. "Multiculturalism, 'Political Correctness,' and the Politics of Identity." *Sociological Forum* 9(4):547–567.

Spencer, R. 1997. "Theorizing Multiracial Identity Politics in the United States." Ph.D. diss., Emory University, Atlanta, GA.

———. 1999. *Spurious Issues: Race and Multiracial Identity Politics in the United States.* Boulder: Westview.

———. 2003. "Census 2000: Assessments in Significance." Pp. 99–110 in *New Faces in a Changing America: Multiracial Identity in the Twenty-First Century,* edited by L. I. Winters and H. L. Debose. Thousand Oaks, CA: Sage.

Spickard, P. R. 1989. *Mixed Blood: Intermarriage and Ethnic Identity in Twentieth-Century America.* Madison: University of Wisconsin Press.

———. 1995. "Pacific Islander American Multiethnicity: A Vision of America's Future?" *Social Forces* 73:1365–1383.

Spickard, P., and G. R. Daniel. 2004. "Independence Possible." Pp. 1–17 in *Racial Thinking in the United States: Uncompleted Independence,* edited by P. Spickard and G. R. Daniel. Notre Dame, IN: University of Notre Dame Press.

Spickard, P., J. L. Rondilla, and D. H. Wright, eds. 2002. *Pacific Diaspora: Island Peoples in the United States and Across the Pacific.* Honolulu: University of Hawai'i Press.

St. Jean, Y. 1998. "Let People Speak for Themselves: Interracial Unions and the General Social Survey." *Journal of Black Studies* 28:398–414.

Stack, C. B. 1996. *Call to Home: African Americans Reclaim the Rural South.* New York: Basic Books.

Stannard, D. E. 1989. *Before the Horror: The Population of Hawai'i on the Eve of Western Contact.* Honolulu: University of Hawai'i Social Science Research Institute.

Steele, A. 2003. "Race Card Is the Sign of a Losing Hand." *Los Angeles Times,* September 18, www.latimes.com/la-oe-steele18sep18,1,2511763.story.

Steinberg, S. 1989. *The Ethnic Myth: Race, Ethnicity, and Class in America.* Boston: Beacon Press.

———. 1995. *Turning Back: The Retreat from Racial Justice in American Thought and Policy.* Boston: Beacon Press.

Steinhorn, L., and B. Diggs-Brown. 2000. *By the Color of Our Skin: The Illusion of Integration and the Reality of Race.* New York: Putnam.

Stephan, C. W. 1992. "Mixed-Heritage Individuals: Ethnic Identity and Trait Characteristics." Pp. 50–63 in *Racially Mixed People in America,* edited by M. P. P. Root. Newbury Park, CA: Sage.

Stets, Jan E., and Peter J. Burke. 2000. "Identity Theory and Social Identity Theory." *Social Psychology Quarterly* 63(3):224–237.

———. 2003. "A Sociological Approach to Self and Identity." Pp. 128–152 in *Handbook of Self and Identity,* edited by Mark R. Leary and June Price Tangney. New York: Guilford Press.

Stoddard, E. R. 1973. *Mexican Americans.* New York: Random House.

Stonequist, E. 1937. *The Marginal Man: A Study in Personality and Culture Conflict.* New York: Russel and Russel.

Storrs, D. 1999. "Whiteness as Stigma: Essentialist Identity Work by Mixed-Race Women." *Symbolic Interaction* 23:187–212.

Strickland, B. R. 2000. "Misassumption, Misadventures, and the Misuse of Psychology." *American Psychologist* 55(3):331–338.

Stryker, S. 1980. *Symbolic Interactionism: A Social Structural Version.* Menlo Park, CA: Benjamin/Cummings.

Stryker, S., and P. J. Burke. 2000. "The Past, Present, and Future of an Identity Theory." *Social Psychology Quarterly* 63(4) (Special Millennium Issue on the State of Sociological Social Psychology):284–297.

Sudbury, J. 2001. "ReConstructing Multiracial Blackness: Women's Activism, Difference and Collective Identity in Britain." *Ethnic and Racial Studies* 24(1):29–49.

Swain, C. 2002. *The New White Nationalism in America: Its Challenge to Integration.* New York: Cambridge University Press.

Swain, C. M., and R. Nieli. 2003. *Contemporary Voices of White Nationalism in America.* Cambridge: Cambridge University Press.

Tafoya, S. M., H. Johnson, and L. E. Hill. 2004. *US Census 2000: Multiracial Identity of Children of Mixed-Race Couples.* Washington, DC: Population Reference Bureau.

Tajfel, H. 1970. "Experiments in Intergroup Discrimination." *Scientific American* 223:96–102.

———. 1979. "Individuals and Groups in Social Psychology." *British Journal of Social and Clinical Psychology* 18:183–190.

Tajfel, H., and J. Turner. 1979. "An Integrative Theory of Intergroup Conflict." Pp. 33–47 in *The Social Psychology of Intergroup Relations,* edited by W. G. Austin and S. Worchel. Monterey, CA: Brooks/Cole.

Takaki, R. 1983. *Pau Hana: Plantation Life and Labor in Hawai'i.* Honolulu: University of Hawai'i Press.

———. 1993. *A Different Mirror: A History of Multicultural America.* Boston: Little, Brown.

Tatum, B. 1997. *Why Are All the Black Kids Sitting Together in the Cafeteria? And Other Conversations About Race.* New York: Basic Books.

Taub, R., D. G. Taylor, and J. D. Dunham. 1984. *Paths of Neighborhood Change: Race and Crime in Urban America.* Chicago: University of Chicago Press.

Taylor, C. 1992. "The Politics of Recognition." Pp. 25–68 in *Multiculturalism and the "Politics of Recognition,"* edited by A. Gutman. Princeton: Princeton University Press.

Texeira, M. T. 2003. "The New Multiracialism: An Affirmation of or an End to Race as We Know It?" Pp. 21–37 in *New Faces in a Changing America: Multiracial Identity in the Twenty-First Century,* edited by L. I. Winters and H. L. Debose. Thousand Oaks, CA: Sage.

Thernstrom, S., and A. Thernstrom. 1999. *America in Black and White: One Nation, Indivisible.* New York: Simon and Schuster.

Thomas, A., and S. Sillen. 1972. *Racism and Psychiatry.* New York: Carol Publishing Group.

Thomas, H. 1997. *The Slave Trade: The Story of the Atlantic Slave Trade, 1440–1870.* New York: Simon and Schuster.

Thornton, M. C. 1997. "Strategies of Racial Socialization Among Black Parents: Mainstream, Minority, and Cultural Messages." Pp. 201–215 in *Family Life in Black America,* edited by R. J. Taylor, J. S. Jackson, and L. M. Chatters. Thousand Oaks, CA: Sage.

Thornton, M. C., L. M. Chatters, R. J. Taylor, and W. R. Allen. 1990. "Sociodemographic and Environmental Correlates of Racial Socialization by Black Parents." *Child Development* 61(2) special issue: Minority Children: 401–409.

Tizard, B., and A. Phoenix. 1993. *Black, White or Mixed Race: Race and Racism in the Lives of Young People of Mixed Parentage.* London: Routledge.

Todd, J. 1992. "Attitudes Toward Interracial Dating: Effects of Age, Sex and Race." *Journal of Multicultural Counseling and Development* (October):202–208.

Tonouchi, L. A. 2001. *Da Word.* Honolulu: Bamboo Ridge Press.

———. 2002. *Living Pidgin: Contemplations on Pidgin Culture.* Käne'Ohe, HI: Tinfish Press.

Toppo, G. 2004. "Integrated Schools Still a Dream 50 Years Later: Decades After 'Brown,' Income, Not the Law, Separates the Races." *USA Today,* April 28, p. 1.

Torres-Saillant, S., and R. Hernández. 1998. *The Dominican Americans.* Westport, CT: Greenwood.

Trask, H.-K. 1999. *From a Native Daughter: Colonialism and Sovereignty in Hawai'i,* revised ed. Honolulu: University of Hawai'i Press.

———. 2000. "Native Social Capital: The Case of Hawaiian Sovereignty and Ka Lähui Hawai'i." *Policy Sciences* 33:149–159.

———. 2003. "Restitution as a Precondition of Reconciliation: Native Hawaiians and Indigenous Human Rights." Pp. 32–45 in *Should America Pay? Slavery and the Raging Debate on Reparations,* edited by Raymond A. Winbush. New York: Amistad.

Trillin, Calvin. 1986. "American Chronicles: Black or White." *New Yorker,* April 14, pp. 62–78.

Tuan, M. 1998. *Forever Foreigners or Honorary Whites? The Asian Ethnic Experience Today.* New Brunswick, NJ: Rutgers University Press.

Tuch, S. A., and J. K. Martin. 1997. *Racial Attitudes in the 1990s.* Westport, CT: Praeger.

Tucker, M. B., and C. Mitchell-Kernan. 1990. "New Trends in Black American Interracial Marriage: The Social Structural Context." *Journal of Marriage and Family* 52:209–218.

Turner, J. C. 1984. "Social Identification and Psychological Group Formation." In *The Social Dimension: European Developments in Social Psychology,* vol. 2, edited by H. Tajfel. Cambridge: Cambridge University Press.

———. 1987. *Rediscovering the Social Group.* Oxford: Blackwell.

———. 1999. "Some Current Issues in Research on Social Identity and Self-Categorization Theories." Pp. 6–34 in *Social Identity,* edited by N. Ellemers, R. Spears, and B. Doosje. Malden, MA: Blackwell.

Turner, J. C., P. J. Oakes, S. A. Haslam, and C. McGarty. 1994. "Self and Collective: Cognition and Social Context." *Personality and Social Psychology Bulletin* 20:454–463.

Turner, M., et al. 2002. *All Other Things Being Equal: A Paired Testing Study of Mortgage Lending Institutions: Final Report.* Washington, DC: Urban Institute.

Tutu, N. 2003. "Afterword." Pp. 321–325 in *Should America Pay? Slavery and the Raging Debate on Reparations,* edited by Raymond A. Winbush. New York: Amistad.

Twigg-Smith, T. 1998. *Hawaiian Sovereignty: Do the Facts Matter?* Honolulu: Goodale.

Twine, F. W. 1997/1996. "Brown-Skinned White Girls: Class, Culture and the Construction of White Identity in Suburban Communities." Pp. 214–243 in *Displacing Whiteness: Essays in Social and Cultural Criticism,* edited by R. Frankenberg. Durham, NC: Duke University Press. Originally published in 1996 in *Gender, Place, and Culture: A Journal of Feminist Geography* 3(2):205–224.

———. 1998. *Racism in a Racial Democracy.* New Brunswick, NJ: Rutgers University Press.

———. 1999a. "Bearing Blackness in Britain: The Meaning of Racial Difference for White Mothers of African-Descent Children." *Social Identities: A Journal of Race, Culture and Nation* 5(2):185–210.

———. 1999b. "Transracial Mothering and Antiracism." *Feminist Studies* 25(3): 727–747.

———. 2001. "Transgressive Women and Transracial Mothers: White Women and Critical Race Theory." *Meridians: Feminism, Race, Transnationalism* 1(2):130–153.

UNESCO (United Nations Educational, Scientific, and Cultural Organization). 1967. *Statement on Race and Racial Prejudice.* Paris: UNESCO.

US Bureau of the Census. 1996. *Population Projections of the United States by Age, Sex, Race, and Hispanic Origin: 1995 to 2050.* Washington, DC: US Government Printing Office.

———. 2001a. *The Black Population: 2000.* August, Retrieved October 27, 2001, from http://www.census.gov/prod/2001pubs/c2kbr01-5.pdf.

———. 2001b. *The White Population: 2000.* August, retrieved October 27, 2001, from http://www.census.gov/prod/2001pubs/c2kbr01-4.pdf.

————. 2001c. *The Two or More Races Population: 2000,* from http://www.census .gov/prod/2001pubs/c2kbr01-6.pdf.

————. 2002. *The Asian Population: 2000.* February, http://www.census.gov/prod/ 2002pubs/c2kbr01-16.pdf.

————. 2003. *Census 2000, Public Use Microdata Sample (PUMS), United States.* Washington, DC: US Census Bureau.

US Congress. House of Representatives. 1993. Subcommittee on Census, Statistics, and Postal Personnel of the Committee on Post Office and Civil Service. Review of Federal Measurements of Race and Ethnicity: Hearing. 103rd Cong., 1st sess., pp. 105–125, 165–171.

US Department of Commerce, Bureau of the Census. 1997. "Results of the 1996 Race and Ethnic Targeted Test." Working Paper No. 18, Population Division, Washington, DC.

US Executive Office, Office of Management and Budget. 1994. "Standards for the Classification of Federal Data on Race and Ethnicity." *Federal Register* Notice 59, 44673–44693.

Urciuoli, B. 1996. *Exposing Prejudice: Puerto Rican Experiences of Language, Race, and Class.* Boulder, CO: Westview.

Vaca, N. 2004. *Presumed Alliance: The Unspoken Conflict Between Latinos and Blacks and What It Means for America.* New York: Rayo.

Valverde, K-L. C. 1992. "From Dust to Gold: The Vietnamese Amerasian Experience." Pp. 144–161 in *Racially Mixed People in America,* edited by M. P. P. Root. Newbury Park, CA: Sage.

Van Ausdale, D., and J. Feagin. 2001. *The First R: How Children Learn Race and Racism.* Lanham, MD: Rowman and Littlefield.

Van Den Berghe, P. L. 1971. "Racial Segregation in South Africa: Degrees and Kinds." Pp. 37–49 in *South Africa: Sociological Perspectives,* edited by H. Adam. New York: Oxford University Press.

Vander Zanden, J. W. 1972. *American Minority Relations,* 3rd ed. New York: Ronald.

van Dijk, T. A., S. Ting-Toomey, G. Smitherman, and D. Troutman. 1997. "Discourse, Ethnicity, Culture, and Racism." Pp. 144–180 in *Discourse as Social Interaction,* edited by T. A. van Dijk. London: Sage.

Van Dyke, J. 2003. "Reparations for the Descendants of American Slaves Under International Law." Pp. 57–78 in *Should America Pay? Slavery and the Raging Debate on Reparations,* edited by Raymond A. Winbush. New York: Amistad.

Van Kerckhove, Carmen. 2005. "Media Exploits Fear of Interracial Relationships." June 10, http://www.tolerance.org/news/article_tol.jsp?id=1234. Reprinted from newdemographic.com.

Vera, H., and A. Gordon. 2003. *Screen Saviors: Hollywood Fictions of Whiteness.* Lanham, MD: Rowman and Littlefield.

Verkuyten, M., W. De Jong, and C. N. Masson. 1995. "The Construction of Ethnic Categories: Discourses of Ethnicity in the Netherlands." *Ethnic and Racial Studies* 18:251–276.

Vickerman, M. 1999. *Crosscurrents: West Indian Immigrants and Race.* New York: Oxford University Press.

Wade, P. 1994. *Blackness and Race Mixture: The Dynamics of Racial Identity in Colombia.* Baltimore, MD: Johns Hopkins University Press.

Wade-Gayles, G. 1996. *Rooted Against the Wind.* Boston: Beacon Press.

Wagley, C., ed. 1963. *Race and Class in Rural Brazil,* 2nd ed. Paris: UNESCO.

Walker, R. 2003. "Whassup, Barbie? Marketers Are Embracing the Idea of a 'Post-Racial' America. Goodbye, Niche Marketing." *Boston Globe,* retrieved October 26, 2004, from LexisNexis Academic database.

Wallace, K. 2001. *Relative/Outsider: The Art and Politics of Identity Among Mixed-Heritage Students.* Westport, CT: Ablex.

Wallerstein, P. 2002. *Tell the Courts I Love My Wife: Race, Marriage, and Law, an American History.* New York: Palgrave.

Ward, Janie Victoria. 1996. *The Skin We're In: Teaching Our Teens to Be Emotionally Strong, Socially Smart, and Spiritually Connected.* New York: Free Press.

Ware, V. 1992. *Beyond the Pale: White Women, Racism, and History.* London: Verso.

Wareham, R. 2003. "The Popularization of the International Demand for Reparations." Pp. 226–236 in *Should America Pay? Slavery and the Raging Debate on Reparations,* edited by Raymond A. Winbush. New York: Amistad.

Warren, J. W., and F. W. Twine. 1997. "White Americans, the New Minority?: Non-Blacks and the Ever-Expanding Boundaries of Whiteness." *Journal of Black Studies* 28(2):200–218.

Waters, M. 1990. *Ethnic Options: Choosing Identities in America.* Berkeley: University of California Press.

———. 1991. "The Role of Lineage in Identity Formation Among Black Americans." *Qualitative Sociology* 14(1):57–76.

———. 1997. "The Impact of Racial Segregation on the Education and Work Outcomes of Second-Generation West Indians in New York City." Jerome Levy Economics Institute Working Paper no. 216.

———. 1998. "Multiple Ethnic Identity Choices." Pp. 28–46 in *Beyond Pluralism: The Conception of Groups and Group Identities in America,* edited by W. F. Katlin. Chicago: University of Chicago Press.

———. 1999. *Black Identities: West Indian Immigrant Dreams and American Reality.* Cambridge, MA: Harvard University Press.

———. 2000. "Immigration, Intermarriage, and the Challenges of Measuring Racial/Ethnic Identities." *American Journal of Public Health* 90:1735–1737.

Waters, M. C., and K. Eschbach. 1995. "Immigration and Ethnic and Racial Inequality in the United States." *Annual Review of Sociology* 21:419–446.

Watson, G. 1970. *Passing for White: A Study of Racial Assimilation in a South African School.* London: Tavistock.

Weber, M. 1949. "Objectivity in Social Science and Social Policy." In *Methodologies of the Social Sciences.* New York: Free Press.

Wei, Deborah, and Rachael Kamel, eds. 1998. *Resistance in Paradise: Rethinking 100 Years of U.S. Involvement in the Caribbean and the Pacific.* Philadelphia: American Friends Service Committee.

Weitzer, R. 1997. "Racial Prejudice Among Korean Merchants in African American Neighborhoods." *Sociological Quarterly* 38(4):587–606.

Welland, S. 2003. "Being Between." *Colorlines: Race, Culture, Action* (Summer): 31–33.

Wellman, D. 1993. *Portraits of White Racism.* Cambridge: Cambridge University Press.

Wellner, A. S. 2001. "A Niche in Time: Multiracials—the Bellwethers of Tomorrow's Markets." *Forecast,* April 21, p. 10.

———. 2002. "The Next Wave of Census Data." *Forecast,* retrieved October 26, 2004, from LexisNexis Academic database.

West, C. 1982. *Prophecy Deliverance! An Afro-American Revolutionary Christianity.* Philadelphia: Westminster Press.

West, S. 1996. "Is Oak Park Really Integrated?" *Journal Express,* February 21, p. 27.

Westley, R. 2003. "Many Billions Gone: Is It Time to Reconsider the Case for Black Reparations?" Pp. 109–134 in *Should America Pay? Slavery and the Raging Debate on Reparations,* edited by Raymond A. Winbush. New York: Amistad.

Wetherell, M., and J. Potter. 1992. *Mapping the Language of Racism: Discourse and the Legitimation of Exploitation.* New York: Columbia University Press.

Whelan, David. 2001. "Casting Tiger Woods: Multiracials Step into the Advertising Spotlight." *Forecast,* May 7, p. 1; retrieved October 26, 2004, from Lexis-Nexis Academic database.

White, J., and T. Parham. 1990. *The Psychology of Blacks: An African-American Perspective.* Englewood Cliffs, NJ: Prentice Hall.

White, J. E. 1997. "'I'm Just Who I Am.'" *Time,* May 5, pp. 32–36.

White, M. J., A. E. Biddlecom, and S. Guo. 1993. "Immigration, Naturalization, and Residential Assimilation Among Asian Americans in 1980." *Social Forces* 72(1): 93–117.

White, W. 1948. *A Man Called White: The Autobiography of Walter White.* New York: Viking.

Wiggins, J., B. Wiggins, and J. Vander Zanden, J. 1994. *Social Psychology.* New York: McGraw-Hill.

Wijeyesinghe, C. 1992. "Towards an Understanding of the Racial Identity of Biracial People: The Experience of Racial Self-Identification of African-American/ Euro-American Adults and the Factors Affecting their Choices of Racial Identity." Ph.D. diss., University of Massachusetts, Amherst, MA.

———. 2003. "Relationships and Black/White Multiracial People." Pp. 160–167 in *Multiracial Child Resource Book,* edited by M. P. P. Root and M. Kelley. Seattle: MAVIN Foundation.

Wilkerson, I. 1998. "Middle-Class Blacks Try to Grip a Ladder While Lending a Hand." Pp. 226–234 in *Race, Class, and Gender in the United States: An Integrated Study,* 4th ed., edited by P. Rothenberg. New York: St. Martin's.

Wilkins-Godbee, V. 1996. Untitled Speech. Multiracial Solidarity March I. Washington DC, August 9.

Will, G. F. 1997a. "Census: Should the 'Other' Category Be Expanded?" *Washington Post,* October 5, http://www.sacbee.com/voices/national/will/more/will_19971005.html.

———. 1997b. "Melding in America." *Washington Post,* October 5, p. C07.

Williams, G. H. 1995. *Life on the Color Line: The True Story of a White Boy Who Discovered He Was Black.* New York: Dutton.

Williams, K. 1998. "Linking Theory and Action: Social Movements Frameworks and Multiracial Activism." Paper presented at Colorlines in the Twenty-First Century: Multiracialism in a Racially Divided World, September 26, Roosevelt University, Chicago, IL.

———. 2003. "Parties, Movements, and Constituencies in Categorizing Race: State-Level Outcomes of Multiracial Category Legislation." Pp. 197–225 in *States, Parties, and Social Movements: Pushing the Boundaries of Institutionalized Politics,* edited by J. Goldstone. Cambridge: Cambridge University Press.

Williams, P. J. 1995. "Alchemical Notes: Reconstructing Ideals from Deconstructed Rights" Pp. 84–94 in *Critical Race Theory,* edited by R. Delgado. Philadelphia: Temple University Press.

———. 1998. *Seeing a Color-Blind Future: The Paradox of Race.* San Francisco: Noonday Press.

Williams, R. 1961. *The Long Revolution.* New York: Columbia University Press.

Williams, R. L. 1980. "The Death of White Research in the Black Community." In *Black Psychology,* 2nd ed., edited by R. L. Jones. New York: Harper and Row.

Williams, T. K. 1996. "Race as Process: Reassessing the 'What Are You?' Encounters of Biracial Individuals." Pp. 191–210 in *The Multiracial Experience,* edited by M. P. P. Root. Newbury Park, CA: Sage.

Williamson, J. 1980. *New People: Miscegenation and Mulattoes in the United States.* New York: Free Press.

Wilson, A. 1987. *Mixed-Race Children: A Study of Identity.* London: Allen and Unwin.

Wilson, J. 1997. "Lost in the Fifties: A Study of Collected Memories." Pp. 147–181 in *The Narrative Study of Lives,* vol. 5, edited by A. Lieblich and R. Josselson. Thousand Oaks, CA: Sage.

Wilson, W. J. 1980. *The Declining Significance of Race: Blacks and Changing American Institutions,* 2nd ed. Chicago: University of Chicago Press.

———. 1987. *The Truly Disadvantaged: The Inner City, the Underclass, and Public Policy.* Chicago: University of Chicago Press.

———. 1999. *The Bridge over the Racial Divide: Rising Inequality and Coalition Politics.* Berkeley: University of California Press.

Winant, H. 1994. *Racial Conditions: Politics, Theory, Comparisons.* Minneapolis: University of Minnesota Press.

———. 1997. "Behind Blue Eyes: Whiteness and Contemporary US Racial Politics." *New Left Review* 225 (September–October).

———. 2002. *The World Is a Ghetto.* New York: Basic Books.

Winbush, R. A. 2003a. "Introduction." Pp. xi–xix in *Should America Pay? Slavery and the Raging Debate on Reparations,* edited by Raymond A. Winbush. New York: Amistad.

———. 2003b. "And the Earth Moved: Stealing Black Land in the United States." Pp. 46–56 in *Should America Pay? Slavery and the Raging Debate on Reparations,* edited by Raymond A. Winbush. New York: Amistad.

Wing, A. K., and S. Merchán. 1995. "Rape, Ethnicity and Culture: Spirit Injury from Bosnia to Black America." Pp. 516–528 in *Critical Race Theory,* edited by Richard Delgado. Philadelphia: Temple University.

Wise, T. 2003. "Debtor's Prison: Facing History and Its Consequences." Pp. 239–250 in *Should America Pay? Slavery and the Raging Debate on Reparations,* edited by Raymond A. Winbush. New York: Amistad.

Wolff, Robert Paul. 1977. *Understanding Rawls: A Reconstruction and Critique of a Theory of Justice.* Princeton, NJ: Princeton University Press.

Woo, D. 2000. "The Inventing and Reinventing of 'Model Minorities': The Cultural Veil Obscuring Structural Sources of Inequality." Pp. 193–212 in *Asian Americans: Experiences and Perspectives,* edited by L. H. Shinagawa. Upper Saddle River, NJ: Prentice-Hall.

Worrell, Frank C., William E. Cross, Jr., and Beverly J. Vandiver. 2001. "Nigrescence Theory: Current Status and Challenges for the Future." *Journal of Multicultural Counseling and Development* 29(3):201–213.

Worrill, C. W. 2003. "The National Black United Front and the Reparations Movement." Pp. 203–208 in *Should America Pay? Slavery and the Raging Debate on Reparations,* edited by Raymond A. Winbush. New York: Amistad.

Wright, Lawrence. 1994. "One Drop of Blood." *New Yorker,* July, pp. 46–55.

Wu, F. 2001. *Yellow: Race in America Beyond Black and White.* New York: Basic Books.

Wuthnow, R., J. D. Hunter, and E. Kurzwell. 1987. *Cultural Analysis.* New York: Routledge and Kegan Paul.

Wynter, L. E. 2002. *American Skin: Pop Culture, Big Business, and the End of White America.* New York: Crown.

Yamamoto, E. 1979. "The Significance of Local." *Social Process in Hawai'i* 27: 101–115.

Yamamoto, E. K., S. K. Serrano, M. S. Fenton, J. Gifford, D. Forman, B. Hoshijo, and J. Kim. 2001. "Dismantling Civil Rights: Multiracial Resistance and Reconstruction." *Cumberland Law Review* 31(3):523–567.

Yancey, G. 1999. "An Examination of Effects of Residential and Church Integration upon Racial Attitudes of Whites." *Sociological Perspectives* 42(2):279–304.

———. 2001. "Racial Attitudes: Differences in Racial Attitudes of People Attending Multiracial and Uniracial Congregations." *Research in the Social Scientific Study of Religion* 12:185–206.

———. 2003a."Integrated Sundays: An Exploratory Study Into the Formation of Multiracial Churches." *Sociological Focus* 36(2):111–126.

———. 2003b. *One Body, One Spirit: Principles of Successful Multiracial Churches.* Downers Grove, IL: Intervarsity Press.

———. 2003c. *Who Is White? Latinos, Asians, and the New Black/Nonblack Divide.* Boulder, CO: Lynne Rienner.

———. 2003d. "A Preliminary Examination of Differential Sexual Attitudes Among Individuals Involved in Interracial Relationships: Testing 'Jungle Fever.'" *Social Science Journal* 49:153–157.

Yancey, W. L., E. P. Ericksen, and R. N. Juliani. 1976. "Emergent Ethnicity: A Review and Reformulation." *American Sociological Review* 41(3):391–403.

Yetman, N. 1999. *Majority and Minority: The Dynamics of Race and Ethnicity in American Life,* 6th ed. Boston: Allyn and Bacon.

Yinger, J. 1995. *Closed Doors, Opportunities Lost: The Continuing Costs of Housing Discrimination.* New York: Russell Sage Foundation.

Yoon, I. 1995. "Attitudes, Social Distance, and Perceptions of Influence and Discrimination Among Minorities." *International Journal of Group Tensions* 25(1): 35–56.

———. 1997. *On My Own: Korean Businesses and Race Relations in America.* Chicago: University of Chicago Press.

Young, A. A., Jr. 1999. "Navigating Race: Getting Ahead in the Lives of 'Rags to Riches' Young Black Men." Pp. 30–62 in *The Cultural Territories of Race: Black and White Boundaries,* edited by M. Lamont. Chicago: University of Chicago Press.

Young, R. J. C. 1995. *Colonial Desire: Hybridity in Theory, Culture, and Race.* New York: Routledge.

Zack, N. 1993. *Race and Mixed Race.* Philadelphia: Temple University Press.

Zebrowski, S. 1999. "Black-White Intermarriages: The Racial and Gender Dynamics of Support and Opposition." *Journal of Black Studies* 30:123–132.

Zhou, H. 2003. "Affirmative Action and Asian Americans." *Chinese Community Center Newsletter,* June 1, p. 34.

Zhou, M. 2001. "Straddling Different Worlds: The Acculturation of Vietnamese Refugee Children." Pp. 187–228 in *Ethnicities: Children of Immigrants in America,* edited by R. G. Rumbaut and A. Portes. Berkeley: University of California Press.

Zuberi, T. 2001/2003. *Thicker Than Blood: How Racial Statistics Lie.* Minneapolis: University of Minnesota Press.

Zubrinsky, C. 2003. "The Dynamics of Racial Residential Segregation." *Annual Review of Sociology* 29:167–207.

The Contributors

Benjamin Bailey is assistant professor in the Department of Communication at the University of Massachusetts at Amherst. He is the author of *Language, Race, and Negotiation of Identity: A Study of Dominican Americans*. His research focuses on negotiations of ethnic and racial identities in face-to-face interaction, the ongoing transformation of US ethnic and racial categories through immigration, and the sociopolitical dimensions of bi- and multilingualism.

Kanika Bell is a clinical psychology postdoctoral fellow at Emory University. Her future research projects include the development of identity assessments and therapeutic interventions targeting African American women.

Eduardo Bonilla-Silva is professor of sociology at Duke University. He is well-known for his 1997 article in the *American Sociological Review*, "Rethinking Racism: Toward a Structural Interpretation," and his book *White Supremacy and Racism in the Post–Civil Rights Era* was the cowinner of the 2002 Oliver Cromwell Cox Award from the American Sociological Association. Professor Bonilla-Silva's other publications include *Racism Without Racists: Color-Blind Racism and the Persistence of Racial Inequality in the United States* and *White Out: The Continuing Significance of Racism*.

David L. Brunsma is assistant professor of sociology and black studies at the University of Missouri at Columbia. He is the author and coauthor of several books and articles, most notably *Beyond Black: Biracial Identity in America* and *The School Uniform Movement and What It Tells Us About American Education: A Symbolic Crusade*. Brunsma is committed to investigating and initiating ways in which scholarship can be actively used to combat structural racial injustices.

Josef Manuel Castañeda-Liles is a graduate student in the Department of Sociology at the University of California at Santa Barbara. His research focuses on the ethnic identities of the offspring of Mexican-white intermarriage and is informed by his personal experience in that area. He currently serves on the advisory boards of the Association of Multi-Ethnic Americans and Multiracial Americans of Southern California.

Erica Chito Childs is assistant professor of sociology at Hunter College of the City University of New York. Her book *Navigating Interracial Borders: Black-White*

Couples and Their Social Worlds explores the societal ideas and beliefs about interracial relationships in white and black communities. Her research and teaching looks at race/gender/sexuality, families, and media/popular culture images.

Kimberly McClain DaCosta is assistant professor of African and African American studies and of social studies at Harvard University. DaCosta is interested in the intersection of cultural ideas about race and the family and is currently completing a book on efforts to create a multiracial collective identity in the United States, based on interviews and fieldwork with members of organizations for interracial families and people of mixed descent.

Heather Dalmage is director of the Mansfield Institute for Social Justice, associate professor of sociology at Roosevelt University in Chicago, and a member of the board of the Chicago Council on Urban Affairs. Dalmage is the author of *Tripping on the Color Line: Black-White Multiracial Families in a Racially Divided World* and editor of *The Politics of Multiracialism: Challenging Racial Thinking.*

G. Reginald Daniel is associate professor in the Department of Sociology at the University of California at Santa Barbara. Since 1989 he has taught "Betwixt and Between," one of the first and longest-standing courses in the United States to deal specifically with the question of multiracial identity. He has published *More Than Black? Multiracial Identity and the New Racial Order* and *Race and Multiraciality in Brazil and the United States: Converging Paths?*

F. James Davis is professor emeritus of sociology at Illinois State University. Dr. Davis conducted research for the Air Force at the University of Washington during the years 1951–1952. He is the author of the classic work *Who Is Black? One Nation's Definition,* as well as *Society and the Law, Social Problems,* and *Minority-Dominant Relations.*

David G. Embrick is a Ph.D. candidate at Texas A&M University. His current research concerns the social, political, and psychological misinterpretations of diversity and inclusiveness within major US corporations. He has publications in *Race and Society, Sociological Forum, Research in Political Sociology,* and *The Journal of Intergroup Relations.*

Abby L. Ferber is director of women's studies and associate professor of sociology at the University of Colorado at Colorado Springs. She is the author of *White Man Falling: Race, Gender, and White Supremacy* and coauthor of *Hate in America: What Do We Know?* and *Making a Difference: University Students of Color Speak Out.* With Michael Kimmel, she coedited *Privilege: A Reader.* Her most recent work is *Home-Grown Hate: Gender and Organized Racism.*

Johanna E. Foster is visiting assistant professor of sociology and the director of gender studies at Monmouth University in West Long Branch, New Jersey. Her previous work has been published in *Gender and Society, Sociological Forum,* and *Research in Political Sociology.* She is currently interested in feminist perspectives on the prison-industrial complex, particularly the ways in which the intersections of inequalities shape women's experiences of incarceration. In 2003, she cofounded College Connections, a college-bound program for women prisoners in Taconic Correctional Facility in Westchester County, New York, where she also volunteers and teaches sociology and gender studies.

Charles A. Gallagher is an associate professor in the Department of Sociology and the race and urban studies concentration director at Georgia State University. His reader *Rethinking the Color Line: Readings in Race and Ethnicity* is used in colleges and universities throughout the country. He is currently finishing a book on race relations based on interviews with 150 whites from around the country and will be starting a project on how racial disparities in access to health care are shaped by social and cultural factors.

Hayward Derrick Horton is associate professor of sociology at the School of Public Health at the State University of New York at Albany. He has published over thirty articles on demography, race and ethnicity, and rural sociology and also introduced a new paradigm into the field of demography, "critical demography." In the March 2000 Special Millennial Issue of the top journal in his field, the *American Sociological Review,* Horton published a groundbreaking article, "Lost in the Storm: The Sociology of the Black Working Class, 1850–1990," in which he redefined the race-class debate and introduced a new measure of social class in the United States. Horton is a coeditor of *Skin Deep: How Race and Complexion Matter in the "Color-Blind" Era.*

Kathleen Korgen is associate professor of sociology at William Paterson University in Wayne, New Jersey. She is the author of *From Black to Biracial, Crossing the Racial Divide: Close Friendships Between Black and White Americans,* and numerous articles on issues concerning racial identity and race relations. Her current work focuses on the relationship between sociology and the "educating citizens" movement in higher education. Korgen's latest book (coauthored with Howard Lune) is *How Sociology Can Save Democracy.*

Tracey Laszloffy is a marriage and family therapist in private practice in Connecticut. She has also served on the faculty at Seton Hill University, where she directed the master's-level marriage and family therapy program. Laszloffy has published extensively in the area of race, oppression, and family therapy.

R. L'Heureux Lewis is a Ph.D. candidate in sociology and public policy at the University of Michigan. His research interests include racial and ethnic studies, educational disparities, and mental health functioning. He is currently an American Sociological Association MFP mental health fellow.

Jeffrey Moniz is assistant professor of education at the University of Hawai'i. He is coeditor of *Crossing Lines: Race and Mixed Races Across the Geohistorical Divide.* He is currently working on a book on hapas in Hawai'i for the University of Hawai'i Press.

Julia Noveske is a doctoral student in sociology at the University of Illinois at Chicago. Her research interests include white racial ideology, qualitative methods, social stigma, and the sociology of health and illness.

Eileen O'Brien is currently an assistant professor of sociology at the University of Richmond in Virginia. She is the author of three books: *Whites Confront Racism: Antiracists and Their Paths to Action, White Men on Race: Power, Privilege, and the Shaping of Cultural Consciousness,* and *Race, Ethnicity, and Gender: Selected Readings.* Her next project will challenge the notion that the United States is about to become a majority nonwhite nation by investigating the processes by which some Latinos and Asian Americans are "becoming white," as did the Irish, Jews, and others before them.

Kwame Owusu-Bempah is a reader in psychology at the University of Leicester, UK, as well as a charted psychologist and associate fellow of the British Psychological Society. His current research interests include identity development and maintenance in children and the relationship between sociogenealogical connectedness and the psychological functioning of separated children. Besides his numerous journal articles and contributions in several edited volumes, his coauthored books (with Dennis Howitt) include *The Racism of Psychology* and *Psychology Beyond Western Perspectives.*

Kerry Ann Rockquemore is associate professor of African American studies and sociology at the University of Illinois at Chicago. She is coauthor of *Beyond Black: Biracial Identity in America* and *Raising Biracial Children.*

Rainier Spencer is associate professor of Afro-American studies in the Department of Anthropology and Ethnic Studies at the University of Nevada at Las Vegas. He is the author of *Spurious Issues: Race and Multiracial Identity Politics in the United States,* as well as several book chapters and journal articles on multiracial identity. His research focuses on interrogating the ways in which biological race is reified in the ideology of the multiracial identity movement in the United States.

Paul Spickard is professor of history and Asian American studies at the University of California at Santa Barbara. He is the author or editor of fourteen books, most recently *Racial Thinking in the United States: Uncompleted Independence* and *Race and Nation: Ethnic Systems in the Modern World.* He is at work on a history of race and immigration in the United States.

Debbie Storrs is associate professor of sociology at the University of Idaho, where she teaches the sociology of inequalities. Her research focuses on the construction and negotiation of multiracial, religious, and transnational identities. Some of her recent publications include *Making a Difference: University Students of Color Speak Out,* "Women's Pursuit of Higher Education and the Negotiated Process of Hegemony: Embedded Resistance Among Mormons" (with Mihelich, in *Gender and Society*), and "Like a Bamboo: Representations of a Japanese War Bride" (in *Frontiers*).

France Winddance Twine joined the Sociology Department at the University of California at Santa Barbara in 1997 after teaching at the University of Washington in Seattle. She has conducted field research in Brazil, Great Britain, and the United States. She is the author of *Racism in a Racial Democracy: The Maintenance of White Supremacy in Brazil* and a coeditor of four volumes, including *Feminism and Antiracism: International Struggles for Justice* and *Racing Research, Researching Race: Methodological Dilemmas in Critical Race Studies.* Her manuscript that examines racism and antiracism in interracial families in England is forthcoming from Duke University Press.

George Yancey is associate professor at the University of North Texas. He specializes in the study of interracial families, multiracial churches, and contemporary race relations. He has published several articles on these topics in academic journals such as *American Sociological Review, Sociological Focus, Sociological Perspectives,* and *Social Science Quarterly.* He is the author of *Who Is White? Latinos, Asians, and the New Black/Nonblack Divide* and coauthor of *United by Faith: The Multiracial Congregation as an Answer to the Problem of Race.* Currently he is seeking a grant to conduct the first national probability study of multiracial families.

Index

Collective black, 33, 37, 39, 40, 47.
See also Latin Americanization
thesis
Collins, Patricia Hill, 240
Colonialism, 23, 24, 64, 66, 68–70, 76,
77, 79–81, 171–172
Color-blind racism/ideology, 37,
46, 105–108, 115–116, 125–128,
136–138, 140–143, 147, 149, 152,
153, 159, 208–211, 213, 214, 235,
236, 243, 244, 267–269, 272–284,
309. *See also* Racial discourse;
Racial ideology
Colorism, 19–20, 30, 46, 143n1. *See
also* Appearance; Pigmentocracy;
Skin color
Color line, 81, 301. *See* Colorism;
Race; Racial classification
Congressional Black Caucus, 28, 137,
144n8
Congress of Industrial Organizations–
International Longshore and Ware-
house Unions, 72
Connerly, Ward, 38, 57, 135, 136, 138–
140, 142, 143. *See also* American
Civil Rights Institute; Racial Privacy
Initiative
Conservatism, 38. *See also* Neo-
conservatism; Republic Party
Consumerism, 110, 184, 190, 194, 195.
See also Advertising; Marketing
Contact hypothesis, 268, 283
Conyers, John Jr., 144n8, 172
Cornell, Stephen, 51
Costa Rican Americans, 40–41
Counseling, 324; and multiracials,
316–318, 320, 321, 323; as "race
therapy," 317–319
Crane, Marie, 268, 269, 283
Creoles, 19, 143n1
Critical demography, 117–118, 120, 121
Cuba, 37
Cuban Americans, 40–42, 45, 57, 62n7
Cultural objects, 332–335. *See also*
Culture, and identity; Multiracial(s),
identity; Multiracial(s), use of
cultural repertoires in
Cultural pluralism, 60
Cultural socialization, 212. *See also*
Racial socialization
Culture, 34, 180n3, 329, 330, 340, 341;
and identity, 286, 294, 329–340,
343–346

DaCosta, Kimberly McClain, 302
Dakar Declaration (2001), 171
Daniel, G. Reginald, 168
Dating, 118, 119
Davila, Arlene, 185, 199n15
Davis, F. James, 92, 315
Day, A. Grove, 67
Deaux, Kay, 251, 262
December 12th Movement, 165
Democratic Party, 133, 144n8
Demography, 36–37, 106; critical,
117–118, 120, 121
Disability Rights Movement, 164
Discourse. *See* Racial discourse
Discrimination, 42, 107, 210, 211, 301,
337, 338
Dominican Americans, 36, 40, 45,
285–297, 299n1
Dominican Republic, 288
Douglas, Nathan, 167, 168, 170
Douglass, Frederick, 178
Douglass, Ramona, 139, 144n9, 167
DuBois, W. E. B., 254, 263
Duke, David, 151, 157

East-West Center, 65
Economic shifts, 106
Edwards, Jeffrey, 305
Egalitarian pluralism, 25, 26, 31, 126,
128, 141, 142. *See also* Liberalism
Ellison, Ralph, 263
Embrick, David G., 147
Epidermic capital, 36. *See also* Pheno-
type; Pigmentocracy; Skin color
Equality, whites' assumptions of,
106–109, 113, 115, 127
Equal opportunity, 108. *See also*
Liberalism
Essentialism, 2–3, 68–70, 73, 80, 141,
150, 151, 153, 167, 176, 239, 244,
286, 328, 329, 339, 343, 344; multi-
raciality reinscribing, 83, 85, 86,
139, 169, 170, 189, 338, 346
Ethnic identity, 51, 52, 255, 257, 330,
343–345
Ethnicity, 49, 287, 288
Ethnonationalism, 37
Eugenics, 151, 152
Exogamy. *See* Interracial marriage;
Interracial relationships

Fair Housing Acts, 307, 309
Families. *See* Interracial families

About the Book

The experiences and voices of multiracial individuals are challenging current categories of race, profoundly altering the meaning of racial identity, and in the process changing the cultural fabric of the nation. Exploring this new reality, the authors of *Mixed Messages* examine what we know about multiracial identities—and the implications of those identities for fundamental issues of justice and equality.

David L. Brunsma is assistant professor of sociology and black studies at the University of Missouri. He is coauthor of *Beyond Black: Biracial Identity in America.*